Brave community

Manchester University Press

Politics, culture and society in early modern Britain

General editors

PROFESSOR ANN HUGHES

DR ANTHONY MILTON

PROFESSOR PETER LAKE

This important series publishes monographs that take a fresh and challenging look at the interactions between politics, culture and society in Britain between 1500 and the mid-eighteenth century. It counteracts the fragmentation of current historiography through encouraging a variety of approaches which attempt to redefine the political, social and cultural worlds, and to explore their interconnection in a flexible and creative fashion. All the volumes in the series question and transcend traditional interdisciplinary boundaries, such as those between political history and literary studies, social history and divinity, urban history and anthropology. They thus contribute to a broader understanding of crucial developments in early modern Britain.

Brave community

The Digger movement in the English Revolution

JOHN GURNEY

Manchester
University Press

Manchester and New York

distributed exclusively in the USA by Palgrave

Published by Manchester University Press
Oxford Road, Manchester M13 9NR, UK
and Room 400, 175 Fifth Avenue, New York, NY 10010, USA
www.manchesteruniversitypress.co.uk

Distributed exclusively in the USA by
Palgrave, 175 Fifth Avenue, New York, NY 10010, USA

Distributed exclusively in Canada by
UBC Press, University of British Columbia, 2029 West Mall,
Vancouver, BC, Canada V6T 1Z2

British Library Cataloguing-in-Publication Data
A catalogue record for this book is available from the British Library

Library of Congress Cataloging-in-Publication Data applied for

ISBN 978 0 7190 6102 8   *hardback*

First published 2007

16 15 14 13 12 11 10 09 08 07   10 9 8 7 6 5 4 3 2 1

Typeset in Scala by Florence Production Ltd, Stoodleigh, Devon
Printed in Great Britain by CPI, Bath

'For then we shall see
Brave Community,
When Vallies lye levell with Mountaines'.

Robert Coster, *A Mite Cast into the Common Treasury* (1649), p. 6.

For my parents,
Joyce and Dick Gurney

Contents

Preface

John Coulton, a yeoman living in the parish of Cobham in Surrey, drew up his will on 15 June 1652. The will contained no lengthy preamble or dedicatory clause, and Coulton expressed only his desire to settle his 'estate for the peace and quiett of my children and friends after my decease'. Jane, his wife, was made sole executrix, and bequests ranging from 20s to £30, and amounting in total to £117, were made to seven of his children and one grandchild.[1] Coulton's family had long been settled in Cobham, and he was an established member of his local community. He had inherited a customary holding of approximately thirty acres in the Cobham tithing of Downside, and had for many years played a major role in manorial and parochial affairs. He was a long-standing member of the Cobham manorial homage, and during the Civil War he had helped to assess and collect wartime taxes and to compile accounts of the costs incurred by Cobham's parishioners in their contributions to the parliamentary war effort.[2] Coulton's career is at first sight unremarkable, and many of the activities in which he engaged were typical of those of respected members of the 'middling sorts' in parishes across southern England. What is unusual about his will, however, is the reference in it to 'my friend Jerrard Winstanly', whom he named as one of the overseers appointed to assist in its execution. Winstanley was also one of the three witnesses to the will, which was proved on 14 September following.[3]

It was just three years before the signing of this will that Gerrard Winstanley had achieved widespread fame as leading figure in the Digger movement, a movement that had set out to declare the earth a common treasury and to call for an end to all private property and buying and selling. Winstanley and his companions had attempted to put their vision into action in April 1649 by digging and planting the waste lands on St George's Hill in the neighbouring parish of Walton-on-Thames, and by asserting the right of all poor people to work the land in common. The Diggers' programme represented a deliberate challenge to existing and familiar patterns of property holding, and their activities provoked furious opposition.

It has often been thought that the Diggers were outsiders to the communities in which they sought to operate, their disruptive activities leading to their swift ejection from the commons by angry locals. The reality is however more complex. John Coulton – a yeoman farmer and solid member of his local community – was one of those who joined Winstanley on St George's Hill in 1649, and he remained with the Diggers until they finally abandoned their work in April 1650. Coulton was, moreover, by no means alone among Cobham inhabitants in joining or sympathising with the Diggers. Although many Diggers would have had few local connections, it is apparent that throughout the digging episode some of Winstanley's most active supporters were from Cobham. Popular opposition to the Diggers in Walton-on-Thames was intense and unremitting, and from the start the Diggers were treated there as outsiders. Their experiences in Cobham, where they transferred their activities in August 1649 and where they remained until April 1650, were rather different, and feelings towards them in that parish were much more mixed than had been the case in Walton.

For Cobham's inhabitants, the Digger episode did not represent an imposition from the outside, or sudden incursion into an unsuspecting rural community by radicals with no local ties. It was, rather, an episode rooted in local experience, and one that reflected tensions and conflicts that had long affected the community. A major aim of this book is, therefore, to explore the local background to the Digger movement and to assess the very different reactions to the Diggers' activities in Walton and Cobham. Chapter 1 will therefore seek to provide a detailed account of social relations and social change in Cobham in the decades preceding the Diggers' occupation of the commons, and in the following chapter the impact of civil war in the local community will be examined.

The Digger movement has attracted considerable scholarly interest in recent years, not least as a result of Christopher Hill's pioneering work on radical ideas in the English Revolution in his 1972 book *The World Turned Upside Down*.[4] Yet with the exception of brief but important studies by Sir Keith Thomas and Brian Manning,[5] most recent work on the movement has focused on the thought of Gerrard Winstanley, rather than on those who joined him in digging and planting the common lands.[6] The focus on Winstanley is understandable, given his extraordinary interest as writer and thinker. It is also the case that without Winstanley there would have been no Digger movement. The Diggers were very different from the Levellers or early Quakers, among whom there were several figures who could be seen to have played a leading role. In the case of the Diggers, however, it was Winstanley whose vision led them to St George's Hill and who promoted and defended the Diggers' cause in print. Gerrard Winstanley remains an enigmatic figure, and the subject of much controversy. While the main focus of this book is on the Digger movement as a whole, a subsidiary aim is therefore to reassess Winstanley's career and intellectual development in the light of new evidence, and to call into question many of the assumptions currently held about his background, connections and ideas.

NOTES

1   The National Archives (hereafter TNA), PROB11/224, fol. 307v.

2   Below, pp. 2, 6–7, 32, 39, 43, 132, 173.

3   TNA, PROB11/224 fol. 307v.

4   Christopher Hill, *The World Turned Upside Down: Radical Ideas During the English Revolution* (London, 1972).

5   Keith Thomas, 'Another Digger broadside', *P&P*, 42 (1969), pp. 57–68; Brian Manning, *1649: The Crisis of the English Revolution* (London, 1992), pp. 109–32.

6   David W. Petegorsky, *Left-Wing Democracy in the English Civil War: A Study of the Social Philosophy of Gerrard Winstanley* (London, 1940); Olivier Lutaud, *Winstanley: Socialisme et Christianisme sous Cromwell* (Paris, 1976); T. Wilson Hayes, *Winstanley the Digger: a Literary Analysis of Radical Ideas in the English revolution* (Cambridge, Massachusetts, 1979); Timothy Kenyon, *Utopian Communism and Political Thought in Early Modern England* (London, 1989); George Shulman, *Radicalism and Reverence: the Political Thought of Gerrard Winstanley* (Berkeley, 1989); Andrew Bradstock, *Faith in the Revolution: the Political Theologies of Müntzer and Winstanley* (London, 1997); David Boulton, *Gerrard Winstanley and the Republic of Heaven* (Dent, 1999). See also the important chapter on Winstanley and the Diggers in James Holstun, *Ehud's Dagger: Class Struggle in the English Revolution* (London, 2000), pp. 367–433.

Acknowledgements

The origins of this book go back some years. My first proper acquaintance with Winstanley and the Diggers came in William Lamont's English Revolution undergraduate special subject seminar at the University of Sussex. Willie was an inspirational teacher and later a most generous and supportive DPhil supervisor, and my decision to embark upon this project owes much to his persistence and encouragement. Although my doctoral thesis on Surrey and the English Revolution focused largely on political conflicts in the county during the 1640s, I became aware while writing it that there remained much still to be said about the Digger movement, and I therefore included in it a brief section on the Diggers in which several of the arguments advanced in this book were first aired. I was subsequently given the opportunity to develop these arguments in my first published article, and I am grateful to John Morrill, the external examiner of my thesis, for encouraging me to go into print. Ann Hughes has supported the current project from its inception, and has provided valuable help with access to Winstanley's early writings. At Manchester University Press, Alison Welsby and her colleagues have been consistently understanding and helpful.

In the course of research for this book I have incurred many debts to fellow historians and archivists. At Sussex in the late 1980s I learned much about England's rural past from conversations with Alun Howkins, Linda Merricks, Mick Reed, Brian Short, Roger Wells, Barry Reay and Reg Hall. For more recent help with sources, advice and general encouragement I am grateful to James Alsop, the late Gerald Aylmer, Jeremy Boulton, Andrew Bradstock, Colin Brooks, Ian Bullock, Nicholas Cooper, Robert Dalton, Jude Dicken, Mark Forrest, Julia Hall, Rachel Hammersley, Michael Hawkins, John Henderson, John Hodgson, Jim Holstun, Sean Kelsey, Peter Lambert, Richard Olney, Christopher O'Riordan, Ron Ramdin, Michael Roberts, Nigel Smith, Lawrence Spring, David Stoker, David Taylor, Christopher Whittick, Andy Wood, Blair Worden and Brian Young. I began writing this book while working for the Historical Manuscripts Commission, and I wish to thank my former colleagues there for all their encouragement. I should also like to thank the staff of the Surrey History Centre; The National Archives; Bodleian Library; British Library; Guildhall Library; House of Lords Record Office; John Rylands University Library of Manchester; National Library of Wales; St George's Chapel Archives and Chapter Library; Berkshire Record Office; Centre for Buckinghamshire Studies; Cheshire and Chester Archives and Local Studies; East Sussex Record Office; Corporation of London Records Office; Croydon Archives Service; Hampshire Record Office; Centre for Kentish Studies; Lancashire Record Office; The Record Office of Leicestershire, Leicester and Rutland; Liverpool Record Office; London Metropolitan Archives; Northamptonshire Record Office; Somerset Archive and Record Service; West Yorkshire Archive Service, Leeds; the Worshipful Company of Skinners; the National Monuments Record; National Register of Archives; International Institute of Social History, Amsterdam; Institute of Historical Research; Society of Genealogists; Dr Williams's Library; and the University libraries of Sussex, Newcastle and London. Kingston Borough Archives, which are now held by Kingston Museum and Heritage Service, were consulted at the former Surrey Record Office, Kingston.

My parents, who inspired my interest in history and to whom this book is dedicated, have provided constant support; and it is undoubtedly the case that without their help this book could never have been written. My wife Rachel has provided inspiration, companionship and intellectual stimulation. She read through the entire manuscript and made many valuable suggestions. Neither she nor our son Thomas, who arrived just as the finishing touches were being put to the book, can be blamed for any remaining errors.

List of abbreviations

Repositories:

BL	British Library
CKS	Centre for Kentish Studies
CLRO	Corporation of London Records Office
ESRO	East Sussex Record Office
GL	Guildhall Library
HLRO	House of Lords Record Office
HRO	Hampshire Record Office
JRULM	John Rylands University Library of Manchester
KMHS	Kingston Museum and Heritage Service
LLRRO	The Record Office for Leicestershire, Leicester and Rutland
LMA	London Metropolitan Archives
LRO	Lancashire Record Office
NLW	National Library of Wales
Northants RO	Northamptonshire Record Office
St George's CAL	St George's Chapel Archives and Chapter Library
SHC	Surrey History Centre
TNA	The National Archives

Publications:

BIHR	*Bulletin of the Institute of Historical Research*
CCAM	*Calendar of the Committee for Advance of Money*
CCC	*Calendar of the Committee for Compounding*
CJ	*Journals of the House of Commons*
CSPD	*Calendar of State Papers Domestic*
DNB	*Dictionary of National Biography*
HJ	*Historical Journal*
HMC	Historical Manuscripts Commission
JBS	*Journal of British Studies*
LJ	*Journals of the House of Lords*

N&Q	*Notes and Queries*
ODNB	*Oxford Dictionary of National Biography*
P&P	*Past and Present*
PR	*Calendar of the Patent Rolls held in the Public Record Office*
Sabine, *Works*	George H. Sabine, ed., *The Works of Gerrard Winstanley* (Ithaca, 1941)
SAC	*Surrey Archaeological Collections*
SRS	Surrey Record Society
THSLC	*Transactions of the Historic Society of Lancashire and Cheshire*
TRHS	*Transactions of the Royal Historical Society*
VCH	*Victoria County History*

Chapter 1

Parish, community and social relations in Cobham

The parish of Cobham, where the Digger movement had its origins, was a large, irregularly shaped parish of a little under 5,300 acres, with a population in 1649 of around five hundred. It lay in a central position in mid-Surrey between the North Downs and the River Thames, and administratively it belonged to Elmbridge hundred and the middle division of Surrey. The parish occupied an important position on the London to Portsmouth Road, a road that not only linked the capital to England's major naval port, but also served as the main route between Surrey's two principal towns of Guildford and Kingston-upon-Thames.[1]

Despite being one of the smaller English counties, Surrey was noted for the exceptional diversity of its landscape, and Cobham too was a place of contrasts.[2] The northern parts of the parish lay principally on Bagshot sands, while London clay predominated in the south. Although the parish lay at some distance from the Thames, it was bisected by the River Mole, which contributed to the diversity of its soil types through deposits of alluvial beds and gravel. Cobham had a dispersed pattern of settlement, and this was reflected in the administrative division between the three tithings of Church Cobham, Street Cobham and Downside. The tithing of Church Cobham contained Church Street, a nucleated settlement that had developed at an early date around the twelfth-century parish church of St Andrew. Street Cobham's houses, shops and inns had largely grown up along the Portsmouth Road.[3] Downside contained a small hamlet and several scattered farms, as well as Down Field, the largest at 153 acres of the manor of Cobham's 482-acre common arable fields. Church Field, which was only slightly smaller, lay between Street Cobham and Church Street.[4] The parish also contained substantial quantities of unenclosed common or waste, including Downside Common, Fairmile, Chatley Heath, the Tilt, Stoakes Heath and Little Heath.[5] Beyond the parish boundary, to the north-west of Church Cobham and Street Cobham, lay St George's Hill, the southernmost part of the extensive commons of the manors of Walton and Walton Leigh. The commons of Esher, Ockham, Little Bookham and Stoke d'Abernon also adjoined the parish.

Cobham lay in an area of mixed farming. At the turn of the seventeenth century just under half the demesne of the manor of Cobham was under arable cultivation and just over a quarter pasture, with the rest woodland or meadow; roughly 47% of the leasehold lands of the manor were also under arable cultivation.[6] The holdings of customary tenants in Cobham typically included scattered parcels of land in the common arable fields and more substantial parcels of old enclosed ground, as well as more recent encroachments from the commons and wastes.[7] For Cobham's wealthier farmers the extensive local commons also provided land for profitable stock rearing for the London market, while the meadows along the banks of the Mole were regarded as valuable assets that could change hands for considerable sums of money.[8]

Surviving Cobham inventories from the late-sixteenth and seventeenth centuries show arable fields sown with oats, barley or rye, a somewhat smaller acreage being sown with peas or beans. Wheat was also grown in the parish, though this was often intermixed with other crops.[9] The mixed husbandry practised by John Coulton, a husbandman of Oxcombes in Downside, and direct ancestor of the Digger John Coulton, was characteristic of the pattern followed by Cobham's farmers. Coulton died in April 1585 leaving a holding of two virgates or roughly twenty-five acres of land.[10] At the time of his death his fields were sown with eight acres of winter corn, five acres of oats and two-and-a-half acres of peas, tares and beans, valued at £4, £1 5s and 10s respectively, while in his barns were one quarter each of rye and barley, three bushel of oats and four of malt. Coulton also possessed a flock of forty sheep and sixteen lambs, a small number of cows, bullocks and draft animals and a stall of bees.[11] References in other probate inventories to buckwheat, hay, hemp, hops, fruit growing, rabbit keeping, coppicing and cheese making provide further evidence of agricultural diversity in this area of varied soils.[12]

Most occupiers of agricultural land in Cobham were tenants of the former Chertsey Abbey manor of Cobham or Coveham, which was by far the largest and most important manor in the parish. The manor's boundaries were not coterminous with those of the parish: the manors of Esher Episcopi and Esher Wateville or Milbourne intruded into the parish, and included within their boundaries Northwood Farm and Stoakes Heath, while the manor of Cobham extended into the parish of Ockham, where some parishioners held their lands as tenants of the Cobham manor.[13] These included members of the Freeland family, one of whom was to join the Diggers.[14] The small manor of Ham or Ham Court consisted of a principal messuage in the parish of Chertsey and scattered freehold and copyhold tenements in Cobham and other neighbouring parishes, the bulk of its properties being concentrated in Cobham. Its holdings in the parish included the White Lion Inn, Tan House, Appleton Farm and

Tyrell's Croft, as well as meadowland at Stewards Mead near Cobham mill.[15] Ham Court's status was that of a subordinate manor, and the Dean and Canons of Windsor, the lords of the manor, were included in Cobham manorial surveys and quit rentals as freehold tenants of the larger manor for properties they held in the parish of Cobham.[16] Reputed manors in Cobham included Downe, Heywood and Chilbrook, but these were dormant by the seventeenth century and no longer subject to manorial organisation.[17]

Tenants of the manor of Cobham held their lands by a mixture of customary tenure (either copyhold or at will), freehold and leasehold. Copyhold remained the most significant form of landholding on the manor in the early years of the seventeenth century, though freehold tenure was by no means negligible, and leasehold lands were becoming increasingly important to the manorial lords as a reliable source of income. Copyholders in Cobham held their estates by inheritance rather than for lives, and holdings passed to the eldest son, despite the high incidence locally of the practice of Borough English, in which holdings passed to the youngest son or daughter.[18] A 1598 survey of the manor of Cobham listed fifty customary tenants, including both copyholders and tenants at will, sixteen leasehold tenants and nineteen freeholders. Nine of the freeholders also held land by customary tenure, as did seven of the leasehold tenants.[19] The number of customary holdings on the manor remained fairly stable during the sixteenth and seventeenth centuries at around fifty, with the most common size of holdings being between one and five acres; perhaps as many as four fifths of tenants in 1598 held less than twenty acres each of customary land.[20] It was not unusual however for even small property holders in Cobham to hold land in other manors and parishes. John Melsham the elder, a Cobham yeoman who died in 1620, owned freehold property in the Surrey parish of Great Bookham as well as holding both freehold and copyhold land in Cobham.[21] Edward Lee, a Cobham husbandman who drew up his will in September 1640, was able to leave a recently-purchased house and land in Wonersh to his daughter, while members of the Marsh family of Cobham, a prosperous yeoman family, held property in Walton-on-Thames and Effingham as well as in Cobham.[22]

FAMILY, OCCUPATION AND SOCIAL STRUCTURE

The parish of Cobham contained no resident greater gentry, and the only knight noted in the parish registers in the period 1552–1640 was the Calvinist writer and controversialist Sir Humphrey Lynde (1579–1636), who settled in Cobham late in life and whose daughter Margaret married Vincent Gavell, lord of the manor of Cobham. The Gavells, and the related families of Sutton and Downe, were Cobham's leading families in terms of wealth and status, but they were of importance at parish rather than county or national level. In parish registers, testamentary records and manorial documents the heads of these families

3

tended to be described as 'Gentleman' or 'Mr' rather than as 'Esquire', and of the Gavells only Vincent Gavell, who died in 1643, was regularly described in the parish registers as 'Esquire'.[23]

The Gavell family had gained possession of the manor of Cobham in the mid-1560s through the marriage of Robert Gavell of Nonsuch to Dorothy, daughter of George and Elizabeth Bigley. The latter had purchased the manor from the Crown in 1553, following the dissolution of Chertsey Abbey and the confiscation of its lands.[24] Elizabeth Bigley had previously been married to Richard Sutton, the last lessee of Cobham manor from Chertsey Abbey, and her descendants from this marriage continued to exert an influence in parish affairs, as minor gentry and prosperous yeomen farmers, for much of the seventeenth century.[25] Properties owned or occupied by members of the Sutton family included Heywood, Norwood Farm, Pyports, the White Lion and the Tan House in Cobham, as well as land in Byfleet and Thames Ditton.[26] Thomas Sutton, the head of the family at the time of the digging episode, was a regular member of the Cobham manorial jury and also of the grand jury at assizes.[27] His kinsman John Downe, who lived at Downe Place in the Cobham tithing of Downside, was another representative of a long-established minor gentry family, and also served regularly as a grand juror at the assizes.[28] Both Downe and Sutton were to clash with Gerrard Winstanley in the months before the digging, and Sutton was to play a leading part in the local campaign against the Diggers.[29]

Another local family on the fringes of the gentry were the Bickerstaffes, one of whom, Henry Bickerstaffe, was to join Winstanley on St George's Hill. The family had first acquired freehold and copyhold property in Cobham, including the George Inn in Street Cobham, soon after 1540.[30] In the early years of the seventeenth century they acquired further land in Walton-on-Thames and established their principal residence at Pains Hill, a crown estate on the borders of Walton and Cobham.[31] The family also had extensive property interests in the east Surrey town of Croydon.[32] Like many gentry families who settled in mid-Surrey at this time, the Bickerstaffes had connections with the court. At least four generations of Bickerstaffes held minor court office, and the Digger's father Robert was half-brother of Hayward Bickerstaffe, a page of the bedchamber to Charles I.[33] Several members of the family were also involved in the London cloth trade: Anthony Bickerstaffe (*c.* 599–1654), the eldest son and eventual heir of Robert Bickerstaffe, became a liveryman in the Skinners' Company and a prominent London linen draper, and two of his brothers, including the future Digger, were active in the cloth trade for at least part of their careers.[34]

Cobham's economy was predominantly rural, with most adult males involved in agriculture or related occupations. Occupations were recorded systematically in Cobham's parish registers for only a brief period in the years 1610 to 1619, when the occupations listed included labourer, husbandman, yeoman, miller, blacksmith, gardener, butcher, tanner and glover. Labourers formed the largest single occupational group, with twenty-five individuals, roughly a third of the total, being described as such in the registers. Other, non-agricultural occupations listed included shoemaker, tailor, clothworker, weaver, innkeeper, bricklayer, glazier and sawyer.[35] Evidence from the registers and other sources, including testamentary and taxation records, suggests that occupations connected with clothworking were, as elsewhere in Surrey, more common in the parish at the start of the seventeenth century than at the time of the Civil War. The Surrey cloth industry suffered a disastrous reverse at the beginning of the 1630s, when hundreds of workers were reported to have been forced out of work as markets contracted.[36] At least fifteen individuals noted in the Cobham parish registers in the years 1610–19 were involved in the cloth industry. One of these was Edmund Starr, a clothworker who died in May 1638. None of his five surviving sons seems to have followed him in this trade; his eldest son was a Cobham copyholder, while Thomas, a younger son who was to join the Diggers on St George's Hill, became a shoemaker.[37] Members of the Melsham family, who were settled in the parishes of Cobham and Stoke d'Abernon, and who were to become involved in the campaign against the Diggers, continued to work as tailors until after the Civil War, but they were also substantial farmers.[38] The Foster family appears to have swapped clothworking for farming after the death in 1623 of the tailor Robert Foster.[39] Although the cloth industry had not disappeared completely from Cobham by the middle years of the century, involvement in it was by that time confined to just a small number of individuals.

Building work may well have been less precarious as a profession, given the extraordinary range of building activity that took place in Surrey in the early years of the seventeenth century.[40] Major houses constructed near Cobham in this period included Ashley House in the parish of Walton-on-Thames, built for Lady Jane Berkeley in the years 1602–7, Sir Dudley Carleton's house at Imber Court in Thames Ditton, and the house built in the 1630s for the lawyer George Shiers at Slyfield in Great Bookham.[41] Local building workers were also employed at Oatlands Palace in Weybridge, where extensive work took place in the early years of the century.[42] Robert Maybank, a Cobham bricklayer who died in 1610, was a member of a Surrey family that had been active in the building trade since the early sixteenth century and involved in building work as far afield as Loseley in Surrey and Sheriff Hutton in Yorkshire. Maybank's son seems to have followed him in his trade.[43] Henry Mills, a Cobham glazier, was employed in 1603–4 in glazing Lord Buckhurst's house at Horsley, and, with Maybank, also worked on repairs to Cobham's parish church.[44] When Mills died in 1638, he left all his 'utensills & materialls which appertaine to my trade of Glazinge & paintinge' to two of his sons, Matthew, later a Digger or Digger sympathiser, and Gowen, who was still described as a glazier at the time of his death in 1667.[45] Another local family active in the building trade were the Taylors of Walton and

Cobham, who combined work as carpenters and bricklayers with sheep farming on the extensive commons around St George's Hill.[46] The carpenter John Taylor, who as a young man assisted his father and uncle in carpentry work at Ashley House, was to become one of the Diggers' leading opponents in 1649.[47]

The high level of building activity in mid-Surrey in the early years of the seventeenth century also reflected the attraction that the county held for courtiers and wealthy Londoners. Surrey's gentry community was unusually cosmopolitan, with more than two thirds of those included in the heralds' visitations of 1662–68 having fathers or paternal grandfathers from outside the county.[48] Two courtier families from outside Surrey who settled in the vicinity of Cobham were the Drakes, farmers of the Crown manor of Walton on Thames, and the Vincents, owners of the manor of Stoke d'Abernon. Richard Drake, who was granted the lease of Walton manor during the 1590s, also acquired the neighbouring manor of Esher, which was to be owned later in the seventeenth century by a succession of prosperous London merchants.[49] The manor of Sandon, a small manor in Esher, was purchased in 1636 by the London merchants William and Gerard Gore, and was to remain in their family's hands until 1715.[50] Several Londoners also settled in Cobham or acquired property there. Among those buried in the church or churchyard in the first half of the century were Roger Bellow, citizen and brewer of London, who died in 1614, Aminadab Cooper, a citizen and merchant taylor who died in 1618 and Ralph Cox, citizen and silkman of London, who was buried in the chancel of the parish church in 1631.[51] The hamlet of Hersham, a settlement in the parish of Walton just over a mile from Cobham, was home from 1636 to the astrologer William Lilly, who moved there from London after suffering a bout of 'Hypocondraick Melancholy' following the death of his wife. He returned briefly to London in 1641, but later settled permanently in Hersham, 'intending by the Blessing of God, when I found it convenient, to retire into the Country, there to end my days in Peace and Tranquility'.[52]

At the heart of the local social system in Cobham was a complex network of neighbourhood and kinship ties.[53] Long-settled families such as the Suttons had extensive local kinship links, which helped reinforce their position of authority in the parish community. Kinship reached across social divisions: the Gavell family included small farmers as well as the owners of the manor, and among the large network of Cobham Suttons were husbandmen, brewers and tanners as well as small gentry and yeomen.[54] The will of Edward Sutton, a Cobham yeoman who died in 1622, showed that he was related to, and had retained close contacts with, members of the local families of Dalton, Stint, Inwood and King, as well as being related to the parish's wealthiest families, the Gavells and Downes.[55] The Digger John Coulton, as head of an established local yeoman family, also played an influential role in the community, serving as overseer of the wills of at least three Cobham inhabitants and as witness to the wills of at least two more.[56] Members of the Mills, Starr and Bickerstaffe families were also frequently to be found as overseers or witnesses to their neighbours' wills.[57]

Although most households would have been dominated by a male head, there were, in Cobham as elsewhere, exceptions to this. One of the largest copyhold and leasehold tenants noted in the 1598 survey of Cobham was Alice Smyth, widow of John Gavell and William Smyth.[58] The Marsh family of Marsh Place in Cobham was headed for many years by Ann Wisson (d. c1650), widow of Robert Marsh.[59] Her sons James Marsh, who died in 1641, and John Marsh, who died the following year, both made her sole executrix to their wills and left her the bulk of their property, James Marsh being quoted in his nuncupative will as acknowledging that he had received the greatest part of his substance from her.[60] Cobham manorial custom could, in certain circumstances, also allow women precedence over men in disputes over the descent of copyholds. In 1613, for instance, following the death of Thomas Rayner, the manorial homage presented his sister rather than his uncle as rightful heir by the custom of the manor.[61]

MANOR AND PARISH

The manor and the parish were the two institutions that served to bring Cobham's male householders together on a regular basis, and to provide a focus for the life of the community. The court baron for the manor of Cobham, which dealt primarily with land transactions, the raising of entry fines and presentments for the infringement of manorial custom, was held twice a year, most often in the spring and autumn.[62] The meeting of the view of frankpledge or court leet, at which constables and other sub-officers were elected, and at which the attendance of all householders was required, was normally an annual event. Before 1630 the view of frankpledge met in the autumn, but for the remainder of the century meetings were usually held in March or April.[63] Separate entries were made in the court rolls for the view of frankpledge and court baron, but the business of both courts was often transacted at the same session. Members of the homage at the court baron invariably also served as jurors at the view of frankpledge, but the latter's jury was in many cases slightly larger, and included some residents who never served at the court baron. Membership of the homage and jury seems, by the seventeenth century, to have been generally restricted to more substantial tenants and those from well-established families. Some forty-four tenants served in the years 1613–22, forty-one in the years 1623–32 and forty in the years 1637–48, compared with seventy-eight individuals who served in the nine years from 1570 to 1579.[64]

Courts for the manor of Cobham were kept most often by a steward – usually a local gentleman with legal training – or his deputy. John Derrick, who was steward in 1594, was a Guildford attorney and coroner, and owner of property in west Surrey and in St Giles-in-the-Fields.[65] George Duncombe was a Clifford's Inn lawyer and substantial local landowner who served as steward for several Surrey manors, including the Countess of Arundel's manor of Ashtead.[66] Cobham's steward in the later 1640s and 50s, Henry Baldwin, was like Derrick a Guildford attorney, and served as mayor of that town on three occasions.[67] It is apparent from surviving court rolls and minutes that these highly experienced stewards helped to ensure that Cobham's manorial structure remained relatively secure throughout the first half of the century. Juries continued to raise essoins and fines for default of court, and to present tenants and other residents for quite minor infringements of manorial custom. Cobham's view of frankpledge was a more active institution than was the case in some other areas, where many of the functions of courts leet had by this time fallen into abeyance.[68] Pindars and ale tasters continued, for instance, to be elected on a regular basis alongside constables and tithingmen, and presentments for breaking the assize of ale, and for other breaches of the peace, were not uncommon.[69]

Courts for the small manor of Ham Court were held much less frequently, and the business there appears largely to have been restricted to recording surrenders and admissions, many of which had taken place out of court.[70] These courts were in theory held by the Dean and Canons of Windsor or their steward, but most lessees held courts themselves or through their own stewards.[71] Many of the tenants who served on the homage at the Ham Court court baron were also tenants of the manor of Cobham, and their names can be found among those of jurors at Cobham's manor court.

Parochial officeholding was the second area of activity in which a wide range of Cobham's male inhabitants participated. Some sixty-nine individuals served as churchwarden, overseer of the poor or waywarden in Cobham in the years 1656–72.[72] Most of those who served as churchwarden had previously served as overseer or waywarden, though by no means all who had served in these more junior offices succeeded in being appointed churchwarden. The Digger Gerrard Winstanley was to serve twice as waywarden and once as overseer before he became a churchwarden in 1667.[73] Of those who held office in the years 1656–72, 17% were described as 'Mr' or 'Gentleman', but at least a quarter of the officeholders who can be matched with entries in the 1663 hearth tax assessment were assessed at only one or two hearths, and may have been of quite modest status.[74]

It is not certain whether a formal, select vestry had evolved in the parish by the time of the Civil War, but it is evident that a determined effort was made at the end of the 1620s to reverse a period of neglect by parochial officeholders.[75] The accounts for the year 1629–30 by the churchwardens Robert Coulton and Richard Phillips were the first for several years to be entered in the Cobham

'Church Book', and were preceded by a declaration that 'by the space of 23 years last past ther hath bene a neglect of setting downe the Church Accounts as hath bene comendablye in former tymes effected by our predicessours', and that 'nowe this booke is provided to reforme this neglect and to revive the former comendable course for the benefit of the present & future tymes'.[76]

Involvement in parochial office also brought Cobham's inhabitants into contact with the wider activities of the state. In the dearth year of 1630–31, Cobham's churchwardens, Richard Phillips and Henry Mills, travelled several times to Leatherhead to consult with JPs about the poor and about the price of corn; while in the following year, the churchwardens Henry Mills and Robert Bickerstaffe were required to attend monthly meetings instituted by Surrey's JPs to enforce the implemention of the provisions of the Privy Council's Book of Orders.[77] These provisions included setting the poor to work, apprenticing poor children, punishing vagrants and suppressing superfluous alehouses, practices that were put into effect throughout Surrey's middle division during the 1630s.[78] Between 24 June and 16 November 1633, three apprentices were put out in Cobham and twelve vagrants punished, while between the latter date and 10 February following, three absentees from church were fined, the fines going towards the relief of the poor.[79] In the spring of 1636, four vagrants were punished in Cobham: John Chambers, his wife and Isaac Peter, who were sent to Lancaster, and Mabel Lewis, who was sent back to Windsor.[80] All these activities were reported to the middle division's JPs and by them to the Council of State.

Dilatoriness or non-compliance with orders from justices of the peace or deputy lieutenants could lead to local officials being called to account for their actions. In March 1632, for instance, the names of Thomas Sutton and John Perior of Cobham were returned to the Privy Council for their failings in raising money for the county's muster master, and a messenger was despatched to obtain their answers. Sutton, as high constable, was accused of having 'delayed to make return of the warrant directed to him for the levying of the muster masters enterteynment', while Perior, the parish constable, 'will neither levy the monie nor returne the names and answers of those that doe deny payment of it but excuse themselves that they will not deny it but yet will not pay it'.[81] In August 1638 John Downe of Cobham was among the forty-eight Surrey ship money collectors ordered to appear before the Privy Council for failure to perform their duties adequately.[82]

POPULATION

Cobham's mid-seventeenth-century population had more than doubled since the second decade of the sixteenth century.[83] The disparate sources available for the study of population in Cobham suggest figures of slightly more than two hundred inhabitants in the 1520s, just under three hundred at the end of the 1560s, and between three-hundred-and-fifty and four hundred in 1603.[84] By the mid-1660s Cobham's population was in the range of between 486 and 516.[85] Taken together, these figures indicate a substantial rise in population between the 1520s and the middle years of the seventeenth century, though the trends may be exaggerated by under-assessment in the 1525 subsidy assessment, from which the earliest population figures are extrapolated, or by too low an estimation of the number of communicants in the parish in 1603.[86] Population trends elsewhere in Surrey do, however, also reveal a steadily rising population in the century before 1640, with the most rapid increases occurring in the pastoral regions of west Surrey and in built-up areas near London.[87]

It is impossible to establish precise population figures for Cobham. The parish registers, which begin in 1562, are incomplete, and they contain no entries for the years 1565–1610 and several gaps for later years. The original registers no longer survive, and the extant eighteenth-century transcripts are deficient in several respects, with names frequently mistranscribed and inaccurate dates inserted.[88] Used with caution, however, the registers do provide valuable, additional information about population trends in the parish. Rough comparisons between numbers of baptisms and burials recorded can be made for twenty-nine of the thirty-four years in the period 1610–43. In the years 1610–26 baptisms exceeded burials by approximately thirty-five, despite an outbreak of plague which caused several deaths in 1625, while in the years 1632–43 burials exceeded baptisms by twenty-seven.[89] This would suggest that the natural rise in Cobham's population was checked in the decade leading up to the Civil War. While this shift no doubt reflected the general levelling off of population that affected much of the south-east in the middle years of the seventeenth century, Cobham appears also to have experienced a mortality crisis of its own at the end of the 1630s.[90] Ninety burials were recorded in the registers in the years 1638–40, with thirty-five of these occurring in 1640 alone; in both 1639 and 1640 the number of recorded burials was more than double the parish's annual average for the first half of the century of just over fourteen.[91] An outbreak of plague was reported in the vicinity of Cobham in August 1640, the month before the largest number of burials, so there is a strong likelihood that epidemic disease was to blame for the unusually high number of deaths that year.[92]

Cobham, unlike many other rural parishes in south-east England, experienced a renewed natural increase in population in the second half of the century, and this too would suggest that the high death rate in 1638–40 represented a temporary, if severe, local population crisis.[93] Population levels would also have been sustained by the steady flow of incomers into the parish, evidence for which can readily be found in the parish registers. 139 surnames appeared in the baptismal registers in the years 1610–49, at an average of 61.5 per decade.

Twenty-three new surnames were recorded during the 1620s, twenty-five during the 1630s and twenty-four during the 1640s.[94] Surnames appearing in the registers throughout this period tended to be those associated with settled manorial tenants and families of middling status; labourers and other inhabitants whose surnames did not figure in manorial documents were most likely to appear only fleetingly in the registers.

POPULATION PRESSURES

The steady rise in Cobham's population was accompanied by a noticeable shift in the balance of wealth within the community. Comparisons between the 1525 subsidy assessment and the hearth tax returns of the mid-1660s suggest that the proportion of Cobham's least wealthy inhabitants rose between these two dates, largely, it would appear, at the expense of those immediately above them in the social scale.[95] The trend in Cobham is not unlike the one identified by David Levine and Keith Wrightson in the Essex parish of Terling, where the proportion of least wealthy rose from just under a third to just over half the population between 1524/25 and 1671.[96] In 1525 thirteen Cobham inhabitants, or 27.7% of the total number assessed, were rated at £1 in wages, the usual figure for labourers or poor cottagers, while in the years 1664–66 the proportion of householders assessed at one hearth or excused payment of the hearth tax on grounds of poverty was in the range of 37.5% to 45.1%.[97] While these figures should be treated with caution, since any under-assessment of the poorest sections of society in 1525 could lead to an exaggeration of the differences between the 1520s and the 1660s, they do suggest that the parish of Cobham was becoming more unequal as well as more populous in these years.[98]

This trend was of course by no means exceptional, and a similar process of social differentiation was experienced in other Surrey parishes besides Cobham. The percentage of occupied houses in Elmbridge hundred exempted from the hearth tax in 1664 was approximately 29%, though figures per parish in the hundred ranged from 12.12% to 44.22%.[99] Exemption rates elsewhere in Surrey in 1664 could be much higher: the percentage of non-chargeable households in the parish of Bisley, for instance, was 60% and in Windlesham and Bagshot 75%, while in Blackheath hundred more than 40% of households were exempt in eight of the hundred's eleven parishes.[100] What seems significant in the figures for Cobham is not just the rise in numbers of poorer inhabitants between the 1520s and 1660s, but also the relative diminution in numbers of inhabitants of lesser husbandman or craftsman status – those inhabitants who might be assessed at £2 in goods or lands in 1525 or at two hearths in 1664.[101] While the relative numbers of poor inhabitants rose between the 1520s and 1660s, and the numbers of gentry and yeoman inhabitants remained relatively stable, the position of those between the middling sorts and the poor appears to have weakened. 31.9% of Cobham taxpayers in 1525 were assessed at £2, while the proportion of householders assessed at two hearths in 1664–66 (and not excused payment of the hearth tax on grounds of poverty), was between 17.7% and 18.33%.[102] Although the changes suggested by these figures may have been subtle ones, they are indicative of a gradual sharpening of social differences within the community and of a widening gulf between wealthy and poor.

By the seventeenth century, differences in wealth and status were clearly to be seen reflected in house size and in housing standards, room use and furnishings. Cobham Court, the manor house of Cobham manor, was, with thirteen hearths, not particularly large for a gentry house, but it did contain a hall suitable for the holding of manorial courts.[103] The Bickerstaffes' house at Pains Hill contained, in 1650, a wainscoted hall and parlour with five chambers above and two garrets, and substantial service rooms including kitchen, brewhouse, larder, dairy room, pastry room and washhouse.[104] Similarly, the home of Katherine Sutton, widow of the Diggers' opponent Thomas Sutton, included in 1675 a hall and a parlour, both with bedchambers above. The parlour was furnished with table, leather chairs and court cupboards, indicating that it was used solely as a day-room rather than doubling, as was the case in many smaller houses, as a bedchamber.[105] While there is evidence by the middle years of the seventeenth century that yeoman houses might contain parlours that were used exclusively as rooms for entertainment and eating, the houses of husbandmen tended to retain beds in their parlours.[106]

In Cobham, as elsewhere, many houses were rebuilt or enlarged in the late sixteenth and early seventeenth centuries.[107] In May 1594 Nicholas Foster, a Cobham copyholder, gave evidence before the Court of Requests that he had known several tenants to 'pull downe their olde howses and build newe', while other tenants had made use of locally-available timber to repair their homes.[108] One of those who rebuilt was Anthony Bickerstaffe, who obtained a licence in 1572 to take elms from his copyhold lands for building on his freehold estate.[109] The more substantial structures built in Cobham in this period included end-smoke bay houses and lobby-entrance houses with central stacks, though the smallest houses would have been of just one chamber.[110] Typical of a smaller house was that of Francis Terrell of Stoke D'Abernon and Cobham, who died in 1665 and whose house was inventoried by John Hayman, a former Digger. Terrell's house contained a hall, workhouse and buttery or milkhouse, each with a chamber above, but only the hall appears to have been heated, and from the nature of the fire irons listed it apparently also served as the kitchen.[111] The house of Margaret Starr (d. 1609), grandmother of the Digger Thomas Starr, also seems to have been quite small, for its lofts were fitted out with beds, painted cloths and other hangings.[112] A similar arrangement was to be found in the house of Richard Taylor (d. 1587) of Cobham, which had a bedchamber behind the hall and two boarded bedsteads in one of the lofts.[113]

References to furniture, bedding and household goods in wills and inventories also point to the increasing prosperity of Cobham's yeoman inhabitants, and to clear disparities of wealth even among those who had sufficient property to make wills. In 1585 the husbandman John Coulton had left a house that was only modestly furnished: many of the items inventoried were described as old, and the total value of his furniture and bedding was estimated at just £6 2s. Beds in Coulton's house consisted of an old featherbed and two old flock beds, while the hall furniture consisted of an old table, a form and an old chair.[114] Forms remained the most common type of seating in husbandmen's houses for much of the first half of the following century, but by mid-century they had given way to chairs in the day-rooms of many yeoman houses.[115] The well-furnished parlour in the house of Thomas King, a Cobham mercer-cum-yeoman who died in 1669, contained a drawing table and side table, a court cupboard and glass cupboard, several leather chairs, a wainscot chair, a green bench and three joined stools, as well as two striped carpets and an India cupboard cloth.[116]

King's inventory, which is the most detailed to survive from these years, is testimony to the comfortable existence that might be enjoyed by Cobham's wealthier inhabitants. His shop and warehouses, which were evidently attached to his house, contained a wide range of foodstuffs, broadcloth, clothing and other provisions. The house itself was relatively modest, though of a size not untypical for a member of the middling sorts, and contained a kitchen, parlour, a hall with bed, washhouse, cellars, garret, and well-furnished bedchambers over both shop and kitchen. King's books, which included a statute book and two bibles, and which were valued in total at £1 10s, were housed in the chamber over the shop. Hearths were to be found in the kitchen, parlour and kitchen chamber, and a copper and brewing vessels in the washhouse. King's by-occupation as a yeoman farmer was reflected in the references in the inventory to wheat and oats on the ground, to threshed and unthreshed wheat and rye in barns, and to the timber, logs and firewood in his possession. The sum total of the inventory was £474 13s 6d, though as much as £200 of this related to several debts owed to King, many of them classified as desperate.[117]

Testators of King's status were increasingly likely to leave specific items of value in their wills. Katherine Sutton's will included references to a silver watch and to other goods made of silver or silver gilt, and similar bequests were mentioned in wills of Cobham inhabitants of yeoman or small gentry status in 1616, 1630 and 1641; bequests of pewter or brass were more often found in the wills of husbandmen, such as those of Richard Taylor (d. 1587), Robert Palmer (d. 1610) and John Marsh (d. 1619).[118] References to beds and bedding could be found in wills at all levels of local society, but bequests of clothing appear to have been less common in Cobham than may have been the case in certain other communities.[119] Clothes were mentioned most often in wills drawn up by widows, where particular items of clothing might be divided between daughters, and in wills drawn up by male testators who sought to dispose of the clothes of a deceased spouse. Margaret Starr, for instance, left her best gown to her daughter Frances and her second gown to her daughter Jane; Henry Mills left to his daughter Katherine her mother's best gown, while his second wife was to have her riding suit and horse furniture, as well as 'my great byble and my warming pan'.[120]

Any increase in numbers of poorer inhabitants in Cobham during the early part of the seventeenth century was almost certainly fuelled by migration. This had also been the case in the pastoral regions of north-west Surrey, where extensive, and often unstinted commons proved attractive to cottagers and squatters. In a survey drawn up in 1615 of out-of-town cottages in west Surrey, 73% of cottages noted in Godley hundred were described as 'new built', including forty-nine of the fifty-two cottages noted in the parish of Chertsey.[121] A 1630 survey of recent encroachments in Windsor Forest provided details of 145 cottages built in the bailiwick of Surrey, which covered those parts of Surrey lying to the west of the river Wey and to the north of the Hogs Back. Of the cottages listed, at least sixty-one were said to pay no rent, only five had the legal minimum of four acres of land attached and 103 had half an acre or less. The number of cottages had, the surveyors complained, grown 'to that excesse and nomber wee conceave to bee paste Cure and Reamedy for those which are allreadye erected', while the 'further increase . . . daylie growes uppon the fforreste'. The cottages in Windsor Forest were branded 'the Ruyne and distruction both of his Majesties Woodes and Game, and the shelter of Dearestealers and all disorderly persons'; they were 'a greate hyndrance . . . and a great ympoverishinge to the ffree holders, and inhabitants of the said Bayliewick'.[122]

In Cobham, pressures of in-migration led the manorial and parish authorities to combine in restricting new settlement in the parish. Presentments against inmates were made at the manor court in October 1613, when the jury also ordered that no inhabitant within the precincts of the court leet, and no tenant of the manor, should, upon pain of 40s, let any farm or take in 'any fforeyner' without first providing sureties to the parish authorities to 'save the Parishioners harmeles from all charge and damage that shall or may arise thereby'. A further order, made at the court baron in September 1615, and also designed to protect Cobham's parishioners from the danger of having to maintain 'such fforryners and their Children borne & to be borne and all their ffamilyes', raised the pain to £10 for each offence, with half the money going to the lord of the manor and half to the collectors for the poor in the parish of Cobham.[123] Presentments for taking inmates continued to be made on a regular basis in later years. Four Cobham inhabitants were presented at the view of frankpledge in October 1630, for instance, while in April 1637 William Ansell was accused of receiving inmates and was ordered to 'avoyde them' within two months on pain of 20s per month. At the same court John Manby was presented 'for that hee doth not avoide this parrish, and for lying loytering and pilfering in mens lands, both for broome stalves and Broome'; Robert Ellis was presented for harbouring him.[124]

Much is now known about patterns of crime in early modern England, and about connections between rising crime levels and population pressure in the period of greatest population increase.[125] Levels of crime in Cobham are, however, difficult to measure, given the almost total loss of Surrey quarter sessions records from before 1659.[126] The few surviving records of indictments of Cobham inhabitants at the assizes do suggest that the incidence of petty crime remained fairly constant throughout the late sixteenth and early seventeenth centuries, with an occasional increase in prosecutions in years of high prices following poor harvests.[127] Cobham inhabitants prosecuted for theft at the assizes appear to have come predominantly from among the poorer sections of village society, and their victims or accusers largely from among the parish's middling and wealthier residents. George Grey, a Cobham shoemaker, who married in April 1613, and whose first child was baptised later that year, had already been presented before the manorial court for wood stealing when in July 1614 he was indicted at the Southwark assizes for having stolen eight ells of cloth, a frock and 4 lbs of onion seeds in Cobham.[128] He had also been presented, at the view of frankpledge in October 1613, for having received John Thatcher into his cottage as an inmate. Thatcher, a baker, was also to be indicted at the assizes in 1614, accused of having stolen a quantity of wool from the house of James Sutton at Heywood in Cobham.[129] Members of the Sutton family appear in the records as victims of theft on more than one occasion, and the same is true of members of the Gavell and Downe families.[130]

References to witchcraft accusations in Cobham occur only once in the assize records, when Joan Gowse, wife of Roger Gowse, was found guilty in 1565 of having bewitched to death an ox belonging to James Adowne.[131] One crime particularly associated with Cobham and the surrounding area was highway robbery.[132] The stretch of Portsmouth Road between Esher and Street Cobham, where the road crossed Fairmile Common, was a notorious spot for attacks on travellers. It was here that in August 1633 a royal messenger travelling to Viscount Montagu's house at Cowdray in Sussex was ambushed at gunpoint, killing his assailant when he fought back.[133] St George's Hill, to the north-west of Cobham, was another place where travellers might be attacked.[134] In most reported cases, however, neither the assailants nor their victims were local, and this was a crime that would rarely have had any direct impact on the community.

The loss of Surrey's early-seventeenth-century quarter sessions records, and also of Archdeaconry of Surrey church court records for the same period, make it difficult to judge whether Cobham experienced, like Terling in Essex or the town of Dorchester, a 'reformation of manners' in response to increased social pressures.[135] It is, nevertheless, evident that puritanism had strong roots in mid-Surrey, and that the godly played an important part in parish affairs in Cobham. The Gavell, Sutton and Bickerstaffe families had demonstrable puritan connections, and William King, who served as vicar of Cobham from 1626 until the mid-1640s, was a leading figure in mid-Surrey's godly community.[136] Despite Samuel Pepys's later recollection of King as a dull preacher, 'of whom we made so much scorn' when he was minister of Ashtead, he was clearly a popular and influential figure in Cobham.[137] Several Cobham testators are known to have left him small bequests in their wills, most often for preaching their funeral sermons, and at least four named him overseer; he acted as witness to several more wills.[138] Henry Locksmith, for instance, who died in 1637, requested in his will that King would 'take the paines to teach and instruct the congregacon assembled at my buryall in the way to eternall happines which God grante they may followe', and he appointed his 'lovinge friend' as one of his overseers and left him 40s.[139] It is possible that it was King's arrival in the parish that led to the revival of the Cobham 'Church Book' at the end of the 1620s, and to a more rigorous keeping of churchwardens' accounts.[140] Actions taken against Cobham alehouse offenders in the 1620s and 1630s may also have reflected his influence – though such actions may just as likely have been the result of central government pressure or of decisions taken by JPs at quarter sessions.[141]

A more traditional response to the problem of poverty in the local community, and one for which there is a good deal of evidence in Cobham, was for testators to leave bequests in their wills to the local poor, or to provide for the setting up of parochial charities.[142] Several small charities were established in Cobham during the first half of the seventeenth century, suggesting that levels of poverty in the parish were such that local needs could not be fully met by the poor rate. £1 a year in bread to the poor was, for instance, left in 1614 by Roger Bellow out of Church Stile House in Cobham; £2 a year was left by Edmund Sutton in 1629, and £1 a year by Owen Peter in 1641.[143] Sara Cox, a member of the Sutton family who died in 1632, left £50 in her will for the poor of Cobham; her mother and executrix Cicelly Darnelly added a further £30, and the sum of £80 went in 1639 to acquiring land in Ripley principally for the benefit of Cobham's poor.[144] By the late 1660s at least twenty-five inhabitants a year were in receipt of assistance from these Cobham charities, as well as from the Henry Smith charity which benefited a number of Surrey parishes besides Cobham.[145]

LANDLORDS AND TENANTS

The parish of Cobham, like many communities across England, experienced protracted landlord-tenant conflict in the late sixteenth and early seventeenth centuries. These disputes, which revolved around contested tenurial rights and customs, were to have a lasting impact in the parish. They appear to have begun almost immediately after the Gavell family acquired the manor of Cobham, for as early as 1566 a case was brought against Robert Gavell in the Court of Requests by William Wrenn, a prominent copyholder.[146] Wrenn's case related to the size of the customary rent payable for his estate, and also to the confiscation by Gavell of thirty-eight acres of his copyhold lands following disagreement over the tenant's right to sublet.[147] The case was submitted to arbitration, and Wrenn's complaint that at 30s his customary rent was 2s more than it should have been was upheld; Gavell was ordered by the court to pay Wrenn £30 in compensation.[148] In 1577 Gavell was accused by Wrenn in the Court of Requests of having felled timber on his copyhold lands, contrary to the custom of the manor, and of having held on to the thirty-eight acres at the centre of the 1566 action.[149] Wrenn also alleged that Gavell was evading his responsibilities towards the community by not contributing sufficiently to assessments: Gavell had, he claimed, got the greatest and most profitable part of the manor into his hands and now 'laye a hevy burden uppon the poorer tenants contrarye to the ancient usage, equitie and consciens'.[150]

The case between Wrenn and Gavell was followed by a series of actions brought by Cobham copyholders against the Gavells, as the family attempted to challenge and overturn manorial customs which, by the later sixteenth century, must have appeared increasingly disadvantageous to them. The active peasant land market that had developed in Surrey during the fifteenth century had continued to flourish after 1500, and there is much evidence in the court rolls of a high turnover in land in Cobham and of frequent subletting of copyholds by more substantial tenants.[151] At a time of high inflation, the Gavells might stand to gain financially from their leasehold rents, but customary rents from copyholds of inheritance were largely immune from inflationary pressures, and on the manor of Cobham, receipts from these rents remained stable throughout the late sixteenth and early seventeenth centuries at around £20 a year.[152] For the Gavells to improve their income from copyholds they would need to seek profits from other sources, notably entry fines and fines to demise copyhold tenements and to take timber. Cobham's tenants claimed in an action in 1594 that their entry fines should be no more than two years' customary rent, and that copyholders might take the timber growing on their holdings for new building as well as for repairs. They also claimed the right to demise their tenements for a fixed fine of 4d per year. Robert Gavell and his son Francis, against whom actions were brought in the Court of Requests, argued that entry fines were uncertain and that timber could only be taken by tenants for repairs to their premises; they also sought to demonstrate from the court rolls that tenants had, in the past, willingly paid uncertain fines to demise their tenements.[153] From detailed depositions taken in this case, it is evident that while most tenants entering copyholds had continued to pay fines of two years' customary rent, a small number had, crucially, been prepared to pay more, and at least four tenants had in recent years agreed to pay fines of above 4*d* per year for permission to demise their tenements.[154]

Cobham's manorial customs were quite distinct from those of neighbouring manors, and it would seem that in mid-Surrey manorial custom varied quite widely over a relatively small area. Tenants of Ham Court, for instance, paid one year's rent of assize upon descent or alienation, and upon descent a heriot of a best beast with the benefit of common of pasture and sheep walks.[155] By 1603, tenants of the manor of Walton were paying two years' value – or market rent – for entry fines, a level perhaps more common in southern England at the turn of the century than one or two years' customary rent.[156] Entry fines in Walton Leigh were, by 1650, said to be 'meerely arbitrable at the will of the lord'.[157] Tenants of the manor of Walton could take timber growing on their copyholds for repairs, though they claimed there were too few trees on their land for this, while Walton Leigh's tenants could take for both repairs and new building. Some Walton Leigh copyholds were subject to the payment of heriots, but not all.[158] On a number of manors in the vicinity of Cobham, including Ashtead and the crown manor of Chertsey Beomond, there is evidence from the early seventeenth century of tenants agreeing to compound with their landlords in exchange for reasonable entry fines.[159] On the mid-Surrey manor of West Humble in Mickleham, for instance, Sir Francis Stydolfe agreed in 1608 not to raise entry fines or to take timber growing on his tenants' copyholds, on the undertaking of the tenants to take such timber only for necessary repairs.[160]

One of the Cobham tenants most actively involved in the 1590s action against the Gavells was William King, originally a native of Fetcham, who had married Judith, daughter and heir of William Wrenn. Through his acquisition of Wrenn's copyhold, King had become one of Cobham's largest customary tenants, with holdings of more than 130 acres.[161] Other leading tenants who took part in the action included James Sutton and Anthony Bickerstaffe, men whose wealth and social standing was hardly less than that of the Gavells.[162] King was singled out by the Gavells as one of their most troublesome opponents. Their attempt to deprive him of his copyhold premises for refusing to pay an entry fine of £20 – rather than the equivalent of two years' worth of his annual rent of 28*s* – failed when in 1593 the Court of King's Bench ordered that he be allowed quiet possession of the premises.[163] The Gavells countered by claiming that King had infringed their rights by keeping unlicensed rabbit warrens on his holding, and they suggested that the tenants' claims to timber for new building were 'surmised and new found customes' that had been 'espetially contrived' by King.[164]

By the end of the 1590s, it seems that the dispute between landlords and tenants had been resolved in the Gavells' favour. Entries in the court rolls which showed that fines had, in a few cases, been higher than the customary fines claimed by the tenants may have been enough to persuade the judges that Cobham's entry fines were arbitrary rather than fixed. In 1598, following the conclusion of the tenants' action, the Gavells commissioned from the land surveyor Ralph Agas a comprehensive survey of the manor of Cobham. Agas was one of the pioneers of the new form of surveys by admeasurement, and his survey of the manor contained detailed descriptions of tenants' holdings measured by acreages rather than by the more traditional, and imprecise, Surrey virgates.[165] Entry fines recorded in court rolls from the early years of the seventeenth century were consistently higher than those imposed before 1590, and when William King's son was admitted to his holdings in 1614, the fine was put at £100, approximately 25% more than the estimated yearly value of the estate and one eighth of the sale value it was to realise seventeen years later.[166]

The Gavell family had good reason to seek to maximise their income from Cobham's customary holdings, and to adopt a course of action that was widespread among landlords at this time. Neither Robert Gavell, who died in 1595, nor his son Francis was particularly wealthy, and both had large families. Robert Gavell's lands in the Surrey parishes of Buckland and Reigate were left to a younger son rather than to his heir, and his property in Suffolk had to be sold to pay for legacies to his other children.[167] Francis Gavell, who inherited only the manor of Cobham and a small number of adjoining properties, was survived by nine children when he died in 1610, and he tried to leave substantial legacies to each of them.[168] He had already built up debts of nearly £2,000, including sums of between £30 and £40 owed to his servants and labourers in Cobham, and these, together with the legacies to his children, amounted to a total debt at the time of his death of £3,295.[169]

The Gavells' financial troubles brought them and their tenants increasingly within the sphere of influence of their wealthy neighbours the Vincents of Stoke d'Abernon. Sir Francis Vincent was a baronet, deputy lieutenant and JP, and was to serve as knight of the shire for Surrey in 1626.[170] The highest office held locally by Francis Gavell was as treasurer for maimed soldiers in Surrey's west and middle divisions.[171] As Gavell's debts built up, Vincent became increasingly involved in his neighbour's affairs. In 1609, only months before Gavell's death, Cobham Court, the manorial demesne and Chatley Farm were mortgaged to Vincent for £1,300, but the money raised by this had mostly been wasted by the time Gavell died. After Gavell's death several leasehold properties of the manor, and outlying properties in Cobham, were sold off, many of them to Vincent; Gavell's widow married Vincent, and his heir, also named Francis

Gavell, was made Vincent's ward and later married Vincent's daughter.[172] The younger Francis Gavell also fell heavily into debt, and in 1623 is said to have conveyed much of his estate to his father-in-law. After his death in January 1633, his son Vincent Gavell was in turn made a ward of Sir Francis and Sir Anthony Vincent.[173]

The Vincents held courts in Cobham in the years 1613–17, and also for much of the 1620s and 1630s, and they appear to have made the most of their control over the manor and its resources.[174] Sir Francis Vincent was, for example, accused in the 1630s of having secured grants of large parts of the younger Francis Gavell's estates, many without licence from the Court of Wards.[175] In 1634 a pardon was obtained for the alienation without licence by Francis Gavell, a week before his death in January 1633, of Chatley and the Hurst in Cobham to Sir Francis and Sir Anthony Vincent, while in 1638 an order of the Court of Wards was issued to restrain Sir Francis and Sir Anthony from fishing and felling trees on the land of their ward Vincent Gavell.[176] In an action brought after 1633 on Vincent Gavell's behalf, Sir Francis and Sir Anthony were charged with having taken the profits of the ward's estates, and of having 'receaved great sums of mony for fynes and making of estates, and made waste by cutting downe of woods and trees, and have gotten all the wrightings and evidences concerning the plaintiff's lands into theyr hands'.[177]

By the end of the 1630s, Cobham's tenants had experienced prolonged periods of conflict with their manorial lords and uncertainties over the future ownership and control of their manor. After years spent seeking to uphold their customary rights against the demands of the financially-embarrassed Gavells, Cobham's tenants had found themselves forced to contend with a more powerful, and by all accounts even more predatory family in the Vincents. The Gavell family did regain full control of the manor of Cobham when Vincent Gavell came of age, but his early death in 1643 was to create further uncertainty for Cobham's inhabitants. Within six years of Vincent Gavell's death Gerrard Winstanley and his fellow Diggers were occupying parts of the manorial waste, denouncing lords of manors and calling on tenants to boycott manorial courts and withhold all customary dues. It would of course be an exaggeration to claim that the rise of the Digger movement came as a direct consequence of the pre-1640 landlord-tenant conflicts in Cobham, for similar stories of conflict could be told from numerous manors and parishes across southern England. Cobham's experience of conflict was, however, likely to have helped exacerbate the local social divisions which Winstanley later exploited to good effect. But for Winstanley to develop his revolutionary programme, and to gain the local support he needed to put it into practice, would require the additional experiences of the impact of civil war, a breakdown of settled church government in the locality, and exposure to the radical religious ideas that circulated in the aftermath of war.

NOTES

1 *Victoria County of History of Surrey* (hereafter *VCH Surrey*), vol. 3 (1911), pp. 442–3. For Cobham's population, see below, pp. 9–11.

2 G. J. Copley (ed.), *Camden's Britannia: Surrey and Sussex* (London, 1977), p. 2; Thomas Fuller, *The Worthies of England*, ed. John Freeman (London, 1952), p. 542; Peter Brandon, *A History of Surrey* (London, 1977), pp. 14–16; Peter Brandon and Brian Short, *The South East from AD 1000* (London, 1990), pp. 6–8.

3 T. E. C. Walker, 'Cobham: manorial history', *Surrey Archaeological Collections* (hereafter *SAC*), 58 (1961), pp. 47–78; David Taylor, *Cobham: A History* (Chichester, 2003), pp. 1–2.

4 Walker, 'Manorial history', p. 71. Church Field contained roughly 140 acres.

5 Walker, 'Manorial history', pp. 68–75; *VCH Surrey*, 3, pp. 442–3. As late as 1793 the manor of Cobham still contained 1,314 acres of common and waste, besides c2,789 acres of 'old enclosures': Walker, 'Manorial history', pp. 73–4.

6 Surrey History Centre (hereafter SHC), 2610/29/3, fols 1–5. Figures for the demesne were c45% arable, 26.5% pasture, 17.5% woodland and 11% meadow.

7 SHC, 2610/29/3; TNA, REQ2/34/23.

8 SHC, 3817/1; 2610/29/3; London Metropolitan Archives (hereafter LMA), DW/PA/7/10, fol. 280; DW/PA/7/11, fol. 443; Brian Short, 'The South East', in Joan Thirsk (ed.), *The Agrarian History of England and Wales*, vol. 5, part I (Cambridge, 1984), pp. 288, 291; Brandon and Short, *South East*, p. 182.

9 Hampshire Record Office (hereafter HRO), 1585B18/2; 1587B84/2; 1608B72/2; TNA, PROB4/15639. Cf. HRO, 1625B16/2; East Sussex Record Office (hereafter ESRO), GLY303.

10 HRO, 1585B18/1; SHC, K44/1/6; 2610/29/3, fols 19v–20. For the late survival of virgates in Surrey, see Mark Forrest, 'The Estates of Chertsey Abbey: Land Management and Rural Society 1300–1550' (unpublished PhD thesis, Royal Holloway, University of London 2002), pp. 36, 40, 120.

11 HRO, 1585B18/2.

12 HRO, 1587B84/2; 1608B72/2; 1625B16/2; TNA, PROB4/15639; REQ2/159/13; SHC, 835/37.

13 SHC, 165/49; Walker, 'Manorial history', p. 71.

14 Below, pp. 129, 166.

15 St George's Chapel Archives and Chapter Library (hereafter St George's CAL), Parliamentary Surveys, vol. II, fols 93–8; MS XI. M3, fols 108v, 109v, 110v; *VCH Surrey*, 3, p. 445; Walker, 'Manorial history', p. 78; David C. Taylor, *Cobham Houses and Their Occupants* (Cobham, 1999), pp. 12, 146.

16 SHC, 2610/29/3, fols 25v–26; TNA, LR2/190, fol. 265v; SC12/22/34.

17 *VCH Surrey*, 3, p. 444; Walker, 'Manorial history', pp. 52–6 for Downe and Heywood; TNA, E41/167 for Chilbrook.

18 Borough English was practised on the manors of Walton and Walton Leigh: TNA, E317/Surrey/56, p. 11; SHC, G52/7/3. Cf. TNA, E317/Surrey/31; E317/Surrey/46, p. 15; SHC, K10; K58/3/3/2; 351/1/5–6. Primogeniture and copyholds of inheritance appear to have been standard on former Chertsey Abbey manors: Forrest, 'Chertsey Abbey', pp. 184, 208.

19 SHC, 2610/29/3. 19 freeholders were also listed in a Cobham rental copied into a 1550 Court of Augmentation ledger of rentals of monastic lands: TNA, LR2/190, fols 264–74.

20 SHC, 2610/29/3. For numbers of customary holdings, see also Forrest, 'Chertsey Abbey', p. 195 (for holdings in 1490); TNA, LR2/190, fols 264–74 (c1550); SC12/22/34 (1626).

21 LMA, DW/PA/7/10, fol. 144; SHC, 2610/11/8/33; John H. Harvey, 'Thomas Clay's plan of the manor of Great Bookham, 1614–1617', *Proceedings of the Leatherhead and District Local History Society*, 2, 10 (1966), pp. 281–3.

22 LMA, DW/PA/7/13, fols 222, 354v; TNA, PROB11/208, fol. 446.

23 SHC, COB/1/1.

24 *VCH Surrey*, 3, pp. 443–4; Walker, 'Manorial history', pp. 48–9; *Calendar of the Patent Rolls preserved in the Public Record Office* (hereafter *PR*), *Philip and Mary, AD 1553–54*, p. 169; *PR, Eliz. I, 1563–66*, pp. 262–3. Robt and Dorothy Gavell held their first court in 1566, and the manor remained in the Gavell family's possession until its sale in 1708.

25 LMA, DW/PA/5/1617/120; DW/PA/7/5, fol. 127; DW/PA/7/10, fols 20–1, 254–5v; DW/PA/7/11, fols 548v; 559v; TNA, E331/5, fol. 68; PROB11/227, fols 134v–35; SHC, K44/2/1; K145/5, 9; 296.

26 SHC, K145/9; 296/1–2; 1974/40, pp. 5, 20; COB/5/1; St George's CAL, MS XI. M3, fols 110v, 115, 116, 117; LMA, DW/PA/7/10, fols 20–1; *VCH Surrey*, 3, p. 444; Walker, 'Manorial history', pp. 48, 75; Taylor, *Cobham Houses*, pp. 12, 147–9.

27 TNA, ASSI 35/92/8, 12; ASSI 35/93/5, 7, 10, 11; ASSI 35/94/7; SHC, K44/1/7–9; 2610/11/8/33; 4398/1/1,4–6, 8–10; COB/6/16; George H. Sabine (ed.), *The Works of Gerrard Winstanley* (Ithaca, 1941), pp. 433, 435.

28 TNA, PROB/11/306, fols 1–1v; ASSI 35/84/1; ASSI 35/92/12; ASSI 35/93/5, 7, 10, 11; LMA, DW/PA/7/8, fol. 6.

29 Sabine, *Works*, pp. 433, 435; below, pp. 77, 171–2, 193–4.

30 TNA, LR2/190, fols 266, 270v; C. A .F. Meekings (ed.), *Abstracts of Surrey Feet of Fines 1509–1558* (Guildford, Surrey Record Society (hereafter SRS, 1946), p. 68.

31 TNA, E134/9 Jas I/H7; E134/19 Jas I/T2; E317/Surrey/44; National Library of Wales (hereafter NLW), Wynnstay 161, fol. 103v. They had acquired a reversionary interest in Pains Hill in 1572: TNA, E41/117.

32 Croydon Archives Service, 'Calendar of deeds and documents relating to Croydon from the earliest date to 1743'; Croydon parish registers 1538–1679 (copies), *passim*; Manor of Croydon minute book, vol. 1 (1582–1722) (typed transcript, ed. Clarence G. Paget, nd), pp. 7, 12, 13, 17–18, 20, 22, 24, 26–7, 29, 34, 38–9, 41, 43, 45–7, 49, 53, 59, 69, 99, 113, 134, 139; Clarence G. Paget (ed.), *Abstracts of the Ancient Muniments of the Whitgift Foundation, Croydon* (Croydon, 1934), pp. 104–5, 108, 126–30, 139; A. C. Ducarel, *Some Account of the Town, Church and Archiepiscopal Palace of Croydon* (London, 1783), appx, pp. 78, 149–50, 154.

33 TNA, E115/31/95; E317/Surrey/44; W. Bruce Bannerman (ed.), *The Visitations of the County of Surrey . . . 1530, 1572 and 1623* (London, Harleian Society, 1899), p. 106.

34 TNA, E317/Surrey/44; PROB11/248, fols 393v–95; Skinners' Hall, register of apprenticeships and freedoms 1601–94 (now in the Guildhall Library), fols 48, 83, 87, 108v; Corporation of London Records Office (hereafter CLRO), CF1/25/131v.

35 SHC, COB/1/1.

36 TNA, SP16/175/105; 177/56; 182/38. Cf. C. W. Chalklin, *Seventeenth-Century Kent: A Social and Economic History* (London, 1965), p. 121.

37 SHC, COB/1/1, p. 39; 2610/11/8/33; LMA, DW/PA/7/12, fol. 495; D. L. Powell with H. Jenkinson (eds), *Surrey Quarter Sessions Records: Order Book and Sessions Rolls 1663–1666* (Kingston, SRS, 1938), p. 241. Edm. Starr was described as a fuller in 1622: J. S. Cockburn (ed.), *Calendar of Assize Records: Surrey Indictments, James I* (London, HMSO, 1980), p. 325.

38 TNA, E179/257/28; SHC, 2610/11/8/33; LMA, DW/PA/7/10, fol. 144; DW/PA/7/11, fol. 498v.

39 Kingston Museum and Heritage Service (hereafter KMHS), KP4/14/1; LMA, DW/PA/7/10, fol. 289v; DW/PA/7/11, fol. 43; SHC, 361/14/6.

40 For evidence of building activity in Cobham in the late-16th cent., see SHC, K44/1/5; TNA, REQ2/159/13 (depositions of John Derrick, Nich. Foster, Thos Adowne, Jas Sutton, Jas Hypkin).

41 M. E. Blackman (ed.), *Ashley House Building Accounts 1602–1607* (Guildford, SRS, 1977); Nicholas Cooper, *Houses of the Gentry, 1480–1680* (New Haven and London, 1999), pp. 131, 137, 176–8; John Gurney, 'Lady Jane Berkeley, Ashley House, and architectural innovation in late-Elizabethan England', *Architectural History*, 43 (2000), pp. 113–20; TNA, SP16/153/69; SP16/158/48, 54.

42 ESRO, GLY 227, 235–51.

43 SHC, COB/1/1, pp. 5,11; LMA, DW/PA/7/4, fol. 167; DW/PA/7/8, fol. 105; HRO, 1561B124–5; TNA, PROB4/3124; Centre for Kentish Studies (hereafter CKS), U269 A 2/1, fol. 19; West Yorkshire Archive Service, Leeds, TN/SH/G2, G3, G4, G11; Anne Daly (ed.), *Kingston upon Thames Register of Apprentices*, (Kingston, SRS, 1974), p. 23; J. Evans, 'Extracts from the private account book of Sir William More, of Loseley', *Archaeologia*, 36 (1855), pp. 297–301.

44 SHC, COB/5/1; CKS, U269 A2/1.

45 LMA, DW/PA/7/12, fol. 484; DW/PC/5/1667/26; TNA, E179/257/28. Henry's great bible was left to his wife Mary.

46 TNA, PROB11/118, fol. 264; PROB11/272, fol. 346v; Guildhall Library (hereafter GL), 9051/6, fol. 143v; MS 21742/1; LMA, DW/PA/5/1575/42; DW/PA/7/11, fol. 442; DW/PA/7/12, fol. 100v; DW/PA/7/13, fol. 308; SHC, 793/1; 2381/1/1, p. 5; HRO, 1587B/84/1–2; Daly, *Kingston Register of Apprentices*, p. 23; J. S. Cockburn (ed.), *Calendar of Assize Records: Surrey Indictments, Elizabeth I* (London, HMSO, 1980), p. 510.

47 Blackman, *Ashley House Building Accounts*, xix, pp. 23, 54, 56–7, 68, 70. For Taylor's opposition to the Diggers; below, pp. 155–6, 157.

48 Figures derived from G. J. Armytage (ed.), *A Visitation of the County of Surrey 1662–1668* (London, Harleian Society, 1910).

49 SHC, 442, fols. 37–55; ESRO, GLY 276A; TNA, SP28/335, fol. 473; SP28/291 (unfol.), papers re dispute Francis Drake and the parish of Walton, c1650; *VCH Surrey*, 3, pp. 448–49, 469–70; P. W. Hasler (ed.) *The History of Parliament: The House of Commons 1558–1603* (London, HMSO, 1981), vol. 2, pp. 55, 558–9.

50 *VCH Surrey*, 3, p. 450; TNA, LR2/226, fol. 208.

51 SHC, COB/1/1; John Aubrey, *The Natural History and Antiquities of the County of Surrey* (1718–19), vol. 3, pp. 131–2.

52 William Lilly, *History of his Life and Times from the Year 1602, to 1681*, ed. Elias Ashmole (1715), pp. 34–5, 37, 68.

53 Keith Wrightson and David Levine, *Poverty and Piety in an English Village: Terling, 1525–1700* (revised edn, Oxford, 1995), pp. 73–109; Keith Wrightson, 'The politics of the parish in early modern England', in Paul Griffiths, Adam Fox and Steve Hindle (eds), *The Experience of Authority in Early Modern England* (London, 1996), pp. 13–14; Keith Wrightson, *Earthly Necessities: Economic Lives in Early Modern Britain* (New Haven and London, 2000), pp. 31–68.

54 LMA, DW/PA/7/5, fol. 127; DW/PA/7/10, fols 254–5v; DW/PA/7/11, fols 482, 548v; SHC, COB/1/1, pp. 30, 40, 42; K145/9; 296; 2610/29/3, fols 11–12, 13v–14; TNA, SC12/22/34; PROB11/227, fols 134v–35; HRO, 1608B72/1; St George's CAL, MS Xl. M3, fols 109v–10v, 116.

55 LMA, DW/PA/7/10, fols 254–5v.

56 LMA, DW/PA/7/11, fols 373, 482; DW/PA/7/12, fol. 300v; DW/PA/7/13, fols 228, 403v.

57 LMA, DW/PA/7/9, fols 220v–21; DW/PA/7/10, fol. 289v; DW/PA/7/11, fol. 482; DW/PA/7/12, fols 73, 389v, 495; DW/PA/7/13, fols 186, 218v; TNA, PROB11/175, fols 97v–98.

58 SHC, 2610/29/3, fols 7v–8, 20v–21; TNA, E41/167.

59 SHC, K44/1/8; TNA, SP16/192/66. Her second husband John Wisson sat on the court leet jury in right of his wife: K44/1/8.

60 LMA, DW/PA/7/13, fols 178v, 222. Cf. DW/PA/7/12, fol. 217v.

61 SHC, 1974/40, p. 9. Cf. 181/17/5.

62 SHC, K44/1/5–9; K176/10/2; 181/17/5; 2610/11/8/33; 4398/1/1, 3–6, 8–10; TNA, SC2/204/43.

63 Sources as in the preceding note. Meetings took place most often in October (before 1630) and April (after 1630).

64 SHC, K44/1/5, 7–9; 2610/11/8/33; 4398/1/1, 3–6, 8–10; TNA, SC2/204/43. No information available for October 1642–April 1646.

65 LMA, DW/PA/7/8, fol. 242; TNA, REQ2/159/13.

66 SHC, K10/2–3; K44/1/8; 439; 2610/11/8/33. Duncombe was accused by tenants of the manor of Woking of interfering in the way manorial officers were chosen; they later accused their landlords of having employed 'sundrie uniust stewards': TNA, E134/7CarI/M39; House of Lords Record Office (hereafter HLRO), Main Papers 1646, 30 July.

67 Owen Manning and William Bray, *The History and Antiquities of the County of Surrey*, vol. I (London, 1804), p. 39; B. D. Henning (ed.), *The House of Commons 1660–1690* (London, History of Parliament Trust, 1983), vol. I, p. 584.

68 For the 16th-cent. decline of courts leet in Norfolk, see Jane Whittle, *The Development of Agrarian Capitalism: Land and Labour in Norfolk 1440–1580* (Oxford, 2000), pp. 55–6.

69 SHC, 2610/11/8/33, p. 28; 4398/1/9. For 16th-cent. presentments for breaches of the peace and insulting language, see TNA SC2/204/3; SHC, K44/1/5.

70 St George's CAL, MS Xl. M3.

71 St George's CAL, Parliamentary Surveys, vol. II, fols 86–91; MS Xl. M3, fols 109v, 110v, 112, 113, 113v, 114v, 115.

72 SHC, COB/5/1. Cf. Mark Goldie, 'The unacknowledged republic: officeholding in early modern England', in Tim Harris (ed.), *The Politics of the Excluded, c. 1500–1850* (Basingstoke, 2001), pp. 163–4. Parish officers in Cobham were chosen at meetings held on Easter Monday: COB/5/1.

73 SHC, COB/5/1, accounts for 1659, 60, 66, 67, 68.

74 TNA, E179/257/30: SHC, COB/5/1.

75 For the rise of vestries see esp. Steve Hindle, 'The political culture of the middling sort in English rural communities, c. 1550–1700', in Harris, *Politics of the Excluded*, pp. 125–52.

76 SHC, COB/5/1, accts for 1629–30.

77 SHC, COB/5/1, accts for 1630–31, 1631–32.

78 TNA, SP16/182/7, 190/65, 192/66, 242/79, 250/69, 260/66, 267/75, 272/22, 314/25–6, 328/68, 328/73, 348/95, 363/123, 363/132, 364/128, 383/31, 386/110, 395/24, 395/119, 426/88.

79 TNA, SP16/250/69, 262/46.

80 TNA, SP16/328/68. See also SP16/314/25.

81 TNA, SP16/214/99. Sutton also appeared before the Privy Council in 1640, on an unrelated matter: PC2/52, fol. 286v.

82 TNA, PC2/49, fols 196, 201.

83 TNA, E179/188/481; E179/258/4; C. A. F. Meekings (ed.), *Surrey Hearth Tax 1664* (Kingston, SRS, 1940), ci–cii; Anne Whiteman (ed.), *The Compton Census of 1676: a Critical Edition* (British Academy, Records of Social and Economic History n.s. 10, Oxford 1986), p. 96.

84 TNA, E179/184/141, 149; SP12/50, fols 44–4v, 137; British Library (hereafter BL), Harl. MS 595, fol. 248. 47 householders in Cobham were assessed in the 1525 assessment for the second payment of the 1523 subsidy; 44 had been assessed for the first payment in 1524. 67 male Cobham inhabitants were listed in the 1569 muster returns. A multiplier of 1.54 used with the 1603 communicant returns, to take account of the estimated 35% of the population too young to be included in the returns, produces a population figure of roughly 370. Cf. E. A. Wrigley and R. S. Schofield, *The Population History of England 1541–1871* (London, 1981), p. 569.

85 TNA, E179/188/481; E179/258/4. A multiplier of 4.3 used with the 1664 hearth tax roll and Cobham hearth tax returns c. 1664–66 produces population figures of 516 and 486 respectively; a multiplier of 1.54 used with the Compton Census of 1676 produces a population figure of around 450.

86 For problems involved in estimating population totals from such sources, see especially Tom Arkell, 'A method for estimating population totals from the Compton census returns', in K. Schurer and T. Arkell (eds), *Surveying the People* (Oxford, 1992), pp. 97–116, and for the problem of under-assessment and evasion in 1524–25, Whittle, *Agrarian Capitalism*, pp. 204–9.

87 BL, Harl. MS 595, fols 242–50; Meekings, *Hearth Tax*, lxxxix–cxxxiii; Jeremy Boulton, *Neighbourhood and Society: A London Suburb in the Seventeenth Century* (Cambridge, 1987), pp. 18–27, 34. Cf. Brandon and Short, *South East*, pp. 191–6.

88 SHC, COB/1/1.

89 SHC, COB/1/1.

90 Wrigley and Schofield, *Population History*, pp. 677–9; Wrightson and Levine, *Poverty and Piety*, pp. 63–5, and cf. *ibid.*, pp. 46–7; Jeremy Greenwood, 'A lost seventeenth-century demographic crisis: rural Surrey', *Local Population Studies*, 23, 1979, pp. 39–40; Brandon and Short, *South East*, p. 191.

91 For the century as a whole the annual average of burials was approximately 12.6.

92 7 burials, or a fifth of the year's total, took place in September 1640: SHC, COB/1/1. For reports of the plague in Weybridge in August 1640, see M. E. Blackman and J. S. L. Pulford, *A Short History of Weybridge* (Weybridge, 1991), p. 23. A serious outbreak of plague had also taken place in Surrey in 1637: TNA, SP16/343/36, 58; 344/62; 349/13; 355/130; 359; 364/112; PC2/48, p. 111.

93 In the period 1659–1701 recorded baptisms averaged at c. 16.6 and burials at c. 11.2 per annum; the average for the whole period 1610–1701 was c. 15.69 baptisms and c. 12.6 burials per annum.

94 Figures taken for the whole period 1610–49. No information is available for the years 1628–30, and only partial information for the years 1644–49.

95 TNA, E179/184/141, 149; E179/188/481, 504; E179/257/30; E179/258/4; E179/346.

96 Wrightson and Levine, *Poverty and Piety*, pp. 32–6. Cf. Marjorie Keniston McIntosh, *A Community Transformed: The Manor and Liberty of Havering, 1500–1620* (Cambridge, 1991), pp. 165–6, 170–1.

97 TNA, E179/184/149; E179/188/481; E179/258/4. 45 out of 120 households with 1 hearth or excused in the 1664 returns, and 51 out of 113 in an undated assessment of 1664–66. Cf. E179/346 for a Cobham exemption certificate from November 1672 containing 37 names.

98 Cf. Whittle, *Agrarian Capitalism*, pp. 204–9.

99 Meekings, *Hearth Tax*. The lowest figure (12.12%, or 19 households) relates to Walton on Thames and may be too low. A Walton exemption certificate from November 1670 lists 22 alms takers and 32 other poor people for whom exemption was claimed: TNA, E179/346.

100 Meekings, *Hearth Tax*. Exemption rates were also high in the built-up areas near Southwark.

101 Categories adapted from those used by Wrightson and Levine, *Poverty and Piety*, pp. 34–5.

102 TNA, E179/184/149; E179/188/481; E179/258/4. 15 out of 47 in 1525; 22 out of 120 in 1664; 20 out of 113 in 1664–66. 22 households were in this category in 1663 and 24 in 1672–73: E179/257/30; E179/188/504. The percentages of the wealthiest two categories in 1525 and 1664 were, for gentry inhabitants and very large farmers, 10.6% and 14.2% respectively, and for yeomen and prosperous craftsmen 29.8% and 30%. Cf. Wrightson and Levine, *Poverty and Piety*, pp. 34–5.

103 TNA, E179/257/30; Walker, 'Manorial history', p. 49.

104 TNA, E317/Surrey/44, p. 1.

105 TNA, PROB11/351, fols 138–9v. Cf. PROB4/12962.

106 LMA, DW/PA/7/8, fols 86v, 354; DW/PA/7/11, fol. 506; DW/PA/7/13, fols 160, 319; TNA, PROB4/15639.

107 For a recent overview, see Colin Platt, *The Great Rebuildings of Tudor and Stuart England*, (London, 1994), pp. 1–27.

108 TNA, REQ2/159/13. See also SP15/33/74.

109 SHC, K44/1/5; TNA, REQ2/159/13.

110 National Monuments Record Centre, Surrey Domestic Buildings Research Group report 3550; English Heritage statutory lists, Cobham; Taylor, *Cobham*, pp. 41–3; Taylor, *Cobham Houses*, pp. 19, 31–2, 85, 101, 107, 111, 125–6, 141, 145–6, 179, 183.

111 SHC, 835/37.

112 LMA, DW/PA/7/8, fol. 86v.

113 HRO, 1587B84/2.

114 HRO, 1585B18/2.

115 LMA, DW/PA/7/8, fols 86v, 350; HRO, 1587B84/2; SHC, 835/37; TNA, PROB11/351, fol. 138–9v.

116 TNA, PROB4/15639.

117 TNA, PROB4/15639. Thos King was assessed at five hearths in 1662 and 1664: E179/257/30; E179/188/481.

118 LMA, DW/PA/7/8, fol. 354; 9, fols 310v–11; 10, fols 220–21v; 11, fol. 559v; 12, fol. 241v; 13, fol. 191v; HRO, 1587B84/1. Cf. TNA, PROB11/297, fols 141–2.

119 TNA, PROB11/216, fols 218v–219; LMA, DW/PA/7/8, fol. 354; 10, fols 220v–21; 11, fol. 559v; 13, fols 21v, 160; SHC, K165/224/1. For bequests of clothing, see esp. Wrightson and Levine, *Poverty and Piety*, pp. 38–9.

120 LMA, DW/PA/7/8, fol. 86v; 12, fol. 484. Cf. DW/PA/7/13, fol. 181v.

121 SHC, LM 637.

122 TNA, SP16/165/59. Cf. Buchanan Sharp, *In Contempt of all Authority* (Berkeley, 1980), p. 163, for new cottages bordering Blackmore and Chippenham forests, of which 162 out of 213 had no land.

123 SHC, K44/1/8. Cf. K44/1/7. The order, with other presentments, was signed by Robt Bickerstaffe and John A. Downe. For similar orders made in Walton's manor court in 1610, see 442, fol. 42b. Cf. Steve Hindle, 'Persuasion and protest in the Caddington Common enclosure dispute 1635–1639', *P&P*, 158 (1998), pp. 49–50, for similar orders made in Beds in 1610–12.

124 SHC, 2610/11/8/33; 4398/1/6.

125 Joel Samaha, *Law and Order in Historical Perspective: the Case of Elizabethan Essex* (New York, 1974); J. A. Sharpe, *Crime in Early Modern England, 1550–1750* (London, 1984). Cf. Cynthia B. Herrup, *The Common Peace: Participation and the Criminal Law in Seventeenth-Century England* (Cambridge, 1987), pp. 38–41.

126 D. L. Powell, *Guide to Archives and Other Collections of Documents Relating to Surrey: Quarter Sessions Records* (London, SRS 1931); H. Jenkinson and D. L. Powell (eds), *Surrey Quarter Sessions Records: Order Book and Sessions Rolls 1659–1661* (Kingston, SRS, 1934), p. 41.

127 Indictments for theft peaked in 1587, following the poor harvest of 1586: Cockburn, *Surrey Indictments: Eliz. I*, pp. 304–10.

128 TNA, SC2/204/43; Cockburn, *Surrey Indictments: Jas I*, p. 116.

129 SHC, K44/1/8; Cockburn, *Surrey Indictments: Jas I*, p. 114.

130 Cockburn, *Surrey Indictments: Eliz. I*, pp. 244, 288, 332, 382, 472; Cockburn, *Surrey Indictments: Jas I*, pp. 96, 114, 142.

131 Cockburn, *Surrey Indictments: Eliz.* I, p. 50.

132 *PR 1557–58*, p. 143; Cockburn, *Surrey Indictments: Eliz. I*, pp. 8, 93, 129, 142, 158, 160, 212–13, 215, 240, 350; Cockburn, *Surrey Indictments: Jas I*, pp. 70, 159.

133 TNA, SP16/244/80.

134 Cockburn, *Surrey Indictments: Eliz.* I, p. 93.

135 Wrightson and Levine, *Poverty and Piety*, esp. pp. 177–83, 198–200; David Underdown, *Fire from Heaven: Life in an English Town in the Seventeenth Century* (London, 1992), pp. 90–166. Cf. William Hunt, *The Puritan Moment: The Coming of Revolution in an English County* (Cambridge, Massachusetts 1983), pp. 79–84, 140–4; Robert von Friedeburg, 'Reformation of manners and the social composition of offenders in an East Anglian cloth village: Earls Colne, Essex, 1531–1642', JBS, 29 (1990), 347–85; Tom Webster, *Stephen Marshall and Finchingfield* (Chelmsford, 1994), pp. 5–9.

136 TNA, PROB11/171, fols 220v ff; PROB11/233; PROB11/248, fols 393v–95; PROB11/338; A. G. Matthews, *Calamy Revised* (Oxford, 1937), pp. 86, 391.

137 TNA, E331/5; Robert Latham and William Matthews (eds), *The Diary of Samuel Pepys*, vol. 4 (London, 1971), p. 247; T. E. C. Walker, 'Cobham incumbants and curates', *SAC*, 71 (1977), pp. 208–10. King was from Surrey, but does not appear to have been closely related to the King family of Cobham. His will shows that he held free and copyhold land in Leatherhead, which may indicate that this was where his family originated: TNA, PROB11/338.

138 LMA, DW/PA/7/11, fol. 482, 548v; DW/PA/7/12, fols 217v, 241v, 300v, 389v, 484; DW/PA/7/13, fols 21v, 218v, 354v, 403v; TNA, PROB11/216, fols 218v–219.

139 TNA, PROB11/175, fol. 98.

140 Above, pp. 8–9

141 SHC, 2610/11/8/33, p. 28; TNA, SP16/190/65; SP16/314/25.

142 For bequests to the poor, see LMA, DW/PA/7/8, fol. 324 (6s 8d left by Geo. Marsh, yeoman, 1602); fol. 6 (£5 left by John A. Downe, gent, 1607); DW/PA/7/11, fol. 443 (10s left by Nich. Foster, yeoman, 1627); fol. 482 (10s left by Geo. Sutton, husbandman, nd [c1628]); fol. 559v (20s left by Joane Sutton, widow, 1630); DW/PA/7/12, fol. 241v (5s left by Wm Otway, 1631); fol. 73 (20s left by Edmond Maisters, gent, nd [c1632]); DW/PA/7/13, fol. 222 (5s left by John Marsh, yeoman, 1638), fol. 149v (£5 left by Owen Peter, yeoman, 1640); fol. 191v (10s left by Rich. Flint, yeoman, 1641); fol. 160 (£5 left by Rich. King, yeoman, 1641); TNA, PROB11/175 (50s left by Henry Locksmith, gent, 1637); PROB11/208, fol. 446 (40s left by Geo. Marsh, yeoman, 1648); PROB11/227, fols 160–1v (10s in money or bread left by Wm Sponge, yeoman, 1650); PROB11/297, fols 141ff (£3 left by Mary Vaghan, widow, 1657); PROB11/351, fols 138–9v (£5 left by Katherine Sutton, widow, 1675). Cf. Steve Hindle, 'Power, poor relief and social relations in Holland Fen, c. 1600–1800', *HJ*, 41 (1998), pp. 83–4 on the significance of bequests to the poor.

143 LMA, DW/PA/7/11, fol. 548v; DW/PA/7/13, fol. 149v; P76/JS1/133; SHC, COB/5/1; COB/6/2; Taylor, *Cobham Houses*, p. 34; *VCH Surrey*, 3, p. 447.

144 SHC, COB/6/17–19; COB/5/1; Surrey Record Office, *County Archivist's Half-Yearly Report*, 27 March 1984. See also Cicelly Darnelly's 1654 will: TNA, PROB11/258, fols 263v–4v.

145 SHC, COB/5/1. Cf. TNA, C93/31/6.

146 TNA, E41/123.

147 TNA, E41/123; REQ2/34/23.

148 TNA, E41/123. Wrenn received £15 of this sum on 12 April 1566. Gavell was allowed to retain possession of the disputed lands for a year.

149 TNA, REQ2/34/23; REQ2/159/192.

150 TNA, REQ2/159/192. cf. REQ2/159/51. Gavell's practice in the payment of the fifteenths was contrasted with custom from the time the manor belonged to Chertsey Abbey: E133/10/1626.

151 TNA, SC2/204/43; SHC, K44/1/5. For a detailed discussion of the Surrey land market in the 15th and 16th centuries, Forrest, 'Chertsey Abbey', pp. 185, 197–230.

152 TNA, SC12/22/34; Forrest, 'Chertsey Abbey', p. 126.

153 TNA, REQ2/159/13; SP15/33/74; SHC, K44/1/5.

154 TNA, REQ2/159/13; SP12/15/33/4.

155 St George's CAL, Parliamentary surveys, vol. II, fol. 98.

156 TNA, LR2/226, fols 259–60. Further afield, Pirbright tenants were said to pay two-and-a-half years' purchase: SP23/195, p. 53.

157 TNA, E317/Surrey/55, p. 11. The entry fine paid in 1636 and 1650 for Great Rummors, a tenement with twelve acres in Walton held of the manor of Walton Leigh, was £12: SHC, 351/1/5–7.

158 TNA, E317/Surrey/55, p. 11; LR2/226, fols 259–60.

159 SHC, 6200/(632) for Chertsey Beomond, where the tenants agreed in 1627–29 to pay the Crown £1,086 in exchange for confirmation that entry fines should not exceed one year's rent; *VCH Surrey*, 3, p. 249, for Ashtead. Cf. Eric Kerridge, *Agrarian Problems in the Sixteenth Century and After* (London, 1969), pp. 54–5.

160 SHC, G63/1/12.

161 SHC, 2610/29/3. Cf. John Gurney, 'William King, Winstanley and Cobham', in Andrew Bradstock (ed.), *Winstanley and the Diggers 1649–1999* (London, 2000), p. 43.

162 TNA, REQ2/159/13; SP15/33/74. Cf. Hindle, 'Persuasion and protest', pp. 66–72, 75 for involvement of substantial copyholders in anti-enclosure agitation in the Chilterns.

163 TNA, SP46/19/212.

164 TNA, SP15/33/74; REQ2/159/13.

165 SHC, 2610/29/3. For Agas, see Kerridge, *Agrarian Problems*, p. 29; R. W. Hoyle (ed.), *The Estates of the English Crown 1558–1640* (Cambridge, 1992), pp. 67, 205–6, 307.

166 TNA, SC2/204/43; C10/22/86; SHC, 1974/40; 2610/11/8/33, pp. 47–9.

167 LMA, DW/PA/7/7, fols 36–6v. His two youngest sons were apprenticed to London tradesmen: DW/PA/7/7, fol. 36v; TNA, E40/5697.

168 TNA, PROB11/117, fol. 221.

169 TNA, SP15/40/48; SHC, 4398/2/1.

170 John Gurney, 'The County of Surrey and the English Revolution' (unpublished DPhil thesis, University of Sussex, 1991), pp. 359–61.

171 TNA, SP12/171.

172 TNA, SP15/40/48; SHC, 4398/2/1. £900 worth of land was reserved for Vincent's use, including Yeating farm, of roughly 190 acres, which was to remain in his family's hands until 1674: SHC, 2715/1/49.

173 SHC, 4398/2/1; TNA, C2/CHASI/G10/18.

174 TNA, SC2/204/43; SHC, K44/1/8; 2610/11/8/33, pp. 7, 11, 15, 19, 25, 29.

175 SHC, 4398/2/1.

176 SHC, 181/15/19; 2610/1/38/22.

177 SHC, 4398/2/1.

Chapter 2

———◆———

The parish of Cobham and
the Civil War

The Civil War reached Cobham in the autumn of 1642, a fortnight after the armies of king and parliament had met at the battle of Edgehill. As the king's field army advanced upon London at the beginning of November, royalist forces entered Surrey from the west; by 10 November London newsbooks were reporting that parties of horse had come as far as Cobham, St George's Hill and Oatlands and that 'they plunder all they come by'.[1] The king arrived at Oatlands Palace on 14 November, and spent the next four nights there, entertaining members of the local gentry who felt it prudent to make a show of their loyalty.[2] On the 19th his forces withdrew from the county, having plundered the town of Kingston and the homes of parliamentarians from across Surrey.[3] In the parish of Walton-on-Thames the homes of the MP Francis Drake, Captain John Inwood and Stephen Cheeseman were plundered, and in Chertsey the homes of Matthew Carleton, Elizabeth Hammond and Thomas Hayes.[4] Byfleet's parishioners claimed losses of £200 from plunder by the king's army, and Egham's parishioners losses of as much as £1,901 3s.[5] Among those left behind by the royalists when they withdrew from Surrey were 'a captain among the cavaliers with his boy', whose burials were recorded that November in the Walton-on-Thames parish register.[6]

Aside from this brief incursion by the King's field army in 1642, Surrey was largely spared the worst excesses of the Civil War, the county's proximity to London ensuring that it was brought rapidly under the control of parliament's forces. It would be wrong, however, to assume that the county and its inhabitants were little affected by the Civil War or by the political and religious changes that accompanied it. The people of Cobham and the surrounding parishes were, from the calling of the Long Parliament in November 1640 to the execution of the king in January 1649, involved to an unprecedented level in wider political developments, both as active participants and through their experience of taxation, free quarter and political conflict. In the early stages of

31

the conflict, this popular participation was linked to the need for opposing parties to compete for mass support.[7] For some below the gentry, however, it could later come to manifest itself in the pursuit of political and religious causes far removed from those they had originally been called on to support.

THE COMING OF WAR

The county's inhabitants were drawn increasingly into the political process in the months preceding the outbreak of war. In January 1642, signatures were gathered in parishes across the county for two anti-episcopal and pro-parliament petitions from Surrey which were carried up to Westminster on 4 February, and for which the support of 10,000 knights, gentlemen, freeholders and other inhabitants of the county was claimed.[8] A Surrey petition in favour of episcopacy, which was circulated at the county's quarter sessions, claimed the support of just 428 signatories.[9] In February and early March, adult males across Surrey took the protestation oath in support of parliament, and over the following two months collections were taken in parish churches for the relief of protestant victims of the rebellion that had broken out in Ireland the previous November.[10] Cobham's initial contribution towards Irish protestants in April amounted to £12 3s. Thirty-four named individuals each contributed sums of between 2s and £1, with the two largest sums being paid in by Thomas Sutton and John Downe. 'Mr Goldwire, his scollers' contributed 7s 6d, and 'the young men and maydes with some other Inhabitants' £3 2d.[11] 10s was paid in by the future Digger John Coulton, the same amount being contributed in Walton-on-Thames by another future Digger, Henry Bickerstaffe.[12]

The propositions scheme, which parliament had introduced in June as a means of raising money through loans repayable on the 'public faith', was successfully implemented in the middle division of Surrey during the summer and autumn of 1642. The first recorded contribution was from Richard Byfield, rector of Long Ditton, who paid in the substantial sum of £50 on 25 July, and further collections were made in the division in August, September and October.[13] Some 130 inhabitants of the middle division contributed just over £1,400 on the propositions, with contributions being made by inhabitants of each of Elmbridge Hundred's eight parishes. The surviving returns demonstrate the importance to parliament of middling sorts support in Surrey at the outbreak of war, with the largest number of contributors in mid-Surrey, or just under half, being described as yeomen.[14] Contributions from Cobham in September and October included £5 from the vicar, William King, and £20 from the schoolmaster John Goldwire; John Downe lent £6 4s 2d in plate, and John Coulton £2.[15] Sir Anthony Vincent of Stoke d'Abernon is known to have lent £100, but there is no record of any loan having been made by Vincent Gavell, lord of the manor of Cobham.[16] While propositions loans were being collected, attempts were also being made to raise forces for parliament in Surrey's middle division. In August 1642, John Hammond of Chertsey began raising a troop of horse from among his neighbours in Elmbridge and Godley hundreds. A number of local inhabitants, including at least three from Walton-on-Thames, sent in money or horses, while others are known to have joined his troop.[17] A second troop of horse, based initially in Kingston, and commanded by the poet George Wither, was raised at the beginning of September, its members being drawn from parishes across mid- and west Surrey.[18]

Although there was considerable popular and gentry support for parliament in Surrey in 1642, neutralist and royalist views were by no means absent. As in other counties, the early optimism generated by the calling of the Long Parliament in November 1640 came to be matched by concerns about the possible consequences of far-reaching changes, particularly as pressure grew for the removal of bishops from the House of Lords and for root-and-branch reform of the church. In Surrey, as elsewhere, gentry fears of popular religious radicalism contributed to the eventual destruction of the anti-Laudian consensus of 1640, and helped encourage the growth of increasingly determined support for the existing church hierarchy and liturgy.[19] At the outbreak of war, antipathy towards parliament's reform programme might be expressed through support for the royalist cause or, as was clearly more prudent in a county close to London, through the adoption of a neutralist stance. Only two of the eleven justices of the peace in Surrey's middle division were active parliamentarians during the civil war years, and eight of the remaining nine were neutrals.[20] Sir Anthony Vincent of Stoke d'Abernon was one local JP who cooperated with parliament while avoiding active involvement in the war effort, and he later came under suspicion due to his wife's open support for the royalist cause.[21]

Below the level of the county's elite, several prominent Kingston residents joined the county's sheriff, George Price of Esher, in refusing to assist in raising money for parliament in October 1642, and twelve of them were arrested.[22] Kingston's inhabitants were also suspected by parliament's more zealous supporters of being too eager to allow the king into their town in November 1642, and the subsequent plundering of the town was seen by some as 'a just repay of Cavalieran-gratitude, for their so basely and perfidiously inviting such unmannerly guests'.[23] In west Surrey George Wither, whose troop took control of Farnham Castle for parliament in October 1642, suspected that 'most of the neighbouring Villages (aswell as the Towne) were at best, Newters, if not ill-willers, to our Cause'.[24] The undisciplined behaviour of the king's forces when they entered the county, and the widespread plunder that took place while they were there, served however to strengthen support for parliament in Surrey in the months following the king's departure. The parliamentary cause also benefited from the moderate policies pursued by Surrey's parliamentarians under the leadership of Sir Richard Onslow, who was the dominant figure in

Surrey from the outbreak of war until 1649. Onslow and his allies consistently sought to prevent the needless exacerbation of political divisions in the county, aiming to influence local opinion in favour of parliament while attempting to ensure that the county's contribution to the war effort was kept within manageable bounds.[25]

Patterns of civil war allegiance in Surrey reflected the religious complexion of the county, with the areas initially most favourable to parliament generally being those in which puritanism had strongest roots. The county cannot be said to have displayed the clear, regionally-specific patterns of allegiance identified by David Underdown in the West Country: Surrey's landscape was too diverse, and its natural and economic regions too fragmented and disparate, for the type of socio-cultural differences described by Underdown to be easily identifiable here.[26] The evidence from Surrey does however add support to the view that downland areas were among the least parliamentarian parts of the country, and that parliament gained some of its strongest support from cloth-making towns and villages.[27] Puritanism was well established in the west Surrey clothmaking region around Guildford, Godalming and Wonersh, and, in mid-Surrey, in a small concentration of parishes around Cobham. It was from these parishes, which included Kingston, Long Ditton and Thames Ditton, that some of the most generous financial contributions to the war effort came in 1642. In the south-east corner of the county, by contrast, many of the parishes on the North Downs and in the Vale of Holmsdale appear to have been largely untouched by puritanism or religious conflict, and to have made only a small contribution to the parliamentary war effort.[28]

RURAL POPULAR PROTEST

Political developments in Surrey in the years 1640–42 took place against a background of sustained rural protest.[29] The most visible and widespread protests were those that broke out in north-west Surrey in 1641. These protests, which led to the destruction of large numbers of deer in Windsor Forest, reflected the unpopularity of the revival in the 1630s of forest law in the western third of the county. Although only part of the county had been directly affected by the imposition of forest law, it was an issue that aroused interest across a much wider area, and at all levels of society. The rioting which broke out in 1641 was to continue, at least in a sporadic form, through the civil war years, at a time when other forms of rural social conflict were also beginning to make an appearance. While few direct links between the rural rioters of the early 1640s and the Diggers can be identified, the earlier protests were an important part of the background to the Digger movement. The Digger agitation of 1649–50 was by no means the first manifestation of open social conflict in Surrey during the 1640s, and it is significant that the Diggers were to make their appearance in a county whose inhabitants had considerable recent experience of organised protest against agrarian grievances.

The revival of forest law in Surrey dated from September 1632, when at a justice seat held by the Earl of Holland, it was confirmed that the whole county to the west of the River Wey between Weybridge and Guildford bridge, and to the north of the Hog's Back from Guildford to the Hampshire border, lay within the bounds of Windsor Forest.[30] There were already some 1,075 red deer in this Surrey bailiwick in April 1630, and the revival of forest law brought a substantial increase in numbers.[31] Opposition to these developments came particularly from local farmers and cottagers who feared that their crops were endangered by the deer and who faced the loss of established common rights. Much of their anger was directed against the forest keepers, whose responsibility it was to protect the deer, and who would later be accused of having prevented the locals from driving the deer from their crops, from felling woods and from exercising 'their rights in taking ferne and heath in their grounds and commons'.[32] In Egham, the parishioners lost their right to pasture their cattle in Windsor Great Park.[33] Privileges granted to inhabitants of the forest areas by Queen Elizabeth and James I, in exchange for their preservation of the deer, were also eroded during the 1630s. In 1633 and 1634, for instance, the inhabitants of the Surrey bailiwick found that they could no longer claim exemption from the carriage of ship timber, the Privy Council stating firmly that in matters concerning the safety and defence of the realm 'fforresters are noe more to bee exempted then other subjects'.[34]

Much recent work on rural riot in the English Revolution has emphasised the autonomous nature of social protest in these years. In his important study of civil war rural riots in the south-west of England, Buchanan Sharp has suggested that agrarian popular protest had little connection with the issues at stake in the struggle between king and parliament. Rioters were more concerned with specific local grievances than with broader political, social or religious issues, and although a degree of class hatred may have been present in the riots, these disorders could be seen as being 'essentially non-ideological and nonrevolutionary in character'.[35] Keith Lindley, in his detailed account of fenland riots during the revolution, has – from a rather different perspective – come to similar conclusions, emphasising the indifference of the common people in the fens to Westminster issues.[36] Although rural protest in Windsor Forest and the surrounding area may eventually have developed along these lines, in its early stages it seems to have been closely linked to broader political issues, with protestors appearing firm in the belief that their actions were consistent with parliament's reform programme.[37]

In Windsor Forest, rioting did not begin in earnest until parliament had made clear its determination to deal with the particular abuses connected with the revival of forest law. The Surrey parts of Windsor Forest remained quiet until August 1641, when parliament's act for the limitation of forests was passed.[38] This act was taken as a signal for large-scale popular action against the deer in the forest. On 8 September 1641, the MP Sir Simonds D'Ewes noted in his diary that 'divers people in Surrie and Barkeshire' had risen and had 'by scores and hundreds' destroyed large numbers of deer, an action taken, he suspected, 'under pretence of the late statute which was passed for the limiting the boundes of forrests'.[39] Those who carried out attacks on the deer did not act in isolation. While the destruction of deer continued, plans were being made to establish a commission to inquire into the bounds of the forest in Surrey, the initiative being taken locally by minor gentry and yeoman inhabitants of the parishes of Chertsey, Egham and Horsell.[40] The case for a commission was successfully made in parliament by Surrey MPs, but its meeting was delayed by opposition from the House of Lords, which had, since the collapse of Star Chamber, taken the lead in seeking to suppress disorder in the countryside.[41]

Actions against the deer continued throughout the autumn. In a petition read in the House of Lords on 27 October, the keepers of Egham Walk claimed that the forest rioters threatened to 'stabb or shoote them if they offered to come into them'.[42] On 25 October Sir Arthur Mainwaring, lieutenant of the forest, had warned that although a House of Commons order against the killing of deer had been published in churches and at the forest's swanimote court, the 'insolent killing the deere' continued unchecked. The destruction of deer around Egham was so serious, he suggested, that unless 'some speedy Course' was taken to restrain the rioters, 'if it shalbe adjudged fforest hereafter, there wilbe noe deere to keepe in it'.[43] The Lords ordered the arrest of Surrey rioters on 27 October, but on 11 November they were informed that those arrested by their messenger had been rescued by local sympathisers.[44] Two months later, on 7 January 1642, the commission to inquire into the bounds of the forest in Surrey finally met in Guildford, despite a further order of the House of Lords for the meeting to be postponed.[45]

The inquisition, which declared that no part of Surrey lay any longer within the bounds of Windsor Forest, reflected a broad range of opinion from across west and mid-Surrey. The nineteen sworn members of the inquisition jury were drawn from fourteen Surrey parishes, including Cobham, Walton-on-Thames and Weybridge. The Cobham juror was John Downe, an experienced member of the county's assize grand jury, while the Walton representative was the future Digger Henry Bickerstaffe.[46] In deciding to meet and in declaring that the county was free from forest law, the inquisition's commissioners and jurors had taken a decisive political step, choosing not only to defy the wishes of the House of Lords but also, in so doing, to provide a degree of legitimation for the actions of their neighbours in ridding the county of deer. This combination of gentry and middling sorts legalism with popular protest was to be demonstrated most clearly in a petition from Egham the following May, when a request for the restoration of local rights to pasture cattle in Windsor Great Park was accompanied by warnings of what might happen if the request was not granted:

> This is the desire of those who have a respect aswell to his Majesty's right, as to theire owne, and for the prevention of a great inconvenience by reason that the rude multitude have threatned to pull downe the pales of the park, and lay it all to common, if they may not be in some measure satisfied in this particular. And their late disorders in the destructon of his Majesty's red deere maugre the best meanes that either the messingers of the parliament or the magistrates of the Countrey could use to prevent it makes them iustly feare that where they have a colourable pretence they will not be lesse riotous and disorderly then when they had no pretence at all.[47]

When the Surrey commissioners attempted to file the return of the inquisition in Chancery, they were prevented by the House of Lords from formally registering their findings.[48] As a result, uncertainty remained over the legal status of the Surrey bailiwick, and the deer killing and unrest continued into the spring and summer of 1642. A noticeable change in the attitude of forest rioters became apparent in these months, for it would seem that the Lords' intransigence helped to disabuse them of any remaining belief that their actions were connected with, or in any way legitimised by, parliament's programme to reverse the policies of personal rule. In April 1642, large numbers of deer were destroyed in the Finchampstead bailiwick of Windsor Forest by inhabitants of the Surrey parishes of Chobham, Weybridge and Ash, many of the deer being driven into Hampshire on 7 April. In their reports on the disturbances, the forest keepers made much of the supposed violence and lawlessness of the deer-stealers. Rioters were said to have threatened to pull down the house of the underkeeper of the bailiwick and to have shot at the keepers. Thomas Symonds, a Chertsey shoemaker, was accused of shooting dead the horse of John Barnes, constable of Windlesham, after the latter had confronted Symonds and three other Surrey deer-stealers on 9 April. In his deposition to the Lords, Barnes claimed that the deer-stealers had responded to his command 'in the Kings name to stand and obey his warrant' with the words that 'they cared not neither for the King nor Parliament neither would they obey his warrant'.[49]

By September 1642 protests had spread beyond the forest parishes to other parts of Surrey. On 20 September, the House of Lords ordered the county's deputy lieutenants and sheriff to prevent disorders from taking place on the Earl of Dover's estate at Coombe Park near Kingston, and to preserve the deer and cattle in the park there from 'tumultuous meetings'.[50] Two days later, a further order was issued for the protection of the Surrey home of the royalist Lord Dunsmore at Apps Court in Walton-on-Thames, where 150 acres of land had recently been emparked.[51] A similar order was made on 3 October, for the protection of a 400-acre rabbit warren near Farnham which had been threatened with attack by local people who had already destroyed the deer in the Marquis of Hertford's park and had started killing the deer in the Bishop of Winchester's two parks at Farnham.[52] The Farnham rioters were described as a 'multitude of disorderly' people, but among them were said to be 'men of abilitie'. At least one was a subsidy payer and lent £1 on the propositions.[53] While bishops' and royalists' lands were the main targets of the rioters, the latter's targeting of deer parks and recent encroachments suggests that more deep-seated agrarian grievances were also important as motives for their actions. The reporting of the Farnham riots could certainly lend weight to the fear that the county's non-gentry inhabitants were seeking to take advantage of political divisions among the landed elite. The keeper of Farnham Great Park made a point of emphasising the rioters' professed lack of interest in the parliamentary cause:

> And also they threatned to kill your petitioner for reproveing them for their said misdemeanors and telling them it were more fitting they should be at Church on the ffast day according to the Order of Parliament then in that rioutous manner. Whereto they replied they cared not what the Parliament did or said.[54]

The royalist invasion of Surrey in November 1642, and the subsequent consolidation of parliament's control over the county, brought a lull in large-scale rural protest. Further orders from Westminster for the protection of property began, however, to appear again in the spring of 1643. In April and June 1643, the House of Lords issued orders to protect the Little and Great Parks at Nonsuch, and in May the Westminster committee of sequestrations warned that the Earl of Arundel's house and park at Albury would be spoiled unless care was taken for their protection.[55] Orders for the preservation of Apps Court from 'waste and spoile' were made once more in May, while in September the Commons instructed its local supporters to preserve the deer and woods within Richmond Park.[56]

THE IMPACT OF WAR

Responsibility for the maintenance of order in Civil War Surrey fell to the parliamentarian county committee and its divisional sub committees, which evolved in a piecemeal fashion in late 1642 and early 1643.[57] The county committee's headquarters were established at The Crane, a large inn situated in Kingston's High Street just to the south of the town's market place. Here the county's leading parliamentarians met regularly, issuing orders for the raising of money and men, examining accounts, directing the operations of the county forces and overseeing the business of sequestration and composition. The sub-committee which assumed responsibility for wartime administration in the middle division also sat at The Crane, the bulk of its work being handled by a small group of committed parliamentarians including Sir John Dingley of Kingston, Sir Matthew Brend of West Molesey and Francis Drake of Walton-on-Thames.[58]

Traditional institutions of local government and social control were undermined by the war, but they did not disappear completely. No assizes were held in Surrey between August 1642 and September 1644, but the work of local magistrates continued, in a limited form at least, throughout the course of 1643. In May 1643, the mid-Surrey JPs Sir Anthony Vincent, Sir Thomas Evelyn and Robert Hatton held meetings at The George Inn in Cobham to examine churchwardens' and overseers' accounts from parishes in Elmbridge hundred, and in the following month they summoned alehouse keepers and victuallers to appear before them at The George to renew their licences.[59] In April and May 1643 they were also involved in the collection of money for the relief of Ireland, appointing John Downe of Cobham as collector in Elmbridge hundred.[60] These JPs were civil war neutrals, but were prepared to continue participating in those areas of local government that remained unaffected by the war, while their more committed neighbours concentrated on harnessing the county's resources towards the war effort.

The parliamentarian administration in Surrey spawned an extensive net-work of officials, drawn predominantly from among the county's non-gentry inhabitants. These officials included the committee's doorkeeper, housekeeper, gamekeeper, marshal and muster master, as well as officials engaged primarily in the business of raising revenue from the sequestered estates of royalists and recusants.[61] Many of the committee's employees were from Kingston, but they also included residents of outlying parishes. Ephraim Carter, whose son would become one of Cobham's first Quakers, was employed as gamekeeper to the committee.[62] Among the most active of the committee's servants was Henry Sanders of Walton-on-Thames, a yeoman who served as messenger to the committee at Kingston and who was involved in, among other things, the arrest of suspected royalists, the collection of arrears of taxes and the valuation of delinquents' goods.[63] In April 1649 Sanders would be the first to report to the Council of State the activities of the Diggers on St George's Hill.[64]

Cobham's middling sorts were also actively involved in raising money for parliament. In May 1643 six Cobham inhabitants, including Thomas Sutton, John Downe and the future Digger John Coulton, were ordered by the county committee to make assessments in the parish for the three-month weekly assessment.[65] In the three years from October 1642 at least eighteen individuals took part in the collection of taxes in the parish.[66] Others volunteered, or were compelled, to serve as soldiers in the parliamentary forces. When, in December 1643, orders were given for pressing 400 men from the county's east and middle divisions for service in Sir William Waller's army, Cobham's quota was set at ten men, a substantial number for a parish of its size.[67] In the following summer, Surrey's forces joined those of Hampshire and Sussex in the protracted and unsuccessful siege of the royalist stronghold of Basing House. Horses and riders from Cobham were provided by Margaret Gavell, Thomas Sutton, John Downe and Ann Wisson; while John Coulton, George Marsh and John Nortridge – a Cobham cottager – served at Basing as foot soldiers in the militia forces commanded by Major John Yates of Kingston.[68] Further orders for pressing men from parishes across Surrey's middle division were issued in 1645, to supply the newly-created army under Sir Thomas Fairfax. The number of men pressed in Cobham on this occasion is not known, but it is likely to have been considerable given that in 1645 and 1646 the small parishes of Fetcham and Petersham supplied six and eight soldiers respectively, while Weybridge supplied eight.[69]

Local involvement in the parliamentarian war effort extended well beyond the raising of men and money. Surrey's county committee showed genuine enthusiasm for reform of the church, and the religious changes imposed on the county during the war had an impact upon the lives of all who lived in the middle division. The ministers and churchwardens of parishes in Elmbridge hundred were ordered to publish the Vow and Covenant in their churches in July 1643, and to take the solemn League and Covenant before the county committee at Kingston in February 1644; their parishioners were to take the covenant the following month.[70] Copies of the new directory of public worship were purchased and distributed to parishes in the spring of 1645, while in October 1645 orders were issued by the committee for, among other things, the removal of altar rails, fonts, superstitious pictures and crosses, the levelling of chancels and surrender of all books of common prayer 'both public and private'.[71] Meetings of Surrey ministers, paid for by the committee, took place regularly in Kingston, and a weekly lecture was established in the town.[72] Surrey was one of the few counties in which a concerted effort to establish a Presbyterian scheme of church government was made in the later 1640s.[73] The directory of public worship had been put into use in Cobham by September 1646 at the latest, when James, son of Thomas Parrish, was baptised without godparents and at the desk rather than at the font.[74]

The parish of Cobham was also affected by the clerical ejections which took place in between a quarter and a third of Surrey parishes during the 1640s. The enforced departure of so many ministers provided those who remained with the opportunity to seek preferment to wealthier livings.[75] Among the Surrey ministers who took advantage of the newly created vacancies was Cobham's vicar William King, who was instituted rector of Ashtead in September 1643.[76] A note added some years later to Cobham's parish register suggests that King departed from Cobham in 1644 through fear of being 'taken by some of the king's party and punished for speaking against his majesty and justifying the proceedings of parliament'.[77] The date and reason given in the register are questionable, and it seems most likely that King was attracted to Ashtead by the promise of an income far more generous than he could hope to earn from Cobham's impropriate living. John Goldwire, Cobham's schoolmaster, briefly took over King's duties in the parish, but he became rector of Millbrook in Hampshire in March 1646. Cobham had no settled minister between the time of King's departure and 1656, when Edward Carter became vicar.[78]

Evidence of religious radicalism, and of dissatisfaction with a national church, began to appear in Surrey during the mid-1640s. Sectaries from London, including the Baptists Thomas Lamb, Thomas Collier and Samuel Oates spent time in the county on preaching and dipping tours, and the town of Kingston emerged as a centre of radical religious activity and a site of open conflict between sectaries and Presbyterians.[79] The Kingston chamberlains' accounts for 1643–44 recorded that 25s was spent by the town on 'carrying the Anabaptists to the parliament two sevrall tymes', and in August 1644 the county committee paid Henry Dennis, the town's marshal, for taking an 'Anabaptist' to London.[80] Dr Edmund Staunton, Kingston's minister and a member of the Assembly of Divines, would later be praised by his biographer Richard Mayo for having 'wrought a general reformation throughout the Town', but his time at Kingston was also said to have been disturbed by 'wrangling persons', without whom 'a Minister might live as comfortable a life amongst them, as amongst any people in England'.[81] Staunton's temporary successor in Kingston, Thomas Thorowgood, also came to describe the town as a 'quarrelling place'.[82]

Some indication of the radical views believed to be circulating in Kingston can be found in the writings of Staunton's Surrey colleague on the Assembly of Divines, Richard Byfield, rector of Long Ditton. In a pamphlet based on two sermons given at the Kingston lecture in February 1645, Byfield spoke out against the 'diseasednesse of the Congregation of Kingston', which was now spreading through the church, and attacked those 'Sensuall Separatists . . . that walke after their lusts; Mockers, that jugling with the Scriptures broach bruitish-damnable Tenets'.[83] Byfield, who would later record in the preamble to his will his 'utter detestation of all Popery as noe other then Antechristianisme, and of all Arminianisme, Socianianisme, Anabaptisme, with all the dreames and furyes of Enthusiasts, Quaqers and ffamilistes', sought to use his Kingston pamphlet to promote 'solid substantiall truths' over 'watery trash'. He denounced, among others, those who sought to bring people 'into astonishment, and a trance upon the conceit of the great power of God in them, and some inspirations of the Holy Ghost', and those who tried to 'alleviate the threats of Gods word with vain words, and to promise liberty; and to turne Gods grace into wantonnesse':

> They conceive they have a great light, and a new light; when their new great light, is either some old errour raised from Hell again and new painted, or some matter

of opinion which is very doubtfull and controversiall, or somewhat of lesser moment, urged and pursued with such zeale that the great things of the Law and Gospel are neglected, the very disposition of the Pharisees of Old.

Also among his targets were those who 'disgrace the publique and solemn Assemblies, . . . troubling them by barbarous confusion'; 'if they may not have liberty to speak in the Publick Assemblies . . . they will deny their presence to the Publick, and fling dishonour upon them all they can'.[84]

At the time that Byfield was preaching his Kingston sermons, the most prominent separatist group in mid-Surrey was one associated with John Fielder, a Kingston miller, whose congregation was to supply at least one Digger and would later come to form the nucleus of the town's first Quaker meeting. Fielder had served as a volunteer in the parliamentarian forces in Surrey in 1642, and had returned home to Kingston in 1644 following the siege of Basing. In Kingston he began holding conventicles with others of like mind, 'being unsatisfied in the use of the Common-prayer'. These meetings attracted the attention of the town authorities and the county committee, and in January 1645 Fielder and eleven others were arrested at his house, four of them subsequently being imprisoned in the town's court of guard. A second imprisonment followed in March, after watermen, soldiers and apprentices rioted against the separatists as they met at the house of Peter Gosse, a Kingston heel-maker.[85] Those arrested with Fielder included Robert Dixon, later quarter-master to Colonel Robert Lilburne, and Urian Worthington, a Kingston maltster who in 1649 would join the Diggers on St George's Hill.[86] In spite of the actions taken against them, Fielder and his companions continued to meet after 1645, and would come to establish links with radicals beyond Kingston, including Gerrard Winstanley, his fellow Digger Henry Bickerstaffe and the Leveller leader John Lilburne.[87]

Political as well as religious radicalism was in evidence in civil war Surrey, with conflicts between competing parliamentarian factions leading to the open expression in the county of radical political ideas. Challenges to the moderate Onslow regime were mounted several times by militant parliamentarians between mid-1643 and early 1647, though on each occasion Sir Richard Onslow and his allies on the county committee emerged victorious.[88] Among Onslow's most persistent critics was the poet George Wither, who had been appointed a committee-man in 1643. In a series of pamphlets at least partly inspired by the conflicts in Surrey, Wither advanced arguments which, in the emphasis they placed on the accountability of MPs to their electors, bore a strong resemblance to later Leveller arguments.[89] Wither was praised by John Lilburne in 1645, and in the same year the influential pamphlet *Englands Miserie and Remedie* quoted at length the passage from Wither's *Vox Pacifica* which ended with the warning that 'there is, on earth, a greater-thing/Then, an unrighteous Parliament, or King'.[90] Wither sought, but failed, to take command of forces raised in Surrey's east and middle divisions in 1644, and in the following year he unsuccessfully attempted to stand for parliament at Guildford against Nicholas Stoughton, an Onslow supporter whom he had publicly accused of infringing the freedoms of the people.[91] His 1646 work *Justitiarius Justificatus*, in which he directly attacked Onslow for betraying the parliamentary cause, and complained that 'men of large fortunes, and little conscience' had for too long dominated positions of power and trust, was burned by the county committee's marshal on market day at Kingston and Guildford, and Wither was fined and imprisoned.[92] The significance of writings of this sort lay not only in the views expressed in them, but also in the fact that their authors sought to reach a wide readership beyond the confines of the established political elite. Outspoken authors such as Wither thereby set an important precedent for their more radical successors of the late 1640s and 1650s. As a result of their well-organised propaganda campaigns, advanced ideas that challenged the dominance of parliamentarian grandees, and championed the rights of electors against their representatives, were able to circulate widely in Surrey well before the rise of the Leveller movement and emergence of the Diggers.

THE COSTS OF WAR

Recent research has provided detailed evidence of the impact of Civil War exactions on local communities across England.[93] It is possible to gain some notion of the costs of war in Cobham from the accounts submitted by the parish to the Surrey sub-committee of accounts in late 1645. Although these accounts give only a partial picture of the costs of war, omitting, for instance, any mention of the local costs of royalist plunder in 1642, it is fortunate for us that John Goldwire, Thomas Sutton, John Downe and John Coulton, the inquisitors who compiled the accounts, provided a level of detail rarely to be found in such documents.[94] Cobham's 1636 ship money assessment of £30 10s was dwarfed by the financial exactions imposed on the parish during the war.[95] The three-month weekly assessment brought in £43 14s 8d from Cobham in May 1643, and the two-month assessment £25. Other taxes included the £3 5s per week payable on an assessment for the garrison at Farnham Castle – which raised £244 10s in the parish between 1 February 1644 and February of the following year – and, from April 1645, the monthly assessment for the New Model Army and assessments for the army in Ireland.[96] By September 1645, at least £427 had been raised in Cobham on wartime assessments, £74 on pre-war assessments collected after the outbreak of war, and £142 on the excise tax introduced in 1643.[97] In addition, those who were suspected of having failed to lend adequately, or not at all, on the propositions were subject to the fifth and twentieth part assessment, which was imposed in Surrey in 1643 and which brought in further contributions from at least nine Cobham inhabitants.[98]

Much more costly than formal assessments, at least during the period covered by the accounts, was free quarter, the seizure of horses and the taxes on provisions imposed by armies quartered in the locality. Some of the highest costs of free quarter in Surrey were experienced in west Surrey, in parishes lying close to Windsor or Farnham castles. The parishioners of Egham, in north-west Surrey, claimed in the spring of 1645 to have been subjected to free quarter charges of as much as £1,124 17s since the beginning of the war. The individual bills included in the Egham parish accounts ranged from the theft 'by 3 dutch souldiers' of a widow's clothes to an innkeeper's bills left unpaid by soldiers 'which would not tell their names but call for meate and drinke saieing they would pay but afterwards denied'.[99] Other Surrey parish accounts, though usually less detailed than those of Egham, also testify clearly to the destructive impact of free quarter. The parishioners of West Horsley, for instance, declared that they had added £100 to their bill for free quarter and the seizure of horses, in order to take account of 'the spoyle of horses in the service and the losse of tacklinge there imployeinge, and the most extravagant abusivenes of souldiers in our goods'.[100]

Cobham's free quarter charges and charges for horses seized were among the highest recorded in Surrey. Although Cobham lay at some distance from the nearest garrisons, soldiers regularly passed through the parish along the main London to Portsmouth road. Cobham's parishioners recorded in their accounts that twenty-nine of their horses, worth just under £140, had been taken away by soldiers during the war, eighteen of them being 'lost and taken away by souldirs that wee know not under what captains they weare', and 'some of them lost in a jerny into the west with the lord of Essex's being prest to draw aminishtion'. They also estimated that they had spent at least £959 3s 8d on free quarter by September 1645, and they added another £120 to the accounts for the cost of 'many souldiers passing from London to the West and out of the West to London being billited by the constables in severall mens houses' along the road. Uniquely for Surrey, the accounts make reference to householders being forced from their homes through the pressure of free quarter, stating that this 'great burden' had 'caused some of the parish to forsake there habitations not being able to continue'.[101]

The Diggers were to make much of the costs of free quarter, and Gerrard Winstanley, who settled in Cobham in 1643, would later claim that 'in the burthen of Taxes and much Free-quarter, my weak back found the burthen heavier than I can bear'.[102] The iniquitous way in which some parish officials spread those burdens among householders was emphasised in Winstanley's writings, and was to be described with particular force in *The Law of Freedom*:

In many parishes two or three great ones bears all the sway, in making Assessments, over-awing Constables and other Officers; and when time was to quarter Souldiers, they would have a hand in that, to ease themselves, and over-burden the weaker sort; and many times make large sums of money over and above the Justices Warrant in Assessments, and would give no accompt why, neither durst the inferior people demand an accompt, for he that spake should be sure to be crushed the next opportunity; and if any have complained to Committees or Justices, they have been either wearied out by delays and waiting, or else the offence hath been by them smothered up; so that we see one great man favored another, and the poor oppressed have no relief.[103]

It is quite possible that Winstanley wrote this from experience, and that tensions of this sort were thought to be present in Cobham during the 1640s. Winstanley was certainly by no means alone in these years in complaining that the costs of quartering soldiers had not been shared equitably, and that the common people had suffered a disproportionate share of these costs. In August 1647, for instance, while the New Model was quartered in and around Kingston, complaints were made that MPs and 'other rich men' in the parts occupied by the army were being exempted from quartering soldiers, 'whereby the poorer sort are much oppressed and overburdened'.[104] Newswriters recognised that the fault lay largely with local officials rather than with the army, 'for they proportion the quarters, Officers of the Army onely appoint the townes'.[105]

SOCIAL CONFLICT

One consequence of the war in Surrey was the departure of many gentry families for the relative safety of London, and the shutting up of their houses and laying off of servants. Gentlemen who served as members of parliament inevitably spent much of their time in the capital, often accompanied by their families. Francis Drake of Walton-on-Thames, who served as an MP for Amersham in Buckinghamshire, lodged during the war at his neighbour Lord Dunsmore's London house in Charterhouse Yard, while the Haslemere MP Sir Poynings More of Loseley lived at various addresses in Covent Garden, St Clement Danes and Charing Cross in 1644 and 1645.[106] Sir William Elyott of Busbridge in Godalming made plans in March 1643 to move his family and goods to London, though he was still in Surrey in the autumn because of his wife's reluctance to leave and the difficulty of finding suitable accommodation in London.[107] By mid-1644 Jane Evelyn, whose brother George had recently moved from Wotton to London, could claim that there were 'scarce five gentlemen in our County but have left off house keeping'; her brother's husbandmen remained at Wotton, but he planned to 'put them away at Christmas, and hire men by the week'.[108]

The flight of gentry families to the capital contributed to the sense of social dislocation that became increasingly evident in Surrey in the mid-1640s. The county experienced a noticeable exacerbation of social conflict in the civil war years, closely associated with the mounting pressures of war. As the war progressed, the threat to property in the countryside came less from organised protests of the sort witnessed in Windsor Forest in 1641 and 1642, than from the more limited and disparate actions of local inhabitants acting variously through necessity, the assertion of perceived customary rights or a willingness to take advantage of the weakening of traditional structures and agencies of social control.[109]

The activities of poorly paid and undisciplined soldiers added to these local tensions. On the More estate at Loseley, frequent complaints were made in 1644 and 1645 of the unruliness of parliamentarian soldiers living on free quarter. In May 1644, it was reported that soldiers were killing Sir Poynings More's rabbits, threatening to break into Loseley House and attempting to destroy the head of the great pond in the park.[110] When challenged, the soldiers were said to have replied that they were unpaid and were quartered in poor houses 'where ther is scant bread for them'; their lieutenant was reported to have claimed that 'he nor none could order them except the state allowe them ther pay'.[111] As More's neighbour John Wight complained, 'it is a miserable condition that this poor division is in, to pay weekly for ther provision, quarter freely, and yeat are dayly in danger of pillaging'.[112] In December More was warned not to ride late at night for fear of being robbed; two of his tenants had been robbed by soldiers, while another inhabitant had lost £100 and his horses near St Catherine's Hill. A tenant of More's in Guildford was asking for his holding to be taken off him, for 'it lyeth open to the parke he can make nothing of it the souldyers tooke away all the pales'.[113] In February 1645 Wight informed More that 'wee are afrayd one to goe to the other the souldyers be so untoward at home and so pilfring abroad'; iron bars had been removed from windows at Loseley and doors to the new building there broken.[114]

At the Queen's house and park at Wimbledon, which had been bought by the Crown in 1639 and expensively improved by Inigo Jones, Nicholas Stone and André Mollet, efforts to protect the deer and to maintain the gardens from depredations by soldiers and the local poor continued throughout the war.[115] Regular payments were made for the repair of the park pales and for routine work on the gardens, as were payments for feed for the Queen's deer, turtle doves and jermy hens. The banqueting house in the garden was repaired, and glass for covering muskmelons and boxes for orange trees purchased.[116] From 1643, the Wimbledon steward's accounts noted with increasing frequency payments for protecting the park against deer-stealers and wood-stealers. Writs were issued in 1643 for the arrest of 'dyvers for stealing of wood in the Park', and in 1645 and 1646 the costs of arresting wood and deer-stealers were entered into the accounts; in June 1646 a local resident was employed to preserve the wood in the park and to watch at night to guard the deer.[117] The Queen's hens, fed on a special diet of French wheat, survived until early 1649, when, not long after the execution of the King, they finally succumbed to the attentions of hungry soldiers.[118]

In parishes across Surrey, the evidence points to the poor taking matters into their own hands as the pressures of war increased. In February 1645 it was reported that Camberwell Woods had recently been enclosed and converted to arable, since they could no longer be maintained as woodland 'by reason of the multiplicity of the poor that lay upon them'.[119] The 'poorer sorts' in the parishes of Frensham and Wrecclesham were among those accused of 'hacking and lopping' trees across the Hampshire border in Alice Holt Forest.[120] During the winters of 1644–45 and 1645–46, parties of poor people made regular forays into Guildford Park to cut down trees and carry away the wood. The keeper of the park, which was owned by James Maxwell, gentleman usher to the House of Lords, alleged that when he had 'reproved them in a gentle manner for such their doeings', the intruders had

> in a violent and raging sorte told this deponent that they would come and fetch wood there in despight of him or any man els, and that if this deponent did but offer to hinder them in such their doeinges they would cleave his head to his shoulders: And that they cared not for Mr Maxwell or any man els, for that they wanted wood, and would have it, as long as it was to be had, either in his parke or elswhere.[121]

Also near Guildford, on the More estate at Loseley, local residents were accused in 1646 of felling ash trees in Sir Poynings More's coppice woods, and of taking the hooks and hinges off the gates leading to Loseley House.[122] More's great pond at Frensham was fished regularly in 1646 by groups of poachers, who came in disguise and who were said to be too numerous and well-organised to be halted.[123] John Wight of Artington, who watched over Loseley during More's absences on parliament business at Westminster, warned him in May 1646 that if measures were not taken to secure the arrest of the poachers 'they will destroy your pond'.[124]

In September 1644 it was reported that no deer remained in the Surrey bailiwick of Windsor Forest, nor in Moat Park near Windsor. Alexander Hayes, a Windsor gentleman who had endeavoured to protect Moat Park, described in October 1644 the opposition he received from soldiers and local inhabitants:

> And there lay in the Parke for the most parte every night do what the looker to the Parke could 30 or 40 beast and horse out of the fforrest by reason the Soldiers that came hourely to fell the trees would breake downe the gates pales and hedges to lay all to comon and threaten to beate and kill any that would resist them. I lost two good heifers out of the Parke and never found them. And Richard Lodge lost one. And it cost mee 3 or 4 weeks worke to seeke out the rest for I had at least 16 which were maliciously driven out in the night into the heath countrey by those that would daily sweare the Parke should bee a comon do what I could . . . I found some of the rest so driven away in the Holt 5 mile beyond south Ffarnham.[125]

In the Surrey and Berkshire parts of Windsor Forest, much of the unauthorised tree felling and deer killing that took place during the Civil War was done by soldiers from the garrison at Windsor Castle, and it would be tempting to see this mainly as the work of outsiders rather than locals. It is clear, however, that many of these soldiers came from parishes around Windsor, and were known as wood or deer-stealers before they joined the garrison forces.[126] As soldiers in the parliamentary armies, such men could enter the forest armed and without fear of the forest officers.[127] Richard Greenaway, a local gentleman who was authorised to cut wood for parliament, claimed in 1644 that he was unable to halt the abuses committed by soldiers from Windsor, for when he tried to restrain them 'they held up hatchetts and swore they would knocke out his braines'.[128] When Colonel Christopher Whitchcot replaced the London MP John Venn as governor of Windsor Castle in 1645, he complained that many of the garrison soldiers were

> very aged and unserviceable, part of them such riffe raffe of the Country that know not how els to live and under the Color of Castle souldiers; and wantinge pay will hardly be comaunded but quarter upp and downe in the Country where they can either begg or gett victualls [and] in the case of danger will doe little service.[129]

Edward Jeffrey, a carter from New Windsor, was told by castle soldiers in 1644 that 'their Officers when they aske their paye bid them goe into the Countrey and shift for themselves'. Wood felled by soldiers was said to have ended up in the hands of brewers and other tradesmen in the vicinity of the castle, the soldiers being joined in this trade by locals who were described as people 'who doe little other worke or labour but steale wood'.[130] Garrison soldiers were also involved in attacks on the deer of the forest, often alongside civilians. When, in 1645, the under keeper of Windsor Great Park tried to secure the punishment of soldiers who had shot dead his son in a clash between keepers and poachers, he complained that civilian deer-stealers were threatening 'to knocke him on the head' for prosecuting the soldiers.[131]

As Christopher O'Riordan has suggested, parliament's ordinance of October 1643 for supplying fuel to the poor, which was aimed in part at preventing further destruction of timber quality trees, may actually have contributed to the widespread loss of timber in counties near London.[132] The existence of this ordinance could be used by wood-stealers to justify their actions in taking fuel for their families, but it could also serve as cover for the illegal and systematic exploitation of timber by wealthier members of the community. Depositions taken in 1644 suggested that wood cut for fuel in Chertsey by order of parliament was sold to 'rich people and men of qualitie' when it reached Scotland Yard in Westminster, rather than going to the poorer sorts for whom it was intended. Other wood from Chertsey was sold illegally to local craftsmen or to coopers further along the Thames in Southwark.[133] When parliament investigated the wartime depredations in Windsor and Alice Holt forests, similar stories of the exploitation of forest resources were reported from across Surrey, Berkshire and Hampshire.[134]

The costs of war could also lead to the drying up of rents, thereby contributing to increased conflict between landlords and their tenants.[135] The parliamentary assessment ordinances contained clauses setting out the respective responsibilities of landlords and tenants in the payment of taxes, but much of the detail relating to apportionment was left to local committees to decide.[136] When Surrey's county committee introduced the weekly assessment for the Farnham garrison in February 1644, the instructions issued to high constables in the middle division stipulated that tenants were to pay one third of the amount laid upon the land they occupied, with landlords abating the remaining two parts out of the tenants' rent.[137] It is not certain how smoothly such arrangements worked in practice. On one farm in Cobham in the later 1640s, the landlord does appear to have borne the cost of parliamentary assessments.[138] In the parish of Weybridge, on a warren held of the Crown by Sir John Trevor, it was only in 1649 that an agreement over allowances for tax was arranged with the warrener, enabling the latter to begin paying off the substantial rent arrears that had accrued since the start of the war.[139] On Sir Poynings More's estate at Loseley, the tenants argued in September 1644 – apparently unsuccessfully – that their landlord should bear two-thirds of the cost of an assessment towards the relief of the poor, citing the precedent established in the Farnham assessments.[140] The letters of John Wight to Sir Poynings More contain frequent reference to the failure of tenants to pay their rents, and to their threat to leave their holdings if pressure was brought on them to pay.[141]

THE MANOR OF COBHAM DURING THE CIVIL WAR

Manorial administration across Surrey was widely disrupted by the Civil War. In Cobham, manor courts were held in April and October 1642, but no further sittings are recorded in the surviving draft court rolls until January 1646.[142] It is possible that documents relating to other courts were destroyed or misplaced in the confusion of war, for it was claimed in 1655 that a number of Cobham rentals, boundaries and other manorial documents 'were lost in the late troubles'.[143] Other relevant manorial documents may well have disappeared in more recent times.[144] Internal evidence does however indicate that few if any manor courts were held in Cobham while the war was at its height.[145] What the surviving court rolls do show is a determination on the part of the lord of the manor and substantial tenants to continue to protect established manorial custom. The occasional meetings of the manor court in the 1640s were by no means limited to the appointment of officials or recording of land transfers, and presentments for infringements of the customs of the manor and breaches of court leet regulations were common. At a view of frankpledge held in 1642, for instance, four Cobham victuallers, Elizabeth Perrier, Robert Jenman, Arnold Champion and Laurence Johnson, were presented and fined for breaches of the assize of ale, while at the court baron Anthony Wrenn, a future Digger, was fined for digging and selling turves from the manorial waste.[146] In November 1642, Vincent Gavell exercised his rights as lord of the manor when he impounded a riderless horse that had found its way on to a tenant's farm following the fighting at Brentford.[147]

Vincent Gavell died in the following May, and it was not long before his widow Margaret married again, to John Platt, minister of West Horsley and grandson of the agricultural writer and inventor Sir Hugh Platt.[148] Platt had arrived in the parish of West Horsley in or before 1645, having been placed in the living by Surrey's county committee following the sequestration of the previous incumbent, Dr Thomas Howell.[149] On his marriage to Margaret Gavell, Platt gained control of the manor of Cobham in right of his wife and her young son Robert Gavell, and he continued to seek to uphold the interests of the manorial lords. At the court baron of 8 January 1646, three Cobham inhabitants, Nicholas Corby, William Bonsey and John Nortridge, were presented for having illegally erected cottages on the manorial waste at Poynter's Green, Downside Common and Randalls Pit.[150] On 10 April, at a court baron held before the steward George Duncombe, presentments were made against Elizabeth Perrier, Richard Woods and Luke Chinold for digging and carrying away turves from the common. Each of them was fined 10s. Perrier and a further five Cobham inhabitants were also presented and fined 10s for digging peat on the common.[151]

The circumstances surrounding these actions are unclear. None of those presented in April 1646 came from the poorest level of local society, and we cannot be certain whether they were digging turves and peat for their own use, for sale or for the use of others. Elizabeth Perrier was an innholder in Street Cobham, as was Richard Jenman.[152] Jenman, who was tenant of the Bickerstaffe family at The George Inn, was sufficiently wealthy to be assessed for a loan of £10 towards the costs of the siege of Basing House in 1644.[153] Gowen and Edward Mills were the sons of the Cobham glazier Henry Mills, who had died in 1638, and brothers of the Digger or Digger sympathiser Matthew Mills. Gowen Mills was, like his father, a glazier, and in 1663 would be charged on five hearths in the hearth tax; his younger brother Edward was a clothier, with a house assessed at four hearths in 1663.[154] Gowen was chosen tithingman for Street Cobham at the view of frankpledge held on the same day as the court baron at which he was presented for digging peat, and in later years he would serve as waywarden and overseer in the parish.[155] Susan Whitrow was of a gentry family from Enfield in Middlesex, and had moved to Cobham with her husband and mother during the 1630s.[156] Another recent arrival among those fined was

Gerrard Winstanley, who had moved to Cobham from London in 1643 following the collapse of his cloth business.[157]

With the exception of widow Perrier, the peat diggers of 1646 were all relatively young, and most had young families. Gowen Mills was thirty in 1636, and his wife had given birth in 1642 and 1643; Edward Mills was twenty-seven, and had become a father in 1644.[158] Susan Whitrow had six children living in June 1636, with three more born to her by the time she was widowed in September 1640.[159] The peat diggers all appear to have been inhabitants rather than tenants of the manor, and they would therefore have lacked the customary right of tenants to take fuel from the commons. It is not certain whether non tenants in Cobham had previously enjoyed informal use-rights to the natural resources of the commons, of the sort permitted in many areas in lieu of formal poor relief.[160] Presentments for taking fuel from Cobham's commons before 1640 appear mostly to have been made against individuals who were neither tenants of the manor nor settled inhabitants of the parish, and when the Cobham inhabitant Anthony Wrenn was presented before the manor court in 1642 for taking turves it was presumably as much for selling them as for digging them.[161] The 1646 presentments are unusual for the numbers of inhabitants involved, and for the absence of any suggestion that the fuel was taken for sale rather than for personal use. It is conceivable that the action of the manor court represented a move to restrict non-tenant use-rights, which, unlike tenants' established customary rights, were enjoyed only at the will of the lord of the manor and manor court.[162]

The Cobham peat digging incident may have been of more than just local significance. The parliamentary ordinance of October 1643, which had been designed to provide for the controlled distribution of wood for fuel to the poor, but which had come increasingly to be used by the poor to justify their own actions in taking wood, had been extended in 1644 to allow for the cutting of turf as well as wood.[163] The ordinance could bolster arguments from necessity voiced by those who lacked ownership of or customary rights to local natural resources; turf and peat diggers might also now argue that their actions were warranted by parliamentary ordinance, irrespective of particular local custom. Cobham's inhabitants were not alone in Surrey in the later 1640s in illegally taking peat and turves from the manorial waste. The parishioners of Wandsworth in east Surrey cited the 1644 ordinance in June 1647 when they complained to the House of Lords that 'now certain idle persons in the parish make this their whole employment and dig more turf than was dug in time of the greatest scarcity', thereby 'ruining the common, and depriving the poor and others of the benefit of pasture for their cattle'.[164] In June and July 1649, several inhabitants of Thorpe, Egham and Chertsey were to be indicted before the Surrey assizes of digging and carrying away turves from Chobham Common.[165]

For the future Digger leader, the Cobham incident may have had particular significance. In his Digger writings, Winstanley would attack not only lords of manors, but also wealthier villagers who, he believed, connived with them in using manorial custom to deprive the poor of their natural right to subsistence. Local custom remained an arena of contention and negotiation between rich and poor in the mid-seventeenth century, and could be turned to advantage by those seeking to uphold communal rights against aggressive seigneurialism.[166] The language of custom could also however – as Winstanley found – just as easily be used by settled tenants against their less secure and less privileged neighbours.[167] In Cobham, established manorial tenants who had long experience of conflict with the Gavell family over manorial custom were equally adept at protecting their rights against the claims of non tenants. When Winstanley came later to defend the rights of the poor, he pointedly avoided using arguments derived from custom. Rather than seeking to challenge the legitimacy of exclusive definitions of local custom, or to appropriate the language of custom on behalf of the poor, Winstanley would, like other civil war radicals, portray custom as a barrier to the advancement of community; his New Law would 'change times and customs'.[168] In the *Law of Freedom*, Winstanley would argue that 'whatsoever Law or custom doth deprive brethren of their Freedom in the Earth, it is to be cast out as unsavory salt'; an essential part of a parliament's work should be to abolish all oppressive laws and customs.[169] Manorial custom was, for Winstanley, the preserve of the wealthiest members of local society: 'In Parishes where Commons lie, the rich Norman Freeholders, or the new (more covetous) Gentry, over-stock the Commons with Sheep and Cattle; so that inferior Tenants and poor Laborers can hardly keep a Cow, but half starve her'.[170] The claims of lords of manors to the commons were based not on the force of any statute but on 'only an ancient custome, bred in the strength of Kingly Prerogative'.[171] Winstanley, a stranger to Cobham – and perhaps even to rural society – before 1643, came face to face in Cobham with the realities of rural social organisation and control. It is quite possible that his experience in Cobham of the survival of strong manorial control, at a time when in many places such constraints remained weakened in the aftermath of war, helped influence him in his later adoption of arguments that transcended the limitations of the conventional defence of popular customary rights.

The impact of the war on Winstanley's neighbours in Cobham had been profound. In the early stages of the conflict they had been witness to widespread rural unrest, as parliament struggled to establish control over the county. From late 1642, Cobham's inhabitants were drawn into providing material and ideological support for the parliamentary war effort, and they came to suffer the effects of financial exactions and free quarter at a rate at least as high as any experienced in Surrey. Economic dislocation brought about by war was accompanied in Cobham by bankruptcies, the disposal of estates and the abandonment by some parishioners of their homes. The manorial court's determination to re-establish control over use-rights restricted the opportunities available to Cobham's poorer sorts to exploit the manorial waste as an aid to subsistence, in contrast to the opportunities available in areas where manorial administration had failed during the war. The impact of religious change was also felt in Cobham. The lack of a settled minister, after the long-serving William King's departure to a more lucrative living, removed an important barrier to the spread of heterodox ideas in the parish. The war was a powerful solvent of established ideas and customs, and it seems certain that in a community of Cobham's circumstances, size and situation, radical ideas stood a much greater chance of gaining a sympathetic reception at the end of the war than could possibly have been the case in 1640 or 1642.

NOTES

1 *A Perfect Diurnall of the Passages in Parliament* (7–14 November), p. 5; *England's Memorable Accidents* (7–14 November); *A Continuation of Certain Speciall and Remarkable Passages* (12–17 November 1642), p. 6; H. E. Malden, 'The Civil War in Surrey, 1642', *SAC*, 22 (1909), pp. 108–14.

2 Bodleian Library, Nalson MS XIV 37; BL, Harl. MS 383, fol. 207.

3 *A Continuation of Certain Speciall and Remarkable Passages* (12–17 November), pp. 3, 6; *A Perfect Diurnall* (14–21 November 1642); Gurney, 'Surrey and the English Revolution', pp. 89–93.

4 TNA, SP19/98/90A; SP28/11, fol. 170; SP28/177 (unfol.), Chertsey parish accts; SP28/180 (unfol.), Walton-on-Thames parish accts (abstract); SP28/244 (unfol.), answers of Surrey and Sussex fee-farmers, 21 November 1643; BL, Harl. MS 164, fols 290–90v.

5 TNA, SP28/177 (unfol.), Byfleet parish accts; SP28/178 (unfol.), Egham parish accts.

6 SHC, 2381/1/1, p. 3.

7 On popular allegiance and mobilisation see esp. Brian Manning, *The English People and the English Revolution* (2nd edn, London 1991), pp. 242–350; Joyce Lee Malcolm, *Caeser's Due: Loyalty and King Charles 1642–1646* (London, 1983); David Underdown, *Revel, Riot and Rebellion: Popular Politics and Culture in England 1603–1660* (Oxford, 1985), esp. pp. 1–8, 136–45, 183–207; Mark Stoyle, *Loyalty and Locality: Popular Allegiance in Devon During the English Civil War* (Exeter, 1994); John Walter, *Understanding Popular Violence in the English Revolution: the Colchester Plunderers* (Cambridge, 1999), ch. 8; Andy Wood, 'Beyond post-revisionism? The civil war allegiance of the miners of the Derbyshire "Peak Country"', *HJ*, 40 (1997), pp. 23–40.

8 *Three Petitions Presented Unto the High Court of Parliament* (1642), pp. 4–6. Cf. Anthony Fletcher, *The Outbreak of the English Civil War* (London, 1981), pp. 191–227. The precise number of signatories is not known, but even hostile observers accepted a figure of above 2,000: Edward Hyde, Earl of Clarendon, *The History of the Rebellion*, ed. W. D. Macray (Oxford, 1888), book 4, 272.

9 *To the Honourable Court of Parliament; The Nobility, Knights, Gentry, Ministers, Freeholders and Inhabitants of the County of Surrey* (1642); Fletcher, *Outbreak of the Civil War*, p. 287. This was probably the pro-episcopacy petition presented to parliament

on 4 February 1642: *Journals of the House of Commons* (hereafter CJ), 2, p. 412; BL, Harl. MS 383, fol. 197.

10 H. Carter (ed.), 'Surrey protestation returns', *SAC*, 59 (1962), pp. 35–69; Cliff Webb (ed.), *Surrey Contributions to the Relief of Protestant Refugees from Ireland, 1642* (London, 1981).

11 TNA, SP28/194, fol. 31; SP28/179 (unfol.), Cobham parish accts, 1645.

12 Webb, *Surrey Contributions*.

13 TNA, SP28/177 (unfol.), accts of Henry Hastings; SP28/178 (unfol.), Kingston parish accts; SP28/179 (unfol.), Long Ditton parish accts; accts of Henry Hastings and John Redfern; SP28/298, fol. 218.

14 TNA, SP28/177 (unfol.), accts of Henry Hastings; accts of Henry Hastings for Anth. Fane; SP28/178 (unfol.), Kingston parish accts; SP28/179 (unfol.), accts of Henry Hastings and John Redfern; accts of John Redfern; Cobham and Long Ditton parish accts; SP28/180 (unfol.), Long Ditton, Newdigate, Richmond and Walton-on-Thames parish account abstracts.

15 TNA, SP28/177 (unfol.), acct of Henry Hastings; SP28/179 (unfol.), accts of Henry Hastings and John Redfern; Cobham parish accts.

16 TNA, SP28/177, accts of Henry Hastings.

17 TNA, SP28/1A, fols 94, 99, 127; SP28/179 (unfol.), parish accts of West Molesey and Pirbright; SP28/180 (unfol.), parish accts (abstracts) of Walton-on-Thames; LMA, DW/PA/7/13, fol. 308.

18 TNA, SP28/177 (unfol.), accounts of Henry Hastings for Col. Fane; SP28/334 (unfol.), acct book of Rich. Wither, fol. 7; SP28/267, fols 145, 149v, 151v; George Wither, *Justitiarius Justificatus: the Justice Justified* (1646), p. 8.

19 Fletcher, *Outbreak of the English Civil War*, pp. 91–123; John Morrill, 'The religious context of the English Civil War', *TRHS*, 5th series, 35 (1985), pp. 172–3, 175–7. See also John Morrill, *Revolt in the Provinces: The People of England and the Tragedies of War 1630–1648* (2nd edn, Harlow 1999), pp. 70–1; John Morrill, *Cheshire 1630–1660* (Oxford, 1974), pp. 36–7, 49–51. Developments in Surrey are discussed in Gurney, 'Surrey and the English Revolution', pp. 41–2, 50–6, 67–8.

20 Gurney, 'Surrey and the English Revolution', appx 4.

21 TNA, SP28/214 (unfol.), sequestration accts of Henry Wilcock.

22 *CJ*, 2, pp. 811, 818–19, 820, 859, 902; *CJ*, 3, p. 574.

23 John Vicars, *God on the Mount* (1643), p. 217; *A Looking Glasse* (1643), p. 7.

24 George Wither, *Se Defendendo: A Shield, and Shaft, against Detraction* (1644), p. 7.

25 Gurney, 'Surrey and the English Revolution', pp. 74, 94–6, 103, 124–81.

26 Underdown, *Revel, Riot and Rebellion*, pp. 73–105.

27 Underdown, *Revel, Riot and Rebellion*, pp. 167, 170, 179, 206, 277–8; John Morrill, 'The ecology of allegiance in the English revolution', *JBS*, 26 (1987), pp. 462, 467; Stoyle, *Loyalty and Locality*, pp. 157, 160–1, 200, 202; Walter, *Understanding Popular Violence*, pp. 308–14.

28 Gurney, 'Surrey and the English Revolution', pp. 108–12, 114–18.

29 For the spread of rural protest in England in the years 1640–3, see esp. Morrill, *Revolt in the Provinces*, p. 51; Manning, *English People*, pp. 266–81; John Morrill and John

Walter, 'Order and disorder in the English Revolution', in John Morrill, *The Nature of the English Revolution* (London, 1993), pp. 359–91; Andrew Charlesworth (ed.), *An Atlas of Rural Protest in Britain 1548–1900* (London, 1983), pp. 39–41, 56–8, 77–80; Andy Wood, *Riot, Rebellion and Popular Politics in Early Modern England* (Basingstoke, 2002), pp. 91–2, 137–40.

30 TNA, SP29/442/164(1); *Calendar of State Papers Domestic* (hereafter *CSPD*) *1631–33*, p. 417.

31 TNA, SP16/165/59; SP16/206/67; E178/6049.

32 Manning and Bray, *Surrey*, 3, appx, lxxxi.

33 TNA, SP16/384, p. 123.

34 TNA, SP16/178/21; SP16/234/21; SP16/246/77; SP16/259/29; SP16/267/1.

35 Sharp, *In Contempt of All Authority*, pp. 7–8, 220–1.

36 Keith Lindley, *Fenland Riots and the English Revolution* (London, 1982), pp. 139–43, 160.

37 Cf. Walter, *Understanding Popular Violence*, pp. 294–306, for the popular appropriation of parliamentarian rhetoric by Essex rioters.

38 S. R. Gardiner (ed.), *The Constitutional Documents of the Puritan Revolution 1625–1660* (3rd edn, Oxford 1906), pp. 192–5.

39 BL Harl. MS 164, fol. 96v; Fletcher, *Outbreak of the English Civil War*, p. 80.

40 HLRO, Main Papers 1647–48, 1 January, petition of Humph. Goulde and others; *Forresta de Windsor in Com. Surrey. The Meets, Meers, Limits and Bounds of the Forrest of Windsor, in the County of Surrey* (London, 1646), p. 5; Manning and Bray, *Surrey*, 1, xii.

41 On the significance of parliament's assumption of the responsibility of prosecuting riot, see Morrill and Walter, 'Order and disorder', pp. 360–1.

42 HLRO, Main Papers 1641, 27 October, humble information of keepers of Egham Walk.

43 HLRO, Main Papers 1641, 27 October, Sir Arth. Mainwaring to Hen. Lucas (letter dated 25 October).

44 *Journals of the House of Lords* (hereafter *LJ*), 4, pp. 406–7, 434; Manning, *English People*, p. 272.

45 *LJ*, 4, pp. 473, 503–504; *Forresta de Windsor*, p. 7.

46 *Forresta de Windsor*, p. 13.

47 TNA., SP16/384, pp. 122–4; Manning, *English People*, pp. 272–3.

48 *LJ*, 4, p. 506; HLRO, Main Papers 1647–48, 1 January, petition of Humph. Goulde and others.

49 HLRO, Main Papers 1642, 21 May, affidavits of John Barnes and Fras Beard; Main Papers 1642, 23 July, affidavit of Fras Beard; TNA, E178/6049; Manning, *English People*, p. 273.

50 *LJ*, 5, p. 365; Manning, *English People*, p. 276.

51 *LJ*, 5, p. 367. Cf. TNA, SP20/1, p. 51. Dunsmore had received a licence to enclose 150 acres at Apps Court for a park in 1639: *VCH Surrey*, 3, p. 473.

52 HLRO, Main Papers 1642, 3 October, petition of Fras Nicholls of Westminster, poulterer; Manning, *English People*, p. 276.

53 HLRO, Main Papers 1642, 5 October, petition of Thos Hyde; TNA, SP28/334 (unfol.), account book of Rich. Wither, fol. 6.

54 HLRO, Main Papers 1642, 5 October, petition of Thos Hyde.

55 TNA, SP20/1, p. 34; *LJ*, 6, pp. 11, 108.

56 TNA, SP20/1, p. 51; *CJ*, 3, p. 245.

57 For the development of county committees, see D. H. Pennington and I. A. Roots (eds), *The Committee at Stafford 1643–1645* (Manchester, 1957), xvi–xvii; Alan Everitt, *The County Committee of Kent in the Civil War* (Leicester, 1957), p. 10; Alan Everitt, *Suffolk and the Great Rebellion 1640–1660* (Ipswich, 1961), p. 22; Clive Holmes, *Seventeenth Century Lincolnshire* (Lincoln, 1980) p. 181; Morrill, *Cheshire*, pp. 82–3; Ann Hughes, *Politics, Society and Civil War in Warwickshire, 1620–1660* (Cambridge, 1987), pp. 170–82; Morrill, *Revolt in the Provinces*, pp. 90–100.

58 Gurney, 'Surrey and the English Revolution', pp. 124–5.

59 TNA, SP28/244 (unfol.), warrants to the high constables of Elmbridge hundred, 6 and 29 May 1643.

60 TNA., SP28/244 (unfol.), warrants to the high constables of Elmbridge hundred, 21 April and 1 May 1643.

61 Gurney, 'Surrey and the English Revolution', pp. 182, 375.

62 TNA, SP28/214 (unfol.), accounts of Henry Willcock, warrants to Willcock 4 August, 4 November 1648; warrants to SP28/244 (unfol.), warrants to Sackford Gunson, 30 September, 27 December 1645; SP28/245 (unfol.), warrants to Gunson, 26 March 1646, 5 January 1647.

63 TNA, SP28/177 (unfol.), accounts of Sackford Gunson; SP28/214 (unfol.), warrants to Henry Willcock, 30 May, 28 August 1645, 9 March, 8 June 1648; SP28/244 (unfol.), warrants to Gunson, 26 September 1644, 3, 10, 22, 24 July, 26 August, 30 September, 21 October 1645; SP28/245 (unfol.), warrants to Gunson, 4, 19 December 1645; SP23/252/68; *CSPD 1648–49*, p. 180.

64 Below, p. 121.

65 TNA, SP28/35, fol. 359. The other three were Nich. Foster, Thos Parrish and Fras Stint.

66 TNA, SP28/179 (unfol.), Cobham parish accts, 1645; SP28/245 (unfol.), acct of Wm Dyer, 1645.

67 TNA, SP28/244 (unfol.), warrant to the high and petty constables and headboroughs of Elmbridge hundred, 8 December 1643.

68 TNA, SP28/35, fols 356–7; SP28/179 (unfol.), Cobham parish accts, 1645. This was presumably John Coulton junior (d. 1659), son of John Coulton of Cobham.

69 TNA, SP28/245 (unfol.), bills for impressment charges, 1645–46.

70 TNA, SP16/497/103; SP16/500/44; SP16/501/37.

71 TNA, E179/187/468A (unfol.), warrant to Rich. Wither, 8 April 1645; BL, Add. MS 71,534, fol. 178. Cf. Morrill, *Nature of the English Revolution*, pp. 152–3.

72 TNA, SP28/245 (unfol.), warrants to Sackford Gunson 11 September, 14 November 1645, 30 January 1646, 21 January 1647.

73 W. A. Shaw, *A History of the English Church during the Civil War and under the Commonwealth, 1640–1660* (London, 1900), vol. 2, pp. 433–5; Morrill, *Nature of the English Revolution*, pp. 156–7.

74 SHC, COB/1/1.

75 Clerical ejections in Surrey are discussed in Gurney, 'Surrey and the English revolution', pp. 109–11, 281 note 74.

76 SHC, COB/1/1, p.47; Matthews, *Calamy Revised*, p. 310; Walker, 'Cobham incumbents and curates', p. 209; *CJ*, 3, p. 253. The House of Lords did not confirm his institution until May 1647: *LJ*, 9, p. 203.

77 SHC, COB/1/1, p. 47.

78 SHC, COB/1/1, p. 47; T.N.A., SP28/179 (unfol.), Cobham parish accounts, 1645; Matthews, *Calamy Revised*, p. 226; Walker, 'Cobham incumbents and curates', p. 210.

79 Thomas Edwards, *Gangraena* (1646), Book 1, p.92, Book 2, pp. 146, 148.

80 KMHS, KD5/1/2, p. 63; TNA, SP28/244 (unfol.), warrant to Sackford Gunson 15 August 1644.

81 Richard Mayo, *The Life and Death of Edmund Staunton* (London, 1673), pp. 11–12.

82 B. Cozens-Hardy, 'A Puritan moderate: Dr Thomas Thorowgood, S.C.B., 1595 to 1669', *Norfolk Archaeology*, 22 (1926), pp. 333–4.

83 Richard Byfield, *Temple-defilers Defiled* (1645), epistle dedicatory, pp. 33–4.

84 *Ibid.*, pp. 16–34; TNA, PROB11/317, fol. 9. Cf. Keith Lindley and David Scott (eds), *The Journal of Thomas Juxon, 1644–1647* (Camden Fifth Series, vol. 13, Cambridge, 1999), p. 150; Richard Byfield, *The Gospels Glory* (1659), p. 262.

85 John Fielder, *The Humble Petition and Appeal of John Fielder of Kingston, Miller, to the Parliament of the Common-wealth of England* (1651), pp. 1–2, 4–5, 14–17, 20–2; TNA, SP24/61 (unfol.), Lidgold v Fielder.

86 Fielder, *Humble Petition and Appeal*, pp. 2, 4; Sabine, *Works*, p. 277. For Worthington see also SHC, 181/10/4; 181/10/6a-b; LMA, DW/PA/7/9, fol. 265v; DW/PA/7/10, fol. 94.

87 See below, pp. 76–8. For Fielder and Winstanley, see L. F. Solt, 'Winstanley, Lilburne and the case of John Fielder', *Huntington Library Quarterly*, 45, 2 (1982), pp. 119–36.

88 Gurney, 'Surrey and the English revolution', pp. 123–97; John Gurney, 'George Wither and Surrey politics, 1642–1649', *Southern History*, 19 (1997), pp. 74–98.

89 See esp. Wither's *The Speech Without Doore* (1644), *Letters of Advice Touching the Choice of Knights and Burgesses* (1644; 2nd edition 1645), *Vox Pacifica* (1645), *Justitiarius Justificatus* (1646) and *Opobalsamum Anglicanum* (1646). For the development of Wither's political ideas, see David Norbrook, 'Levelling poetry: George Wither and the English revolution, 1642–1649', *English Literary Renaissance*, 21, 2 (1991), pp. 217–56; David Norbrook, *Writing the English Republic: Poetry, Rhetoric and Politics 1627–1660* (Cambridge, 1999), pp. 87–90, 140–58.

90 William Haller (ed.), *Tracts on Liberty in the Puritan Revolution* (New York, 1934), pp. 291–3; David Wootton (ed.), *Divine Right and Democracy* (Harmondsworth, 1986), pp. 52–4, 282. Cf. Norbrook, 'Levelling poetry', pp. 244–5.

91 SHC, BR/OC/5/21; Wither, *Justitiarius Justificatus*, p. 9.

92 Wither, *Justitiarius Justificatus*, p. 7; *CJ*, 4, pp. 505, 639–40; *CJ*, 5, p. 337; BL, Add. MS 10,114, 10 April, 7 August 1646; Add. MS 31,116, fols 264v, 280; *Perfect Occurences of Both Houses in Parliament*, week ending 14 August; *A Perfect Diurnall*, 3–10 August 1646; *The Moderate Intelligencer*, 6–13 August 1646, p. 592.

93 Morrill, *Revolt in the Provinces*, chs 2 & 3; Ian Roy, 'England turned Germany? The aftermath of the Civil War in its European context', *TRHS*, 28 (1978), pp. 127–44; Hughes, *Warwickshire*, pp. 255–71; Philip Tennant, 'Parish and people: South Warwickshire in the Civil War', in R. C. Richardson (ed.), *The English Civil War: Local*

Aspects (Stroud, 1997), pp. 157–86; Underdown, *Revel, Riot and Rebellion*, pp. 148–53; Christopher Clay, 'Landlords and estate management in England', in Thirsk, *Agrarian History*, 5, 2, pp. 119–45; Martyn Bennett, *The Civil Wars in Britain and Ireland 1638–1651* (Oxford, 1997), pp. 169–202.

94 TNA, SP28/179 (unfol.), Cobham parish accts, 1645. For a discussion of the accuracy of parish accounts, see Hughes, *Warwickshire*, pp. 258–60.

95 TNA, SP16/347/6.

96 The Farnham garrison cost Surrey's inhabitants at least £18,779 in the period August 1643–March 1645: TNA, SP28/135, 178 (unfol.), accts of Col. Samuel Jones.

97 TNA, SP28/179 (unfol.), Cobham parish accts, 1645. Cf. SP28/177 (unfol.), accts of Sackford Gunson, 1645; SP28/178 (unfol.), warrants to the high constables of Elmbridge hundred, 20 December 1643, 10 January 1644.

98 TNA, SP28/179 (unfol.), Cobham parish accts, 1645.

99 TNA, SP28/178 (unfol.), Egham parish accts, 1645 Cf. Hughes, *Warwickshire*, p. 258; Morrill, *Cheshire*, p. 109.

100 TNA, SP28/177 (unfol.), West Horsley parish accts. Cf. Gurney, 'Surrey and the English Revolution', pp. 174–7, 200–1.

101 TNA, SP28/179 (unfol.), Cobham parish accts, 1645. Cf. SP28/244 (unfol.), warrant to Sackford Gunson, 14 September 1644 and appended bill for free quarter in Cobham September 1644.

102 Sabine, *Works*, p. 315.

103 *Ibid.*, p. 506.

104 *A Perfect Diurnall* (9–16 August 1647); John Rushworth, *Historical Collections* (London, 1721), vol. 7, p. 773.

105 *Perfect Occurences of Every Day Iournall in Parliament* (13–20 August 1647), p. 222.

106 SHC, LM Cor. 5/16, 18, 33, 34–39; TNA, SP28/244 (unfol.), answers of farmers and fee-farmers of Surrey and Sussex, 21 November 1643.

107 BL, Harl. MS 382, fols 113, 120.

108 W. G. Hiscock, *John Evelyn and his Family Circle* (London, 1955), p. 15.

109 Morrill and Walter, 'Order and disorder', p. 366. Cf. John Walter, 'The impact on society', in John Morrill (ed.), *The Impact of the English Civil War* (London, 1991), p. 110; Hughes, *Warwickshire*, pp. 265–6. See also Linda Merricks, 'Forest and waste in seventeenth-century England: the enclosure of Ashdown Forest, 1600–1700', unpublished DPhil thesis, University of Sussex 1989, pp. 114–17; Linda Merricks, ' "Without violence and by controlling the poorer sort": the enclosure of Ashdown Forest 1640–1693', *Sussex Archaeological Collections*, 132 (1994), pp. 115–28, for the exploitation of resources in Ashdown Forest in Sussex.

110 SHC, LM Cor. 5/36.

111 SHC, LM Cor. 5/37.

112 SHC, LM Cor. 5/36.

113 SHC, LM Cor. 5/57. Cf. LM Cor. 5/55, 60; LM Cor. 7 (unfol.), Anne Gresham to Jas Gresham (nd).

114 SHC, LM Cor. 5/62. Cf. LM Cor. 5/66.

115 John Harris and Gordon Higgott (eds), *Inigo Jones: Complete Architectural Drawings* (New York, 1989), pp. 236–7; John Harris, Stephen Orgel and Roy Strong (eds), *The King's Arcadia: Inigo Jones and the Stuart Court* (London, Arts Council of Great Britain, 1973), pp. 138, 148, 158–9.

116 NLW, Wynnstay 167, fols 3–4; 170, fols 2, 42, 42v–43v, 48, 59, 59v; 171, fols 65v, 68, 82, 85, 88, 104.

117 NLW, Wynnstay 170, fol. 42v; 171, fols 25v, 65v, 67v–68, 83.

118 NLW, Wynnstay 170, fols 59–60, 171, fol. 65v, 103v, 172, fol. 4. For wartime costs incurred in Richmond Park and Little Park, see HRO, 44M69/E6/107–108, 168; F4/16/1, 8–9.

119 TNA, SP28/139, part 10, accts of Capt. Charles Ghest.

120 TNA, E178/6049. For the survival and defence of this custom in Frensham in the 18th cent. see E. P. Thompson, *Whigs and Hunters* (revised edn, Harmondsworth, 1977), pp. 136, 244.

121 HLRO, Main Papers 1646, 2 June, affidavit of Wm Smith. (One of those accused by Smith of entering the park, Nich. Tooth of Guildford, labourer, was later indicted at the assizes for stealing a sheep: TNA, ASSI35/88/8.)

122 SHC, LM Cor. 5/83.

123 SHC, LM Cor. 5/79.

124 SHC, LM Cor. 5/83.

125 TNA, E178/3049.

126 Cf. Christopher O'Riordan, 'Popular exploitation of enemy estates in the English Revolution', *History*, 78, 253, pp. 191, 195–6, for attacks on royalist estates by tenants who had enlisted as parliamentarian soldiers. I am grateful to Christopher O'Riordan for providing me with a copy of this article.

127 More than one deponent before parliament's 1644 commission to investigate abuses in the royal forests alleged that 'most parte of the Castle Souldiers when they come to spoile wood bring their swords with them': TNA, E178/6049.

128 TNA, E178/6049. Greenaway was agent to Dan. Blagrave, treasurer of the Berks county committee and later MP for Reading, for whom see David Underdown, *Pride's Purge: Politics in the Puritan Revolution* (London, 1971), pp. 50–1.

129 HLRO, Main Papers 1645, 5 July, petition of Col. Whitchcot.

130 TNA, E178/6049.

131 HLRO, Main Papers 1645, 30 June, petition of Thos Shemonds.

132 O'Riordan, 'Popular exploitation', p. 189–90. For the ordinance, see C. H. Firth and R. S. Rait (eds), *Acts and Ordinances of the Interregnum* (London, 1911), vol. I, pp. 303–5.

133 TNA, E178/6049. The contractors could claim that they were only selling windfalls, but these included one tree described by an informant as being 'as workeman like cut downe as any tree could bee'.

134 TNA, E178/6049.

135 Clay, 'Landlords and estate management', pp. 120–3, 125–8; C. B. Phillips, 'Landlord-tenant relationships 1642–1660', in R. C. Richardson (ed.), *Town and Countryside in the English Revolution* (Manchester, 1992), pp. 235–7, 238, 246.

136 Firth and Rait, *Acts and Ordinances*, I, pp. 85–100; Morrill, *Revolt in the Provinces*, p. 85.

137 TNA, SP28/244, warrants to the high constables of Kingston and Elmbridge hundreds, 6 February 1644. In east Surrey landlords were to abate the sum out of their next half year's rent: SP 28/244 (unfol.), warrant to the high constables of Brixton and Wallington hundreds, 3 February 1644. See also the warrant of 6 January 1644 to the high constable of Kingston hundred re the assessment for horse, arms and pay for Waller's army, also in SP28/244.

138 TNA, C10/22/86.

139 ESRO, GLY 300.

140 SHC, LM Cor. 5/48.

141 SHC, LM Cor. 5/40–3, 52–3, 60, 70. Cf. Hughes, *Warwickshire*, pp. 264–6.

142 SHC, 4398/1/9.

143 TNA, C10/22/86. Some of the documents said to have been lost are, however, now in the Surrey History Centre: SHC, 2610/11/8/33.

144 See David Taylor, 'Gerrard Winstanley at Cobham', in Bradstock, *Winstanley and the Diggers*, p. 39, for the reuse of 1640s Cobham manorial documents as packing in a container holding estate papers.

145 Minutes of the court baron of January 1646 follow on without a break from those of the court baron of October 1642; court business in 1646 included records of land transfers dating from the civil war years: SHC, 4398/1/9.

146 SHC, 4398/1/9.

147 TNA, SP28/244 (unfol.), warrant to the high constables of Elmbridge hundred, 7 June 1643.

148 For Platt's ancestry, see below, p. 151n.214. His father appears to be wrongly identified in Joseph Foster, *Alumni Oxonienses 1500–1714* (Oxford, 1891–2) and Matthews, *Calamy Revised*.

149 HLRO Main Papers 1646, 16 June, petition of John Platt; TNA, SP28/177 (unfol.), West Horsley parish accts, 1645. Platt was formally admitted to the living in December 1647: Matthews, *Calamy Revised*, p. 391.

150 SHC, 4398/1/9. See also 580/1.

151 SHC, 4398/1/10; Taylor, 'Winstanley at Cobham', p. 39. The five others presented were Rich. Jenman, [Susan] Whitrow, Gowen Mills, Edw. Mills and Gerrard Winstanley.

152 SHC, COB 5/1; TNA, C10/468/162.

153 TNA, SP28/177 (unfol.), acct of Sackford Gunson; SP28/300 (unfol.), receipt of Gunson of £10 from Jenman, 6 June 1644.

154 TNA, E179/257/28, 30. Both were residents of Street Cobham: E179/188/481.

155 SHC, 4398/1/10; COB 5/1. Edw. Mills served as waywarden in 1667–68.

156 TNA, PROB11/183, fols 365–365v; SHC, COB1/1; Marc Fitch (ed.), *Index to the Administrations in the Prerogative Court of Canterbury*, vol. 6 (London, British Record Society, 1986); J. Matthews and G. F. Matthews (eds), *Year Books of Probates 1630–39*, p. 51; *1640–44*, p. 42. She was daughter of Robert and Frances Jason of Green Street in Enfield and brother of Sir Robert Jason, 1st Bart, for whom, see David Pam, *A Parish Near London: A History of Enfield*, vol. I (Enfield, 1990), pp. 157–8.

157 See below, p. 71.

158 SHC, COB 1/1.

159 TNA, PROB11/183, fols 365–5v; SHC, COB1/1.

160 For the sanctioned access to fuel on Norfolk commons, see Sara Birtles, 'Common land, poor relief and enclosure: the use of manorial resources in fulfilling parish obligations 1601–1834', *P&P*, 165 (1999), pp. 74–106, esp. pp. 91–3.

161 SHC, 4398/1/6, 9.

162 For attempts to regulate the cutting and digging of turves, peat and heath in Witley in 1657, see SHC, G70/38/4.

163 *LJ*, 6, p. 639; *CJ*, 3, p. 554; O'Riordan, 'Popular exploitation', p. 190.

164 HMC, *Sixth Report, Appx* (London, HMSO 1877), p. 185; O'Riordan, 'Popular exploitation', p. 190.

165 TNA, ASSI 35/90/8; SHC, 4398/1/10.

166 For the politics of custom in early modern England, see especially E. P. Thompson, *Customs in Common* (London, 1991), esp. pp. 1–12; Wrightson, 'Politics of the parish', pp. 22–5; Wrightson, *Earthly Necessities*, pp. 72–5; Andy Wood, *The Politics of Social Conflict: the Peak Country 1520–1770* (Cambridge, 1999), esp. pp. 127–9; Andy Wood, 'Custom and the social organisation of writing in early modern England', *TRHS*, 6th Series, 9 (1999), pp. 259–60; Wood, *Riot, Rebellion and Popular Politics*, pp. 11–12, 43–4, 77, 94, 192.

167 Andy Wood, 'The place of custom in plebeian political culture: England, 1550–1800', *Social History*, 22, 1 (1997), pp. 46–60, esp, pp. 50–1; Wood, *Politics of Social Conflict*, pp. 127–9, 176–8.

168 Sabine, *Works*, p. 121. Cf. *ibid.*, p. 490.

169 *Ibid.*, pp. 533, 558–9.

170 *Ibid.*, p. 506. Cf. *ibid.*, p. 273.

171 *Ibid.*, p. 322.

Chapter 3

Gerrard Winstanley

G errard Winstanley was thirty-four when he arrived in Cobham, and thirty-nine when he led the Diggers on to St George's Hill. Born in Wigan, Lancashire, he had served an eight-year apprenticeship to Sarah Gater of St Michael Cornhill, the widow of a London merchant taylor.[1] Having gained his freedom from the Merchant Taylors' Company in February 1638, Winstanley set up independently as a cloth merchant in the London parish of St Olave Old Jewry.[2] In September 1640 he married Susan King of St Martin Outwich, the daughter of a London barber surgeon.[3] His business had little chance to grow before England's cloth trade was hit by wars against the Scots, the Irish Rebellion and the outbreak of civil war.[4] By late 1643 Winstanley was on the verge of bankruptcy, and before the end of the year he had ceased trading and had left London for Surrey.

FAMILY BACKGROUND

The basic outline of Winstanley's life has been familiar since 1940, when David Petegorsky drew together the few certain facts then known about Winstanley's life and career in his *Left-Wing Democracy in the English Civil War*.[5] Much more has been discovered since then, thanks largely to the researches of Richard Vann, Robert Dalton, David Taylor and, above all, James Alsop.[6] Despite these recent advances, significant gaps in our knowledge of Winstanley's life remain. We still know little about his background and social class, about the circles he moved in in Wigan, London or Cobham, or about the circumstances surrounding his emergence as a radical thinker. The brevity of his public career, which lasted only from 1648 to 1652, has created particular problems of interpretation, and it has proved difficult to explain this short period of openly radical activity in the context of the much longer periods of quiescence either side of the Digger episode.[7] Winstanley can still appear as an obscure figure, who remains difficult to place within the broader picture of political and religious change in mid-seventeenth-century England. It is tempting for historians to try to explain Winstanley's radicalism as a temporary reaction to his business failure, to present it as something of an aberration, or to see it as what one recent historian has wryly characterised as 'a mid-life crisis of epic proportions'.[8] A closer look at Winstanley's family background and at the contacts he made before his arrival in Cobham may, however, reveal a rather more complex picture, placing Winstanley within a series of surprisingly influential and cosmopolitan networks of kinship and affinity.

Gerrard Winstanley was almost certainly the son of Edmund Winstanley, a Wigan mercer, rather than the Edward Winstanley who is usually identified as his father.[9] There were at least two Edmund Winstanleys resident as heads of households in the large parish of Wigan at the time Winstanley was born, one of them living in the township of Pemberton and another, possibly Winstanley's father, living in the town of Wigan.[10] An Edmund Winstanley of Wigan served as churchwarden in the town in 1625, and in September 1634 a Wigan mercer of that name was involved in a land transaction with the surviving feoffee of the land and rents of Wigan Grammar School.[11] It is impossible to say for certain that this was Winstanley's father, for the name was not uncommon in Wigan and the surrounding area, but the coincidence of forename and occupational description may make him a likely candidate.[12]

The Winstanley family was long established in the parish of Wigan, and by 1609 the parish and its constituent townships contained several Winstanley households.[13] The family was originally settled in, and took its name from, the township of Winstanley, which lay in the south-west part of Wigan parish between the townships of Billinge and Pemberton.[14] The hall and estate at Winstanley, which had been in the possession of a senior branch of the family since at least the late twelfth century, was sold in 1596 to James Bankes, a London goldsmith of Lancashire origin.[15] Edmund Winstanley, the vendor, had settled some years before in Presteigne in Radnorshire, where he died without a male heir in 1612.[16] Other closely related branches of the family included the Winstanleys of Blackley Hurst in Billinge, a detached part of the township of Winstanley, and the Winstanleys of Hough Wood in Billinge.[17] Although these branches of the Winstanley family were minor gentry, and were not themselves particularly wealthy or influential, they had close ties of kinship with several of Lancashire's greater gentry families, including the Rigbys of Peel and Middleton,[18] the Moores of Bankhall[19] and the Gerards of Ince and Newton.[20] Another branch of the Billinge Winstanleys had settled in Liverpool, where John Winstanley acted as agent and legal adviser to John and Edward Moore of Bankhall, as well as serving as Liverpool's town clerk from 1641 to 1662.[21] A Gerrard Winstanley of Liverpool would be chosen bailiff for the town in 1684.[22]

Connections between these gentry Winstanleys and the Digger leader are difficult to determine, for members of the family were, as James Alsop has remarked, to be found at all levels of society in Wigan.[23] Gerrard Winstanley's social status has been a subject of much debate, and his father's occupation as a mercer has led many commentators to conclude that his background was a solidly middling-sorts one.[24] A London apprenticeship of the sort undertaken by Winstanley was also, of course, a common route towards social advancement for members of the provincial middle sorts.[25] What has rarely been noticed, however, is that the Digger was one of the few members of the extended Winstanley family network to be regularly accorded the title 'gentleman', a compelling, if not conclusive, sign in the seventeenth century of gentry status.[26] Gerrard Winstanley was described as gentleman in Cobham manorial court rolls in April 1648, a year before the start of the digging venture, and in legal documents dating from 1660 to 1676.[27] The designation 'Mr' was also frequently applied to him.[28] By contrast, his kinsman James Winstanley, a yeoman's son who also came to London as an apprentice merchant taylor in the 1630s, was described most often as Citizen and Merchant Taylor of London, despite having a career that turned out to be far more successful and long lasting than that of the Digger.[29]

Several Winstanleys made the journey from Wigan to London to enter the cloth trade or the law, but there was one in particular with whom Gerrard Winstanley can be shown to have had close, and hitherto unnoticed, links.[30] This was another James Winstanley, a Gray's Inn lawyer originally from Hough Wood in Billinge, who was to become the most successful member of the family in his generation.[31] His career deserves to be looked at in some detail, since it helps to throw light on the circles with which the future Digger leader came into contact after his departure from Wigan. James Winstanley entered Gray's Inn in 1624, and in 1636 he married Katherine Mosse, daughter of a wealthy London attorney and merchant taylor, Clement Mosse of St Michael Bassishaw and Edmonton.[32] By the 1640s he had built up a prosperous legal practice, partly through his exploitation of kinship ties with leading Lancashire gentry families but also through his development of business links with major landed families in the south-east.[33] He served as a manorial steward in Essex and Middlesex, and as a JP in the latter county.[34] Among the Lancashire interests he represented during the Civil War were those of his kinsmen the royalist Gerards and the MP and regicide Colonel John Moore of Bankhall.[35] He was also involved in land purchases with the regicide John Bradshaw – another lawyer with kinship ties to many of the same leading Lancashire parliamentarian families – and with Bulstrode Whitelocke.[36] Later, in 1659, he would serve as counsel for another regicide, Colonel Robert Lilburne, and the republican Luke Robinson, in a dispute over elections to Richard Cromwell's parliament.[37]

Like many parliamentarian lawyers, James Winstanley invested heavily in land during the 1640s and 1650s, acquiring in 1651 the Braunstone estate in Leicestershire from the royalist Hastings family.[38] Here he settled his family, and in 1653 he was made Recorder of Leicester.[39] Although he lost this office in 1662, and was removed from the Gray's Inn bench the following year, his family's fortunes survived the Restoration.[40] In part this was due to the astute marriages of his children. His son and heir Clement Winstanley married Catherine, daughter of Sir Francis Willoughby of Middleton, while his daughter Catherine married the rising politician and groom of the bedchamber Silius Titus, who in 1657 had collaborated with the Leveller Edward Sexby in the production of the republican and anti-Cromwellian tyrannicide tract *Killing Noe Murder*.[41] Catherine Titus was made Lady of the Privy Chamber in Ordinary to the Queen in December 1665.[42]

Winstanley the Digger was evidently also part of this family network, for when he was in need of legal representation in the 1650s and 1660s it was to James Winstanley that he turned. The latter acted for Winstanley's wife's parents in 1658, when they appeared to be in danger of being defrauded of their estate, and in 1660 and 1661 he successfully represented Winstanley against attempts to recover a disputed debt dating back to 1643.[43] The Braunstone Winstanleys are known to have given legal and financial support to other members of their extended family. James Winstanley, for instance, provided legal backing over several years for his brother Edmund's attempt to recover the Holme Cultram estate in Cumberland, which he claimed by right of his marriage in 1639 to Dorothy Lamplugh.[44] In 1668 James Winstanley's son Clement offered, through Edward Moore of Bankhall, to give financial support to two of the daughters of John Winstanley of Liverpool, in order to help them set up a shop in the town; John Winstanley also asked for Clement's help in obtaining a position for his son Peter in the service of Colonel Titus.[45] Gerrard Winstanley's debt to the Braunstone Winstanleys was no doubt reflected in the choice of name for his son who was born in Cobham in 1670, and who was christened Clement Winstanley.[46]

Another member of his family with whom Gerrard Winstanley is known to have had contacts while in London was the merchant taylor James Winstanley.[47] He was one of three brothers who came to London from Haigh in Wigan, and was apprenticed in 1637 to Robert Holt of Basinghall Street, a wealthy haberdasher and merchant taylor of Lancashire origin.[48] He gained his freedom in December 1644 and set up independently as a merchant, taking his younger brother Roger Winstanley on as his first apprentice.[49] James Winstanley's business survived the Civil War, and he appears to have prospered during the 1650s, despite coming under suspicion in 1651 due to his connections with the Presbyterian minister Christopher Love, to whom he was closely related by marriage.[50] When Love was executed for high treason in August 1651, the

Council of State ordered the Lord Mayor to send for 'James Winstanley his brother-in-law', who was suspected of being 'a principal person' involved in plans to organise a public funeral and mass demonstration from Merchant Taylors' Hall.[51] After the Restoration James and his brother Roger Winstanley were active in the London Whig circles of the City Chamberlain and opposition politician Sir Thomas Player, and had connections with Bishop John Wilkins.[52] In 1676 James Winstanley was one of the four London merchants who petitioned the Lord Chancellor for the release of Francis Jenks, son-in-law of the former Leveller William Walwyn, after Jencks had been imprisoned for making a speech in favour of a new parliament.[53] His son and heir James Winstanley married the daughter of the former Rumper Sir William Leman.[54]

It should not be surprising that Gerrard Winstanley retained links with other members of the Winstanley family who settled in London. Recent research on the London business community and on non-subsistence migration from the provinces has shown how important provincial networks of kinship and regional affinity were in supporting newcomers to the capital.[55] What is perhaps remarkable about the London Winstanleys was the extent and richness of their ties of kinship and affinity, which linked them not only to major landed families in their county of origin but also to leading figures in the worlds of politics and religion. Even if Winstanley had only a marginal connection to these networks, he was clearly not the obscure and unworldly individual he is so often presented as being. The nature of his business contacts before 1643, his evident familiarity in 1649 with army officers and MPs, his success in 1650 in providing legal assistance to the aristocratic Lady Eleanor Davies, and his post-Restoration dealings with the Herefordshire Coningsby family, all point to his membership of an influential community of interest encompassing major gentry families, politicians, mercantile leaders and prominent religious figures.

The business venture in which Winstanley served his apprenticeship also had demonstrable Lancashire connections, as well as connections with influential figures in the wider world. Sarah Gater had, as James Alsop has shown, close kinship ties with the anti-Calvinist Henry Mason, chaplain to the Bishop of London and prebendary of St Paul's Cathedral, who left her many of his books; she was also related to the poet Isaak Walton, whom she named overseer of her will.[56] It is not known whether Winstanley's own business was, from the start, a wholly independent venture or was established as part of a larger family network, but it was certainly not unusual for family-run Lancashire textile businesses to make use of London based members of the family to market cloth in the capital.[57]

What the surviving evidence does suggest is that from at least 1641 Winstanley began to move beyond his Lancashire connections. The merchants with whom Winstanley is known to have traded in the years 1641–43 had no demonstrable links to the county. Richard Aldworth, the prominent London skinner from whom Winstanley purchased more than £400 worth of fustians, dimities, linens 'and such like comodities' in the years 1641–42, was a native of Berkshire, and retained strong links with that county.[58] From Winstanley's later testimony, it would appear that he came to regard Aldworth as a friend as well as a business contact.[59] Winstanley also sold goods worth at least £114 to a Dublin merchant, Philip Peake, and goods worth £150 to Matthew Backhouse, a Staffordshire-born London cloth trader and Barbados merchant.[60] Winstanley's only recorded apprentice, Christopher Dicus, was the son of an Essex minister.[61]

Winstanley also demonstrated an interest in City politics and local administration, serving as an active member of the St Olave Old Jewry vestry from April 1641 until January 1643.[62] Evidence of his independent spirit, and a possible glimpse of his future radicalism, was seen at a vestry meeting on 4 January 1642, at which the City reform movement's campaign to broaden participation in common council elections was discussed. A majority on the vestry refused to support the reformers' proposal to restore to general wardmote assemblies the power to choose common councilmen, preferring instead their 'ancient custom' of restricting participation to their own parishioners. Fourteen members of the vestry took the majority line but three, including Winstanley, insisted on recording their dissent from the vestry's decision.[63]

MARRIAGE

In his marriage, as in his business affairs, Winstanley reached beyond the Lancashire circles of his youth. It is often thought that Susan King, who married Winstanley in September 1640, was the daughter of a Cobham yeoman, but her father William was a prominent London-born surgeon and her mother Susan a midwife.[64] William King (1587–1666) was the second surviving son of Edward King, a citizen and barber surgeon of Cateaton Street in the parish of St Lawrence Jewry.[65] Edward King had died young in 1589, leaving a wife and four children and predeceasing both his parents.[66] Little is known of his career, but it is evident that he had close connections with the families of Quarles and Becher, who were active in late-Elizabethan London as major defence contractors and overseas cloth merchants. In his will he named 'Mistris Judithe Becher, wife of Mr William Becher' as joint executrix with his wife and eldest son, and her brother Edward Quarles as one of the two overseers.[67] William Becher was employed as Sir Thomas Sherley's agent in financing and 'victualling, apparelling and arming' soldiers in the Queen's military campaigns in the Netherlands and France, and was described to Sir Robert Sidney in 1597 as having 'great frendes in Court'.[68] Edward Quarles was also involved in this work, as was William Leveson, King's other overseer.[69] Another of Judith Becher's brothers – and leading business partner of her husband – was the

London draper John Quarles, whose depopulating activities in the Leicestershire parish of Cotesbach helped spark the Midland Rising of 1607, in which the names 'Leveller' and 'Digger' were first heard.[70] Her son was the diplomat, confidant of Buckingham and Clerk to the Privy Council Sir William Becher (1580–1651).[71]

William King was made free of the Barber-Surgeons' Company by patrimony in June 1609, and he settled in Cateaton Street before moving in old age to the parish of St Bartholomew-the-Less. He was licensed as a surgeon in November 1632 and became a leading member of the Barber-Surgeons' Company.[72] In 1643 he was elected one of the four surgeons of St Bartholomew's Hospital, in succession to the celebrated paracelsian John Woodall, and he also held for a time the reversion of a coveted surgeon's place at St Thomas's Hospital.[73] King was one of the feoffees of the Arris lecture in anatomy, and was elected an examiner in surgery for the Barber-Surgeons' company in August 1645, which may have occasioned his gift to the company that year of a great tortoiseshell painted with the company's arms.[74] During the 1640s and 1650s he was involved in the treatment of wounded soldiers and sailors, and in checking surgeons' bills for the parliamentary commissioners for the sick and wounded.[75] He became senior warden of the Barber-Surgeons' Company in 1646 and master in 1650.[76]

Susan King was one of three daughters of William and Susan King to marry in 1640. On 16 April, Elizabeth King had married Richard Price and Mary King had married Giles Hickes in the church of St Lawrence Pountney.[77] Both Price and Hickes were, like their father-in-law, members of the Barber-Surgeons' Company, as was Robert Gill, who married a fourth daughter, Christian King.[78] Hickes, a minister's son, was brother of Jasper or Gaspar Hickes (d. 1677), who served as vicar of Landrake in Cornwall under the patronage of the MP and religious writer Francis Rous, and who was a member of the Westminster Assembly of Divines from its inception in 1643.[79] A committed Presbyterian, he preached before parliament several times, including at the funeral of the parliamentarian William Strode.[80] Giles Hickes served in the parliamentary fleet as surgeon on the Earl of Warwick's flagship, before in 1644 Warwick recommended that he fill William King's reversion of a surgeon's place at St Thomas's Hospital, King having recently been appointed surgeon at St Bartholomew's.[81] Hickes was granted the reversion in 1645, and became surgeon at St Thomas's in 1649 following the resignation of Lawrence Lowe.[82] He was dead by the middle of August 1652, when Oliver Cromwell and William Lenthall wrote to the Hospital to recommend a successor.[83]

Winstanley was the only one of the Kings' sons-in-law not directly engaged in the medical profession. It is possible however that he had some prior connection with the world of medicine through Sarah Gater, whose references in her will to her garden and garden houses in the London suburbs, to her copy of John Gerard's *Herbal* and to her 'Phisick and Chirurgerie Bookes and notes', may hint at some involvement in the apothecaries' trade.[84] Winstanley's interest in medicine and his knowledge of anatomy have been remarked upon by historians, as has his possible acquaintance with the Paracelsan tradition.[85] Such medical knowledge that he had was most likely gained through his association with the King family.[86] William King is known to have possessed a small but well-stocked medical library, which included Ambroise Paré's *Works*, Pliny's *Natural History*, Gerard's *Herbal* and Burton's *Anatomy of Melancholy*, as well as manuscript notes on his own and other surgeons' 'course of practise in chirurgery, phisicke and anatomy'.[87] Several of these works were later said to have ended up in Winstanley's house at Cobham.[88]

The King household appears to have been an unconventional one. Both William and Susan King were active in their respective careers until old age, the latter spending long periods away from home in the West Country as a professional midwife until she was well into her seventies.[89] The property they acquired during their marriage was held jointly, having been 'laboured for and gotten over their lifetimes by theire hard labour and profession'.[90] William King was forced through failing eyesight to relinquish his post at St Bartholomew's Hospital in February 1656, having already had to hand over much of his work to a subordinate, the surgeon Robert Arris.[91] Before this time, his 'sight and hearing being almost gone', and his wife often absent from home, King came to share his house in St Bartholomew-the-Less with a musician, John Stone, who provided him with company while also teaching music to King's unmarried daughter Sarah.[92]

Winstanley's marriage to Susan King may have brought him influential contacts, but it did not necessarily bring great financial reward. Despite William King's eminence as a surgeon, it would seem that he had financial problems even before the onset of his incapacity and his enforced retirement. In part this was the result of over-ambitious attempts to settle generous portions on his four married daughters. By 1655 Robert and Christian Gill had begun a lawsuit against William and Susan King for their failure to settle on them the property promised at the time of Christian's marriage, and further suits were being brought by other daughters and sons-in-law. The Kings' response was to settle their property in trust on the musician John Stone, in the hope of protecting it from their children's suits. Stone, who had apparently expressed an interest in marrying Sarah King, instead made off with the bulk of their lands and goods, with the exception of a copyhold estate in Cobham. William King was arrested for trespass and imprisoned on his attempt to return to his London home, and it was to be some years before he and Susan succeeded in regaining their property.[93]

WINSTANLEY'S BANKRUPTCY

Winstanley's business remained, as James Alsop has shown, a relatively modest one throughout its existence.[94] His business activities were concerned primarily with the buying and selling of cloth: he paid rates on a shop in St Olave Old Jewry from Christmas 1638, but he may also have had some involvement in the cloth mart at Blackwell Hall.[95] At the time of the 1641 poll tax levy, Winstanley's household contained only himself, his wife, his servants Christopher Dicus and Jane Williams, and Richard Whitfield, a lodger possibly also from the Wigan area.[96] This small, high-risk business venture would have been particularly vulnerable to the economic crisis accompanying the outbreak of civil war. In October 1642 Winstanley joined five other merchants in launching an action against the Barbados merchant Matthew Backhouse in the Lord Mayor's Court, having apparently received no money for any of the goods he had sold him in 1641.[97] The Dublin merchant Philip Peake also became indebted to him for more than £100, a sum that was still unpaid as late as 1660.[98] As debts to Winstanley mounted, he found it increasingly difficult to clear his own debts to others. He made only irregular payments to Richard Aldworth in 1642, and apparently none between 29 October 1642 and 30 November 1643, when he attempted to settle his account with Aldworth with a final payment of £79 worth of goods and wares.[99] Aldworth's servants would later claim that £114 of debt remained uncleared at the end of 1643, and it is apparent from later court proceedings that Aldworth was only one of the creditors to whom Winstanley owed money at the time of his bankruptcy.[100]

It has recently been suggested that in his business dealings with Matthew Backhouse, Winstanley was the victim of a fraud, and that this experience was 'the single most influential of Winstanley's life,' without which 'he might never have developed his communist ideology'.[101] There is nothing in the surviving evidence, however, to indicate that Backhouse deliberately set out to defraud Winstanley and the five other merchants who took action against him in the Lord Mayor's Court, or that his debts to them were never subsequently repaid.[102] It is also worth remembering that Backhouse was, as has been shown, only one of the merchants indebted to Winstanley in 1642. Winstanley's experience of mounting debt and eventual business collapse must, however, have come to have a profound effect on him, and he was certainly to draw heavily on his experience of business failure in his published writings.[103] London's 'cheating sons in the theeving art of buying and selling' were, he would later claim, at least partly responsible for his having been 'beaten out both of estate and trade'.[104] His description in his early work *The Saints Paradise* of the troubles inflicting man reveals a deep unease about the practice of trade:

> Again, in his course of trading in the world, if he ask sometimes too little, or sometimes too much for his wares, then he is troubled, and do what he can, his

heart is troubled, because he thinks he might have done better; when business goes crosse to his mind, he is troubled; whether it be fair weather or fowl, if it be not just to his mind, he is troubled.[105]

He was to condemn buying and selling in *The New Law of Righteousnes* as something that had become irrevocably corrupt:

> For matter of buying and selling, the earth stinks with such unrighteousnesse, that for my part, though I was bred a tradesman, yet it is so hard a thing to pick out a poor living, that a man shall sooner be cheated of his bread, then get bread by trading among men, if by plain dealing he put trust in any.
>
> And truly the whole earth of trading, is generally become the neat art of thieving and oppressing fellow-creatures, and so laies burdens, upon the Creation, but when the earth becomes a common treasury this burden will be taken off.[106]

THE MOVE TO COBHAM

Having been 'beaten out both of estate and trade' Winstanley was, as he later wrote, 'forced to accept the good will of friends crediting of me, to live a Countrey-life'.[107] Winstanley's move to Cobham is likely to have taken place after 8 October 1643, when he and other inhabitants of St Olave Old Jewry took the Covenant in their parish church, and before 20 December, when Surrey's county committee ordered rates to be set in Elmbridge hundred for the two months weekly assessment, on which Winstanley was assessed as a Cobham resident.[108] Winstanley's reasons for moving to Cobham are unclear. It has long been thought that his father-in-law was the son of William and Judith King of Cobham, and had inherited a copyhold estate at Stewards Mead in Cobham held of the manor of Ham or Ham Court; it could therefore be supposed that Winstanley moved to Cobham solely because of his family connections with the parish. It is apparent however that the William King who held Stewards Mead, and other more extensive customary property belonging to the manor of Cobham, was not Winstanley's father-in-law, but a Cobham yeoman of the same name who sold his estate and left the parish in 1631.[109]

By the 1650s Winstanley's parents-in-law did possess a copyhold estate of inheritance in the manor of Ham or Ham Court, worth between £30 and £40 a year, and other lands in the parish of Cobham; Gerrard and Susan Winstanley lived there as their tenants.[110] In April or May 1655 they settled this copyhold estate on their lodger John Stone in trust for the use of their daughters, but in 1657, when they feared that Stone was intent on depriving them of their whole estate, they were able to surrender it into the hands of the lord of the manor of Ham. The surrender was for their own use and, after their deaths, for the use of Gerrard and Susan Winstanley.[111] The Kings' property was described in William King's will as a 'tenement or 10 acres of land lately Smythes', and was almost certainly the Cobham tenement occupied in 1631 by Thomas Smythe or Smith, who was charged for one pain in a parish assessment for church palings in May of that year.[112] They also acquired a neighbouring property occupied in 1631 by Thomas Emmett, a Cobham tanner, and they held a lease of meadowland at Mill Field in Cobham from Sir Anthony Vincent of Stoke d'Abernon.[113] Surviving Ham Court records indicate that Emmett's copyhold was of roughly twenty-five acres, and Smythe's of around twelve acres.[114] All these properties appear to have been grouped together, and to have been situated in the Hook in Cobham, close to the parish boundary with Stoke d'Abernon.[115]

It is by no means certain when the Kings acquired this land, nor whether they came into possession of it by purchase or inheritance.[116] It is known that the Cobham area had for some years attracted members of the London medical profession. The physician Othowell Meverell, who in December 1638 had been appointed reader of the anatomical lectures at the Barber-Surgeons' company, owned a house in Chertsey as well as his house in the London parish of St Lawrence Jewry.[117] His son was married to a daughter of Matthew Carleton of Chertsey, who had property interests in Cobham, while one of his daughters was married to the physician Dr George Ent, a kinsman of Cicelly Darnelly of Cobham.[118] The King's physician Dr John Hammond of Chertsey had sought to obtain a lease of Ham Court in 1614, and in 1671 the estate was to become the home of the physician Dr Thomas Willis.[119]

Although the Kings may well have been in possession of their Cobham property before 1643, it remains possible that they acquired it only then or later, perhaps after their daughter and son-in-law had chosen to settle in the parish.[120] Winstanley was described in 1646 as a resident of Street Cobham, and had only moved to Church Cobham, where the Kings' estate was situated, by April of the following year.[121] It is likely that tenancies in Surrey would have been relatively easy to come by during the Civil War, given the large numbers of farms that failed in the 1640s. At least one major Cobham landholder, the London merchant Samuel Carleton, went bankrupt during the war, his lands being sold and new leases granted to tenants.[122] Although Ham manor, as a possession of the Dean and Canons of Windsor, would have been liable to sequestration by the parliamentary authorities in 1643, it appears to have escaped sequestration, since the lessee was the parliamentarian naval commander and commonwealth admiral Sir George Ayscough.[123] Ayscough had held the lease since 1634, in succession to his father, and had made Ham Court his home.[124] Here he was to be visited in 1656 by Hugh Peter and Bulstrode Whitelocke, and by the Swedish ambassador who was 'much taken with the pleasantness of the house garden & orchards seated like a ship, among ponds & waters', where Sir George 'said he had cast anchor'.[125] The possibility that William King, as a surgeon involved with the treatment of wounded soldiers and sailors at St Bartholomew's Hospital, as a senior member of the city company that supplied surgeons for the navy, and as the father-in-law of a naval surgeon serving on the Earl of Warwick's flagship, was able to acquire property in Ham manor through personal contact with Ayscough cannot be ruled out. Ayscough certainly had contacts with surgeons, being involved – like the Earl of Warwick and other naval commanders – in helping to secure preferment for the surgeons who had formerly served under him.[126]

If Winstanley chose in 1643 to settle in Cobham of his own accord, rather than because the Kings already held land there, this may indicate that he had prior links with the parish. If that were the case, he would not have been the only resident of St Olave Old Jewry to have such contacts. At least two prominent St Olave parishioners, the common councilman William Vaghan and the alderman and lord mayor Sir Edmund Wright, are known to have had Cobham connections. Wright was father-in-law of Samuel Carleton, who in the 1630s had come into possession of the large copyhold estate of the Cobham yeoman William King.[127] Vaghan was brother of Edward Vaghan, a London goldsmith who had married Mary, daughter of Cicelly Darnelly of Cobham, and who owned property in the parish.[128] Although Winstanley is bound to have encountered both Wright and Vaghan when he served as a member of the St Olave vestry, there is no evidence to indicate that he was close to either of them. Other, more plausible Cobham contacts may include his fellow Diggers Henry Bickerstaffe and John Coulton. Both had connections with Winstanley independent of the digging venture, and Bickerstaffe was certainly known to Winstanley before the start of the digging.[129] Coulton's son-in-law, William Forder, a citizen and carpenter of London, was part of Winstanley's circle in the 1650s. When Winstanley's brother-in-law, the London surgeon Giles Hickes, died in 1652, Forder joined Winstanley in appraising his goods on the orders of the Lord Mayor's Court.[130] Forder had married Mary Coulton in 1633, when he was a tenant of St Bartholomew's Hospital in the parish of St Bartholomew-the-Less.[131] Another of John Coulton's children, the younger John Coulton, was to become an accomplished almanac writer in the 1650s, and may also have been known to Winstanley.[132] It is possible, though of course by no means certain, that Winstanley had come into contact with Forder, Coulton or Bickerstaffe before he left London in 1643.

Winstanley's time in Cobham is often presented as one of abject hardship, with him being reduced to the status of a labourer herding cattle for his neighbours. By his own account he suffered from the strains of war after his move from London to Cobham, for 'there likewise by the burthen of Taxes and much Free-quarter, my weak back found the burthen heavier then I could bear'.[133] As James Alsop has, however, argued, it seems certain that Winstanley was able to maintain a relatively settled – if precarious – existence in Cobham as a farmer or grazier.[134] It was in this period of his life that he was described as a gentleman in the manorial court rolls.[135] Although his name was included in a list of Surrey taxpayers who had failed to pay their share of the two-month weekly assessment in 1644, this need not, as has sometimes been suggested, indicate that he was unable to pay.[136] Surrey's county committee had been slow to implement the assessment ordinance, and did not order rates to be set in Elmbridge hundred until 20 December 1643, more than four months after the ordinance had been passed; it is quite possible that Winstanley had already paid as a London inhabitant, before his move to Cobham, and that he was unwilling to pay for a second time as Surrey inhabitant.[137]

It is clear that Winstanley maintained close links with London after his arrival in Cobham. He continued, for instance, to visit the skinner Richard Aldworth in London: he 'often saw him', he later claimed, 'and came and visited him severall times'.[138] The most striking example of Winstanley's continued involvement in City politics, and evidence of his commitment to the parliamentary cause, was the attack he launched in 1644 or 1645 against Robert Holt of Bassishaw, the former master of his kinsman James Winstanley. In a closely written deposition, Winstanley denounced Holt to the Committee for the Advance of Money at Haberdashers' Hall for having grossly undervalued his estate when being assessed for his fifth and twentieth part.[139] Holt was also confronted by Winstanley, and was said to have cursed both his interrogator and the committee: 'twitt twatt said he, a fart for the comittee and you too. I have taken my oath & am cleared by law, & I care not what neither you nor they can doe'. Winstanley's response was to draw up a detailed list of questions for the committee to ask Holt, and he urged them to command him to bring in the estate book on which James Winstanley had worked: 'if he will not show it, you may on a good ground suspect a fals oath'.[140] What sparked this incident is unclear, but Winstanley seems to have been particularly concerned by the fact that Holt had apparently lied on oath. It may also have been connected with the committee's allowance to Holt in April 1644 of £23 8d formerly paid in to the treasurers at Guildhall by a 'Charles Winstanley', but turned over to Holt as a debt, this Winstanley 'being poore & having no other meanes to satisffie him'.[141]

SURREY POLITICS

The occasional references in Winstanley's writings to events in Surrey suggest that he may also have taken an active interest in political developments in that county. It seems certain, for instance, that he was present in Kingston on the day in February 1644 when Surrey ministers and members of the county committee met to take the Covenant.[142] Events in Surrey after the end of the first Civil War would have been particularly disconcerting for a committed parliamentarian like Winstanley, as local support for the parliamentary cause rapidly subsided. Widespread popular sympathy for the king was evident in Surrey in August 1647, when people flocked to see him as he was brought under guard to his palace at Oatlands.[143] Renewed support for the established church was, as in other south-eastern counties, expressed in 1647 through opposition to intruded ministers and through the forced reintrusion of ejected ministers.[144]

This growing backlash against parliament was in part occasioned by the disquiet felt at the army's presence in Surrey and neighbouring counties following its march on London in August 1647. Levels of taxation in Surrey in the first half of 1648 were at their highest since the Civil War, and free quarter was once more a major grievance.[145] The pressures of free quarter were felt with particular intensity in a number of parishes in east and mid-Surrey that had escaped relatively lightly during the war. Opposition to free quarter was expressed on several occasions in Surrey in 1647 and early 1648. In December 1647, for instance, a group of east Surrey farmers petitioned Fairfax for the abatement of quartering charges out of their rents, claiming that the costs of free quarter had doubled, and in some cases trebled, since the army's arrival in the county. 'Our Rent so decayeth our Estates', they complained, 'that little Subsistance is for our selves, for our Families, and for those many Labourers employed by us, left for us for the present, and for afterwards likely none at all, unless your Excellency relieve us'.[146] A fortnight earlier, John Turner of Ham in Bletchingley had complained to the House of Commons that the pressures of free quarter had forced several of his tenants to turn 'their farmes into his hands, which lye at wast for that he is not able to manage them'.[147]

The army's commanders and soldiers were well aware of burdens caused by their continued presence near London, and in declarations issued in September and October 1647 the Council of the Army voiced its concerns about this problem.[148] The authors of *The Case of the Armie Truly Stated*, which was subscribed by the Leveller-inspired new agents in Guildford on 9 October, made clear their dislike of the army's enforced reliance on free quarter, and demanded measures to enable soldiers to subsist without burdening the 'distressed Country'.[149] Fairfax reiterated his concerns on 19 November, when he wrote from Kingston to Robert Scawen, chair of the army committee, to complain that the army had been quartered about London 'soe long, and soe much to the oppression of the parts adiacent', that it could not remain there longer 'without intolerable oppression if not undoing to verie many'.[150]

In the spring of 1648 Surrey was one of the first counties to organise in favour of a personal treaty with the king, and some of the most militant support for these moves came from among Winstanley's neighbours in the county's middle division. The Surrey petition for a personal treaty, which called for the king to be restored 'according to the splendor of His Ancestors' and according to the oaths of supremacy and allegiance, 'from which no power on earth can absolve us', was carried to parliament on 16 May 1648, accompanied by several thousand supporters.[151] Clashes between the petitioners and soldiers guarding the Palace of Westminster led to several deaths and injuries, and a number of petitioners were stripped and robbed, including Winstanley's near neighbour George Price of Esher, who had been chosen to present the petition to the House of Commons.[152] The violence of the soldiers at Westminster led to calls for the county's inhabitants to associate together in a posture of defence, and two representatives from each parish were chosen to meet to plan future action; on 20 May a Kingston physician, Job Weale, set off for the Isle of Wight to seek the king's approval for the appointment of a commander-in-chief for the county.[153] On the following day John Evelyn, who had been reporting on the course of events in Surrey to his father-in-law Sir Richard Browne in Paris, was able to speak of 'allmost the utter deffection' of the county from parliament.[154]

Although prompt action by parliament ensured that Surrey's inhabitants did not join those of Kent in taking up arms against parliament at the end of May, a royalist rising did take place in the county just over a month later. At the beginning of July, the Earls of Holland and Peterborough and the Duke of Buckingham sought to raise the county for the king, declaring their support 'for the King and Parliament, Religion and the known Lawes', and their opposition to 'a confused and levelling undertaking to overthrow Monarchy, and to turn order that preserves all our lives and fortunes into a wild and unlimited confusion'.[155] The insurgents gathered first on Banstead Downs, and passed through Dorking, Reigate and Ewell, before engaging with parliamentary forces near Surbiton and retreating to Kingston and over the Thames into Middlesex. Supporters of parliament were plundered by the insurgents, and at least one was killed.[156] Although local involvement in the rising was limited, some Surrey inhabitants did take up arms, including several from parishes in the county's middle division.[157] Among the most prominent of the Earl of Holland's gentry supporters from Surrey were Winstanley's neighbour Sir Francis Vincent, the son and heir of Sir Anthony Vincent of Stoke d'Abernon, and Sir Charles Howard and Thomas Stydolph of the nearby parishes of Great Bookham and Mickleham.[158] Winstanley's later assertion that some of the Diggers' local opponents had been 'cheife promoters of the offensive Surrey petition' and had been involved in the 1648 risings may have had some truth to it. Certainly the Vincent family was to play a leading part in the campaign against the Diggers in 1649 and 1650.[159]

Feelings against parliament and its more radical supporters continued to run high in Surrey in the autumn of 1648. At the Kingston assizes in September 1648, two Surrey inhabitants, Robert Bell, a Southwark tailor, and Daniel Wynne, a shoemaker from Tooting, were indicted for words spoken against the king, Bell for allegedly saying that 'the king is noe more then another man; I have as much power as the king', and Wynne for saying that 'the kinge is a rascally kinge and keepes rascally company and takes rascally wayes'. Both had been denounced by neighbours.[160] It was also at these assizes that the Kingston separatist John Fielder launched an action against the town's former bailiffs

Richard Lidgold and John Childe for having illegally imprisoned him in 1645. Not surprisingly, Fielder failed to make any progress with his action at these assizes: the case was put to arbitration and no agreement was reached.[161]

By the following month Winstanley had himself became embroiled in a conflict with Kingston's authorities, when he sought to defend the reputation of William Everard, a Reading-born prophet who been arrested by the Kingston bailiffs when he stopped overnight in the town.[162] Everard was a former soldier, and had served in the army of the Earl of Essex and in the New Model before being imprisoned and cashiered following the Ware mutiny in November 1647.[163] He seems to have become a Baptist, before renouncing adult baptism and seeking out and confronting those who continued to advocate the practice. Samuel Fisher, at whose house Everard turned up uninvited, presenting himself as a messenger from God, was made to observe his 'speeches, strange extasies, and uncouth deportment, by many prodigious passages, blasphemous pratings, and . . . flatly false pretences', as well as his 'most presumptuous, yet successe-less, undertakings and frivolous fopperies', and concluded that he was 'one of the Archangels of darknesse, which the devil now sends forth a new in the shape of angels of light'.[164] Like his later acquaintance Thomas Tany, Everard felt divinely inspired to take a new name, claiming that God had given him the name Chamberlain or Chamberlin 'for he lived in the secret chambers of the most high'.[165] According to Winstanley, Everard was accused by ministers and others of holding 'blasphemous opinions: as to deny God, and Christ, and Scriptures, and prayer; and they call him a deceiver, and many filthy names'; Winstanley had been 'slandered as well as he (by some of the Ministers) having been in his company'.[166]

After coming to the aid of Everard, Winstanley became involved in John Fielder's renewed action for false imprisonment against the former Kingston bailiffs. Fielder, having failed to secure damages against Lidgold and Childe at the Kingston assizes, resumed his action at the county's Lent assizes in Southwark. The case was again put to arbitration, with Fielder's chosen representatives being Winstanley and his neighbour Henry Bickerstaffe. The bailiffs' case was also put by two prominent Cobham residents, Thomas Sutton and John Downe, both of whom were regular members of the assize grand jury; Downe was also serving as high constable of Elmbridge hundred at this time.[167] Winstanley's published report on the arbitration, 'all writ with his own hand', is of considerable importance for what it shows of his developing understanding of the law, and of the facility with which he was able to make free use of legal argument in his writings. In responding to the claim that Fielder and his friends had been rightfully imprisoned for breach of the statute of 35 Eliz. against not coming to church to hear common prayer, Winstanley and Bickerstaffe argued that this statute was no longer in force, and that even if it were the bailiffs should not have imprisoned Fielder without first ensuring that he was indicted or presented before the quarter sessions for non attendance. Parliament's ordinance of 3 January 1645 to take away the Prayer Book had, they claimed, rendered the 1593 statute obsolete, 'because the matter of the Statute is taken away'; parliament had set up the Directory of Worship in place of the Prayer Book, 'but hath reserved the power of punishment to themselves, for neglect of obedience to their Directory, and as yet hath not declared any punishment'.[168]

Central to Winstanley and Bickerstaffe's argument was a very distinctive interpretation of the Covenant, which anticipated the ways in which Winstanley was to make use of the Covenant and Engagement in his Digger tracts. Winstanley was always willing to cite the Covenant and other parliamentarian oaths to support his case, but, as with the use he made of biblical texts in his writings, he ascribed to them meanings that bore little resemblance to the more conventional interpretations placed on them by others.[169] The Covenant, as Winstanley and Bickerstaffe pointed out, had enjoined those who took it to 'extirpate Popery and Episcopacy and all that Government'; any statutes made in the times of popery and episcopacy, and which upheld that government, must therefore be 'rooted out':

> But to imprison or punish any one for worshipping his Maker, according to the light of his own understanding, is both Popery and Episcopacy (for according to the word of God, every one ought to be perswaded in his own mind,) therefore the Bayliffs have broke their Covenant by imprisoning Fielder and are perjured, and the Statute likewise is proved null.[170]

Fielder, they insisted, had been acting in pursuit of the Covenant, 'endeavouring a Reformation in his place and Calling, as the Covenant requires every one in particular'. The Covenant remained in force, and 'if a Vow be made to the Lord, it must be kept, and one man cannot absolve another from his Vow'.[171]

Winstanley's intervention in Fielder's case had little effect, and the bailiffs' arbitrators refused to agree to the substantial damages demanded by Winstanley and Bickerstaffe. When the action resumed at the Southwark assizes in April 1650, Fielder was to be represented not by Winstanley and Bickerstaffe but by the Leveller leader John Lilburne, who had apparently been following the case since its inception.[172] By then Winstanley and Bickerstaffe were, of course, busy with other matters, having just begun their occupation of St George's Hill. The activities of the Diggers will be examined in chapters five and six, but before that some discussion of Winstanley's early writings and the development of his religious ideas is necessary.

NOTES

1 Society of Genealogists, Wigan parish registers (microfilm copy of Wigan Record Office, P/W1); Josiah Arrowsmith and Fanny Wrigley (eds), *The Registers of the Parish Church*

of Wigan, Christenings, Burials and Weddings 1580–1625 (Wigan, Lancashire Parish Register Society, 1899), p. 74; GL, MF 316/10, p. 91.

2 GL, MF 351/2 (unfol.), 21 February 1637–38.

3 GL, Ms 10,091/22, fol. 184v.

4 Barry Supple, *Commercial Crisis and Change in England 1600–1642* (Cambridge, 1959), pp. 128–31.

5 Petegorsky, *Left-Wing Democracy*, pp. 121–4.

6 James D. Alsop, 'Gerrard Winstanley's later life', *P&P*, 82 (1979), pp. 73–81; James Alsop, 'Gerrard Winstanley: religion and respectability', *HJ*, 28, 3 (1985), pp. 705–9; James Alsop, 'Ethics in the marketplace: Gerrard Winstanley's London bankruptcy', *JBS*, 28 (1989), pp. 97–119; James Alsop, 'A high road to radicalism? Gerrard Winstanley's youth', *The Seventeenth Century*, 9 (1994), 11–24; James Alsop, 'Gerrard Winstanley: what do we know of his life?', in Bradstock, *Winstanley and the Diggers*, pp. 19–36; R. J. Dalton, 'Gerrard Winstanley: the experience of fraud', *HJ*, 34, 4 (1991), pp. 973–84; Richard T. Vann, 'The later life of Gerrard Winstanley', *Journal of the History of Ideas*, 26 (1965), pp. 133–6; Richard T. Vann, 'From radicalism to quakerism: Gerrard Winstanley and friends', *Journal of the Friends' Historical Society*, 49 (1959–61), pp. 41–6; David C. Taylor, *Gerrard Winstanley in Elmbridge* (Elmbridge, 1982); Taylor, 'Gerrard Winstanley at Cobham', in Bradstock, *Winstanley and the Diggers*, pp. 37–42.

7 Alsop, 'Winstanley: what do we know of his life?', pp. 19–20, makes this point forcefully.

8 Mark Kishlansky, *A Monarchy Transformed: Britain 1603–1714* (London, 1996), p. 196. Kishlansky is, of course, not necessarily endorsing this view.

9 Arrowsmith and Wrigley, *Registers*, p. 74 for Edward Winstanley as his father's name. The MS register gives a name that can be read either as Edward or Edmund, and shows signs of correction, possibly from Edward to Edmund: Society of Genealogists, Wigan parish registers (microfilm). Winstanley's entry in the Merchant Taylors' Co. apprentice-ship binding register gives the father's name as Edmund, and describes him as a mercer: GL, MF 316/10, p. 91. The entry does however contain errors (placing Wigan in Lincolnshire), so cannot be regarded as definitive.

10 For Edm. Winstanley of Pemberton see Arrowsmith and Wrigley, *Registers*, p. 105; Lancashire Record Office (hereafter LRO), QSB/1/6/13, 36; The Record Office for Leicestershire, Leicester and Rutland (hereafter LLRRO), DE728/1001; J. Paul Rylands (ed.), *Lancashire Inquisitions Returned into the Chancery of the Duchy of Lancaster, Stuart Period*, Part I (The Record Society for Lancashire and Cheshire, 1880), p. 130; James Tait (ed.), *Lancashire Quarter Sessions Rolls 1590–1606* (Manchester, Chetham Society, 1917), p. 283; J. P. Earwaker (ed.), *An Index to the Wills and Inventories in the Court of Probate at Chester AD 1621–1650* (Record Society, 1881), p. 239. This Edm. Winstanley appears to have been a recusant: *VCH Lancashire*, 4 (London, 1911), p. 58.

11 LRO, QDD/42/F7; George T. O. Bridgeman, *The History of the Church and Manor of Wigan*, Part 2 (Manchester, Chetham Society, 1889), p. 291; Arrowsmith and Wrigley, *Registers*, pp. 56, 68, 99, 114, 205, 233, 239, 263; J. P. Earwaker (ed.), *An Index to the Wills and Inventories in the Court of Probate at Chester AD 1545–1620* (Record Society, 1879), p. 212. Winstanley's mother's name is not known: an Edm. Winstanley married Jane Doman of Wigan in January 1601, while Eliz. wife of Edm. Winstanley of Wallgate in Wigan was buried in May 1619: Arrowsmith and Wrigley, *Registers*, pp. 233, 263.

12 Others of that name include Edm. Winstanley (d. *c.* 1600) of Billinge, for whom see Arrowsmith and Wrigley, *Registers*, p. 46; Earwaker, *Index to Wills 1545–1620*, p. 212,

and Edm. Winstanley (fl. 1603–14) of Ash, for whom see Robert Dickinson (ed.), *The Register of Winwick Parish Church*, Part I (Lancashire Parish Register Society, 1970), pp. 61, 70, 80, 95. Cf. Joyce Bankes and Eric Kerridge (eds), *The Early Records of the Bankes Family at Winstanley* (Manchester, Chetham Society, 3rd series, vol. 21, 1973), p. 43.

13 Alsop, 'High road to radicalism', p. 12 suggests that more than 20 male Winstanleys headed households in the parish in the period *c.* 1600–1620; Arrowsmith and Wrigley, *Registers*; Earwaker, *Index of Wills 1545–1620*, p. 212. The Winstanley surname was also quite common in neighbouring parishes.

14 BL, Harl. MS 1987, fol. 116; *VCH Lancs*, 4, pp. 87–8; James Croston (ed.) *The History of the County Palatine and Duchy of Lancaster by the Late Edward Baines Esq.*, 4 (Manchester, 1891), p. 305; *Burke's Landed Gentry* (1851 edn), p. 1616; (1886 edn), pp. 2015–16.

15 Joyce H. M. Bankes, 'James Bankes and the manor of Winstanley, 1595–1617', *Transactions of the Historic Society of Lancashire and Cheshire* (hereafter *THSLC*), 94 (1942), pp. 56–93; Bankes and Kerridge, *Early Records*, vii; Anon, 'The Sale of the manor of Winstanley in 1596', *Lancashire Record Office Report 1961*, pp. 15–18; *VCH Lancs*, 4, pp. 87–8.

16 TNA PROB11/319, fols 288v–289. He was sheriff of Pembrokeshire in 1590 and of Radnorshire in 1592–93 and 1599–1600: Bankes 'James Bankes', pp. 65–6, 81; Bankes and Kerridge, *Early Records*, vii; 'Sale of the manor of Winstanley', p. 16. The hall at Winstanley was, in his absence, occupied by his cousin, another Edm. Winstanley (d. 1591): J. P. Earwaker (ed.), *Lancashire and Cheshire Wills and Inventories at Chester* (Manchester, Chetham Society NS, 3, 1884), pp. 116–17, Bankes, 'James Bankes', pp. 66, 81–3.

17 BL, Harl. MS 1987, fol. 115; Croston, *County Palatine*, 4, p. 305; *VCH Lancs*, 4, pp. 86, 88.

18 BL, Harl. MS 1987, fol. 115; LRO, DDKE/acc. 7840 HMC/110, 120; Robert Somerville, *Office Holders in the Duchy and County Palatine of Lancaster from 1603* (London and Chichester, 1972), pp. 106–7. Jas Winstanley (fl. 1602–26) of Blackley Hurst was son-in-law of Roger Rigby, Lancs clerk of the peace, and uncle by marriage of the MP and Civil War parliamentarian commander Col. Alexander Rigby (1594–1650).

19 Liverpool Record Office, Moore of Bank Hall MSS 1235, 1237, 1239, 1523, 1657, 1692, 1699–1700, 1717–18, 1720; J. Brownbill (ed.), *A Calendar of that Part of the Collection of Deeds and Papers of the Moore Family of Bankhall, Co. Lancaster Now in the Liverpool Public Library* (Record Society, 67, 1913).

20 Earwaker, *Wills and Inventories*, pp. 24–27; LLRRO, 16 D 66/396–97; TNA, SP23/14, fol. 13v; SP23/89/283; SP46/108, fol. 238; J. H. Stanning (ed.), *The Royalist Composition Papers*, 3 (Record Society, 29, 1896), p. 25; *Calendar of the Committee for Compounding with Delinquents* (hereafter *CCC*), pp. 2424, 2723). Thos Winstanley of Winstanley (d. 1561) was apparently brother-in-law of Sir Wm Gerard (d. 1581), recorder of Chester and chancellor of Ireland.

21 Liverpool Record Office, Moore of Bank Hall MSS 381, 1554, 1575–6, 1625–6, 1629–30, 1635–6, 1641, 1649, 1657, 1660, 1667, 1680, 1686, 1707, 1715, 1717–18, 1722, 1730, 1733, 1737, 1739; Thomas Heywood (ed.), *The Moore Rental* (Manchester, Chetham Society, 1847), p. 93; J. A. Twemlow (ed.), *Liverpool Town Books 1550–1862*, vol. I (Liverpool, 1918); Sir James A. Picton, *Liverpool Municipal Records* (Liverpool, 1883), pp. 148–9,

166, 240–1; Michael Power (ed.), *Liverpool Town Books 1649–1671* (Record Society, vol. 136, 1999); Edith M. Platt, *History of Municipal Government in Liverpool to 1835* (Liverpool, 1906), p. 9. John Winstanley was apparently born in Billinge: John Nichols, *The History and Antiquities of the County of Leicester*, vol 4, Part 2 (London, 1811), p. 629.

22 Heywood, *Moore Rental*, p. 133; Platt, *Municipal Government*, pp. 205, 207, 212, 226. It is not known what connection this Gerrard Winstanley had with the Digger. The choice of forename for both may have reflected connections between the families of Winstanley and Gerard.

23 Alsop, 'High road to radicalism?', pp. 11–12; Alsop, 'Winstanley: what do we know of his life?', p. 21.

24 See Alsop, 'High road to radicalism?', pp. 11–14 for a detailed discussion of the historiography.

25 Christopher Brooks, 'Apprenticeship, social mobility and the middling sort, 1550–1800', in Jonathan Barry and Christopher Brooks (eds), *The Middling Sort of People: Culture, Society and Politics in England, 1550–1800* (Basingstoke, 1994), pp. 52–83.

26 For perceptions of gentility in early modern England, see esp. Keith Wrightson, *English Society 1580–1680* (London, 1982), pp. 20, 23–4, 25–7; Felicity Heal and Clive Holmes, *The Gentry in England and Wales 1500–1700* (London, 1994), pp. 6–19; Ann Hughes 'Politics, Society and Civil War in Warwickshire, 1620–1660' (unpublished PhD thesis, University of Liverpool, 1980), p. 54; Morrill, *Nature of the English Revolution* , pp. 192–9; David Cressy, 'Describing the social order of Elizabethan and Stuart England', *Literature and History*, 3, 1976, 29–37.

27 SHC, K44/1/9; TNA, C5/581/55; C6/188/66; C6/192/31; C6/217/31; C9/412/269; C24/867/102.

28 TNA, PROB11/316, fols 398v ff; SP 28/169 (unfol.), St Olave Old Jewry poll tax account 1641; SHC, COB/1/1. For a discussion of the significance of the designation 'Mr', see Brian Manning, *1649: The Crisis of the English Revolution* (London, 1992), pp. 58–60.

29 TNA, PROB11/319, fols 286–6v; PROB11/379, fols 95v–97; A. W. Hughes Clarke (ed.), *The Registers of St Michael Bassishaw, London, 1626–1735* (Harleian Society, vol. 78, 1943), pp. 15, 16, 103; *CJ*, 8, p. 62.

30 GL, MF 317/10, pp. 91, 527; MF 317/11, pp. 37, 118; MF 317/12, pp. 262, 313. Cf., for the provincial supply of London merchants, Norman Lowe, *The Lancashire Textile Industry in the Sixteenth Century* (Manchester, Chetham Society, 1972), pp. 59, 62–5; Richard Grassby, *The Business Community of Seventeenth-Century England* (Cambridge, 1995), pp. 91, 155, 163.

31 His father's name is not known. His mother was Alice Winstanley of Hough Wood: LLRRO, 16 D 66/22–3. A pedigree drawn up for the family in 1910 is erroneous: LLRRO, DE728/1002, 1008. A James, son of Edm. Winstanley, was baptised in Winwick near Billinge in 1606: Dickinson, *Winwick Register*, Part I, p. 70. Jas Winstanley gave his age as 30 when he married in 1636.

32 LLRRO, 16 D 66/342; Joseph Foster (ed.), *The Registers of Admissions to Gray's Inn, 1521–1889* (London, 1889), p. 174; Foster, *London Marriage Licences 1521–1869* (London, 1887), p. 1490; Clarke, *Registers of St Michael Bassishaw*, p. 55. For Clement Mosse, see TNA, PROB11/207, fols 272v ff. Winstanley was called to the Bar in May 1636 and to the Bench in November 1657, and was admitted to the Pension in February 1659: Reginald J. Fletcher (ed.), *The Pension Book of Gray's Inn*, vol. I (London, 1901), pp. 327, 421, 427.

33 LLRRO, DE728/44, 46–47, 596, 614–15; 16 D 66/396, 398–400; LRO, DDKE/acc. 7840 HMC/110, 120; DDPt 23/91.

34 LMA, ACC/2844/013–014; *Calendar of the Committee for the Advance of Money* (hereafter *CCAM*, p. 809; 'MSS accessions', *BIHR*, 19 (1942–43), p. 53. From 1632 he also held Duchy of Lancaster office as feodary, supervisor and particular receiver in Lancs: LLRRO, 16 D 66/410.

35 LLRRO, 16 D 66/396–97; TNA, SP23/89/283; Liverpool Record Office, Moore of Bank Hall MS 1235, *CCC*, pp. 2424, 2723; Stanning, *Royalist Composition Papers*, pp. 25–6.

36 LLRRO, DE728/840. Other prominent individuals with whom he had business dealings and dealings over land included Sir Henry Blount, Ralph Bovey, Fras Drake, Gerard Gore, Eliab Harvey and Henry Neville of Cressing Temple.

37 J. T. Rutt (ed.), *The Diary of Thomas Burton* (London, 1828), vol. 3, p. 502; *CJ*, 7, p. 611.

38 LLRRO, DE728/21–51. The initial cost to Winstanley was £6,000. The estate remained with the Winstanley family until 1925, when the Corporation of Leicester acquired it for council housing. For the Hastings family of Braunstone, see Thomas Cogswell, *Home Divisions: Aristocracy, the State and Provincial Conflict* (Manchester, 1998), pp. 293–4.

39 Helen Stocks (ed.), *Records of the Borough of Leicester 1603–1688* (Cambridge, 1923), pp. 441–2, 449–51.

40 Stocks, *Borough of Leicester*, pp. 479–80; Fletcher, *Pension Book of Gray's Inn*, p. 447.

41 LLRRO, 16 D 66/402–403; TNA, PROB11/335, fols 405 ff; PROB11/375, fols 71v–72.

42 BL, Egerton MS 1533, fols 41, 43. Titus made good use of the Winstanleys' extensive kinship ties when developing his own contacts with puritans: see, for instance, Liverpool Record Office, Moore of Bank Hall MS 1720. Cf. MSS 1692, 1699.

43 TNA, C6/25/85; C6/26/73; C9/412/269; C24/867/102.

44 LLRRO, 16 D 66/21; *CCC*, p. 1557. For Edm. Winstanley, see TNA, PROB11/307, fols 271–72v; Foster, *Marriage Licences*, p. 1490; Marc Fitch (ed.), *Index to Administrations in the Prerogative Court of Canterbury*, vol. 6: *1631–1648* (London, British Record Society: Index Library, vol. 100, 1986), pp. 246–7; *The Manuscripts of the House of Lords*, vol. 11 (ns): *Addenda 1514–1714* (London, HMSO 1962), pp. 344–5. Dorothy Lamplugh was daughter of Wm Lamplugh of Hampton, Middlesex, clerk of the kitchen and developer of Dungeness lighthouse: Fitch, *PCC Admons 1631–48*, pp. 246–7; *CSPD 1627–28*, p. 79; G. E. Aylmer, unpublished typescript list of government officials, 1625–1642 at HMC; TNA, PROB11/167.

45 Liverpool Record Office, Moore of Bank Hall MSS 1717, 1718.

46 SHC, COB/1/1. This is the only Clement Winstanley known outside the Braunstone Winstanleys. Clement Winstanley of Braunstone was named after his maternal grandfather Clement Mosse.

47 See below, p. 74.

48 GL, MF315/7; MF 317/11, p. 118; TNA, PROB11/232, fols 227v ff; PROB11/267, fols 231–231v, Arrowsmith and Wrigley, *Registers*, p. 118; J. J. Howard and J. L. Chester (eds), *The Visitation of London 1633, 1634 and 1635* (London, Harleian Society, 1880, 1883), Part I; *CCC*, pp. 1117, 2543, 2549; *CCAM*, p. 362; Alsop, 'Ethics in the marketplace', p. 105.

49 GL, MF 317/12, p. 313; MF 351; Hughes Clarke, *Registers of St Michael Bassishaw*, pp. 15, 16, 103.

50 *CSPD 1652–53*, p. 228; *CSPD 1653–54*, pp. 385, 396.

51 *CSPD 1651*, p. 368. Cf. *CJ*, 8, p. 62, where Major Jas Winstanley is described as brother of Mary Love, Chris Love's widow. Mary Love's maiden name was Stone: BL, Sloane MS 3945, fol. 105. Cf. Ernest Axon, (ed.), *Oliver Heywood's Life of John Angier of Denton*, (Manchester, Chetham Society, 1937), p. 129.

52 Gary S. De Krey, 'London radicals and revolutionary politics, 1675–1683', in T. Harris, P. Seaward and M. Goldie (eds), *The Politics of Religion in Restoration England* (Oxford, 1990), pp. 133–62, esp. p. 157. Player was named overseer of Jas Winstanley's will, and was left £5 in Roger Winstanley's will; Player's will was witnessed by Eliz. Winstanley: TNA, PROB11/319, fols 286–6v; PROB11/379, fols 95v–97; PROB11/382. For the connections with John Wilkins, see James Alsop, 'John Wilkins and Winstanley', *N&Q*, 234 (1989), 46–8.

53 *CSPD 1676–77*, p. 232. Cf. De Krey, 'London radicals', pp. 138–40; Melinda S. Zook, *Radical Whigs and Conspiratorial Politics in Late Stuart England* (Pennsylvania, 1999), p. 199.

54 George J. Armytage (ed.), *Allegations for Marriage Licences 1669–1679* (London, 1892), p. 83.

55 Katharine W. Swett, ' "Born on my land": identity, community and faith among the Welsh in early modern London', in Muriel C. McClendon, Joseph P. Ward and Michael Macdonald (eds), *Protestant Identities: Religion, Society, and Self-Fashioning in Post-Reformation England* (Stanford, 1999), pp. 249–65, esp. pp. 259–61; Peter Clark, 'Migrants in the city: the process of social adaptation in English towns 1500–1800', in Peter Clark and David Souden (eds), *Migration and Society in Early Modern England* (London, 1987), pp. 271–6; Grassby, *Business Community*, pp. 90–1; Lowe, *Lancashire Textile Industry*, p. 62. See also Susan E. Whyman, *Sociability and Power in Late-Stuart England: The Cultural Worlds of the Verneys 1660–1720* (Oxford, 1999), pp. 55–84.

56 Alsop, 'High road to radicalism?', pp. 14–15; James Alsop, 'Gater, Sarah', *ODNB*; Alsop, 'Winstanley: what do we know of his life?', pp. 22–4. Alsop suggests that the Masons and Gaters were also almost certainly kinsmen of the Winstanleys: *ibid.*, p. 23. For Gater's will, see TNA, PROB11/254, fols 150–2.

57 Lowe, *Lancashire Textile Industry*, p. 62.

58 TNA, C9/412/269; C6/44/101; C5/415/123; C24/867/102; PROB11/237, fols 1–10v.

59 TNA, C9/412/269. Aldworth may have had a distant Winstanley connection through his friend the London Presbyterian minister Thos Case. In 1643 Case became brother-in-law to John Angier, whose first wife had been Ellen Winstanley (d. 1642) of Wigan: Axon, *Heywood's Life of Angier*, pp. 54–5. For Aldworth and Case, see Case's *ODNB* entry, and TNA, PROB11/237, fol. 1v.

60 TNA, C6/44/101; Alsop, 'Ethics in the marketplace', p. 104; CLRO, MCD1/71. Winstanley's dealings with Backhouse are discussed in detail in Dalton, 'Experience of fraud'. See also James D. Alsop, 'Gerrard Winstanley: a reply', *HJ*, 38, 4 (1995), pp. 1013–15.

61 GL, M/F 316/12, p. 6; Alsop, 'Ethics in the marketplace', p. 99. Dicus was the son of John Dicus, minister of Felsted in Essex, for whom see GL, MS 10,091/6; John Venn and J. A. Venn (eds), *Alumni Cantabrigienses* (Cambridge, 1922); Foster, *Alumni Oxonienses 1500–1714*. For Christopher Dicus's will, see TNA, PROB11/231, fol. 139

62 GL, MS 4415/1, fols 101, 102, 102v, 103, 104, 105, 105v, 109v; Alsop, 'Winstanley: what do we know of his life?', p. 25.

63 GL, MS 4415/1, fol. 104; Alsop, 'Winstanley: what do we know of his life?', pp. 25–6; James D. Alsop, 'Revolutionary puritanism in the parishes? The case of St Olave, Old Jewry', *London Journal*, 15, 1 (1990), pp. 33–4. Winstanley added his signature to those of Patient Wallen and John Mylne. For Wallen, see Keith Lindley, *Popular Politics and Religion in Civil War London* (Aldershot, 1997), pp. 138–45, 183.

64 GL, 10,091/22, fol. 184v; T. C. Dale (ed.), *The Inhabitants of London in 1638* (London, 1931), p. 84. Susan King was 27 when she married Winstanley, having been baptised in St Lawrence Jewry on 13 December 1612: A. W. Hughes Clarke (ed.), *The Registers of St Lawrence Jewry London, 1538–1676*, Part 3 (London, Harleian Society, 1940), p. 33.

65 R. G. Lang (ed.), *Two Tudor Subsidies for the City of London 1541 and 1582* (London Record Society, 1993), pp. 187–94; Clarke, *Registers of St Lawrence Jewry*, p. 21. Richard, the eldest surviving son, died in 1597 aged 16: *ibid.*, pp. 17, 129.

66 TNA, PROB11/75, fol. 16; Clarke, *Registers of St Lawrence Jewry*, p. 125. He had been apprentice to Jas Bates, later master of the Barber-Surgeons' Co., and was made free of the company on 27 January 1579: GL, 5265/1, fol. 18v. He was son of Thos King, and appears to have married Anne or Agnes Helsby in May 1580.

67 TNA, PROB11/75, fol. 16. Their father was the draper John Quarles (d. 1577), for whom see PROB11/60. Edw. Quarles married Anne, daughter of Sir John Allot, lord mayor in 1591, and was post master of the Merchant Adventurers' Co. in 1609: *CSPD 1603–1610*, p. 568.

68 HMC, *De L'Isle MSS* (1934), pp. 266, 281, 285, 325–6; *Salisbury MSS*, vol. 13 (1915), p. 552; F. C. Dietz, *English Public Finance, 1558–1641* (New York, 1932), pp. 452–4. King left Becher a death's head ring worth 40s.

69 *CSPD 1595–97*, pp. 412, 413, 415; HMC, *Salisbury MSS*, vol. 7 (1899), pp. 22, 200–1; vol. 14 (1923), p. 33. Edw. Quarles was described to his distant kinsman Lord Burghley in 1597 as 'a merchant well known to be of very good ability and credit': *Salisbury MSS*, 7, p. 200. Wm Leveson, mercer, was brother of Sir John Leveson and a member of the Russia Co. See the will of their uncle Wm Leveson the elder: TNA, PROB11/82.

70 L. A. Parker, 'The agrarian revolution at Cotesbach 1501–1612', in W. G. Hoskins (ed.), *Studies in Leicestershire Agrarian History* (Leicester, Leicestershire Archaeological Society, 1949), pp. 41–76; John E. Martin, *Feudalism to Capitalism: Peasant and Landlord in English Agrarian Development* (London, 1983), pp. 186–7; Roger B. Manning, *Village Revolts: Social Protest and Popular Disturbance in England, 1509–1640* (Oxford, 1988), pp, 244–5.

71 For Sir Wm Becher, see John Stoye, *English Travellers Abroad 1604–1667* (rev. edn, New Haven and London, 1989), pp. 28–34, 36, 47–54; S. A. Baron, 'Becher, Sir William', *ODNB*.

72 GL, MS 5255/1; MS 5265/1, fol. 48v; TNA, E179/251/22; J. Harvey Bloom and R. Rutson James, *Medical Practitioners in the Diocese of London, Licensed under the Act of 3 Henry VIII c 11: An Annotated List 1529–1725* (Cambridge, 1935), p. 52.

73 Norman Moore, *The History of St Bartholomew's Hospital*, vol. 2 (London, 1918), pp. 623–5; Victor Cornelius Medvei and John L. Thornton, *The Royal Hospital of Saint Bartholomew 1123–1973* (London, 1974), p. 388; Sidney Young, *The Annals of the Barber-Surgeons of London* (London, 1890), p. 9; F. G. Parsons, *The History of St Thomas's Hospital*, vol. 2 (London, 1934), pp. 70–1. For Woodall (*c.* 1556–1643), first surgeon-general of the East India Co. and author of the influential *The Surgeon's Mate* (1617), see John H. Appleby, 'Woodall, John', *ODNB*; J. H. Appleby, 'New light on John Woodall,

surgeon and adventurer', *Medical History*, 25 (1981), pp. 251–68; Medvei and Thornton, *Hospital of St Bartholomew*, pp. 109–13.

74 GL, MS 5257/5, p. 341; Moore, *St Bartholomew's*, 2, pp. 624–5; Young, *Barber-Surgeons*, p. 218; Dalton' 'Experience of fraud', p. 978.

75 TNA, SP18/83/150; Moore, *St Bartholomew's*, 2, p. 303.

76 GL, Ms 5255/1; Moore, *St Bartholomew's*, 2, p. 303.

77 GL, Ms 10,091/21, fol. 73.

78 TNA, PROB/11/239; GL, Ms 10,091/2, fol. 73.

79 Matthews, *Calamy Revised*, p. 260; M. R. Bell, 'Hickes, Gaspar', *ODNB*; *CJ*, 3, p. 663; *LJ*, 7, p. 27. Jasper and Giles Hickes were sons of John Hickes (d. 1655), minister of Great Barrington in Gloucs and Berks: TNA, PROB11/250, fol. 123.

80 Gaspar Hickes, *The Glory and Beauty of God's Portion* (1644); *The Life and Death of David* (1645); *The Advantage of Afflictions* (1646); *CJ*, 3, p. 542; 4, pp. 207, 268, 451, 473; 5, pp. 471, 697; *LJ*, 8, pp. 129, 304, 558; 9, pp. 35, 601, 604. Another brother, Edward (b. 1622), was also a minister, possibly the rector of Buckland, Herts, and St Margaret Pattens, London, who died in 1683: TNA, PROB11/250, fol. 123; PROB11/372; Matthews, *Calamy Revised*, p. 260.

81 Parsons, *St Thomas's*, 2, pp. 70–1, where Warwick's letter is transcribed.

82 *Ibid.*, pp. 69–70.

83 CLRO, MC1/83/232; Parsons, *St Thomas's*, 2, pp. 81–2.

84 TNA, PROB11/254, fols 150–2.

85 For instance, Hill, *World Turned Upside Down*, pp. 240–1.

86 The King connection may explain Winstanley's apparent familiarity, noted by Hill, with arguments contained in Harvey's *Generation of Living Creatures*, which was not published in English until 1653: Christopher Hill, 'William Harvey and the idea of monarchy', *P&P*, 27 (1964), p. 61.

87 TNA, C6/26/73.

88 This was claimed in a court case in 1658: TNA, C6/26/73. King's 'very faire library of books' also included, among other things, the works of Bishops Hall, Lake and Andrewes, Ralegh's *History of the World* and Foxe's *Acts and Monuments*. It was said to have been worth above £80: C6/26/73.

89 TNA, C6/25/85; C6/26/73.

90 TNA, C6/25/85.

91 Moore, *St Bartholomews*, 2, pp. 626–7; Medvei and Thornton, *Hospital of St Bartholomew*, p. 388.

92 TNA, C6/25/85. Stone later claimed to have taught Sarah King 'to play soe well upon the harpsicon as that her teaching was well worth the some of one hundred pounds'. Stone has proved difficult to identify. It is known that his master had died around 1649, and if he was the John Stone who was brought up in the household of Alderman John Warner (d. 1648), then he was brother-in-law of Christopher Love and a kinsman of the Winstanleys. Mrs Monck, the future Duchess of Albemarle, recommended her son's dancing master, John Stone, to be instructor of dancing at court in 1660: *CSPD 1659–1660*, p. 426.

93 TNA, C6/25/85: C6/26/73. The court's findings in favour of the Kings are outlined in C5/413/199.

94 Alsop, 'Ethics in the marketplace', pp. 98–100, 106–7. This article provides by far the best discussion of Winstanley's business dealings.

95 GL, MS 4415/1, fols 90v, 96v, 100v, 106v, 107, 115, 115v. Winstanley was assessed for the scavenger assessment in St Olave's at 1s a year from Christmas 1638 and for the poor rate at 1d a week from 1641. For the suggestion that Winstanley was involved with Blackwell Hall, see Rutt, *Burton's Diary*, vol. I, p. 156.

96 TNA, SP28/169 (unfol.), poll tax account for St Olave Old Jewry; T. C. Dale (ed.), *The Poll Tax for London in 1641* (London, 1939), p. 20; Alsop, 'Ethics in the marketplace', p. 100. The Whitfield families of Diglake and Roby in Lancashire both had connections with members of the Winstanley family of Wigan.

97 CLRO, MCD1/71; Dalton, 'Experience of fraud', pp. 973–4, where the figure of £274 1s 6d is given for Winstanley's losses. It is evident from the depositions that the goods sold by Winstanley were to the value of £150, and that the higher sum of £274 1s 6d included money owing on a bond with a penalty of £300 entered into by Backhouse at the time of his transactions with Winstanley.

98 TNA, C6/44/101; Alsop, 'Ethics in the marketplace', p. 104. Surviving records of the Irish statute staple office indicate that Peake was still trading in 1655: BL, Add. MS 19,843, fol. 151v.

99 TNA, C9/412/269; Alsop, 'Ethics in the marketplace', pp. 100–2. Winstanley later claimed to have paid £51 in May 1643, but this was disputed by Aldworth's servants.

100 TNA, C9/412/269; C6/44/101; Alsop, 'Ethics in the marketplace', pp. 104, 105; Petegorsky, *Left-Wing Democracy*, p. 123.

101 Dalton, 'Experience of fraud', pp. 973–4, 981. Backhouse's subsequent possible involvement in the slave trade has given the episode added significance for some scholars: see, for example, Peter Linebaugh and Marcus Rediker, *The Many-Headed Hydra: The Hidden History of the Revolutionary Atlantic* (London, 2000), pp. 140–2, where Winstanley's opposition to slavery is discussed in relation to this episode.

102 CLRO, MCD1/71; Alsop, 'Winstanley: a reply', pp. 1013–15. The 1642 depositions make no suggestion of fraud, but make it clear that Backhouse's debts were substantial and remained at that date wholly unpaid.

103 Cf. however G.E. Aylmer, 'The religion of Gerrard Winstanley', in J. F. McGregor and B. Reay, (eds), *Radical Religion in the English Revolution* (Oxford, 1984), p. 94, for a warning against overly reductionist explanations for Winstanley's radicalism.

104 Sabine, *Works*, p. 315.

105 Winstanley, *The Saints Paradise* (1648), p. 38.

106 Sabine, *Works*, p. 188.

107 *Ibid.*, p. 315.

108 GL, MS 4415/1, fol. 118; TNA, SP28/178 (unfol.), warrant to the high constables of Elmbridge hundred, 20 December 1643; SP28/245 (unfol.), accounts of Augustine Phillips, 1645.

109 TNA, C10/22/86; PROB11/245, fol. 13; SHC, 2610/11/8/33, pp. 47–9, 53–7; St George's CAL, MS X1. M3, fol. 116. The problems of identification are discussed in Gurney, 'King, Winstanley and Cobham', pp. 42–6.

110 TNA, C6/25/85; C6/26/73; SHC, G3/4/17.

111 TNA, C6/25/85; PROB11/320, fols 103 ff.

112 SHC, COB/5/1; TNA, PROB11/320, fols 103 ff. In the palings assessment the name 'Mr Winstanly' is added in a later hand against that of Smythe. Smythe had inherited this property on the death in 1608 of his father Jas Smythe: LMA, DW/PA/7/8, fols 28–8v; St George's CAL, MS Xl. M3, fols 113v, 114.

113 SHC, G3/4/17; COB/5/1. Thos Emmett was also a tenant of Ham manor and of Cobham manor: St George's CAL, MS Xl. M3, fols 112v, 113v, 114, 114v, 115; SHC, K44/1/8; 2610/11/8/33. In the palings assessment the names of King and Winstanley are added in later hands to that of Emmett.

114 St George's CAL, MS Xl. M3, fols 112v, 113v, 114.

115 St George's CAL, MS Xl. M3, fol. 113v; S.H.C., K44/1/8. Mill Field was on the site of Cobham cemetery: Walker, 'Manorial history', p. 59.

116 If the copyhold was inherited rather than bought, it is possible that it was inherited by Susan rather than Wm King. She was, however, too old to be Thos Smythe's daughter, and there is no mention of a daughter named Susan in Jas Smythe's will or in the Cobham parish registers.

117 TNA, PROB11/205, fols 161v–62; Norman Moore, rev. William Birken, 'Meverell, Othowell', *ODNB*; Young, *Barber-Surgeons*, pp. 367, 405.

118 TNA, PROB11/258, fols 263v–64v; Armytage, *Visitation of Surrey 1662–1668*, p. 81.

119 Aubrey, *Surrey*, 3, pp. 186–7; Dalton, *Manuscripts of St George's Chapel*, p. 338; *CSPD 1611–18*, p. 254.

120 It is even possible that they acquired the property after 1650, in order to help their daughter and son-in-law to return to Cobham following the collapse of the Digger experiment: Gurney, 'King, Winstanley and Cobham', p. 44. Another possibility is that Winstanley acquired the property himself in the 1640s, but that as a possible bankrupt he did so in the Kings' name.

121 SHC, K44/1/9; 4398/1/10; COB/5/1.

122 TNA, C10/22/86.

123 Surrey properties of the Dean and Canons of Windsor in Chiddingfold were sequestered in October 1644: TNA, SP28/214 (unfol.), account of Thomas Byrne and Thomas Higginbotham.

124 St George's CAL, XV.42.47; Parliamentary Surveys, vol. II, fol. 90; Dalton, *Manuscripts of St George's Chapel*, p. 338; Aubrey, *Surrey*, 3, pp. 186–7. For Ayscough (c. 1615–71) see Peter Le Fevre, 'Sir George Ayscue, commonwealth and restoration admiral', *Mariner's Mirror*, 68 (1982), pp. 189–202; Bernard Capp, *Cromwell's Navy: The Fleet and the English Revolution 1648–1660* (Oxford, 1989), pp. 175–6; TNA, PROB11/338, fols 326 ff.

125 Ruth Spalding (ed.), *The Diary of Bulstrode Whitelocke 1605–1675* (Oxford, 1990), p. 446.

126 TNA, SP18/92/9; J. J. Keevil, *Medicine and the Navy 1200–1900*, vol. 2 (Edinburgh and London, 1958), p. 37.

127 TNA, PROB11/191; Howard and Chester, *Visitation of London 1633, 1634 and 1635*, I, p. 135. For Carleton and King, see above, pp. 19, 71.

128 TNA, PROB11/229; 233; 258, fols 263v–264v; 297, fols 141 ff.

129 Below, p. 77.

130 CLRO, MC1/83/232. Cf. Dalton, 'Experience of fraud', p. 978.

131 GL, Ms 10,091/15, fol. 22. For Forder, see also GL, Ms 21742/1; TNA, PROB11/224, fol. 307v; Dale, *Inhabitants of London*, pp. 199–200.

132 John Coulton, *Theoria Contingentium Anni Aerae Christianae 1653* (1653); John Coulton, *Prognostes Astralis de Contingentibus Anni Aerae Christianae 1654* (1654); John Coulton, *Prognostae Astralis Diarium, Or, An Almanack for the Yeare of Christ, 1655* (1655).

133 Sabine, *Works*, p. 315.

134 Alsop, 'Winstanley: what we know of his life?', pp. 27–8.

135 Above, p. 64.

136 Dalton, 'Experience of fraud', p. 975; Gurney, 'Surrey and the English Revolution', p. 245. The list is in TNA, SP28/245 (unfol.).

137 TNA, SP28/178 (unfol.), warrant to the high constables of Elmbridge hundred, 20 December 1643; revised schedule for Elmbridge hundred, 10 January 1644. At least two Walton residents were charged in both London and Walton on the earlier three-month assessment: E179/187/467.

138 TNA, C9/412/269.

139 TNA, SP19/94/153, 155. The incident was first noted in Lindley, *Popular Politics*, p. 330. Lindley suggests, interestingly, that Winstanley may have been acting in an official capacity as an agent of the committee. For Holt (d. 1657), see also GL, MF 315 (vol. 7); TNA, PROB11/267, fol. 231.

140 TNA, SP19/94/153.

141 TNA, SP19/75, p. 295.

142 Sabine, *Works*, p. 326. For the date of this meeting, TNA, SP16/500/44. Cf. SP28/177 (unfol.), accts of Sackford Gunson, December 1643–January 1645.

143 *Perfect Occurences* 33 (13–20 August), pp. 217, 221; *A Perfect Diurnall* 212 (August 1647), p. 1702.

144 For instance, TNA, SP24/1, fols 69v, 85v; A. R. Bax, 'The plundered ministers of Surrey', *SAC*, 9 (1888), p. 260. Cf. Morrill, *Nature of the English Revolution*, pp. 171–3, for the reintrusion of ejected ministers in other counties.

145 For the collection of taxes see TNA, SP28/334 (unfol.), accnt book of Rich. Wither, fols 66, 71, 74, 82, 86.

146 TNA, SP24/47 (unfol.), petition of the farmers of Surrey to Sir Thos Fairfax, read by the Committee for Indemnity, 25 January 1648; Rushworth, *Collections*, 7, p. 936; *CJ*, 5, p. 413; *VCH Surrey*, I, pp. 413–14; Robert Ashton, *Counter Revolution: the Second Civil War and its Origins, 1646–48* (New Haven and London, 1994), p. 130.

147 HLRO, Main Papers 1647, 20 November, petition of John Turner to the House of Commons.

148 Rushworth, *Collections*, 7, pp. 815, 829. Cf. *ibid.*, 7, p. 773; *A Perfect Diurnall of Some Passages in Parliament* (9–16 August 1647).

149 W. Haller and G. Davies (eds), *The Leveller Tracts 1647–1653* (New York, 1944), pp. 66, 71, 83.

150 HLRO, Main Papers 1647, 19 November, Sir Thos Fairfax to Robt Scawen.

151 BL, Add. MS 15,948, fols 13–14; *LJ*, 10, pp. 239, 260–1; HMC, *Portland Manuscripts* (10 vols, London 1891–1931), I, p. 453; Underdown, *Pride's Purge*, pp. 97–8; A. R. Michell, 'Surrey in 1648', *SAC*, 67 (1970), pp. 68–70; Ashton, *Counter Revolution*, pp. 148–9.

152 BL, Add. MS 37,344, fol. 152; *Mercurius Elenticus* 26 (17–24 May 1648); *An Exact Relation of the late Skirmish at White-Hall* (1648); *A True Relation of the Passages Between the Surrey Petitioners and the Souldiers at Westminster* (1648); *The Sad and Bloody Fight at Westminster* (1648).

153 BL, Add. MS 15,948, fols 13–14v; *A Declaration of the Knights, Gentlemen and Freeholders of the County of Surrey* (1648); *The Copy of a Letter from a Well-affected Gentleman of Surrey to a Gentleman in Kent* (1648); *Kingdomes Weekly Intelligencer* (16–23 May 1648).

154 BL, Add. MS 15,958, fol. 15.

155 *The Declaration of the Right Honourable the Duke of Buckingham, and the Earles of Holland, and Peterborough* (1648), pp. 2–3.

156 For accounts of the rising see Lewis Awdeley, *A True Relation Sent to the Honourable Committee at Derby-House of the great Victory of the Parliaments Forces Against Those of Surrey* (1648); Michell, 'Surrey in 1648', pp. 74–8; H. E. Malden, *A History of Surrey* (London, 1900), pp. 245–51.

157 TNA, SP19/86/57; SP24/4/1; *CCC*, pp. 1191, 1498, 1543, 1837, 1946, 1973, 2102, 2762, 2785, 2870, 2922; *CCAM*, pp. 894, 1023, 1034, 1045, 1195, 1222; *CSPD 1648–49*, p. 181.

158 TNA, SP19/86/57; *CCAM*, p. 1222.

159 C. H. Firth (ed.), *The Clarke Papers* (4 vols, London, 1891–1901), 2, p. 218.

160 TNA, ASSI35/89/7; SP24/3, fol. 84; SP24/34 (unfol.), petition of Robert Bell.

161 Fielder, *Humble Petition and Appeal*, p. 3.

162 Winstanley's defence of Everard (and of himself) was published as *Truth Lifting Up its Head Above Scandals* (1649), in Sabine, *Works*, pp. 97–146.

163 Firth, *Clarke Papers*, I, p. 419; Hill, *World Turned Upside Down*, pp. 55, 228–30; Austin Woolrych, *Soldiers and Statesmen: the General Council of the Army and Its Debates, 1647–1648* (Oxford, 1987), p. 294. For biographical details, see Ariel Hessayon, 'Everard, William', *ODNB*.

164 Samuel Fisher, *Baby-Baptism Meer Babism* (1653), pp. 303–5.

165 *Ibid.*, p. 304. It was by this name that Winstanley first knew Everard: Sabine, *Works*, p. 103.

166 Sabine, *Works*, p. 103.

167 Fielder, *Humble Petition and Appeal*, p. 4; TNA, ASSI35/84/1; 35/89/5; 35/92/8, 12; 93/5, 7, 10, 11. For Downe, whose 1657 will shows distinct support for the Anglican church, see also PROB11/306, fols 1–1v.

168 Fielder, *Humble Petition and Appeal*, p. 5.

169 Cf. Christopher Hill, *Religion and Politics in Seventeenth-Century England*, (Brighton, 1986), pp. 209, 210.

170 Fielder, *Humble Petition and Appeal*, pp. 5–6.

171 *Ibid.*, pp.5–6. Cf. Solt, 'Fielder, Winstanley and Lilburne, pp. 121–4.

172 Fielder, *Humble Petition and Appeal*, p. 10; Solt, 'Fielder, Winstanley and Lilburne, pp. 132–3.

Chapter 4

Winstanley: the early writings

The title page of Winstanley's first published work, *The Mysterie of God*, bears the date 1648. We cannot be certain as to precisely when it appeared, for it escaped the attentions of the George Thomason, the London bookseller who noted down the date of acquisition of each of the publications he added to his extensive collection of contemporary tracts.[1] A second work, *The Breaking of the Day of God*, which was printed for the radical London bookseller Giles Calvert, was dated 20 May 1648.[2] Although *The Mysterie of God* carried no printer's name, the similarities between that work and *The Breaking of the Day of God* suggest strongly that both were published by Calvert. Winstanley's third pamphlet, *The Saints Paradise*, appeared during the summer of 1648, to be followed in October by *Truth Lifting Up its Head Above Scandals*.[3] These four publications were to be reissued by Calvert, along with *The New Law of Righteousnes* of January 1649, in a collected edition of the early writings published in December 1649.[4]

Although Winstanley's four earliest pamphlets appear to have been produced in a remarkably short space of time, each had its own quite distinct character. Together these works bore witness to the rapid development of Winstanley's ideas, and to the increasing confidence with which he was able to give expression to them. In these early writings Winstanley drew on established and recognisable traditions of religious radicalism to advance arguments of great originality, combining some quite familiar views in highly unorthodox ways to fashion an optimistic, and uncompromisingly radical, analysis.[5] He did so moreover with a clarity and directness that set these tracts apart from many of the other radical spiritualist and perfectionist writings that were published in the later 1640s. His early writings challenged conventional understandings of God, the Fall and salvation, but also prefigured the arguments used later to advance the Diggers' case.[6] Through these writings it is possible to trace Winstanley's emergence, from within a radical and heterodox tradition of religious mysticism, as an advocate of a communistic solution to the abiding problems facing England and humankind.[7]

The Mysterie of God, which was dedicated to Winstanley's 'Beloved Countrey-men of the County of Lancaster', was an explicitly millenarian work that set out to demonstrate, within a dispensationalist framework and with the help of abundant biblical citation, the case for general redemption and universal salvation. God will 'dwell in the whole Creation, that is, every man and every woman without exception', and he 'will not lose any part of his Creation, Mankind, but will redeem and preserve it, both in particular, & in whole'.[8] Enlightenment will come first to the elect, those whose names are written in the Lamb's Book, but ultimately to all; for everyone will be saved 'without exception, though some at the ninth houre, some at the tenth houre, and some at the last houre'.[9] God 'will dwell in the whole creation in time, and so deliver whole mankind out of that bondage'.[10]

These arguments were developed further in *The Breaking of the Day of God*, in which Winstanley also made explicit his hostility to ecclesiastical authority, his thoroughgoing anti-formalism and his belief in the superiority of experimental knowledge over knowledge gained through study of the scriptures; of the power of the spirit over the written word.[11] Greater emphasis was also placed in this pamphlet on the inner struggle between good and evil, and on the conviction that 'all outward abominations in mens practises came from the indwelling of the Beast in every mans heart':

> If you desire to know the Beast, that treads you and the holy City underfoot: look first into your own hearts, for there she sits; And after that ye have beheld her confused workings there against Christ, then look into the world, and you shall see the same confusion of ignorance, pride, self-love, oppression, and vain conversation acted against Christ, in States, in Assemblies, and in some Churches in the world.[12]

The need to abide by the biblical Golden Rule, 'to doe as we would be done by', was crucial, for only when 'this Son of righteousnesse and love arises in Magistrates and people, one to another, then these tumultuous Nationall stormes will cease, and not till then'.[13]

It was in his third pamphlet, *The Saints Paradise*, that Winstanley first made clear his equation of God with Reason. God, he asserted, should not be seen to be 'in some particular place of glory, beyond the skies'; he is in every creature, and is 'the spirit within you, invisible in every body to the eye of flesh, yet discernable to the eye of the spirit':[14]

> This spirit which is called God, or Father, or Lord, is Reason: for though men esteem this word Reason to be too mean a name to set forth the Father by, yet it is the highest name that can be given him.

> For it is Reason that made all things, and it is Reason that governs the whole Creation, and if flesh were but subject thereunto, that is, to the spirit of Reason within himself, it would never act unrighteousnesse.[15]

It is Reason that enjoins men and women to abide by the Golden Rule, the centrality of which to Winstanley's thought was becoming increasingly clear:

> For let Reason rule the man, he dares not trespasse against his fellow creature, but will do as he would be done unto: For Reason tels him, is thy neighbour hungry, and naked to day, do thou feed him, and cloath him, it may be thy case to morrow, and then he will be ready to help thee.[16]

Winstanley's identification of God with Reason was defended and expanded upon in *Truth Lifting Up its Head Above Scandals*. In seeking to explain his use of the word Reason in place of God, Winstanley acknowledged that a distinction should be made between the 'Spirit Reason, which I call God', and human reasoning:

> For this Spirit Reason, doth not preserve one creature and destroy another; as many times mens reasoning doth, being blind by the imagination of the flesh: but it hath a regard to the whole creation; and knits every creature together into a onenesse; making every creature to be an upholder of his fellow; and so every one is an assistant to preserve the whole: and the neerer that mans reasoning comes to this, the more spirituall they are; the farther off they be, the more selfish and fleshly they be.[17]

Truth Lifting Up its Head Above Scandals was written following the arrest in Kingston of Winstanley's associate William Everard, and the 'slandering' of Winstanley by local ministers, and the pamphlet sought both to explain and justify the ideas that had caused so much offence.[18] Metaphors that had made fleeting appearances in Winstanley's first three pamphlets, and which were later to have a direct bearing on the language advanced to justify the digging experiment, were elaborated upon in this work. The earth had appeared as a metaphor for mankind in both *Breaking of the Day of God* and *The Saints Paradise*, the 'troublesome distempers' afflicting mankind being equated in the latter with the 'thorns and bryars' which now filled the earth.[19] The spirit within would act as the 'cleanser and purger of this poysoned earth', the spirit of righteousness 'taking up sons and daughters out of their imaginary earth, under which they have lien buried'.[20] Christ was come

> to open the prison doors, to pull you up out of the earth of covetousnesse, and self-imagination, under which you have been, and are buried and will set you even as a corne of wheat lies buried under clods of earth, till the warme cherishing, meeke and loving spirit in the earth cause it to sprout, and spring, and shoot out, and so bring forth fruit like himself in great abundance.[21]

Winstanley's understanding of the Fall and of the corruption of the earth was spelled out in greater detail in *Truth Lifting Up its Head Above Scandals*. Man's determination to live upon the objects of creation rather than according to the light of the spirit had poisoned and corrupted the earth, spreading the spirit of contention throughout mankind and to all other creatures.[22] Those who chose to continue living upon the objects of creation were sons and daughters 'of the first man: so that we may see *Adam* every day before our eyes walking up and downe the street'.[23] Two Adams fought for supremacy within each individual, and it was the second Adam, equated at times with Christ and at others with 'the whole bulke of mankinde, when they shall be drawne up to live in the unity of the one spirit', whose time was now fast approaching.[24] The spirit of the first Adam had hitherto ruled over the earth, and had kept the second, his servant, under subjection. The impending triumph of this second Adam would effect the restoration of things to their prelapsarian state, Christ bringing all 'into order again; taking away the bitterness and curse, and making the whole Creation to be of one heart and one Spirit'.[25] The apostles had declared that the spirit that had ruled in Christ would, in the latter days, 'be poured out upon sonnes and daughters; and shall spread in the earth like the shining of the Sun from East to West':

> And this is that which this mouth and pen of mine doe testifie of to all that heare mee: that the same spirit that hath layne hid under flesh, like a corne of wheat for an appointed time, under the clods of earth, is now sprung out, and begins to grow up a fruitfull vine, which shall never decay, but it shall encrease, till he hath filled the earth. This is the Kingdome of God within man. This is the graine of mustard seed, which is little in the beginning, but shall become a mighty tree. This is the fire, that shall dry and burne up all the drosse of mans worke, and turne all things into his owne nature. This is the spirit which is broke out, that will bringe mankinde into one heart, and one minde: For assure your selves, I knowe what I speake. The Thorne bush is burning; but the Vine is flourishing. The Ashes of the Thorne bush is laid at the root of the feet of the Vine, and it growes abundantly.[26]

It seems evident that Winstanley had already come to accept that the inner reappearance of Christ would have far-reaching political and social consequences. In *Breaking of the Day of God* Winstanley had spoken favourably of magistracy – including kingly authority – as a higher power ordained by God to preserve peace in the world, though troubled and corrupted by ecclesiastical power.[27] He had, however, also warned that in restoring the purity of magistracy 'God shakes, and will yet shake, Kings, Parliaments, Armies, Counties, Kingdomes, Universities, humane learnings, studies, yea, shake rich men and poore men', throwing down 'every thing that stands in his way, opposing him in his work'; for when 'God first shakes down and casts out the Beast out of mens hearts, the outward abominations and unjust practises in church and

State, shake together and fall presently'.[28] Positive references to magistracy were largely absent from the succeeding pamphlets. In *The Saints Paradise* 'the Powers, Governours and Armies of the Land' were enjoined 'to worship the Lord in righteousness': 'for assure your selves, you Kingly, Parliamentarie, and Army power, and know this, that all unrighteous powers and actions must be destroyed'.[29] In *Truth Lifting Up its Head Above Scandals*, the victory of the second Adam was linked to the prospect of wholesale change: the second man

> shall have as large a priviledge to fill the earth, as the first man had surely; and he wil change times and customs, & fil the earth with a new law, wherin dwels righteousnes and peace. And justice, and judgment shal be the upholders of his kingdom.[30]

Although it was not until he wrote *The New Law of Righteousnes* that Winstanley would make explicit the crucial connection between private property and the Fall, the arguments behind that work and the later Digger pamphlets were clearly anticipated in his four earliest pamphlets.

INFLUENCES

Little is known about the specific influences to which Winstanley was exposed in the years leading up to the publication of his first tract, or about which radical religious circles, if any, he had come into contact with. It is certainly legitimate to seek to locate his early writings firmly within the vibrant radical religious culture of the later 1640s, and to see close connections between his writings and works from the spiritualist and mystical tradition published or reprinted in that decade. Key texts from within this tradition, including the familist writings of Hendrick Niclaes, works by Jacob Boehme, and the *Theologia Germanica*, had reappeared in print in the 1640s, and could easily have been read by Winstanley, though we cannot be sure that he knew them.[31] Winstanley himself made no reference in his writings to other authors, and he steadfastly refused to acknowledge any intellectual debts. Instead he claimed to have learnt only from what had been revealed to him; from 'what I do receive from a free discovery within'.[32] His well-known account of the intensity of the writing experience, which he included in the preface to *Several Pieces Gathered into One Volume*, bolsters the impression of a writer driven primarily by an inner light:

> Sometimes my heart hath been ful of deadnesse and uncomfortablenesse, wading like a man in the dark and slabby weather; and within a little time I have been filled with such peace, light, life and fulness, that if I had two pair of hands, I had matter enough revealed, to have kept them writing a long time, which have filled my heart with abundance of sweet joy and rest.

Then I took the opportunity of the spirit, and writ, and the power of self, at such over-flowing times was so prevalent in me, that I forsook my ordinary food whole daies together, and if my houshold-friends would perswade me to come to meat, I have been forced with that inward fulnes of the power of life, to rise up from my ordinary labour, & the society of friends sometimes hath been a burden to me, and best I was when I was alone, I was so filled with that love and delight in the life within, that I have sat writing whole winter-daies from morning til night & the cold never offended me, though when I have risen, I was so starke with cold that I was forced to rise by degrees and hold by the table, till strength and heat came into my legges; and I have been secretly sorry when night came, which forced me to rise.[33]

Perhaps, as Nigel Smith has argued, we should recognise the 'the capacity for extreme opinions regarding perfection and scriptural interpretation to develop autonomously through scripture reading and separately from any particular tradition', while at the same time avoiding the temptation to dismiss the possibility of such a link.[34] Winstanley's emphasis on the power of the spirit, his allegorical reading of the scriptures, his adoption of a dispensationalist framework, rejection of external ordinances and internalisation of the millennium certainly echoed many of the key themes from within the broader radical spiritualist tradition, as expressed through the works both of leading historical figures from that tradition and their more recent English followers.[35] Other features of Winstanley's early writings, notably his marked egalitarianism and his emphasis on the importance of the Golden Rule, were already to be found expressed in the works of prominent radical propagandists such as William Walwyn and John Lilburne.[36] Arguments in favour of universal redemption had appeared in the writings of William Erbery, William Batte and others, while, as David Como has shown, hints of a neglected strain of Christian communism could be seen in the works of John Traske and his disciples.[37]

It would be rash to assume, though conclusive evidence to the contrary may be lacking, that Winstanley's exposure to radical ideas was no more than a recent development. His early writings suggest, in the manner of most conversion narratives and works of radical puritan declaration, that he had only recently undergone a sudden and dramatic change of heart, but the richness and complexity of these early works point rather to a sustained period of study and intellectual development. We can be confident that Winstanley did not lead an isolated existence at Cobham, untouched by the religious and political controversies of the 1640s. As has been shown, he retained close contacts with London after his move to Cobham, and Cobham itself, lying as it did close to Kingston and at no great distance from London, was by no means an isolated parish.[38] Winstanley indicated in *Truth Lifting Up its Head Above Scandals* that he had, at some unspecified date, come into contact with Baptist circles and gone through the 'ordinance of dipping'.[39] Whether his experience of adult baptism took place in London or Surrey we cannot say, but it is known that the

London Baptists Thomas Lamb, Thomas Collier and Samuel Oates toured the county on preaching and dipping tours in the mid-1640s, quite possibly passing through Kingston and Cobham on their way to preach at Guildford.[40] The similarity between the views expressed in Winstanley's early works and ideas associated with Seekers has also led to speculation that Winstanley may have spent some time as a Seeker.[41] By 1648, however, he had evidently come to reject any identification with Seekers or Baptists, and he was openly critical of gathered congregations, which, he claimed, represented 'no more but going out of one form into another, not into the unitie of the one Spirit'.[42] Rather than trying to associate the early Winstanley too closely with any one sectarian tradition, it may be more sensible to see him instead as a not untypical product of the early-seventeenth-century puritan underground; of a heterogeneous godly community whose breadth, fluidity and receptiveness to new ideas is only now coming to be fully understood.[43]

Unorthodox belief was by no means new to Surrey, which was a county with a long tradition of radical sectarian religious belief and practice. The Elizabethan magistrate Sir William More of Loseley was for many years engaged in campaigns against 'familist' circles in the south-western parts of the county. More's extensive correspondence and papers contain frequent references to radical activity in west Surrey, including detailed accounts to the activities of a group of supposed familists active in 1561 in and around Wonersh.[44] The group's stated beliefs, which included, among other things, holding goods in common within the group, denial of the Trinity, rejection of an external heaven and hell, nicodemism and a conviction that 'Christ is come forth in their fleshe', may, as Alaistair Hamilton and Christopher Marsh have both argued, have had little to do with the ideas of Hendrick Niclaes and his closest followers, and may instead have represented a local fusion of half-understood or recently-adopted familist ideas with ideas inherited from an earlier sectarian, anabaptist tradition.[45] Christopher Vittells, who was Niclaes's leading follower in England and an inhabitant of Southwark, did however certainly have some acquaintance with these Surrey sectaries.[46] Anabaptist activity in west Surrey was also of concern to More and his fellow justices during the 1560s and 1570s. Two 'anabaptists' were burnt at Guildford in July 1575, and among More's papers are detailed charges against suspected anabaptists in the area around Wonersh, Bramley and Guildford.[47]

It is impossible to know whether the radical ideas circulating in sixteenth-century Surrey were still remembered locally, even if only in some attenuated form, during the following century. Certainly familist influences continued to be felt, for several members or associates of the Family of Love were resident in the county in the early years of the seventeenth century.[48] Among these Surrey familists was Philip Moyse of Cannons in Banstead, a kinsman of the future Digger Henry Bickerstaffe.[49] As late as 1641, the county was still sufficiently closely identified with familism for the story told in the salacious *Description of the Sect called the Familie of Love* to be set in the Surrey woods near Bagshot, the young victim of seduction by a member of the Family being identified as the daughter of a gentleman from Pyrford, a village only a short distance from Cobham.[50]

TOWARDS THE RESTORATION OF COMMUNITY

Although Winstanley's early tracts are rightly seen as being essentially mystical works, it would be wrong to assume that they did not also reflect the very specific political context in which they were produced. The preface to Winstanley's *The Breaking of the Day of God* was completed on 20 May 1648, only four days after Surrey's petitioners for a personal treaty had fought with the parliament guard at Westminster, and at a time when royalists were boasting that the county's inhabitants had abandoned all support for parliament.[51] This work, and the others produced by Winstanley in mid-1648, gave expression to the increasing vulnerability felt by radicals as former parliamentarian strongholds united in support of a settlement with the king. The sense of isolation felt by radicals in 1648 had been reflected in Winstanley's first pamphlet, when he wrote of 'the great bitternesse, envy, reproachfull languages, and expressions of malicious wrath' directed against those who were branded 'sectaries, by severall names', and when he complained that he had 'heard some say, that they would be content to suffer the misery of a new war in England, so that such as they mentioned, might suffer as well as they'.[52] Several references were made in *The Breaking of the Day of God* and *The Saints Paradise* to the popular use of the names 'Sectaries, Schismaticks, Anabaptists, Round-heads' and 'Independents' to attack the saints.[53] The former work was dedicated to 'the despised sons and daughters of Zion, scattered up and down the Kingdom of England', and sought to encourage them to maintain their faith 'in the midst of this cloud of nationall troubles'.[54]

It was not, however, until the end of the year that Winstanley produced a work that fused his religious ideas with a clear programme for action. The preface to *The New Law of Righteousnes* bore the date 26 January 1649, four days before the execution of the king.[55] It was in this work, his longest and most remarkable to date, that Winstanley made explicit the connection between private property and the Fall. While elaborating upon arguments developed in his previous four publications, he used this work to express for the first time his complete rejection of the prevailing social and economic order, and his belief that private property would shortly be abandoned and the earth made a common treasury.[56] *The New Law of Righteousnes* was, like its preceding works, written within a framework of practical Christianity, but this was expressed in a way that shifted the agency from the charitable to the poor themselves. While drawing on traditional languages of popular protest, it sought also to prioritise arguments in favour of rights to subsistence over traditional arguments drawn from custom.

The spirit of visionary, millenarian hope in which this work was conceived was made clear in the preface, which contained a dedication to 'the twelve tribes of Israel that are circumcised in heart, and scattered through all the nations of the earth'. These had suffered 'inward bondage, and outward persecution', yet the seed of Abraham which lay hidden in them, the 'Law and power of righteousnesse' or 'Law of righteousnesse and peace', was ready to break forth in them and throughout the creation. 'This is the one spreading power that shall remove the curse, and restore all things from the bondage every thing groans under'; 'the blessing shall be everywhere'. The 'glory of Jerusalem' was not only to be 'seen hereafter, after the body is laid in the dust'; for, as Winstanley argued, 'I know that the glory of the Lord shall be seen and known within the Creation, and the blessing shall spread in all Nations'.[57]

The metaphor of first and second Adam reappeared in *The New Law of Righteousnes*, and was placed alongside the story of Jacob and Esau.[58] The first Adam had chosen to live off the objects of creation, and man, driven by self-love and covetousness, had fallen out with his maker; all creatures now lay under the curse.[59] The rising of Christ in his sons and daughters, or of the second Adam or Jacob, heralded the restoration of things to their former state and the ultimate victory of righteousness and peace. Christ rising was the second coming; the new Jerusalem, heaven and hell were all to be seen, and experienced within each individual.[60] The Adam metaphor was further refined in *The New Law of Righteousnes*. The first Adam appeared in every man and woman but also, more particularly, 'he sits down in the chair of Magistracy, in some above others'. This Adam was, Winstanley explained, to be understood in a two-fold sense, as the wisdom and power of the flesh in every individual, and as the wisdom and power of the flesh 'broke out and sate down in the chair of rule and dominion, in one part of man-kind over another'.[61]

Political allusions of this kind were to be repeated throughout this work, even though few overt references to current political developments were made. Kings were described as enemies to Christ, and 'Justices and Officers of State' were denounced for frequently multiplying wrongs and for oppressing the poor.[62] Reformation would not be brought by 'the hands of a few, or by unrighteous men, that would pul the tyrannical government out of other mens hands, and keep it in their own heart [hands], as we feel this to be a burden of our age'; 'Truly Tyrannie is Tyrannie in one as wel as in another; in a poor man lifted up by his valour, as in a rich man lifted up by his lands'.[63] The deep anticlericalism evident in this as in the earlier writings was directed not only against the beneficed, university-educated clergy, but also against preachers attached to gathered congregations, who saw that 'light arises much amongst the people', and who sought to exploit this for their own ends.[64] Wars and 'destroying Armies of men' were, for Winstanley, 'but the curse, the burden which the Creation groans under':

> The Kingdoms of the whole world must become the Kingdoms of the Lord Christ; and this the Nations are angry at; Therefore count it no strange thing to see wars and rumours of wars, to see men that are put in trust to act for publike good, to prove fals, to see commotions of people every where like flouds of water stirred up, ready to devour and overflow one another; To see Kings storm against the people; To see rich men and gentry most violent against the poor, oppressing them and treading them like mire in the street, Why is all this anger?
>
> But because the man of the flesh is to die, his day of judgment is come, he must give up the Kingdom and Government of the earth (man-kind) into the hand of his neighbour that is more righteous then he, For *Jacob* must have the blessing, he is blessed, yea and shal be blessed, and *Esau* shal become his servant; *The poor shal inherit the earth.*[65]

The earth metaphor and attendant alchemical imagery that had appeared in the earlier pamphlets were again made use of in *The New Law of Righteousnes*. The earth, or mankind, had been made barren by the unrighteousness of the first Adam, who had 'lifted up mountaines and hils of oppressing powers': 'look upon the mountaines and little hils of the earth, and see if these prickling thorns and briars, the bitter curse, does not grow there'.[66] In this work, as in *Truth Lifting Up its Head Above Scandals*, Winstanley was not content simply to use the earth as a metaphor for mankind. The barrenness and the corruption of the earth, and of all creatures, followed on from the Fall of man, and the receptivity of mankind to the new light would have a direct bearing on the condition of the whole creation.[67] When mankind was to be restored and delivered from the curse,

> then other creatures shall be restored likewise, and freed from their burdens: as the Earth, from thorns, and briars, and barrennesse; the Air and winds from unseasonable storms and distempers; the Cattle from bitternesse and rage one against another. And the law of righteousnesse and love shall be seated in the whole Creation; from the lowest to the highest creature. And this is the work of restoration.[68]

The sandy heaths around Cobham, on which the Diggers were shortly to set to work, would have owed their corrupted state to the condition of mankind; the rising of Christ in sons and daughters would lead not only to the transformation of mankind, but also to the freeing of these barren parts of the earth from their poisoned state.[69] This view fitted well with the annihilationist mortalist beliefs that Winstanley shared with others writing within the radical spiritualist tradition, and which entailed a belief that the soul dissolved into the Godhead at death:

When the bodies of men are laid in the grave, we have a word, That he is either in heaven or hell: Now the senses of the body are not sensible of either such. But now the power that ruled in that body righteously or unrighteously, is fully manifested to it self. If the power of Righteousnesse did rule, now it enters into the Spirit, the great Ocean of glory, the Father himself: If the power of unrighteousnesse did rule, now it enters into the curse, & encreases the body of death, corruption and enmity, and becomes the bondage and Burden of the Creation, that must be purged out by fire.[70]

Winstanley's association of the Fall with man's determination to live upon the objects of creation, and his seeking after worldly goods, was restated in *The New Law of Righteousnes*. Covetousness, 'the selfish power ruling in a man', was 'the kingdome of darknese in that man' and the curse; it was covetousness, above all else, that had corrupted mankind.[71] These sentiments were consistent with those expressed in *Truth Lifting Up its Head Above Scandals*, but now Winstanley made, for the first time, a specific connection between the corruption of mankind and the rise of private property. Equality was the natural condition of mankind, but this 'universal communitie' had long been suppressed.[72] The first Adam had 'damned up the water springs of universall liberty, and brought the Creation under the curse of bondage, sorrow and tears':

But when the earth becomes a common treasury as it was in the beginning, and the King of Righteousnesse comes to rule in every ones heart, then he kils the first *Adam*; for covetousnesse thereby is killed. A man shall have meat, and drinke and clothes by his labour in freedome, and what can be desired more in earth. Pride and envy likewise is killed thereby, for every one shall look upon each other as equall in the Creation; every man indeed being a parfect Creation of himself. And so this second *Adam* Christ, the restorer, stops or dammes up the runnings of those stinking waters of self-interest, and causes the waters of life and liberty to run plentifully in and through the Creation, making the earth one store-house, and every man and woman to live in the law of Righteousnesse and peace as members of one houshold.[73]

The rising of Christ in his sons and daughters, or rising up of 'this universall law of equity', would bring about the restoration of the equality that had existed before the Fall and had, as shown in Acts 4, been practised by the apostles.[74] The impending changes would, however, also represent something new and untried, for this 'universall freedom hath never filled the earth though it hath been fore-told by most of the Prophets'.[75] In the new social order there would 'be no buying nor selling, no fairs nor markets, but the whole earth shall be a common treasury for every man, for the earth is the Lords'.[76] The change would come about peacefully, and by degrees.[77] It could not be imposed by a minority, and must involve no forcible expropriation of property:

I do not speak that any particular man shall go and take their neighbours goods by violence, or robbery (I abhor it) as the conditions of the men of the Nations are ready to do in this fleshly setled government of the world, but every one is to wait, till the Lord Christ do spread himself in multiplicities of bodies, making them all of one heart and one mind, acting in the righteousnesse one to another. It must be one power in all, making all to give their consent to confirm this law of righteousnesse and reason.[78]

Winstanley's programme for change, which had, he claimed, come to him in a vision, was strikingly simple: the poor should work together and eat together, and should no longer work for hire. By working in common the poor could sustain themselves, and by depriving their wealthier neighbours of their labour they would ensure the swift downfall of the system of private property. The poor had lifted the wealthy above them, and they retained the means to bring them back to a level of equality, for in the 'time of *Israels* restoration',

none then shall work for hire, neither shal any give hire, but every one shal work in love: one with, and for another; and eat bread together, as being members of one household; the Creation in whom Reason rules King in perfect glory.[79]

The way forward for the common people was to work upon the commons and waste lands, which, if properly managed, could yield sufficient food for all. Winstanley, like many others who felt that England's agricultural potential had barely begun to be realised, believed that scarcely a third of the country was under cultivation, and that 'here is land enough to maintain all her children'.[80] The arguments for the introduction of communal cultivation contained a strong moral imperative, which was consistent with the centrality of notions of equity and of the Golden Rule to Winstanley's social philosophy. The man of the flesh, Winstanley maintained, accepted the existence of division between rich and poor, but the

spiritual man, which is Christ, doth judge according to the light of equity and reason, That al man-kinde ought to have a quiet substance and freedome, to live upon the earth; and that there shal be no bond-man nor beggar in all the holy mountaine.[81]

No one should starve for want or be forced, as now, to 'rob and steale through povertie', and no one should claim the right to take another's life as punishment for theft.[82] The only punishments which society should allow were corrective ones, 'to make the offender to know his maker, and to live in the community of the righteous Law of love one with another'. 'Imprisoning, whiping and killing' were 'but the actings of the curse'.[83] To 'act of love in righteousnesse', which was more important and effective than to merely talk of love, meant relieving 'the oppressed, to let goe the prisoner, to open bags and barns that the earth may be a common treasury to preserve all without complaining'.[84] The early Christians, Winstanley reminded his readers,

> did not rule in slavery one over another; neither did the rich suffer the poor to beg and starve, and imprison them as now they do: But the rich sold their possessions, and gave equality to the poor, and no man said, that any thing that he possessed was his own, for they had all things common.[85]

In setting out his vision of the communal cultivation of the commons, Winstanley acknowledged that private enclosures would not be brought under common cultivation until such time as they were voluntarily surrendered by their owners.[86] In line with his insistence that land should not be forcibly expropriated, Winstanley was prepared to accept that the system of private property might, at least for a time, continue to exist alongside the system of communal cultivation:

> Therefore if the rich wil stil hold fast this propriety of *Mine and thine*, let them labour their own Land with their own hands. And let the common-People, that are the gatherings together of Israel from under that bondage, and say that the earth is ours, not mine, let them labour together, and eat bread together upon the Commons, Mountains and Hils.[87]

Such statements should not be taken to imply that Winstanley was willing, even at this early stage, to envisage the long-term survival of two forms of land ownership, the communal and the private, or that he accepted that a communistic form of social organisation would only ever be established on the commons.[88] In Winstanley's millenarian vision, there could be no doubt that 'Christ must rise, and the powers of the flesh must fall', and that there 'shal not be a vessel of humane earth, but it shal be filled with Christ'.[89] While no landowners would be forced to give up their property, their continued opposition to the changes taking place around them would ultimately prove futile. Vengeance was promised against the oppressor,[90] and soon no rich man would dare refrain from giving up his wealth:

> And if covetous, proud flesh stil uphold this self-propriety, which is the curse and burden the Creation groans under: Then O thou covetous earth, expect the multiplying of plagues, and the fulfilling of all threatning prophesies and visions for thy downfall and miserie.
>
> But if thou wouldst find mercie, then open thy barns and treasuries of the earth, which thou hast heaped together, and detains from the poor, thy fellow creatures: This is the only remedy to escape wrath: and the door of acceptance to mercie is yet open, if thou do this: The Judge of Truth and Right waits yet upon thy comming in to him.
>
> Therefore, O thou first *Adam*, take notice, that the Lord hath set before thee life and death, now chuse whether thou wilt, for the time is near at hand that buying and selling of land shall cease, and every son of the land shal live of it.[91]

Those who resisted would be 'stripped naked of all', and if they survived the plagues that were sure to befall them they would become 'servants, and not enjoy the benefit of Sonship, til the Spirit of the Son rise up in them, and make them free':[92] the elder brother would soon serve the younger.[93] A similar fate awaited those who continued to work for others, for 'the hand of the Lord shal break out upon every such hireling labourer', who would 'perish with the covetous rich men, that have held, and yet doth hold the Creation under the bondage of the curse'.[94] While Winstanley denied that the new society could be created by 'wars, councels, or hands of men, for I abhor it', he clearly felt that it would be made possible by them, for 'by those the government of Esau shal be beaten down and the enemy shal destroy one another'.[95] The Civil War and ensuing political conflicts had helped to weaken the hold on society of the dominant classes, and had made possible the rise of a new social order. The changes envisioned by Winstanley were revolutionary and all-encompassing, for within a short time no vestige of the old order would survive.

Winstanley had, he said, been enjoined in his vision to declare his message abroad, and having done so, in speech and now in print, all that remained was for him to learn from the Lord 'the place and manner, how he wil have us that are the common people, to manure and work upon the common Lands'. Then Winstanley could

> go forth and declare it in my action, to eat my bread with the sweat of my brows, without either giving or taking hire, looking upon the Land as freely mine and anothers; I have now peace in the Spirit, and I have an inward perswasion that the spirit of the poor, shall be drawn forth ere long, to act materially this Law of Righteousness'.[96]

CONTEXT

In timing as well as content *The New Law of Righteousnes* was a revolutionary work. Completed the day before sentence was passed on the king, and just four days before his execution, it was written in a period of unprecedented political change and millenarian expectation.[97] Parliament had been purged in the first week of December, and in the first week of January the House of Commons had declared that 'the people are, under God, the original of all just power' and that the Commons 'have the supreme power in this nation'.[98] Within two weeks of the appearance of *The New Law of Righteousnes*, the Commons had resolved to abolish both the House of Lords and the monarchy.[99] To the work's author, there could have seemed few impediments at this time to the rising of Christ in his sons and daughters and to the imminent establishment of community in England.

Winstanley's programme, couched as it was in an unambiguously millenarian framework, was a profoundly religious one.[100] Most scholars would now agree that older debates about whether Winstanley's religious language hid a more overtly political, and secularist, message, raised important questions but ultimately proved inconclusive.[101] Andrew Bradstock, in the most detailed recent study of Winstanley's theology, has emphasised the relevance of the Digger leader's religious views to his political programme, and has argued convincingly that Winstanley's religion, while highly unorthodox not least in its emphasis on God's immanence and in its equation of the Fall with the rise of private property, remained in essence Christian.[102] For Bradstock, Winstanley's religious and political views went hand in hand: his aim was 'not to abolish religion altogether but to recast it in an immanent and non-alienating form: to show, that the meek might inherit the earth now'.[103] A similar argument has been advanced from a Marxist perspective by Jim Holstun, who has pointed out that for Winstanley, 'as for so many seventeenth-century writers, the sacred/secular opposition falls flat'.[104]

It remains the case that Winstanley's views, as expressed in *The New Law of Righteousnes*, may to many of his contemporaries have seemed to represent the abandonment of religion as they knew it.[105] One accusation supposedly levelled against the Diggers in 1650 was that they 'do not know God, nor will not come to Church'.[106] *The New Law of Righteousnes* contains a telling allusion to the isolation from worldly society of those who are 'drawn up to wait upon the Lord':

> Now though this man be in prison, be in straits, be forsaken of all his friends in the flesh, none wil buy nor sell with him, because they count him a man of strange opinions and blasphemies, call him an Atheist, a sot, a Papist, a blasphemer that hath forsaken God and goodnesse, because he wil neither preach nor pray, nor say grace when he sitteth down to meat, as the custome of Professours are,
>   Yet this man is not alone, for his Father is with him, The Father lives in him, and he lives in the Father.[107]

Winstanley's theology, with its emphasis on human conduct and its marked egalitarianism, represents a particularly striking example of the anti-formalist, practical Christianity that has come to be seen as a chief characteristic of early modern radicalism.[108] The central concerns of practical Christianity, when expressed with the singularity and force with which they appear in *The New Law of Righteousnes*, might appear barely distinguishable from the concerns of later, more secular radicals, but it would be unhelpful to seek to impose a rigid distinction between the religious and 'secular' aspects of Winstanley's thought or to insist on prioritising one over the other.[109]

The religious imperative to help the poor may be seen as a *leitmotif* of radical religious discourse in the 1640s.[110] The poet and Surrey parliamentarian George Wither lamented in 1645 that:

There is no pittie of the Fatherlesse,
Or, of the poore afflicted Widdowes teares;
No charitable heed of their distresse,
Whose miserie, most eminent appears.[111]

In 1659 he would suggest that the 'Good Old Cause' had foundered as a result of 'our many great unrepented sins; and in special, our hypocrisie, our gross partiality, our self-seekings, and remissness in doing Justice, and in mercifully relieving the oppressed, the Widows, the Fatherless, and the Friendless; which sins, were the principal causes of the Desolation of all Kingdoms, and Republicks, heretofore destroyed, in former Ages'.[112] Also in 1645, John Lilburne warned MPs of the consequences of their failure to relieve those who had become impoverished through their support for parliament: 'the cry of the Widdow and Fatherlesse, the poor and needy, the oppressed, and the afflicted, will cry lowd in the ears of the Lord of Hosts against them, and theirs, for judgement and vengeance'.[113] William Walwyn had, in his 1643 work *The Power of Love*, already condemned the inequalities which his fellow Christians and countrymen appeared all too ready to tolerate.[114]

One theme that comes through clearly in radical writings from the 1640s is that it was offensive to God as well as man for destitution to exist in a land as plentiful as England. The London Levellers' Large Petition of March 1647 called on parliament to provide the means to prevent the poor from being forced to beg, 'that this Nation may be no longer a shame to Christianity therein', while their petition of 11 September 1648 demanded 'some effectual course to keep people from begging and beggery, in so fruitful a Nation as through Gods blessing this is'.[115] For John Cooke, the future prosecutor at the trial of Charles I, there 'ought not to be a Beggar in England, for they live rather like beasts then men'.[116] The physician and Baptist Peter Chamberlen, whose detailed scheme for helping the poor was published by Giles Calvert in April 1649, agreed that 'the most necessary work of mankind, is to provide for the poore'.[117]

For some radicals, one obvious way to help the poor was to return to them those large areas of common land that had been misappropriated and enclosed over many years. Among the most explicit calls for such action was Richard Overton's, in July 1647, when he demanded that enclosures in 'all grounds which anciently lay in Common for the poore, and are now impropriate, inclosed, and fenced in', should be 'cast out, and laid open againe to the free and common use and benefit of the poore'.[118] *The Case of the Armie Truly Stated* of October 1647 contained, as H. N. Brailsford observed, an almost identical demand.[119] The anonymous author of *Englands Troublers Troubled* was another who called for 'all enclosures of fenns and Commons . . . to be layed open'.[120] The Leveller petition of September 1648 was slightly more circumspect on this issue, stating only that the petitioners might have hoped for parliament to 'have laid open all *late* Inclosures of Fens, and other Commons, or have enclosed them onely or chiefly to the benefit of the poor'.[121]

In the later 1640s, the concerns of practical Christianity also found expression in the numerous schemes, many of them inspired by the ideas of Samuel Hartlib's intellectual circle, which were devised to tackle the problem of poverty in the aftermath of civil war.[122] In these, the solution to the problem was seen to lie at least partly in the exploitation of the productive potential of England's commons and wastes for the benefit of the poor. Central to Peter Chamberlen's 1649 scheme, outlined in *The Poor Mans Advocate*, was his proposal that commons, wastes, forests, fens and other land in which the poor had an interest should either be enclosed and rented out or farmed in common by the poor themselves.[123] Lt Col. John Jubbes agreed that England's wastes and commons could be better managed in the interests of feeding the poor and enriching the nation. For Jubbes, all marsh lands, fens and common pastures might be enclosed and divided, with one part granted to tenants of the parishes in which these lands lay, one part to the local poor and the remaining two parts being used to pay for officers' and soldiers' arrears.[124] The author of *An Experimentall Essay touching the Reformation of the Lawes of England*, which appeared in August 1648, had his own suggestions for the reformation of commons and wastes. These, he argued,

> might be surveighed and inclosed, and put into Farmes, and the Rent imployed for the good of the Towne, or that poore people might have rather more than their portion severally inclosed to themselves, and the Rest to be inclosed according to every ones just proportion; and that little parcels of Land lying at so great a Distance, as they now doe in some Common Fields, may by Exchange be laid together, for the best Convenience, and then inclosed.

All this, he stated confidently, could be done in the space of just three months.[125]

It might be tempting to see Winstanley's plan for the poor to work the commons as a contribution to this radical reform tradition. When Winstanley claimed in *The New Law of Righteousnes* that there was sufficient land in England to feed the whole population, but that barely a third of it was under cultivation, he was adding his voice to a long line of agricultural improvers who had supported the conversion of waste grounds to tillage for the benefit of the poor.[126] His understanding of current social problems comes through clearly in *The New Law of Righteousnes*, and it seems certain that he had some familiarity with contemporary arguments in favour of the exploitation of commons and wastes in the interests of the poor. Members of Samuel Hartlib's circle, and Peter Chamberlen and other radical reformers who drew inspiration from their ideas, were, like Winstanley, acutely aware of the inadequacies of conventional poor relief in the post-war years and were conscious that society was failing in its duty to help the poor. Like him, they were impatient with custom, and they displayed a willingness to envisage solutions that departed radically from those associated with traditional measures for relieving the poor. Their proposals for commons and wastes were, in many cases, accompanied by opposition to tithes and by calls for the reform of manorial tenures and for measures to divert concealed charities to their proper uses.[127] Their schemes for reform, like Winstanley's, cannot be divorced from the millenarian expectation of the 1640s, and should be seen as a product of that current of belief, as well as a reflection of genuine concern for the poor.[128]

The differences between Winstanley's programme and theirs were, however, profound, and we blunt the edge of his message if we try to link him too closely to Chamberlen and the Hartlibians. Although Winstanley may have been influenced by the writings of contemporary social reformers, and was evidently addressing many of the same problems as them, his solutions were radically different. A common feature of many of the reform schemes of the 1640s and 1650s was their tendency to view the poor as a potential source of profit, and in their projected treatment of the poor an element of coercion was often to be found.[129] Chamberlen's plans, which entailed the setting up of a joint-stock syndicate to employ the poor on public works, were clearly designed to bring profits to the projectors as well as benefits to society at large.[130] Such projects might plausibly be seen to have owed something to the abortive improvement schemes of the years of personal rule, in which pursuit of profit was combined with a desire both to feed the population and to exert a measure of control over the disorderly poor.[131] For Winstanley, the eradication of poverty and inequality would be effected through the renunciation of private property and of buying and selling, as individuals submitted to the spirit of righteousness and committed themselves to building community by holding and working the land in common. Winstanley's answer to the problems facing the nation involved giving agency to the poor, instead of forcing them to rely on sympathetic reformers to organise them more productively. He differed markedly from other social reformers in his vision of a future without private property: joint-stock syndicates, or state action, would have found no place in Winstanley's programme in 1649, however much such solutions may have owed to the millenarian reforming spirit which had also motivated him and helped shape his ideas.

The gulf between egalitarians such as Winstanley and more moderate reformers was hinted at in 1648 by John Cooke, when he declared that 'I am not of their opinion that drive at a parity to have all men a like, 'tis but a Utopian fiction, the Scripture holds forth no such thing'.[132] The Leveller leaders too, who had been saddled in 1647 with a name not of their own choosing, were anxious throughout the brief life of their movement to disavow any suggestion that they advocated social levelling.[133] All parliaments, they made clear in their petition of 11 September 1648, ought to be 'bound . . . from abolishing propriety, levelling mens Estates, or making all things common', and this was reiterated in the third Agreement of the People of May 1649.[134] Despite several hints in William Walwyn's writings of his sympathy for the voluntary community practised by the primitive Christians, he and his colleagues were adamant that their political programme posed no threat to property. As they made plain in *A Manifestation* of April 1649, which was almost certainly drafted by Walwyn, they had already declared against levelling, 'for which we suppose is commonly meant an equalling of mens estates, and taking away the proper right and Title that every man has to what is his own'.[135] Although their argument was qualified with a discussion of the practices of the early Christians, and with the assertion that any attempt to induce levelling would be 'most injurious, unlesse there did precede an universall assent thereunto from all and every one of the People', their conclusion was clear:

> We profess therefore that we never had it in our thoughts to Level mens estates, it being the utmost of our aime that the Commonwealth be reduced to such a passe that every man may with as much security as may be enjoy his propriety.[136]

For all the Leveller leaders' emphasis on practical christianity and their sympathetic attitude towards the poor, it is possible to discern in their writings an acceptance of conventional distinctions between deserving and undeserving poor. Beggary was often combined with wickedness in Leveller discourse, and in their Large Petition the Levellers criticised the absence of effective means to reclaim poor people and their children from an 'idle and vicious course of life' or to 'reduce them to any vertue or industry'.[137] John Jubbes too combined demands for the 'hinderance and avoiding of all Vagabonds and Beggars' with demands for 'a conscientious and sufficient Relief for all the poor and indigent people, that none may perish with want'.[138] Andy Wood has commented on the 'combination of fear of the poor and Christian sympathy for them' that drove much of Leveller social policy.[139] This may also be seen in the work of Peter Chamberlen, which contained dire warnings to those in authority of any failure to address the problem of the poor. As Chamberlen told the House of Commons, 'Provide for the poor, and they will provide for you. Destroy the poor, and they will destroy you. And if you provide not for the poor, they will provide for themselves'.[140] The freeing up of the king's estates, houses, goods and profits, and of the lands of bishops and deans and chapters, had provided the state with the means to make adequate provision for the poor, and if this opportunity were not grasped:

> 1. Necessity (which hath no law) will break the bonds of all civility and Government, and so bring in confusion.
> 2. Hunger (which breaketh stone-walls) will force the hungry through all fortifications upon all that have bread.

3. Oppression (which maketh a wise-man mad) will, by necessary, and continued Taxes, continue the Counsells of wisemen against the oppressors.
4. Patience (which many sober men have had) if abused, will turne into fury.[141]

The emphasis here is very different from the activist message contained in Winstanley's writings. With his denunciation of covetousness and inequality, and his expectation of far-reaching change arising from within the body of the people, Winstanley comes much closer in *The New Law of Righteousnes* to the social levelling associated with radical sectaries such as George Foster and Abiezer Coppe.[142] The parallels between Winstanley, Coppe and Foster – and, possibly, the early Laurence Clarkson – are such that one might to see them emerging from a common intellectual milieu of Leveller-influenced sectarian radicalism.[143] Clarkson had anticipated Winstanley by over a year when, in his *A Generall Charge* of October 1647, he had identified inner reform and liberation from deference as keys to the overthrow of oppression.[144] Coppe and Foster, however, followed Winstanley into print, and both may have been influenced by his writings, of which Coppe was certainly aware.[145] Both joined Winstanley in openly advocating the holding of all things in common, but their tactics remained very different from his. In place of Winstanley's programme of collective action, Coppe sought, through the use of strikingly confrontational and provocative language, to shock his readers into acknowledging their duties of Christian charity.[146] Foster too combined warnings of the imminent humbling of great men, and destruction of earthly governments, with implorations to his readers to show pity and compassion towards the poor.[147] Clarkson later claimed to have been suspicious of Winstanley's motives in embarking upon the digging experiment, and Coppe sought to make clear that he was not an advocate of 'sword levelling, or digging-levelling'.[148]

One work that was almost certainly known to Winstanley when he wrote *The New Law of Righteousnes* was the anonymous pamphlet *Light Shining in Buckinghamshire*, the first edition of which appeared early in December 1648.[149] Historians have long been aware of the parallels between this work and *The New Law of Righteousnes*, and Eduard Bernstein and Lewis Berens were so struck by the similarities that both believed that Winstanley must have been involved in writing it.[150] David Petegorsky concluded that Winstanley was not the author, but felt that its influence is 'unmistakably reflected' in the *New Law of Righteousnes*.[151] More recently, both Christopher Hill and Olivier Lutaud have argued that the Buckinghamshire pamphlet and its successor, *More Light Shining in Buckinghamshire*, were more directly political and less polished than anything Winstanley would have written at this time; as Hill points out, the 'vigorous, rudely boisterous and bellicose style is hardly Winstanley's'.[152] The authors of the *Light Shining* pamphlets were Levellers or Leveller sympathisers but, in the emphasis they gave to the problems of manorial tenure, enclosure, tithes and market tolls, they were expressing predominantly local concerns rather than those of the movement's leadership and urban core. Their writings serve as a reminder that on the fringes of the Leveller movement it was possible to find more radical views than might have been acceptable to the movement's leadership.[153]

Like Winstanley, the authors of *Light Shining in Buckinghamshire* traced the origins of mankind's problems to the rise of private property, as man became a 'devourer of the creatures, and an incloser, not content that another should enjoy the same priviledge as himself but incloseth all from his Brother',

> so that all the Land, Trees, Beasts, Fish, Fowle, &c. are inclosed into a few mercinary hands; and all the rest deprived and made their slaves, so that if they cut a Tree for fire they are to be punished, or hunt a fowle it is imprisonment, because it is gentlemens game, as they say; neither must they keep Cattle, or set up a House, all ground being inclosed, without hyring leave for the one, or buying room for the other, of the chiefe incloser, called the Lord of the Mannor, or some other wretch as cruell as he, and all must be summoned to a Court Leet, there to acknowledge Fealty and Service, and that with Oathes if required (at least wise if Jurymen) to their Tyrant called Lord of the Mannor; and if a Tenant admitted, if Coppy-holder, he must take an Oath to become a true Tenant, rather Slave, as aforesaid.

This, they claimed in words that recall Winstanley, all came 'at first by murther and cruelty one against the other'.[154] The rise of private property was a breach of the Golden Rule and of equity, and they equated the latter with the apostolic communism described in Acts 2.[155] They also introduced into their argument the concept of kingly power and the theory of the Norman Yoke, both of which Winstanley would later use to great effect in his attempts to promote and defend the Digger experiment.[156] Whether Winstanley had, as some historians have speculated, some contact with the authors of *Light Shining in Buckinghamshire* is impossible to prove.[157] What is certain, however, is that some of the earliest public support for the digging experiment would come from the Buckingham-shire circles which had produced the *Light Shining* pamphlets, and the county would itself be the site of a Digger colony in 1650.[158]

Light Shining in Buckinghamshire and *The New Law of Righteousnes* were, like the works of Jubbes, Chamberlen and Cooke, written against a background of hardship and social dislocation, and this was clearly reflected in the urgent tone of these writings. The winter of 1648–49 was marked by grain shortages, with food prices running at exceptionally high levels following a run of poor harvests.[159] The 1648 harvest was especially bad, made worse by the storms that hit large parts of the country in August.[160] John Evelyn noted in a diary entry for December 1648 that 'this was a most exceeding wet year, neither frost nor snow all the winter of more than six days in all. Cattle died everywhere of a murrain'; on 22 January he recorded that 'Now was the Thames frozen over, and horrid tempests of wind'.[161] In London, poor people were reported to be unable to afford to buy food, while in Lancashire, where high food prices and decay of trade had been made worse by the spread of sickness – 'a three-corded scourge of sword, pestilence and famine' – a petition from Winstanley's home town of Wigan described the 'numerous swarms of begging poore and the many families that pine away at home, not having faces to beg. Very many now craving almes at other men's dores, who were used to give others almes at their dores':

> Most men's estates being much drained by the wars, and now almost quite exhauste by the present scarsity, and many other burdens incumbent upon them, there is no bonds to keep in the infected hunger-starved poore, whose breaking out jeapoard[is]eth all the neighbourhood, some of them already being at the point to perish through famine, have fetch in, and eaten, carion, and other unwholesome food, to the destroying of themselves, and increasing of the infection.[162]

Winstanley's kinsman James Winstanley was one of four London-based natives of Wigan who in May 1649 were deputed to receive contributions for the relief of the distressed inhabitants of Wigan and Ashton-in-Makerfield.[163]

The New Law of Righteousnes, and Winstanley's proposals for the communal working of common land, can only be properly understood in the context of the widespread social and economic problems of the later 1640s. In Surrey, economic hardship was exacerbated in late 1648 and early 1649 by the renewed presence of soldiers in the county and by continued high levels of taxation for the maintenance of the army.[164] Complaints about the costs of free quarter would continue to be voiced in the county during the course of 1649.[165] There is also evidence from Surrey that questions of land use and ownership were coming to the fore at this time. Particular uncertainty attended to the issue of crown and church land, of which there was a high concentration in mid-Surrey. Dean and chapter lands, whose future disposal was under discussion in 1648, included the manor of Ham Court, in which Winstanley's home was located, while crown land in the vicinity of Cobham included the manors of Walton and Walton Leigh, as well as Pains Hill and several other farms and small estates in Walton and Weybridge belonging to the honor of Hampton Court.[166] Parliament had begun selling bishops' lands in 1646 and, although no sales of dean and chapter lands took place before 1649 or of crown land before 1650, there had already been much discussion about how best to dispose of them. It is significant that the authors of *Light Shining in Buckinghamshire* were already calling for crown lands to be made use of for the maintenance of the poor, citing as precedent the injunctions in Leviticus 25, almost two months before the execution of the king.[167] Had London's common council had its way in 1648, the revenues of Ham Court and other decanal estates might even have been diverted towards the augmentation of ministers' salaries and maintenance of a settled ministry.[168] The future of such lands was still unclear at the end of 1648, and it is very likely that Winstanley had current debates about their use in mind when he set out his proposals for England's commons and wastes in *The New Law of Righteousnes*.

Another land issue of the late 1640s, which had a direct bearing on the use of common land in the vicinity of Cobham, related to measures taken by landowners to rebuild their incomes in the aftermath of the war. Scattered evidence from mid- and west Surrey suggests that a number of manorial lords were seeking to raise cash by selling wood or timber growing on the manorial waste, sometimes in order to pay composition fines, but often to raise portions for their children.[169] The surviving evidence dates from both the 1640s and the 1650s, but appears sufficient to indicate that such actions, which were bound to create tensions between landowners and those who claimed use-rights on the manorial waste, were taking place in Surrey on a significant scale at this time. In July 1646, for instance, tenants of the crown manor of Woking had complained to the House of Lords of the actions of Beatrice Zouch, widow of the royalist James Zouch, in committing 'great wast and destruccons upon the timber, and wood belonging to the said Mannor', in areas where the petitioners claimed rights to the mast of the timber.[170] Further destruction of timber in Woking was reported in 1649.[171] In May 1647 George Wither complained to the committee for compounding that Stanislaus Browne was felling trees in the manor of Pirbright to help make up his composition fine.[172] The following February, the parliamentarian Nicholas Stoughton left instructions in his will for trees on Worplesdon and Ganghill commons to be felled towards raising his daughter's marriage portion.[173] In 1651, Francis Drake would turn over to trustees all his 'coppices woods and underwoods' in Walton-on-Thames and Chertsey on the occasion of his marriage, while five years later Francis Vincent of Stoke d'Abernon would settle on trustees his 'coppice land and other wood and trees' growing on the commons and wastes of Stoke d'Abernon to help raise portions for his children.[174] Most of the timber and wood growing on Stoke Common had been felled by the time Vincent drew up his will in 1669.[175] The question of conflicting rights to the natural resources of the commons would be of great importance to the Diggers, who would attack lords of manors for felling and selling 'the Trees and Woods that grow upon the Commons', and announce their intention of selling wood themselves to create a common stock, as early as May 1649.[176] The practice by landowners of exploiting manorial wastes in order to realise capital had, it seems certain, already become an issue of contention by the time Winstanley began formulating his programme for digging the commons.

Winstanley evidently hoped to provide practical solutions to England's problems in the proposals he set out in *The New Law of Righteousnes*: 'Extream necessity', he reminded his readers, 'cals for the great work of restoration'.[177] To acknowledge this is not to deny the centrality of theology in Winstanley's thought, or to seek to refute the suggestion that the digging experiment may also be seen as a symbolic act and as an affirmation of the rising spirit of righteousness in mankind.[178] The experiment should, as Bradstock has argued, be understood on several levels, and the religious aspects of Winstanley's message need not preclude the practical.[179] Winstanley's achievement in *The New Law of Righteousnes* was to fuse a powerful millenarian vision with arguments derived from necessity, in ways that offered close parallels to the chiliastic and egalitarian languages of social criticism long associated with English rural radicalism.[180] These parallels would become even more apparent in the months that followed, as Winstanley and his fellow Diggers developed arguments to advance their cause, elicit active support and justify their actions to the authorities of the new republic. The effectiveness of Winstanley's message would be measured by the extent to which others accepted its logic and were prepared to join him in working the land in common. It was this support that would transform Winstanley from a thinker of unusual interest into the leader of a social movement which lasted more than a year, and which, by the early months of 1650, had spread from Surrey across the south-east and east Midlands.

NOTES

1 Gerrard Winstanley, *The Mysterie of God Concerning the Whole Creation, Mankinde* (London, 1648); G. K. Fortescue (ed.), *Catalogue of the Pamphlets, Newspapers and Manuscripts Relating to the Civil War, the Commonwealth, and Restoration, Collected by George Thomason, 1640–1661*, 2 vols (London, 1908).

2 Gerrard Winstanley, *The Breaking of the Day of God* (London, 1648).

3 Gerrard Winstanley, *The Saints Paradise: Or, the Fathers Teaching the Only Satisfaction to Waiting Souls* (London, 1648); Gerrard Winstanley, *Truth Lifting Up its Head Above Scandals*, in Sabine, *Works*, pp. 97–146.

4 Gerrard Winstanley, *Several Pieces Gathered Into One Volume* (London, 1649).

5 Cf. Tom Corns, *Uncloistered Virtue* (Oxford, 1992), pp. 148–50; Hill, *Religion and Politics*, pp. 194, 203–4; Holstun, *Ehud's Dagger*, p. 375.

6 The most detailed analysis of the early writings remains Hayes, *Winstanley*, pp. 9–144.

7 Detailed accounts of Winstanley's religious ideas are to be found in Bradstock, *Faith in the Revolution*, pp. 71–135 and Nicola Baxter, 'Gerrard Winstanley's experimental knowledge of God (the perception of the spirit and the acting of Reason)', *Journal of Ecclesiastical History*, 39, 2 (1988), pp. 185–201; Hill, *Religion and Politics*, pp. 185–252; Lotte Mulligan, John K. Graham and Judith Richards, 'Winstanley: a case for the man as he said he was', *Journal of Ecclesiastical History*, 28, 1 (1977), pp. 57–75.

8 Winstanley, *Mysterie of God*, pp. 7, 14. Cf. *ibid.*, sig A2v, pp. 6–7, 13, 15–16, 48.

9 *Ibid*, p. 13. Cf. *ibid.*, sig A4r–v, pp 26, 37, 42, 43.

10 *Ibid*, pp. 9–10. Cf. *ibid.*, pp. 6–7, 28.

11 Winstanley, *Breaking of the Day of God*, sig A7r, 6–7, 21/23, 27/29–28/30, 36, 64, 83, 86–7, 89–92, 104, 109–10, 117, 128, 131–3. For anti-formalism see J. C. Davis, 'Against formality: one aspect of the English revolution', *TRHS*, 6th ser., 3 (1993), pp. 265–88; J. C. Davis, *Oliver Cromwell* (London, 2001), pp. 130–5.

12 Winstanley, *Breaking of the Day of God*, pp. 62, 124. Cf. *ibid.*, p. 73.

13 *Ibid.*, p. 136.

14 Winstanley, *Saints Paradise*, sig A3r. Cf. *ibid.*, pp. 55–6.

15 *Ibid.*, p. 78.

16 *Ibid.*, p. 79.

17 Sabine, *Works*, p. 105. Cf. *ibid.*, pp. 107–9. On the particularity of Winstanley's understanding of Reason, see especially Baxter, 'Winstanley's experimental knowledge', esp. p. 191; Corns, *Uncloistered Virtue*, pp. 155–6; Andrew McRae, *God Speed the Plough: the Representation of Agrarian England, 1500–1660* (Cambridge, 1996), pp. 125–6.

18 Above p. 77; Sabine, *Works*, p. 103.

19 Winstanley, *Saints Paradise*, p. 60; Winstanley, *Breaking of the Day of God*, pp. 18, 43, 57, 59. Cf. Nigel Smith, *Perfection Proclaimed: Language and Literature in English Radical Religion* (Oxford, 1989), p. 265; James Holstun, 'Communism, George Hill and the *Mir*: was Marx a nineteenth-century Winstanleyan?', in Bradstock, *Winstanley and the Diggers*, p. 122.

20 Winstanley, *Saints Paradise*, pp. 77–8. Cf. *ibid.*, pp. 65, 81.

21 *Ibid.*, p. 70.

22 Sabine, *Works*, pp. 113–14.

23 *Ibid.*, p. 120. Cf. *ibid.*, pp. 117, 119.

24 *Ibid.*, p. 120.

25 *Ibid.*, pp. 114, 121.

26 *Ibid.*, pp. 123–4.

27 Winstanley, *Breaking of the Day of God*, A7r, pp. 59, 83, 96, 128, 131–3. Cf. J. C. Davis, *Utopia and the Ideal Society: A Study of English Utopian Writing 1516–1700* (Cambridge, 1981), pp. 181–2.

28 Winstanley, *Breaking of the Day of God*, p. 124.

29 Winstanley, *Saints Paradise*, p. 53.

30 Sabine, *Works*, p. 121; Aylmer, 'Religion of Gerrard Winstanley', p. 98.

31 For the appearance and influence of these texts, see T. Wilson Hayes, 'John Everard and the familist tradition', in Margaret Jacob and James Jacob (eds), *The Origins of Anglo-American Radicalism* (London, 1984), pp. 66–7; Smith, *Perfection Proclaimed*, chapters 3–5; B. J. Gibbons, *Gender in Mystical and Occult Thought: Behmenism and its Development in England* (Cambridge, 1996), pp. 103-7, 120–9; J. C. Davis, *Fear, Myth and History: the Ranters and the Historians* (Cambridge, 1986), p. 61; A. L. Morton, *The World of the Ranters: Religious Radicalism in the English Revolution* (London, 1970), p. 127. Many of these texts were published by Giles Calvert.

32 Winstanley, *Several Pieces*, sig. A2r. Cf. Rufus M. Jones, *Mysticism and Democracy in the English Commonwealth* (Cambridge, Massachusetts, 1932), pp. 140–1, for George Fox's similarly unconscious yet immense debt to contemporary movements and spiritual interpreters.

33 Winstanley, *Several Pieces*, sig. A2r–A2v. Cf. Nigel Smith, 'Winstanley and the literature of revolution', in Bradstock (ed.), *Winstanley and the Diggers*, p. 48.

34 Smith, *Perfection Proclaimed*, p. 108.

35 Hill, *Religion and Politics*, pp. 194–200; Smith, *Perfection Proclaimed*, pp. 229–67; B. J. Gibbons, 'Fear, Myth and Furore', *P&P*, 140 (1993), pp. 179–94; Davis, *Fear, Myth and History*, pp. 22, 31, 37, 47–8, 54; E. P. Thompson, *Witness Against the Beast: William Blake and the Moral Law* (Cambridge, 1993), pp. 22–4.

36 Jack R. McMichael and Barbara Taft (eds), *The Writings of William Walwyn* (Athens, Georgia, 1989), pp. 10, 99, 178, 235; G. E. Aylmer (ed.), *The Levellers in the English Revolution* (London, 1975), p. 73. For the centrality of the Golden Rule in radical thought see J. C. Davis, 'The Levellers and Christianity', in Brian Manning (ed.), *Politics, Religion and the English Civil War* (London, 1973), pp. 228–9; Maurice Goldsmith, 'Levelling by sword, spade and word: radical egalitarianism in the English revolution', in Colin Jones, Malyn Newitt and Stephen Roberts (eds), *Politics and People in Revolutionary England* (Oxford, 1986), pp. 65–80; Jonathan Scott, *England's Troubles: Seventeenth-Century English Political Instability in European Context* (Cambridge, 2000), pp. 253–6.

37 Smith, *Perfection Proclaimed*, p. 205; Michael Hunter, Giles Mandelbrote, Richard Ovenden and Nigel Smith (eds), *A Radical's Books: The Library Catalogue of Samuel Jeake of Rye, 1623–90* (Woodbridge, 1999), xlviii; David R. Como, 'The kingdom of Christ, the kingdom of England, and the kingdom of Traske: John Traske and the persistence of radical puritanism in early Stuart England', in McClendon, Ward and MacDonald, *Protestant Identities*, pp. 73–4.

38 Above, p. 1; Alsop, 'Winstanley: what do we know of his life?', p. 27; Dalton, 'Experience of fraud', p. 977.

39 Sabine, *Works*, p. 141; Alsop, 'Winstanley: what do we know of his life?', pp. 28–9.

40 Edwards, *Gangreana*, Book 1, p. 92, Book 2, pp. 146, 148.

41 Hill, *Religion and Politics*, p. 192. Cf. Aylmer, 'Religion of Gerrard Winstanley', p. 95. For the Seekers, see J. F. McGregor, 'Seekers and ranters', in McGregor and Reay, *Radical Religion*, pp. 121–39.

42 Sabine, *Works*, pp. 141, 163; Hill, *Religion and Politics*, p. 192.

43 Peter Lake, *The Boxmaker's Revenge: 'Orthodoxy', 'Heterodoxy' and the Politics of the Parish in Early Stuart London* (Manchester, 2001), *passim*; Como, 'Kingdom of Traske', pp. 81–2. And see now David Como, *Blown by the Spirit: Puritanism and the Emergence of an Antinomian Underground in Pre-Civil-War England* (Stanford, 2004).

44 Alastair Hamilton, *The Family of Love* (Cambridge, 1981), pp. 117, 118–19; J. W. Martin, 'Elizabethan familists and other separatists in the Guildford area', *BIHR*, 51 (1978), pp. 90–2; Christopher W. Marsh, *The Family of Love in English Society, 1550–1630* (Cambridge, 1994), pp. 66, 267–8, 269, 274.

45 Hamilton, *Family of Love*, p. 119; Marsh, *Family of Love*, pp. 66–7.

46 Marsh, *Family of Love*, pp. 66–8, 275. He distanced himself from them in 1579: Hamilton, *Family of Love*, pp. 118–19; Marsh, *Family of Love*, p. 67.

47 SHC, LM/COR/3/182; Martin, 'Elizabethan familists', pp. 92–3.

48 Marsh, *Family of Love*, pp. 163, 278, 281.

49 Bannerman, *Visitations of Surrey . . . 1530, 1532 and 1623*, pp. 149–50, 186. For Moyse see Marsh, *Family of Love*, pp. 163–4, 281.

50 *A Description of the Sect Called the Familie of Love: With their Common Place of Residence* (London, 1641); Marsh, Family of Love, p. 238.

51 Above, pp. 75–6.

52 Winstanley, *Mysterie of God*, pp. 41, 47. Cf. Winstanley, *Saints Paradise*, p. 41.

53 Winstanley, *Breaking of the Day of God*, pp. 101–3, 105; Winstanley, *Saints Paradise*, p. 15.

54 Winstanley, *Breaking of the Day of God*, sig. A2r–A4r.

55 Sabine, *Works*, p. 148.

56 Hill, *Religion and Politics*, p. 212; Aylmer, 'Religion of Gerrard Winstanley', pp. 98–9.

57 Sabine, *Works*, pp. 149–53. Cf. *ibid.*, pp. 169, 170.

58 *Ibid.*, pp. 149, 157, 158, 159, 173, 174, 177, 179, 183, 189, 190, 200, 202, 204, 205, 206, 212, 216, 227, 228.

59 *Ibid.*, pp. 155–6, 174, 186, 221, 226, 235.

60 *Ibid.*, pp. 162, 176–7, 213–19, 224, 226–7, 229.

61 *Ibid.*, p. 158.

62 *Ibid.*, pp. 174–5, 188. Cf. Petegorsky, *Left-Wing Democracy*, p. 146.

63 Sabine, *Works*, pp 181, 198.

64 *Ibid.*, pp. 163, 176, 187, 193, 200, 206, 208–9, 212–14, 219, 223–4, 226, 230, 238–43.

65 *Ibid.*, pp. 208–9, 222 (italics in the original).

66 *Ibid.*, pp. 157, 198, 202.

67 Bradstock, *Faith in the Revolution*, p. 91; Mulligan, Graham and Richards, 'Winstanley', pp. 64–5. Cf. Walter Blith, *The English Improver Improved* (London, 1652), pp. 5–6; Davis, *Utopia and the Ideal Society*, p. 177; Robert Markley, ' "Gulfes, deserts, precipices, stone": Marvell's "Upon Appleton House" and the contradictions of "nature" ', in Gerald MacLean, Donna Landry and Joseph P. Ward (eds), *The Country and the City Revisited: England and the Politics of Culture, 1550–1850* (Cambridge, 1999), p. 91.

68 Sabine, *Works*, p. 169. Cf. *ibid.*, pp. 153, 157, 186, 198–9, 207.

69 Cf. Bernard Capp, 'The Fifth Monarchists and popular millenarianism', in McGregor and Reay, *Radical Religion*, pp. 185–6.

70 Sabine, *Works*, pp. 218–19. Cf. *ibid.*, p. 216. For Winstanley's mortalism, see especially Gibbons, 'Fear, myth and furore', pp. 185–7, 192.

71 Sabine, *Works*, p. 235.

72 *Ibid.*, p. 202.

73 *Ibid.*, p. 159. Cf. *ibid.*, pp. 202–3.

74 *Ibid.*, pp. 184, 204.

75 *Ibid.*, p. 184.

76 *Ibid.*, p. 184.

77 *Ibid.*, pp. 166, 187.

78 *Ibid.*, pp. 182–3.

79 *Ibid.*, pp. 190–1.

80 *Ibid.*, p. 200.

81 *Ibid.*, p. 179.

82 *Ibid.*, p. 201.

83 *Ibid.*, pp. 192–3, 201.

84 *Ibid.*, p. 193.

85 *Ibid.*, p. 204.

86 *Ibid.*, p. 194.

87 *Ibid.*, pp. 195–6.

88 Cf. Hill, *Religion and Politics*, p. 220.

89 Sabine, *Works*, pp. 225, 226.

90 *Ibid.*, pp. 181, 196–7; Manning, *1649*, pp. 116–17.

91 Sabine, *Works*, p. 200. Cf. *ibid.*, pp. 181, 182, 190, 191, 201, 205, 206, 207, 211–12.

92 *Ibid.*, p. 205. Cf. *ibid.*, pp. 185, 191–2.

93 *Ibid.*, pp. 182, 190.

94 *Ibid.*, p. 194.

95 *Ibid.*, p. 205.

96 *Ibid.*, pp. 194–5.

97 Cf. Corns, *Uncloistered Virtue*, p. 159; Blair Worden, *The Rump Parliament* (Cambridge, 1974), p. 40.

98 S. R. Gardiner, *History of the Great Civil War, 1642–1649* (revised edn, London, 1910), vol. 4, p. 290; Underdown, *Pride's Purge*, p. 173.

99 S. R. Gardiner, *History of the Commonwealth and Protectorate*, vol. 1 (London, 1903), p. 3.

100 For the centrality of millenarianism in seventeenth-century thought see William M. Lamont, *Godly Rule* (London, 1969).

101 W. S. Hudson, 'Economic and social thought of Gerrard Winstanley: was he a seventeenth-century Marxist?', *Journal of Modern History*, 17 (1946), pp. 1–21; Perez Zagorin, *A History of Political Thought in the English Revolution* (London, 1954), pp. 43–58; George Juretic, 'Digger no Millenarian: the revolutionalizing of Gerrard Winstanley', *Journal of the History of Ideas*, 36 (1975); Mulligan, Graham and Richards, 'Winstanley'; Hill, *Religion and Politics*, pp. 185–252.

102 Bradstock, *Faith in the Revolution*, pp. 71–133. See also Andrew Bradstock, 'Sowing in hope: the relevance of theology to Gerrard Winstanley's political programme', *Seventeenth Century*, 6 (1991).

103 Bradstock, *Faith in the Revolution*, pp. 94–5. Cf. Hill, *Religion and Politics*, p. 236.

104 Holstun, *Ehud's Dagger*, p. 376. Cf. James Holstun, 'Communism, George Hill and the Mir*', p. 140.

105 See, for instance, *The Discoverer* (1649), pp. 9 ff. For the question of unbelief and atheism in this period see Michael Hunter and David Wootton (eds), *Atheism from the Reformation to the Enlightenment* (Oxford, 1992); David Wootton, 'Unbelief in early modern Europe', *History Workshop Journal*, 20 (1985), pp. 82–100.

106 Sabine, *Works*, p. 434; Manning, *1649*, p. 130. Cf. Winstanley's comment that 'some have said, I had done well if I had left writing when I finished the Saints Paradise': Winstanley, *Several Pieces*, sig. A3v.

107 Sabine, *Works*, p. 232.

108 Zagorin, *Political Thought in the English Revolution*, pp. 48, 52; Davis, 'Levellers and christianity', pp. 229–30, 234–6; Barry Reay, 'Radicalism and religion in the English revolution: an introduction', in McGregor and Reay, *Radical Religion*, pp. 16–18; Scott, *England's Troubles*, pp. 257–60.

109 Holstun, 'Communism, George Hill and the *Mir*', pp. 140–4. Cf. Blair Worden's judicious discussion of secularization in 'The question of secularization', in Alan Houston and Steve Pincus (eds), *A Nation Transformed: England after the Restoration* (Cambridge, 2001), pp. 20–40.

110 Scott, *England's Troubles*, pp. 247–68.

111 Wither, *Vox Pacifica*, p. 65.

112 George Wither, *A Cordial Confection* (1659), p. 26. Cf. *ibid.*, p. 3; George Wither, *British Appeals, with Gods Mercifull Replies* (1651), pp. 15, 56; George Wither, *The Petition and Narrative of George Wither Esq.* (1659), p. 2.

113 John Lilburne, *The Copy of a Letter from Lieutenant Colonell John Lilburne, to a Friend* (1645), pp. 16–17. Cf. John Lilburne, *Englands Birth-Right Justified* (1645), pp. 44–5.

114 Taft and McMichael, *Writings of William Walwyn*, p. 80.

115 A. L. Morton (ed.), *Freedom in Arms: A Selection of Leveller Writings* (London, 1975), pp. 98, 191. Cf. *ibid.*, pp. 168, 177.

116 John Cooke, *Unum Necessarium: Or the Poor Mans Case* (1648), p. 36.

117 Peter Chamberlen, *The Poor Mans Advocate* (1649), p. 1.

118 Aylmer, *Levellers*, p. 87.

119 H. N. Brailsford, *The Levellers and the English Revolution* (London, 1961), pp. 431–2.

120 *Englands Troublers Troubled, Or the Just Resolutions of the Plaine-men of England against the Rich and Mightie* (1648), pp. 7–8. This pamphlet was ascribed by Clement Walker to Henry Marten, though possibly on dubious grounds: Ivan Waters, *Henry Marten and the Long Parliament* (Chepstow, 1973), pp. 41–2.

121 Aylmer, *Levellers*, pp. 135–6 (my italics). Cf. Manning, *English People*, p. 395.

122 Charles Webster, *The Great Instauration: Science, Medicine and Reform 1626–1660* (London, 1975), esp. pp. 259–60, 360–9.

123 Chamberlen, *Poor Mans Advocate*, pp. 43–6, 49 ff.

124 Don M. Wolfe (ed.), *Leveller Manifestoes of the Puritan Revolution* (New York and London, 1944), p. 319; Manning, *English People*, p. 395.

125 *An Experimentall Essay touching the Reformation of the Lawes of England* (1648), p. 6.

126 Sabine, *Works*, p. 200; Manning, *1649*, p. 100.

127 Chamberlen, *Poor Mans Advocate*; Wolfe, *Leveller Manifestoes*, pp. 318–19; *Englands Troublers Troubled*, pp. 7–8; *An Experimentall Essay*, pp. 2, 5; Aylmer, *Levellers*, pp. 86–7, 136.

128 Webster, *Great Instauration*, pp. 362–3, 369; Eduard Bernstein, *Cromwell and Communism: Socialism and Democracy in the Great English Revolution* (revised edn, London 1980), pp. 100–1, 104; Brian Manning, *The Far Left in the English Revolution 1640–1660* (London, 1999), p. 44; Manning, *1649*, p. 100.

129 Buchanan Sharp, 'Rights, charities and the disorderly poor', in Geoff Eley and William Hunt (eds), *Reviving the English Revolution: Reflections and Elaborations on the Work*

of Christopher Hill (London, 1988), pp. 107–37; Manning, *1649*, pp. 97–102; Holstun, *Ehud's Dagger*, pp. 387–8.

130 Chamberlen, *Poor Mans Advocate*; Webster, *Great Instauration*, p. 368.

131 Sharp, 'Rights, charities and the disorderly poor', pp. 117–18; Brailsford, *Levellers*, pp. 434–6; Manning, *1649*, p. 99.

132 Cooke, *Unum Necessarium*, p. 36. Cf. Petegorsky, *Left-Wing Democracy*, pp. 111–12; Manning, *1649*, pp. 105–6.

133 On the acquisition of the Leveller name, see Brailsford, *Levellers*, pp. 309–10; Blair Worden, 'The Levellers in history and memory, c. 1600–1960', in Michael Mendle (ed.), *The Putney Debates of 1647: the Army, the Levellers, and the English State* (Cambridge, 2001), p. 280–2.

134 Aylmer, *Levellers*, pp. 136, 167.

135 *Ibid.*, p. 153. Cf. Petegorsky, *Left-Wing Democracy*, pp. 109–11.

136 Aylmer, *Levellers*, pp. 153–4. For Walwyn's views on property see McMichael and Taft, *Writings of William Walwyn*, pp. 42, 49, 80. Cf. Morton, *World of the Ranters*, pp. 183–7; Manning, *Far Left*, pp. 51–2.

137 Aylmer, *Levellers*, p. 78; cf. *ibid.*, pp. 59, 80, 166.

138 Wolfe, *Leveller Manifestoes*, p. 317.

139 Wood, Riot, *Rebellion and Popular Politics*, p. 169.

140 Chamberlen, *Poor Mans Advocate*, epistle dedicatory.

141 *Ibid.*, p. 3.

142 George Foster, *The Sounding of the Last Trumpet* (1650); George Foster, *The Pouring Forth of the Seventh and Last Viall* (1650); Nigel Smith (ed.), *A Collection of Ranter Writings from the 17th Century* (London, 1983), pp. 80–116.

143 For parallels between Winstanley and Foster and Coppe, see Christopher Hill, 'God and the English Revolution', *History Workshop Journal*, 17 (1984), pp. 24–5; Davis, *Fear, Myth and History*, pp. 31, 51, 57; Gibbons, 'Fear, Myth and Furore', pp. 179–94.

144 Laurence Clarkson, *A Generall Charge* (1648). Cf. Barry Reay, 'Laurence Clarkson: an artisan and the English Revolution', in Christopher Hill, Barry Reay and William Lamont, *The World of the Muggletonians* (London, 1983), pp. 173–5. J. C. Davis points out that Clarkson's tract is less radical than it may at first appear: Davis, *Fear, Myth and History*, pp. 60–1.

145 Smith, *Ranter Writings*, p. 86.

146 Smith, *Ranter Writings*, pp. 87, 96, 100–1, 109–10, 112–13, 114–16.

147 Foster, *Last Trumpet*, pp. 12–20, 27, 29, 37–39, 41–7, 49, 51–2; Foster, *Seventh Viall*, epistle dedicatory; for Foster, see also below, p. 181.

148 Smith, *Ranter Writings*, pp. 86, 182.

149 Reprinted in Sabine, *Works*, pp. 611–23.

150 Bernstein, *Cromwell and Communism*, pp. 96–7, 132; L. H. Berens, *The Digger Movement in the Days of the Commonwealth* (London, 1906), pp. 79–83.

151 Petegorsky, *Left-Wing Democracy*, pp. 138–42.

152 Hill, *World Turned Upside Down*, p. 94; Lutaud, *Winstanley*, pp. 71–2. Cf. Hill, *Religion and Politics*, p. 203; Brailsford, *Levellers*, p. 444; Sabine, *Works*, pp. 605–6.

153 Hill, *World Turned Upside Down*, pp. 94–5.

154 Sabine, *Works*, p. 612.

155 *Ibid.*, pp. 615–16.

156 *Ibid.*, pp. 614–15. Cf. Hill, *Religion and Politics*, p. 216. Their use of these themes were, however, less sophisticated than Winstanley's.

157 Brailsford, *Levellers*, p. 444.

158 Below, p. 135.

159 Peter J. Bowden, 'Statistical Appendix', in Joan Thirsk (ed.), *The Agrarian History of England and Wales*, vol. 4 (Cambridge, 1967), pp. 821–65; Manning, *1649*, pp. 79–96.

160 *Kingdomes Weekly Intelligencer*, 272 (8–15 August 1648).

161 E. S. De Beer (ed.), *The Diary of John Evelyn* (Oxford, 1955), vol. 2, pp. 546–7.

162 George Ormorod (ed.), *Tracts Relating to Military Proceedings in Lancashire During the Great Civil War* (Manchester, Chetham Society, 1844), pp. 277–8. Cf. Manning, *1649*, pp. 80–1.

163 Ormorod, *Lancashire*, p. 278.

164 SHC, 111/10/7; EL/12/1; TNA, SP28/334 (unfol.), acct book of Rich. Wither, ff. 57, 61.

165 *The Moderate*, 30 (30 January–6 February); 59 (21–28 August 1649); Manning and Bray, *Surrey*, 3, p. 674.

166 TNA, LR2/297, fols 129–40; E317/Surrey/38, 44, 55–7, 65–8; above, pp. 3, 4, 6.

167 Sabine, *Works*, p. 616.

168 Christopher Hill, *Puritanism and Revolution* (revised edn, Harmondsworth 1986), pp. 178–9.

169 Cf. Clay, 'Landlords and estate management', p. 145. See also John Evelyn's comments on timber losses in Surrey, quoted in Peter Brandon, 'Land, technology and water management in the Tillingbourne valley, Surrey, 1560–1760, *Southern History*, 6 (1984), p. 92.

170 HLRO, Main Papers 1646, 30 July.

171 TNA, SP19/21, p. 255.

172 TNA, SP23/132, p. 189.

173 TNA, PROB11/203, fol. 388v.

174 TNA, C6/147/9; PROB11/333, fol. 15v; SHC, G3/4/17.

175 TNA, PROB11/333, fol. 15v.

176 Sabine, *Works*, pp. 272–5; below, p. 142.

177 Sabine, *Works*, p. 188.

178 Hudson, 'Economic and social thought', *passim*; Mulligan and Richards, 'Winstanley', pp. 68–9.

179 Bradstock, *Faith in the Revolution*, pp. 105–106.

180 For these see esp. A. L. Morton, *The English Utopia* (London, 1978) *passim*; John Walter, 'A "rising of the people"?: the Oxfordshire rising of 1596', *P&P*, 107 (1985), pp. 90–143; Steven Justice, *Writing and Rebellion: England in 1381* (Berkeley, 1994). *passim*; McRae, *God Speed the Plough*, *passim*; Andy Wood, ' "Poore men woll speke one daye": plebeian languages of deference and defiance in England, c. 1520–1640', in Harris, *Politics of the Excluded*, pp. 67–98.

Chapter 5

The Diggers on St George's Hill

THE FIRST PHASE

On 16 April 1649, the council of state received intelligence from Walton-on-Thames in Surrey, describing in somewhat alarmist terms the start of the Diggers' activities on St George's Hill. The report, which bore no date, showed that the Diggers had set to work on the hill on 'Sunday was sennight last' – Sunday, 1 April – when they 'began to digge on that side the Hill next to Campe Close, and sowed the ground with parsenipps, and carretts, and beanes'. Five Diggers had been present that first day, but their numbers had increased steadily thereafter; and on the following Friday between twenty and thirty of them appeared on the hill and 'wrought all day att digging'. Their plans to put two or three ploughs to work on the Friday were delayed for lack of seed corn, but they managed to acquire this at Kingston market the following day: 'they invite all to come in and helpe them, and promise them meate, drinke, and clothes'.[1]

Henry Sanders, the author of the report from Surrey, was a Walton yeoman and a long-serving agent of the parliamentarian county committee.[2] He would have been familiar with the commons around St George's Hill, and his report clearly reflects local concerns about the disruptive effects of the Diggers' activities: the Diggers had, he pointed out, 'fired the Heath, and burn't att least 40 roode of Heath, which is a very great prejudice to the Towne'.[3] As an employee of the county committee, Sanders had been in recent contact with the council of state, having been instructed by them in March to arrest a Chertsey resident accused of felling timber in the state's woods.[4] While many Surrey officials had wavered in their allegiance in the spring and summer of 1648, Sanders had remained loyal to parliament and had been involved in the arrest of those suspected of supporting the Earl of Holland's rising.[5] In 1650 he was to be appointed agent for Surrey's sequestration commissioners, and he would continue in the state's employment until 1660.[6] The council of state could hardly afford to ignore information from such a trustworthy source, especially at a time when the newly established republic was faced with unrest in the army and with the threat of royalist and Leveller insurrection.[7] A letter, signed by the council's president John Bradshaw, and with Sanders's report enclosed, was dispatched to the Lord General, requesting that he order horse to Cobham to disperse the Diggers.[8] A second letter, addressed to JPs in Surrey's middle division, called for the 'contrivers or promoters or present at those tumultuous and riotous meetings' to be sent for and proceeded against.[9]

The tone of Sanders's report and the council's letters betrays uncertainty as to the intentions of the strange new arrivals on St George's Hill. Sanders, in claiming that the Diggers 'doe threaten to pull downe and levell all park pales, and lay open', was presumably attempting to explain the Digger phenomenon in terms of more familiar forms of agrarian protest. He also identified an element of compulsion and menace in the Diggers' activities, suggesting that they 'threaten the neighbouring people there, that they will make them all come uppe to the hills and worke, and forwarne them suffering their cattell to come neere the plantation'.[10] The council of state's letters combined warnings of dangerous insurrection with the admission that the Diggers' 'actions hitherto have beene onely ridiculous'.[11] The Diggers' dispersal was required, the council insisted, in order to ensure 'that a malignant and disaffected partie may nott under colour of such ridiculous people have any opportunity to randezvouz themselves in order to a greater mischief'.[12]

There was some confusion too in attempts to identify the leaders of the new movement. In these first reports of the Diggers' activities, Winstanley's name was barely mentioned, with attention being focussed on the more flamboyant William Everard, whom Winstanley had defended in print in October 1648 and who now joined him on St George's Hill.[13] Sanders made no reference to Winstanley in his report to the council of state, but he did refer to 'one Everard, once of the army butt was cashiered, who termeth himself a prophett'.[14] Captain John Gladman, who commanded the two troops of horse sent by Fairfax to disperse the Diggers, spoke of 'Mr. Winstanlie and Mr. Everard' as 'the cheife men that have persuaded those people to doe what they have done'.[15] In published accounts of the meeting that took place between the Diggers and Fairfax on 20 April, most newsbook writers assumed that it was Everard who acted as chief spokesman before the Lord General.[16]

Early published accounts of events on St George's Hill reflected the general uncertainty with which news of the Diggers had first been received.[17] The royalist newsbook *Mercurius Pragmaticus* made fun of 'Prophet Everet's' intention to convert 'Oatlands Park into a Wildernesse, and preach Liberty to the oppressed Deer', while warning that 'what this fanaticall insurrection may grow unto, cannot be conceived; for Mahomet had as small, and as despicable a beginning'.[18] Other newsbook writers sought to ridicule the naive visions that had led this 'new fangled people' to dig on St George's Hill, and the Diggers' belief that the barren wastes would miraculously be made fruitful.[19] The Diggers' claim to all common land was also criticised: 'they thought because they were called commons, they belonged to any body, not considering that they are the commons only for the inhabitants of such, or such a place: they are a distracted, crack brained people that were the chief.'[20] Some writers attempted, as Sanders had done, to link the Diggers' activities to more conventional types of protest, claiming that the Diggers were active in Oatlands and Windsor Parks as well as on St George's Hill, and that they had set about destroying park pales.[21] The very name Digger, which was first applied to the new movement by the London press, helped provide a connection with earlier rural protest movements, the name first having been used by anti-enclosure rioters in the Midlands Revolt of 1607.[22]

Marchamont Nedham, in the royalist newsbook *Mercurius Pragmaticus (for King Charles II)*, adopted a somewhat different approach. At a time when royalists were seeking to court the Levellers and to portray them as valiant upholders of liberty against a tyrannical regime, any attempt to associate constitutional Levellers with the more extreme Diggers needed to be firmly resisted. Nedham was alert to the danger that government supporters might seek to tarnish the Levellers with the communistic ideals of the Diggers, and he sought not only to distance the two groups but to play down the significance of the Diggers' ideas and activities. The Levellers, he reminded his readers, aimed not 'at the Levelling of mens Estates, but at the new State-Tyranny'. The Diggers too posed no threat, but were merely 'a few poor people making bold with a little wast-ground in Surrey, to sow a few Turnips and Carrets to sustain their Families'. The significance of the Digger episode was, Nedham suggested, being exaggerated by the government and its pamphleteers 'to the disrepute of the Levellers'; while the sending of 'divers troops of Janiseries . . . prauncing into Surrey' was little more than a *coup de theatre* designed to magnify the threat posed by these 'feeble souls and empty bellies'.[23]

Nedham's response to the Diggers was an astute one, since government propagandists would soon start to make use of Digger tracts, Winstanley's *The New Law of Righteousnes* and the Buckinghamshire *Light Shining* pamphlets, to attack the Levellers and to accuse them of aiming to 'thrust every one out of his proper and lawful possession'.[24] The Levellers' *A Manifestation*, in which the party's leaders felt compelled to disavow any intention of levelling estates, was issued just after the Diggers began work on St George's Hill, and later in the summer Lilburne was driven to disassociate himself from 'all the erronious tenents of the poor Diggers at George Hill'.[25] It cannot have helped matters that the Diggers chose, in their first published declaration, to refer to themselves as True Levellers.[26] Nedham too would later have no qualms about linking Levellers and Diggers, once he became a supporter of the Commonwealth regime. In his chapter on the Levellers in *The Case of the Commonwealth* of 1650 he would recount the lessons from history that proved how the 'leveling, popular form' leads to support for an agrarian law and thence to support for 'absolute community':

> And though neither the Athenian nor Roman Levellers ever arrived to this high pitch of madness, yet we see a new faction started up out of ours known by the name of Diggers. Who, upon this ground that God is our common father, the earth our common mother, and that the original of propriety was men's pride and covetousness, have framed a new plea for a return of all men *ad tuguria*; that like the old Parthians, Scythian nomads, and other wild barbarians, we might renounce towns and cities, live at rovers, and enjoy all in common.[27]

Nedham's brief account of the Diggers in *Mercurius Pragmaticus (for Charles II)* was important in portraying the Diggers in a way that might, however unintentionally, have added to their popular appeal. By playing down the Diggers' ideological motivation, Nedham helped foster an image of them as poor people acting through necessity to feed themselves and their families. This image may have seemed more familiar and palatable to those Winstanley hoped to mobilise – and perhaps less intimidating to those in authority – than the one most likely to be drawn from a close reading of *The New Law of Righteousnes*. It was also one that would be discernable in Digger pronouncements from the earliest days of the movement, though it would become more clearly defined in later months than it was at the start of the digging. When Winstanley and Everard were brought before Fairfax at Whitehall on 20 April, they emphasised the utility of the Diggers' work, and this theme was to be repeated in the first Digger manifesto, *The True Levellers Standard Advanced*, which appeared in the last week of April.[28]

The meeting with the Lord General followed Captain Gladman's expedition to St George's Hill on 19 April. Gladman had not been impressed by what his soldiers had found on the hill. There had, as he informed Fairfax, been no more than twenty people involved in digging since the start of their activities: 'Indeed the business is not worth the writing nor yet taking nottis of: I wonder the Council of State should be so abused with informations.'[29] Before leaving St George's Hill, Gladman had however carried out his orders to disperse the small gathering of Diggers, who had managed to dig only around one acre of ground but had started making caves and dens on the hill.[30] He had also persuaded Winstanley and Everard to appear before the Lord General the following day, though he warned Fairfax that 'I believe you will be glad to bee rid of them againe, espeshially Everard who is no other then a madd man'.[31] For the two Diggers, the meeting with Fairfax provided a useful opportunity to publicise their activities on St George's Hill. The published account of their speeches before Fairfax represents the first serious attempt to describe the Digger programme, free from the speculation and distortions found in the early newsbook reports on the digging. It may well have been a journalist's abridgement of a paper written by Winstanley – perhaps even an early draft of *The True Levellers Standard Advanced* – for it does appear to reflect with reasonable accuracy the stated aims of the Diggers in the early days of the movement. The people's freedoms, which had been lost under the Norman Conquest, would, they claimed, soon be restored to them in enjoying the fruits and benefits of the earth; through digging and ploughing the earth, they would restore the Creation 'to its former condition':

> And that as God had promised to make the barren Ground fruitfull: So now, what they did was to renew the ancient Community of the enjoying the fruits of the Earth and to distribute the benefit thereof to the Poore and needy, and to feed the Hungry, and to cloath the Naked.

Private property would be left alone, and no park pales or enclosures thrown down, for work would take place only on common and untilled land 'to make it fruitfull for the use of man'; the Diggers were, however, confident that 'the time will suddenly be that all men should willingly come in, and give up their Lands and Estates, and willingly to submit to this Community'. No force would be used against their opponents, but they would 'submit unto Authority, and wait till the promised opportunity be offered which they conceive to be neer at hand'.[32]

The Diggers' first published manifesto, *The True Levellers' Standard Advanced*, made its appearance between 20 April, the date of its introductory epistle, and 26 April, when the London bookseller George Thomason obtained copies.[33] *The True Levellers Standard* set out to explain and justify the activities of the Diggers on St George's Hill, and to encourage others to follow their example. The work was clearly written by Winstanley, but in its references to the Norman Yoke, and in its echoes of the opening paragraphs of *Light Shining in Buckinghamshire*, it showed the influence of others.[34] As with later Digger manifestos, Winstanley's was only one of several names of subscribers appended to it, and it is likely that in writing it Winstanley sought to articulate the views of fellow Diggers as well as his own.[35] *The True Levellers Standard* contained a skilful distillation of the arguments for digging advanced by Winstanley in *The New Law of Righteousnes*, and it proclaimed the Diggers' faith in the inevitably of restoration. The earth was bound to become a common treasury again, 'for all the Prophesies of scriptures and Reason are Circled here in this Community, and mankind must have the Law of Righteousnesse once more writ in his heart, and all must be made of one heart, and one mind'.[36] The very choice of St George's Hill as the site of their work – a place that 'in view of Flesh, be very barren' – was proof of their confidence in the success of the venture.[37] Winstanley's 'Voice in Trance, and out of Trance', which had impelled him to launch the digging experiment, was recounted in detail, including the injunction that none should work for hire. Only through obedience to these commands would the curse be lifted and the work of restoration fulfilled.[38] The digging on St George's Hill was but the beginning, for

> not only this Common, or Heath should be taken in and Manured by the People, but all the Commons and waste Ground in England, and in the whole World, shall be taken in by the People in righteousness, not owning any Propriety; but taking the Earth to be a Common Treasury, as it was first made for all.[39]

The millenarian vision of *The True Levellers Standard* was deeply anti-formalist, and drew on Winstanley's earlier writings in calling for the rejection of outward teachers and rulers. The 'teaching and ruling power' had led 'the Earth, mankind, into confusion and death', making man 'a stranger to the Spirit that is within himself'; mankind's restoration from bondage was dependant on the will to free himself from deference to these powers in favour of the law of righteousness or light of Reason.[40] As in Winstanley's earlier writings, the criticism of teachers and rulers went beyond criticism of the clergy to encompass secular government and lawyers; it was also mankind's subordination to the teaching and ruling power which had, together with covetousness, made possible the rise of private property and the dominion of one part of mankind over another.[41] 'Civil Propriety' was the curse, and

> so long as we, or any other, doth own the Earth to be the peculiar Interest of Lords and Landlords, and not common to others as well as them, we own the Curse, and hold the Creation under bondage; and so long as we or any other doth own Landlords and Tennants, for one to call the Land his, or another to hire it of him, or for one to give hire, and for another to work for hire; this is to dishonour the work of Creation; as if the righteous Creator should have respect to persons, and therefore made the Earth for some, and not for all: And so long as we, or any other, maintain the Civil Propriety, we consent still to hold the Creation down under that bondage it groans under, and so we should hinder the work of Restoration, and sin against Light, that is given into us, and so through the fear of the flesh man, lose our peace.[42]

Alongside these now familiar themes were arguments drawn from necessity, which helped provide a justification of the Diggers' actions in ways that chimed with more traditional languages of popular protest. To a greater extent even than *The New Law of Righteousnes*, *The True Levellers Standard* succeeded in emphasising the moral case for digging. The rise of private property and the inclosure of the Earth had left wealth in the hands of some, while others lived in 'miserable povertie and straits'; England's recent upheavals had, the powers of England were informed, reduced the common people to a morsel of Bread, as well as 'confounding all sorts of People by thy Government, of doing and undoing'.[43] The people had borne their share of the costs of defeating 'the former oppressing Powers' through taxation, free quarter and bloodshed, and 'yet thou hast not given us our bargain'.[44] Through their covetousness, pride and hypocrisy the rich had become incapable of responding to the 'affliction of others, though they dy for want of bread, in that rich City, undone under your eys'.[45] If the Earth were made a common treasury once more, then 'every one that is born in the Land, may be fed by the Earth his Mother that brought him forth, according to the Reason that rules in the Creation'; the oppressed would be set free and 'Poor peoples hearts comforted'.[46] The Diggers 'would have none live in Beggery, Poverty, or Sorrow, but that every one might enjoy the benefit of his creation'; and they were confident that through their work 'Bondage shall be removed, Tears wiped away, and all poor People by their righteous Labours shall be relieved, and freed from Poverty and Straits'.[47] They reiterated their refusal to countenance violent action, for 'there is no intent of Tumult or Fighting, but only to get Bread to eat, with the sweat of our brows; working together in righteousness, and eating the blessings of the Earth in peace'.[48]

Despite its renunciation of violence, *The True Levellers Standard* contained, like *The New Law of Righteousnes* before it, threats of punishment against those who failed to heed the message received and communicated by the Diggers. The time of deliverance had come, and 'thou proud Esau, and stout-hearted Covetousness, thou must come down, and be lord of the Creation no longer'; 'if thou wilt find Mercy, Let Israel go Free'.[49] In promising vengeance against oppressors, and in declaring to the latter that their obedience to the Diggers' message was required rather than merely requested, *The True Levellers Standard* again offered echoes of established languages of popular protest, though in this case of a more militant and chiliastic strain.[50] These languages were also to be found reflected in the work's polarised image of rich and poor, and in its depiction of landlords as thieves who had stolen the land – the inheritance of all – from their fellow creatures.[51] Added force was provided by the reminder to the poor that they were complicit in their own oppression, by having sold their labour and paid rent to 'lift up Tyrants to rule over them', and that they had a central part to play in their own deliverance.[52] The poor were required to act, through withholding their labour and through coming together to dig the commons.[53] The emphasis on agency in the Diggers' message was clear: in *The New Law of Righteousnes* Winstanley had expressed his belief that the 'spirit of the poor, shall be drawn forth ere long, to act materially this Law of Righteousness', and this was spelt out again in *The True Levellers Standard*.[54] Having declared their intentions by word of mouth and in print, the Diggers had 'now begun to declare it by Action, in Diging up the Common Land, and casting in Seed, that we may eat our Bread together in righteousness'.[55] The digging venture was, for its participants, a demonstration of the primacy of action over words, and this was a theme to which Winstanley would return repeatedly in the pamphlets he produced over the coming months.

IDENTIFYING THE DIGGERS

Appended to *The True Levellers Standard Advanced* were the names of fifteen men who had chosen to join Winstanley in working upon St George's Hill.[56] A second Digger publication, *A Declaration From the Poor Oppressed People of England*, which followed at the end of May, contained the names of forty-five Diggers.[57] What is immediately apparent from the lists of signatories to these, and later Digger manifestos, is the presence in them of local names.[58] Henry Sanders had suggested that the five Diggers who had first begun work on the hill were 'all living att Cobham', and among them he named 'one Stewer and Colton'.[59] These are readily identifiable as Thomas Starr and John Coulton, both of whom put their names to *The True Levellers Standard* and *A Declaration From the Poor Oppressed*. Starr was a shoemaker and a resident of Church Cobham. He had been baptised in December 1615, a younger son of Edmund Starr, a Cobham clothworker who had died in 1638.[60] In 1647 and 1648 Starr was named as a defaulter at the view of frankpledge; he served as headborough or tithingman for Church Cobham in 1660, and as a parish waywarden in 1672.[61] He was assessed at six hearths for the hearth tax in 1663 and 1664, and at three hearths in 1672–73.[62] He died in March 1697.[63] Coulton, whom we have encountered before, was a copyhold tenant of the manor of Cobham, and was in possession of a holding of roughly thirty acres in the tithing of Downside.[64] He had for many years played an active part in manorial and parochial affairs, and during the Civil War he had been employed in the assessment and collection of wartime taxes in Cobham and in compiling Cobham's parish accounts.[65]

Another signatory to *The True Levellers Standard* was Henry Bickerstaffe, the second surviving son of Robert Bickerstaffe of Pains Hill and Cobham, and Katherine, daughter of John and Alice Lambert of Perrotts manor in Banstead.[66] Bickerstaffe was baptised in 1606 in White Notley, Essex, where his uncle Anthony was vicar, and in 1626 he was apprenticed to his elder brother Anthony, a linen draper resident in the London parish of Christ Church, Newgate Street.[67] He was made free of the Skinners' company in April 1633, and by 1636 was living in the parish of St Gregory by St Paul.[68] By January 1640 he had returned to the family home at Pains Hill, and he continued there after the death of his father in September of that year.[69] Although Anthony Bickerstaffe inherited the Pains Hill lease in 1640 and was admitted tenant to the family's Cobham copyhold properties, he remained in London where his business and political interests lay; Henry therefore took on the responsibility for managing the estate in his brother's absence.[70] Henry Bickerstaffe was, as we have seen, one of the commission jurors who found in January 1642 that no part of Surrey remained part of Windsor Forest, and he was acquainted with Winstanley before the start of the digging.[71]

Another local inhabitant who was active from the start of the digging was Henry Barton.[72] He was a Street Cobham householder and was named as a defaulter at the view of frankpledge in 1640, 1647 and 1648.[73] His son became an innholder in Street Cobham and a customary tenant of Cobham manor; he was a regular member of the manorial homage in the years 1680–1700, as well as serving as overseer of the poor and waywarden.[74] John Hayman, who had joined the Diggers by May 1649, was another inhabitant of Street Cobham, and was also named as a defaulter at the view of frankpledge in 1648.[75] He was married to Constance Johnson, daughter of Laurence Johnson, a Cobham victualler who was among those presented at the manor court in 1642 for breach of the assize of ale.[76] Johnson later took as his apprentice the son of the Digger Daniel Freeland.[77] Hayman and Johnson both witnessed the will of Francis Stint the elder, a Cobham husbandman, in 1658, and in 1665 Hayman inventoried the goods of Francis Terrell of Stoke d'Abernon.[78] In 1667 he was witness to and overseer of the will of Gowen Mills of Cobham, who in 1646 had been fined with Winstanley for digging peat on the manorial waste, and whose brother Matthew had been a Digger or Digger sympathiser.[79] Hayman served as tithingman for Street Cobham in 1660, and as waywarden for the parish in 1669–70.[80] He was assessed at three hearths in 1663, 1664 and 1672–73, and died in December 1675.[81]

Daniel Freeland, a resident of Church Cobham, was also a defaulter at the 1642 and 1648 views of frankpledge.[82] He was a member of the extensive Freeland family which had settled chiefly in the parishes of Ockham, Pyrford, Wisley and Byfleet.[83] He had died by October 1657, and his widow was in receipt of parish relief in 1662; she was listed as having one hearth in the 1664 hearth tax and died in December of that year.[84] Samuel Webb, a resident of Downside, was another defaulter at the 1648 view of frankpledge, as was William Taylor, a resident of Street Cobham.[85] Anthony Wrenn of Church Cobham had been presented as a defaulter the previous year; in 1642 he had been fined for digging and selling turves from the manorial waste.[86] Until 1649 he was tenant of George Evelyn of Wotton to a warren house at Stoakes Heath, but a new lease, to William Philips of Cobham, was issued in February 1650.[87] Wrenn was listed as a copyhold tenant of the manor of Cobham in 1657 and 1676, and in 1670 he was exempted from payment of the hearth tax.[88]

Anthony Wrenn appears to have joined the digging only in its later stages. One Digger who was present from the start, and who remained with the colony until its dispersal in April 1650, was John Palmer. A John Palmer, son of a Cobham blacksmith of the same name, was apprenticed to William Stedwell, a Kingston baker, for ten years from May 1626.[89] Between December 1630 and May 1631 John Palmer of Cobham – possibly the father – received 5s 6d from the Henry Smith charity during a period of sickness.[90] In March 1641, Thomasin, daughter of John Palmer, was baptised in Cobham.[91] John Palmer had two hearths in 1664 and was exempted from the hearth tax.[92] Other possible Cobham Diggers included John South, John South junior and Thomas South. Thomas South of Cobham, who was to marry Phoebe Coulton in 1658, was a bricklayer, and he was assessed at two hearths in 1663 and 1664.[93] In 1682 he was to be presented by the court baron for encroaching on the manorial waste.[94] John South, also known as 'Ould South', was exempted from payment of the hearth tax on his single-hearth house in 1664 and 1670.[95] He was in receipt of parish relief in the years 1668–70, and died in 1672.[96]

It is also possible to provide a tentative identification of a small number of Diggers from parishes in the vicinity of Cobham. Thomas Edsaw or Edcer, who was present from the start of the digging, may be identified with Thomas Edsaw of Stoke d'Abernon, a member of a family long settled in that parish. He had two children baptised there in 1656 and 1663; he was assessed at one hearth and was exempted from the hearth tax in 1664 and in 1670.[97] Richard Maidley or Medley, who signed *The True Levellers Standard Advanced* and who was still active in the Digger movement in April 1650, may have been the Walton-on-Thames inhabitant of that name. A son of his was buried in Walton in December 1640, and he had two children baptised there in 1642 and 1643.[98] Edward Longhurst's place of origin is uncertain, but the surname was a quite common one in Cobham and its neighbouring parishes. The name was, for instance, to be found in the parish of West Horsley, where an Edward Longhurst was a freehold tenant of West Horsley manor in the 1640s.[99] The Longhurst family of Ewhurst also had known connections with Cobham, and members of that family had held land of Cobham manor.[100] An Edward Longhurst, husbandman of Ewhurst was indicted for assault at the quarter sessions in 1661, and was assessed at one hearth (exempt) in 1664.[101]

Richard Goodgroome and Abraham Pennard alias Goodgroome may also have been local residents. The Digger Richard Goodgroome has sometimes been identified as the army preacher and fifth monarchist Richard Goodgroom, who has also been linked to the 1656 proto-Harringtonian tract *A Copy of a Letter from an Officer of the Army in Ireland*.[102] There is however no evidence to prove that the Digger, fifth monarchist and 'R.G.' who wrote *A Copy of a Letter* were the same person.[103] Goodgroomes and Pennards were to be found in the parish of Richmond-upon-Thames, where both families owned property and worked as tile makers.[104] The families were apparently connected, and their names were listed consecutively in a Richmond quit rental of January 1649.[105] A Richard Goodgroome's admission to half an acre of land in Richmond was recorded in the manorial estreats for January 1649; he had died by March 1654, when his son Richard was admitted to a cottage, tile kiln and land in Richmond.[106] The name Goodgroome alias Pennard was also found in parishes across the Thames in Middlesex. An Elizabeth Goodgroome, daughter of Anne

Goodgroome alias Pennard was, for instance, licensed to marry William Hogray of Hanwell, Middlesex in 1639.[107]

Finally, it is possible that a handful of Diggers may have come from the town of Kingston-upon-Thames. The name Nathaniel Yates features several times in Kingston parish and borough records, and it is probable that there was more than one Kingston resident with this name in 1649.[108] One of them, who seems unlikely to have been a Digger, was a prominent baker and member of Kingston corporation.[109] A more plausible candidate is the Nathaniel Yates of Kingston who later become a Quaker.[110] The Digger Urian Worthington or Worlington is easier to identify. He was a Kingston maltster, the son of a husbandman of Thorpe and grandson of a New Windsor yeoman.[111] During the Civil War he became involved with John Fielder's separatist circle, and he was one of those arrested by the Kingston constable and bailiffs in January 1645.[112] The following year he sold for £50 his interest in one acre of meadow ground in Pyrford that had been left to him by his grandfather.[113] Worthington also later became a Quaker, and in 1664 was presented at the quarter sessions for absence from church.[114]

Attempts to identify individual Diggers are, of course, fraught with difficulty. The limitations of Cobham's fragmentary parish records and manorial documents have already been discussed: entries in the parish registers ceased during the Civil War, and only some of the missing information from the 1640s was added retrospectively after 1656. Further problems occurred when the original registers were later disposed of, to be replaced by an inaccurate eighteenth-century transcript.[115] In addition, it is important to acknowledge that many Diggers must have come from further afield, being drawn to St George's Hill by Winstanley's appeal to well-wishers to join the colony. Where signatories to Digger manifestos had common surnames, we cannot be sure – in the absence of additional, supporting evidence – that the bearers of these names in Cobham and the surrounding area were the Diggers of the same name.[116]

Nevertheless, despite these caveats, it would seem that there is sufficient evidence to indicate that perhaps as many as a third of the seventy-four Surrey Diggers whose names we know were local inhabitants, and that of these the greatest number came from Cobham. Moreover, these local Diggers were among the most active supporters of the movement: approximately three quarters of those who signed three or more Digger pamphlets, and a similar proportion of those involved in legal actions relating to the Diggers' activities, appear to have been from Cobham or from parishes in the vicinity.[117] Occasional references in Winstanley's writings also point to the local origins of many of the Diggers. In *An Humble Request*, for instance, Winstanley complained of the destruction of Digger houses by opponents who were heedless of the 'cries of many little Children, and their frighted Mothers, which are Parishioners borne in the Parish'.[118] Elsewhere he referred to Diggers sharing the costs of quartering soldiers while on St George's Hill – another indication that some at least of the Diggers had a settled existence as householders in the local community.[119]

In seeking to explain why these locals were prepared to join Winstanley and Everard in digging upon the commons, we should avoid looking for any single, overriding motive. The Diggers were clearly a disparate group, and Winstanley's message was designed to appeal at various levels. Radical religious enthusiasm, economic hardship brought on by the pressures of war, and long-standing antagonism towards the local gentry, may each have contributed to the appeal of the Digger programme. Winstanley was able to skilfully exploit existing local discontents, and he was adept at drawing on traditional languages of popular protest in ways that helped soften his message and make his views more palatable to those whose support he hoped to attract. The absence of a settled minister in Cobham, following William King's departure in 1644, might also have enabled Winstanley to build up a local following unhindered by the sort of opposition normally encountered by radical proselytisers.

Certain common features may nevertheless be discerned. The Cobham Diggers were not all from among the poorest sections of the population, but most appear to have been on the fringes of local society; all may have been vulnerable to the heavy burdens to which Cobham was exposed during the Civil War. Several of the Diggers were members of, or were related to, families at the centre of parish affairs, but only one, John Coulton, had ever played a major part in Cobham's parish and manorial administration. Coulton himself cannot be classed among the most prosperous of Cobham's 'middle sorts', despite his prominent involvement in local affairs. His copyhold tenement at Oxcombes in Downside was, at around thirty acres, of moderate size, and appears not to have been supplemented by any extensive freehold or leasehold property.[120] While the Coultons enjoyed relative security of tenure on their copyhold estate, with a fixed annual rent of 15s, the size of their holding is unlikely to have been sufficient to insulate them from the heavy local costs of civil war or from the steeply rising prices of the immediate post-war years.[121] Like other families of similar status, they may also have been vulnerable to the longer-term increase in entry fines on the manor of Cobham during the seventeenth century.[122]

Henry Bickerstaffe was a member of a prominent local family, but it was one that had only recently joined the ranks of the gentry. The Digger's paternal grandfather, who died in 1599, was the first in the family to be identified as a gentleman rather than yeoman, and he was only regularly described as such in the last decade of his life.[123] The Bickerstaffes remained on the fringes of the gentry thereafter, and it was no accident that in Surrey heralds' visitations their younger, more successful cousins, the courtier Bickerstaffes of Godstone and Chelsham, were made to appear the senior branch of the family.[124] Careers in the church had attracted earlier generations of Bickerstaffes, and two of the

Digger's paternal uncles were in holy orders.[125] Each of Henry Bickerstaffe's brothers was, like him, involved in trade or the professions. The Digger was one of three surviving sons of Robert Bickerstaffe to enter the cloth trade, while a fourth began serving an apprenticeship to a London merchant taylor before switching to a career as a barber surgeon.[126] Another of Henry's brothers was employed at the time of the digging as steward to the bibliophile and virtuoso Thomas Wendy of Haslingfield in Cambridgeshire, who would later become brother-in-law of Winstanley's kinsman Clement Winstanley of Braunstone.[127] Much of the Bickerstaffe inheritance was to be dissipated in the later 1650s and 1660s as family members fought to secure a share of the ownership of the Bickerstaffe Surrey properties.[128]

Henry Bickerstaffe's social position was always somewhat precarious. Like Winstanley, he was evidently unable to make a success of his business career in London. There is no record of him ever having taken on an apprentice, and the Skinners' Company had no knowledge of his whereabouts when company members were assessed for the 1641 poll tax.[129] He had – again like Winstanley – spent much of the decade before the digging living on a family property to which he apparently had no title, and which he stood little chance of inheriting.[130] Bickerstaffe was forty-two at the start of the digging, and had a sizeable family. Two daughters – Sara and Mary – had been born in London in 1636 and 1637, and a further three children were baptised in Cobham in 1640, 1641 and 1643.[131] It is likely that further children were born after baptismal entries in the Cobham registers ceased during the Civil War, for in May 1654 he had eight children still living.[132] Other local Diggers also had young families. Henry Barton had children baptised in Cobham in October 1640 and September 1643.[133] Daniel Freeland had children baptised in October 1642 and November 1643, and John Hayman had a son baptised in February 1643; John Palmer, Samuel Webb and William Taylor also had young children to feed at the time of the digging.[134]

All the Cobham Diggers apart from Coulton were residents of the parish rather than manorial tenants in 1649, and by no means all were housekeepers. Daniel Freeland may have had a claim to family property in Ockham, but he never gained control of it: in 1657 his son was left £20 by Elizabeth Freeland of Hyde in Wisley, on condition that he did not contest her decision to leave her tenement in Ockham to another relative.[135] John Palmer may have been a lodger or inmate rather than a householder.[136] John Hayman, Anthony Wrenn, Daniel Freeland and Henry Barton were each presented at the assizes in 1650 for the illegal erection of cottages with less than four acres of land; their position in local society was clearly a marginal one, at least at the time of the digging.[137]

It is noteworthy that several Diggers had connections with the brewing and aleselling trades. Urian Worthington was, as we have seen, a maltster, while Henry Bickerstaffe's family owned the George Inn in Cobham; in October 1649, after he had left the digging, he purchased a tenement with malthouses in Kingston.[138] Thomas Ward, who stood surety for Bickerstaffe when he was prosecuted for digging on St George's Hill, may have been the Cobham victualler of that name.[139] Ward was to be presented at the assizes in 1653 for running a disorderly alehouse in Cobham, along with Laurence Johnson, father-in-law of the Digger John Hayman and master of Daniel Freeland's son.[140] Henry Barton's son was also a Cobham innholder.[141] At a time when alehouses were commonly regarded as a source of disorder and as ripe for reformation, these Diggers' links with brewing and alehouse-keeping could be seen as another sign of their marginality.[142] One charge levelled by the Diggers' opponents in 1649 – and indignantly denied by Winstanley – was that the Diggers were drunkards. This accusation may well have stemmed from the occupational background of some of the Diggers.[143]

The presence among the Diggers of sectaries such as Urian Worthington is a reminder of the centrality of radical religion to the Digger movement. Religious enthusiasm reached across social boundaries, enabling those whose interests might otherwise diverge to find common cause.[144] The Digger cause attracted middling sorts as well as poor, and in its social composition it thus showed similarities to early Quakerism, another predominantly rural movement that in the 1650s was to combine religious radicalism with social and political protest.[145] Urian Worthington moved from sectary to Digger to Quaker, and it seems that a number of other Surrey Diggers became Quakers later in life.[146] Members of the Hayman and Barton families of Cobham were also active in Quaker circles after the Restoration. A widow Barton of Cobham – possibly Henry Barton's widow – was buried as a Quaker in 1672, while in 1674 the registers of the Kingston monthly meeting recorded the birth of a Constance Hayman of Cobham.[147] The Quaker Thomas Hayman of Thames Ditton, who married Sarah Stuchbury, a cousin of Winstanley's widow, in 1702, was almost certainly a descendant of the Digger John Hayman.[148] Thomas Starr is also known to have shown sympathy towards local Quakers, for in 1665 he was presented at the Guildford quarter sessions for refusing to assist Cobham's constable in the arrest of Quakers meeting in the parish.[149]

R. T. Vann has drawn attention to the possibility that some Diggers who later became Quakers originated from Buckinghamshire.[150] Digger surnames were certainly found among Buckinghamshire Quakers, and among those involved in anti-tithe agitation in Buckinghamshire and Hertfordshire in the later 1640s. A Giles Child was, for instance, a signatory to *The Husbandmans Plea against Tithes* of 1647, while a Giles Childe senior put his name to the Digger manifesto *A Declaration from the Poor Oppressed*; more than one Amersham Quaker bore this name in the latter half of the seventeenth century.[151] Although we cannot be sure that any Buckinghamshire inhabitants did join the Diggers on St George's Hill, Vann's claim is a valid one, since public support for the Digger movement was to come from radical circles in Buckinghamshire as early as May 1649. In *A Declaration of the Wel-affected in the County of Buckingham-shire*, which appeared on or before 10 May, the aims of the Digger experiment were explicitly endorsed.[152] The Buckinghamshire *Declaration* included resolutions to support the poor in manuring and digging the commons, and to further the work of those who 'joyn in community in Gods way, as those *Acts* 2, and desire to manure, dig, and plant in the waste grounds and Commons'.[153] Significantly, the authors also referred to the felling of woods growing on the waste to provide a stock for those who dug the commons.[154] This practice was soon to be taken up by the Diggers, but they did not advocate it in print before the end of May.[155] It seems certain therefore that those who wrote the Buckinghamshire *Declaration* had had some contact with the St George's Hill Diggers, and were aware of the details of policies being developed by Winstanley and his associates in the early days of the Digger settlement.

The Buckinghamshire *Declaration* originated from the same milieu as the Leveller-influenced *Light Shining in Buckinghamshire* of December 1648. This work, as we have seen, had affinities with Winstanley's *New Law of Righteousnes* and with *The True Levellers Standard Advanced*.[156] It had been re-issued in March, to be followed at the end of the month by *More Light Shining in Buckinghamshire*, a pamphlet that combined criticism of the Officers' *Agreement of the People* with calls for social reform, including a demand for bishops' and crown lands, commons and forests to be turned over to the poor.[157] The Buckinghamshire *Declaration* of May 1649 purported to be 'a Representation of the Middle Sort of men' within the three Chiltern hundreds of Desborough, Burnham and Stoke and part of Aylesbury hundred.[158] The resolutions contained in the *Declaration* were adopted at a meeting in the town of Aylesbury, and those who attended the meeting were described in newsbook reports as Levellers.[159] In view of the support given in all three Buckinghamshire pamphlets to the broader Leveller cause, this description does not seem wholly unwarranted.

The evidence from Buckinghamshire suggests that sympathy for the Diggers' aims was to be found among some provincial groups of Leveller supporters, and it therefore raises important questions about connections between the two movements. The Leveller leaders' robust rejection of social levelling, and their determination to deny future representatives the power to make all things common, remained consistent and must be taken as the definitive Leveller position on community of property.[160] No doubt the frequent restatement of this position was in large part a reflection of the Levellers' defensiveness in the face of attempts by their enemies to portray them as favourers of community. It may also however have been related, as Christopher Hill and Brian Manning both suggested, to their desire to rein in some of their more extreme supporters, for whom the voluntary, apostolic communism described in Acts 2 and Acts 4 might appear to offer an acceptable model of social organisation.[161]

Hill's view that there existed a broad spectrum of Leveller thought and action, which at one extreme was difficult to distinguish from True Levellerism, found echoes in Manning's identification of a revolutionary 'far left' that was characterised by a commitment to egalitarianism and a willingness to take militant action in pursuit of its aims.[162] The *Light Shining* pamphlets, in which the Leveller cause was associated with a Digger-like notion of restoration and with a radical reinterpretation of the Levitical institution of jubilee, could be seen to demonstrate most clearly the existence of just such a convergence of Leveller activism with True Leveller ideas.[163] A degree of caution is of course necessary when dealing with the Buckinghamshire pamphlets, since little is known about who wrote them; and it is impossible to judge how representative they were even of Leveller opinion in that county. Nevertheless, it does appear that Leveller activity in Buckinghamshire was notable for its militancy and radicalism. In High Wycombe, where the mayor and corporation were involved in a series of disputes in the years 1647–50 with those they termed 'Levellers and such as beare with them', radical activism seems to have converged with traditional forms of popular protest on behalf of the poor. Opponents of the corporation were accused of diverting profits from market stalls to the use of the poor, and of instigating 'tumults and ryotts' in which the market toll and substantial quantities of toll corn were seized by the crowd.[164] 'Levellers' were also reported to have broken open High Wycombe's gaol, and, in a suggestive combination of the popular and the radical, to have publicly insulted the mayor as a cuckold while threatening to 'have him brought to an Account for that Money he had cheated the Country of'.[165] It is likely that the detailed criticism of urban corporations contained in the *Light Shining* pamphlets reflected such local experience of urban conflicts.[166]

The parallels between the *Light Shining* pamphlets and Digger writings should not however be taken too far. In tone as well as content, the last two Buckinghamshire pamphlets – *More Light Shining in Buckinghamshire* and the *Declaration of the Wel-Affected in the County of Buckinghamshire* – bore at least as much similarity to the radical, insurrectionary writings associated with the military unrest of the spring and early summer of 1649 as they did to early Digger publications. Parliament and the army grandees were dismissed in *More Light Shining* as betrayers of the radical cause, while soldiers and other 'dear brethren' were urged to 'stand every one in his place, to oppose all Tyranny whatsoever, and by whomsoever, intended against us'.[167] The Buckinghamshire *Declaration* had particular affinity with *Englands Standard Advanced*, the declaration with which William Thompson had launched his military insurrection at Banbury only days before on 6 May.[168] Whereas the Buckinghamshire radicals opted for outright confrontation with parliament and army commanders, Winstanley and his associates would always be careful to engage with the state authorities, and to at least give the impression of seeking to persuade them of the justice of the Diggers' cause.

Nor should we lose sight of the possible influence that more moderate Leveller ideas may have had in generating support for the Digger experiment. Leveller interest in the countryside may have been limited, but rural issues were never quite so peripheral to the movement as has sometimes been suggested. Calls for the throwing open of enclosed commons and fens, and for the abolition of tithes and base tenures, were heard throughout the life of the Leveller movement, and helped ensure that the movement continued to reach beyond its London base for support.[169] Even at the height of political crisis in December 1648, John Lilburne secured the insertion of a reference to the abolition of base tenures into the second Agreement of the People.[170] During the course of 1649, Derbyshire miners were to gain Leveller support in their conflict with the Earl of Rutland, while in 1650 Lilburne and John Wildman were to take up the cause of the fenland inhabitants of Epworth in Lincolnshire.[171] The *Moderate* newspaper, as Roger Howell and David Brewster have pointed out, was apparently already trying to present the Levellers as a movement with 'an agrarian, nationwide programme'.[172] Despite the Leveller leaders' vocal rejection of any association between their movement and support for community of property, their willingness to campaign against rural grievances must have given some comfort and inspiration to rural protestors whose ambitions went further than theirs. It may therefore have served, however unintentionally, to blur the boundaries between the Leveller movement and other, more radical groups in the countryside.

ST GEORGE'S HILL

In choosing St George's Hill as the site of their first colony, the Diggers confirmed the profoundly millenarian nature of their programme. As those scholars who have emphasised the symbolic, mystical aspects of the Diggers' activities have argued, the choice of St George's Hill provided firm evidence of the Diggers' reliance on divine blessing for the success of their undertaking. The restoration of all things would be actual as well as metaphorical, and the regeneration of man would go hand in hand with the return to fruitfulness of the barren earth.[173] St George's Hill was, as Winstanley had readily acknowledged, an unproductive spot; and other observers agreed.[174] Parliament's surveyors described Sir John Trevor's warren, which lay on the western flank of St George's Hill, and which they surveyed in April 1650, as 'in itselfe extreame barren being nothing but a bare heath & sandy ground'; Walton's commons were also regularly described as 'hethy & sandy groundes'.[175] Walter Blith, when discussing the Diggers' activities in his *The English Improver*

Improved of 1652, declared bluntly that 'if there be not thousands of places more capable of Improvement than theirs, and that by many easier waies, and to far greater advantages, I will lay downe the Bucklers'.[176] While human agency may have been important for advancing the Diggers' cause, that cause could not prosper in such a setting without the divine intervention of which the Diggers felt assured.[177]

There were however some quite sensible and pragmatic reasons for choosing this site. St George's Hill was situated on the southern fringe of Walton's extensive commons, which contemporaries estimated variously at 2,000 acres and between ten and fourteen miles in compass.[178] Henry Sanders had indicated that the Diggers were working on 'that side the Hill next to Campe Close', which suggests that their settlement was in or close to the Iron Age stronghold that was situated at the top of the hill and linked by road to Pains Hill and Street Cobham.[179] For the bulk of Walton's inhabitants, this part of the hill was one of the remotest spots in their parish, and it was certainly more accessible for the inhabitants of Church Cobham and Street Cobham than it was for those who lived in the riverside settlement of Walton-on-Thames. Of all the sites that the Diggers could have chosen for their activities, this was probably the one least likely to cause disruption for local tenants.

Also significant was the fact that Walton heath, of which St George's Hill formed a part, had for many years been subject to a lesser degree of manorial control than Cobham's commons. In the latter years of the sixteenth century, Walton heath was effectively unstinted, for inhabitants as well as manorial tenants; and cottagers had been able to build their houses on the common without hindrance. The 'dyvers cottages newly erected' were said by local residents to 'have had comon without any rate or stynt' on Walton heath, 'yf they have any thing to putt uppon yt'.[180] Inhabitants of other parishes, including Cobham, had also been able to graze cattle – both cattle reared locally and cattle bought at fairs – on the heath.[181] Steps were taken in succeeding years to regulate Walton's commons, but although stints were in place by the middle years of the eighteenth century, there was no mention of any in the parliamentary surveys of March 1650.[182] Manorial tenants also claimed unrestricted rights in 1650 to dig turf, sand, gravel and loam, and to cut heath or ferns, 'in any place' on the commons.[183] This laxity must in part have been due to a lack of pressure on resources in a parish containing large reserves of waste grounds.[184] It was also due to the fact that the heath was shared between two quite distinct manors, those of Walton and Walton Leigh, and had never been formally divided; the heath also extended into neighbouring parishes, some of whose inhabitants enjoyed common of pasture.[185] Jurors at the 1603 Walton court of survey were unable to state the extent of their commons, since they 'lyeth in severall lordships, which are enter commoners the on[e] with the other'; the parliamentary surveyors of Walton Leigh confirmed in 1650 that 'the wastes and commons' in the parish of Walton-on-Thames were 'never severed or divided in soe much that wee cannot precisely sett downe or bound forth what partes or porcons' belonged to each manor.[186] The lack of precise boundaries inevitably created difficulties for those tenants who wished to see tighter control over access to the manorial waste.[187]

St George's Hill was also crown land, and therefore of uncertain status in the months following the abolition of the monarchy. The Diggers emphasised the point when Fairfax visited their colony towards the end of May, reminding him that the hill was crown as well as common land, and 'the King that possest them by the Norman Conquest being dead, they were returned againe to the Common people of England' to improve them.[188] Francis Drake, the farmer of the manor of Walton, had until recently been a figure of some influence in Surrey, having served as a member of the Long Parliament, county committee man and justice of the peace. By April 1649, however, his authority in the county was much reduced. As a prominent supporter of the treaty of Newport, he had been imprisoned at Pride's Purge, and he was removed from the Surrey bench when it was remodelled in February 1649; his last recorded involvement with the work of Surrey's county committee was on 19 October 1648.[189] In addition, Drake was in dispute in 1649 with his Walton neighbours over abatements he was claiming on monthly assessment contributions stretching back to 1645, and his accounts were to remain uncleared the following year.[190] His fee farm rent on the manor of Walton was also seriously in arrears at this time.[191] Drake's financial problems had been made worse by civil war, which had seen the plunder of his house by the king's forces in 1642, and the deliberate destruction of a 'new built farme of his' by parliamentarian soldiers in 1643.[192] He was also involved in a number of dubious financial ventures in the 1640s and 1650s, which included large-scale borrowing – from, among others, Winstanley's relative James Winstanley of Gray's Inn – the mortgaging of properties to several different people at the same time, attempts to sell heavily-mortgaged land as unencumbered property, and speculation in offices.[193] At the time of the digging, his estate at Walton was apparently in the hands of trustees, namely his kinsmen Sir Ralph Verney, Thomas Viscount Wenman and Richard Winwood.[194] Although Drake would later become involved in the local campaign against the Diggers, he was no longer the powerful enemy that he would have been only a short time before.

Francis Drake was not the only local JP to be removed from office in 1649. Also absent from the Surrey bench was Sir Anthony Vincent of Stoke d'Abernon, who, despite his civil war neutrality, had remained active as a JP as recently as 1648.[195] Vincent had lost influence in the county as a result of his son's involvement in the Earl of Holland's rising, and his departure from the bench removed one of the few remaining mid-Surrey JPs who had been a leading participant in local administration before the Civil War. A new appointee in 1649 was Sir George Ayscue, lessee of Ham Court in Chertsey and Cobham, but he was away on active service for most of the year as Admiral of the Irish Seas.[196] Benjamin Weston, son of Lord Treasurer Portland and lessee of Walton Leigh manor was still a JP in 1649, but no longer seems to have played a particularly active part in local government; and the same was true of the former mid-Surrey county committee men Sir John Dingley and Sir Matthew Brend.[197] Few members of mid-Surrey's wartime administration continued in office after the end of 1648, and it is evident that in the early months of 1649 something of a power vacuum existed in this part of the county. There could have been no better time for the Diggers to start work on the remote summit of St George's Hill.

Although the soils of St George's Hill were notoriously poor and unyielding, the Diggers' attempts to plant crops there were not wholly unrealistic. Techniques for improving difficult soils were well established on the Surrey heaths and downlands by 1649, and are likely to have been familiar to those Diggers who had who had experience of farming on Cobham's mixed soils. John Evelyn in 1676 explained to John Aubrey how 'in these forty Years', the 'barren Hills' near Wotton had been 'exceedingly improv'd by Devonshiring, as we call it, that is, by paring off, drying, burning, and spreading the Swarth'.[198] Mid-seventeenth-century estate leases at Portnall Park in Egham required tenants to denshire the heaths, while the cutting of heath for lime-burning was taking place on the waste of the manor of Witley by the second decade of the century at the latest.[199] One 1583 lease of an estate of pasture-land in Cobham required the lessee to 'digg and stubble, gruble and ridd, cutt downe and plucke upp' the thorns, hollies and other unwanted growths on the estate and to 'reduce the same to tillage, meadowe or other commodities'.[200] On the Bickerstaffes' Pains Hill estate on the southern fringes of St George's Hill, fields that had chiefly been used for grazing were enclosed and successfully converted to arable use during the first half of the seventeenth century.[201] Oats, rye, barley, tares and wheat had been grown at Ashley Farm to the north of St George's Hill near Oatlands Park, before the land there was emparked to serve Lady Jane Berkeley's new Ashley House.[202] One of the first acts of the Diggers was to burn at least forty rood – or ten acres – of heath on the hill. Presumably this was principally to clear the land for the planting of crops, but the large acreage involved may suggest that a form of denshiring was being practised.[203]

The Diggers appear from the start to have to have attempted to combine spade husbandry and conventional ploughing. One crop sown by the Diggers in April was barley, which was widely grown in the area around Cobham and Walton. Since some barley was said to have come up already when Fairfax visited St George's Hill at the end of May, this may have been of an early-ripening variety, of the sort most suitable when the weather was poor and when it was prudent – as in the Diggers' case – to harvest the crops as quickly as possible.[204]

In sowing the ground with parsnips, carrots and beans, the Diggers were again drawing on local practice. Spade husbandry was becoming increasingly popular in Surrey in the mid-seventeenth century, and the Diggers were not alone in attempting to practise this on marginal land. As Thomas Fuller remarked in 1662, numerous Surrey inhabitants had, in gardening for profit, 'made their rent, lived comfortably, and set many people on work'.[205] The almanacs produced by John Coulton the younger of Cobham were full of advice about planting and growing onions, leeks, parsnips, carrots, artichokes, beans and garden herbs, as well as grain crops.[206] Gardening took place on the Surrey heaths as well as on more fertile alluvial soils, with carrots being grown on heathland close to St George's Hill at Weybridge.[207] Tithes were levied on garden produce and root vegetables in a number of Surrey parishes by the middle years of the seventeenth century, suggesting that production for profit was already widespread; at Chobham, for instance, a few miles to the west of where the Diggers were operating, the vicar claimed tithes on 'what is planted with the spade by digginge and delveinge within the said parish'.[208]

One attraction of spade husbandry was the high yields that could be achieved on relatively small acreages.[209] Fuller, commenting on Surrey gardening, pointed to the 'incredible profit by digging of ground'; "Tis incredible how many poor people in London live thereon, so that in some seasons gardens feed more people than the field'.[210] Sir Richard Weston of Sutton Place in Woking may have had local Surrey practices in mind, as well as his own observations on agricultural innovations in the Low Countries, when he made similar comments at the end of the 1640s.[211] Root crops were, as Malcolm Thick has shown, increasingly recognised as one of the best sources of food for the poor, particularly in times of dearth.[212] Richard Gardiner had, as early as 1599, publicised his success in feeding Shrewsbury's poor on carrots and cabbages during a period of scarcity, and recommended the like for other urban populations.[213] One of the first to advocate the use of parsnips, carrots and turnips as food for the poor was the agricultural writer Sir Hugh Plat, whose *Sundrie New and Artificiall Remedies against Famine* appeared in 1596 – and whose grandson, John Platt, was lord of the manor of Cobham in 1649.[214]

It would clearly be wrong to see the Diggers as having no practical, achievable ends in mind when they set to work on St George's Hill. Arguments from necessity had been advanced in their first manifesto, and were to be expressed with even greater force in subsequent publications.[215] Early reports of the Diggers' activities showed that they spoke of extending their activities to Newmarket, Hounslow and Hampstead heaths, which were some of the most extensive open spaces within reach of London.[216] The Diggers' reported intentions suggest that from the beginning they had plans to create large, self-supporting agricultural colonies around the capital; they were certainly not content to restrict their ambitions to digging and ploughing upon the difficult soils of St George's Hill.[217] The practical side of the Digger project was most evident in the proposals made in the second Digger manifesto, *A Declaration from the Poor Oppressed People of England*, which appeared at the end of May. *A Declaration*, like *The True Levellers Standard Advanced* before it, was unmistakably the work of Winstanley, while incorporating arguments that no doubt reflected the views of fellow Diggers. It was in this work, which contained the largest number of signatories of any Digger pamphlet, that plans to raise a stock to finance the project were first outlined.[218] The Diggers had, they announced, resolved to 'cut and fell, and make the best advantage we can' of the woods and trees growing upon the commons; woodmongers were to be encouraged to buy only from 'such as may be appointed by us to sell it', and not from those landowners who wrongly claimed ownership. Those woodmongers who ignored this plea were liable to have their carts stopped and the wood converted 'to our own use, as need requires'. Accounts of how the stock was used – 'either in victualls, corn, ploughs, or other materialls necessary' – would be made known 'publikly in Print or writing to all'.[219]

In justifying their proposal to fell and sell wood, the Diggers pointed to their necessitous condition, 'seeing and finding our selves poor, wanting Food to feed upon, while we labor the Earth, to cast in Seed, and to wait tell the first Crop comes up; and wanting Ploughs, Carts, Corn, and such materials to plant the Commons withal'.[220] The Diggers must have been well aware that a successful sale of wood might raise substantial sums of money, as it had for cash-strapped landowners who had sold wood to raise funds in the aftermath of civil war. For it is evident that they were already thinking far beyond the success of the initial St George's Hill venture, and were aiming to 'Dig and Plough up the Commons, and waste Lands through England'; the stock they raised would be used for both the St George's Hill Diggers and 'our poor Brethren, through the Land of England, to plant the Commons withal; and to provide us bread to eat, till the Fruit of our labors in the Earth bring forth increase'.[221] It would be of benefit not only for the present generation, but also for 'our children after us';

> for we shall endeavour by our righteous acting not to leave the earth any longer intangled unto our children, by self-seeking proprietors; But to leave it a free store-house, and common treasury to all, without respect of persons.[222]

What seems to have been envisaged by those who subscribed to *A Declaration from the Poor Oppressed* was the creation of a national movement of Digger communities, which they hoped would have sufficient staying power to continue from one generation to the next. Support for such an ambitious project was, however, bound to highlight tensions in Digger thought between the belief in an imminent and thoroughgoing transformation of the *whole* of society, and advocacy of the creation of a system of propertyless and moneyless communities which would exist alongside, but independently of, the existing legal and property system.[223] Winstanley could comfortably play down these tensions for so long as he believed that the spirit would eventually induce all to throw in their lot with the Diggers; and in *A Declaration from the Poor Oppressed* he reiterated his belief that landlords would come to 'cast up your Lands and Goods, which were got, and still is kept in your hands by murder, and theft'.[224] In later pamphlets, however, such tensions would not so easily be resolved, as increasing emphasis was – of necessity – placed on justifying the occupation of the commons and on defending the Diggers' right to remain there without interruption. The change in emphasis was due above all to the realisation that the transformation of society would take much longer than Winstanley had originally hoped. Although Digger numbers had increased in the first few weeks of their activities, the St George's Hill colony remained perilously small. Forty-five men may have put their names to *A Declaration from the Poor Oppressed*, but when Fairfax stopped off at the hill on 26 May, he found only nine men and three women at work.[225] The planned mass withdrawal of wage labour, which was so crucial to the success of Winstanley's initial scheme, had not taken place, and from the start Winstanley and his small band of associates had been subjected to violent local opposition. Although they had been careful to pick a remote spot in a parish with extensive commons and wastes, the Diggers quickly found that some Walton inhabitants would not tolerate their presence on St George's Hill under any circumstances. It was this intense local opposition that led to their eventual departure from the hill; it also forced them to reassess their strategy and to try to develop new arguments to advance their cause and persuade others to join them.

NOTES

1 Firth, *Clarke Papers*, 2, pp. 210–11.

2 Above, p. 39.

3 Firth, *Clarke Papers*, 2, p. 210.

4 TNA, SP25/62/63.

5 *CSPD 1648–49*, p. 180.

6 TNA, SP23/252/20; Jenkinson and Powell, *Surrey Quarter Sessions Records 1659–1661*, pp. 8–9.

7 On the political unrest see Gardiner, *Commonwealth and Protectorate*, 1, pp. 31–6, 44–9; Worden, *Rump Parliament*, pp. 188–90.

8 TNA, SP25/94, p. 93; Firth, *Clarke Papers*, 2, pp. 209–10.

9 TNA, SP25/94, p. 94.

10 Firth, *Clarke Papers*, 2, pp. 210–11.

11 TNA, SP25/94, p. 94.

12 Firth, *Clarke Papers*, 2, p. 210.

13 Above p. 77.

14 Firth, *Clarke Papers*, 2, p. 210.

15 *Ibid.*, 2, p. 211.

16 *A Perfect Diurnall of Some Passages in Parliament* (16–23 April), p. 2448; *A Modest Narrative of Intelligence*, 3 (14–21 April); *The Moderate*, 41 (17–24 April 1649); *The Declaration and Standard of the Levellers of England* (1649).

17 For a valuable summary of responses to the Diggers, see Petegorsky, *Left-Wing Democracy*, pp. 162–6.

18 *Mercurius Pragmaticus* (17–24 April 1649).

19 *The Kingdomes Faithfull and Impartial Scout* (20–27 April); *The Moderate Intelligencer*, 214 (19–26 April 1649).

20 *A Perfect Summary of an Exact Diarie* (16–23 April 1649).

21 *Perfect Occurences of Every Daies Journall in Parliament*, 120 (13–20 April), p. 452; *A Perfect Summary of an Exact Diarie* (16–23 April); *Declaration and Standard of the Levellers of England*; *Mercurius Pragmaticus* (17–24 April 1649). Cf. Firth, *Clarke Papers*, 2, p. 211, for Henry Sanders's assumption that the Diggers planned to pull down park pales.

22 BL, Harl. MS 787, fol. 9v; *The Moderate*, 41 (17–24 April); *The Kingdomes Faithfull and Impartiall Scout* (20–27 April 1649). Winstanley had begun referring to his companions as Diggers by early June: Sabine, *Works*, pp. 284, 295.

23 *Mercurius Pragmaticus (for King Charles II)* (17–24 April 1649).

24 *The Discoverer* (1649), pp. 9–14. Cf. Petegorsky, *Left-Wing Democracy*, pp. 170–1.

25 Haller and Davies, *Leveller Tracts*, p. 449; Manning, *English People*, pp. 398–9; above pp. 107–8. *A Manifestation* was dated 14 April 1649.

26 Sabine, *Works*, p. 245.

27 Marchamont Nedham, *The Case of the Commonwealth of England, Stated*, ed. Philip A. Knachel (Charlottesville, 1969), ch. 4, esp. p. 109.

28 Sabine, *Works*, p. 245.

29 Firth, *Clarke Papers*, 2, pp. 211–12.

30 *A Perfect Diurnall of Some Passages in Parliament* (16–23 April), p. 2450; *A Perfect Summary of an Exact Diarie* (16–23 April); *Perfect Occurences of Every Daies Journall in Parliament*, 120 (13–20 April 1649), p. 452.

31 Firth, *Clarke Papers*, 2, p. 212. Cf. *Mercurius Pragmaticus*, 17–24 April 1649.

32 *A Perfect Diurnall of Some Passages in Parliament* (16–23 April 1649), p. 2448.

33 The introductory letter of 20 April was signed by a John Taylor, whose identity is unclear. He was certainly not, as has sometimes been assumed, John Taylor the Water Poet.

34 Sabine, *Works*, pp. 247, 251–2, 259.

35 *Ibid.*, pp. 266, 277, 413–14.

36 *Ibid.*, p. 253. Cf. *ibid.*, pp. 252, 257–8, 260, 260–1, 263.

37 *Ibid.*, p. 260. Cf. Hayes, *Winstanley*, p. 148.

38 Sabine, *Works*, pp. 261–2.

39 *Ibid.*, p. 260.

40 *Ibid.*, pp. 252, 255. Cf. *ibid.*, pp. 253, 254, 263, 265.

41 *Ibid.*, pp. 252–3, 255, 258–9, 265.

42 *Ibid.*, pp. 257–8.

43 *Ibid.*, pp. 252, 255.

44 *Ibid.*, p. 256.

45 *Ibid.*, p. 265.

46 *Ibid.*, pp. 257, 260.

47 *Ibid.*, pp. 262, 263.

48 *Ibid.*, p. 266. Cf. *ibid.*, pp. 256–7.

49 *Ibid.*, p. 264.

50 *Ibid.*, p. 265.

51 *Ibid.*, pp. 254, 256, 258, 259, 262, 265. Cf. Wood, ' "Poore men woll speke one daye" ', pp. 67–98. For the centrality of binary opposition to the early modern world view, see Stuart Clark, 'Inversion, misrule and the meaning of witchcraft', *P&P*, 87 (1980).

52 Sabine, *Works*, pp. 258, 260, 262.

53 *Ibid.*, pp. 261–2. On the central importance of the withdrawal of labour to the Digger programme, see esp. Davis, *Utopia and the Ideal Society*, p. 187.

54 Sabine, *Works*, pp. 194–5.

55 *Ibid.*, p. 261.

56 *Ibid.*, p. 266. The absence of female signatories may explain the discrepancy between this figure and the figure of 20 to 30 Diggers given by Henry Sanders earlier in April.

57 *Ibid.*, p. 277.

58 The following is based on the identification of Diggers given in Gurney, 'Surrey and the English Revolution', pp. 217–47, 325–33, and John Gurney, 'Gerrard Winstanley and the Digger movement in Walton and Cobham', *HJ*, 37 (1994), pp. 775–802. For an important, though rather different exercise in identifying local Diggers, see David Mulder, *The Alchemy of Revolution: Gerrard Winstanley's Occultism and Seventeenth-Century English Communism* (New York, 1990), pp. 304–31.

59 Firth, *Clarke Papers*, 2, p. 210.

60 SHC, COB/1/1; LMA, DW/PA/7/12, fol. 495.

61 SHC, K44/1/9; 4398/1/11; COB/5/1. It is not known whether his mother was Edm. Starr's wife Dorothy Rogers, whom he married in 1611, or his wife Mary who survived him. Edm. Starr died in May 1638; Mary was apparently still alive in 1647: 44/1/9.

62 TNA, E179/188/481, 504; E179/257/30.

63 SHC, COB/1/1.

64 SHC, 4398/1/11.

65 SHC, COB/6/17–19; K44/1/7–9; 2610/11/8/3, 2610/29/3, fol. 19v; 4398/1/1, 3–6, 8–11; TNA, SC2/204/43; SC12/22/34; SP28/35, fol. 359; SP28/179 (unfol.), accts of Hen. Hastings and John Redfern; Cobham parish accts; SP28/194 , fol. 31; Daly, *Kingston Register of Apprentices*, 489.

66 SHC, COB/1/1; LMA, DW/PA/7/13, fol. 95; W. H. Challen (ed.), *Carshalton Parish Register, Marriages: 1538–1837* (Croydon, 1928), entry for 14 August 1597; Bannerman,

Visitations of Surrey 1530, 1572 and 1623, pp. 149–50; *VCH Surrey*, 4, p. 257; *Some Account of the Family of Lambert* (privately printed, 1886), p. 15. For Bickerstaffe see also John Gurney, 'Bickerstaffe, Henry', *ODNB*.

67 Society of Genealogists, Mf. 492; GL, Skinners' Co. register of apprenticeships and freedoms 1601–1694 (formerly at Skinners' Hall), fols 48, 83, 87, 117, 124, 145v, 154, 155; TNA, PROB11/248, fols 393v–95.

68 CLRO, CF1/25/131v; GL, Skinners' Co. Register 1601–94, fol. 108v; Ms 10, 232.

69 SHC, COB/1/1. His son Edw. was baptised in Cobham on 1 January 1640.

70 TNA, E317/Surrey/44; LMA, DW/PA/7/13, fol. 95; TNA, C5/592/2; C10/468/162; E115/51/44; above p. 4.

71 Above, p. 36.

72 For his early involvement in the digging, see TNA, ASSI 35/91/4.

73 SHC, K44/1/9; 4398/1/8. He is probably the Hen. Burton elected as constable of Street Cobham in April 1642: 4398/1/9.

74 SHC, COB/5/1; K176/10/2; 181/17/5.

75 SHC, K44/1/9.

76 SHC, COB/1/1; above p. 50. Cf. TNA, ASSI35/94/12.

77 SHC, COB/5/1.

78 TNA, PROB11/298, fol. 300; SHC, 835/37. Nath. Coulton, John Coulton's nephew, was overseer of Stint's will.

79 LMA, DW/PC/5/1667/26; above, pp. 50–1.

80 SHC, 4398/1/11; COB/5/1.

81 TNA, E179/188/481, 504; E179/257/30; E179/258/4; SHC, COB/1/1. His widow survived until 1698.

82 SHC, K44/1/9; 4398/1/8.

83 LMA, DW/PA/7/8, fols 117, 350; 13, fols 126, 396; TNA, PROB11/230, fol. 206v; SHC, G165/49/1–4; Meekings, *Surrey Feet of Fines 1509–1558*, p. 40.

84 SHC, COB/1/1; COB/5/1; TNA, E179/188/481; PROB 11/269, fol. 219.

85 SHC, K44/1/9. Webb was also presented in 1646: 4398/1/10. Taylor was chosen ale taster for Street Cobham in 1660: 4398/1/11.

86 SHC, K44/1/9; 4398/1/9; above, pp. 50, 51.

87 Walker, 'Manorial history', p. 76. Cf. David C. Taylor, 'Old Mistral, Cobham: a 16th century warrener's house identified' *SAC*, 79 (1989), pp. 117–24.

88 SHC, K176/10/2; 4398/1/11; TNA, E179/346. Cf. E179/258/4. He was waywarden 1674–75: SHC, COB/5/1.

89 Daly, *Kingston Register of Apprentices*, p. 36. A John Palmer, illegitimate son of Julian Palmer, was baptised in Cobham on 3 November 1611: SHC, COB/1/1.

90 SHC, COB/5/1. John Palmer was buried 5 February 1640: SHC, COB/1/1.

91 SHC, COB/1/1.

92 TNA, E179/188/481.

93 TNA, E179/188/481; E179/257/30; SHC, COB/1/1; LMA, DW/PC/5/1665/25, 26.

94 SHC, 181/17/5, p. 43.

95   TNA, E179/188/481; E179/258/4; E179/346.

96   SHC, COB/1/1; COB/5/1.

97   TNA, E179/188/481; E179/346; W. Bruce Bannerman (ed.), *The Parish Registers of Stoke d'Abernon* (London, 1911), pp. 4, 6, 7.

98   SHC, 2381/1/1, pp. 2, 3, 4.

99   John Rylands University Library of Manchester (hereafter JRULM), Nicholas MS 5.

100 TNA, REQ2/157/503 .

101 Jenkinson and Powell, *Surrey Quarter Sessions Records 1659–61*, p. 129; Meekings, *Hearth Tax*.

102 See, for instance, Christopher Hill, *Liberty Against the Law: Some Seventeenth-Century Controversies* (Harmondsworth, 1996), p. 277. The authorship of this tract is discussed in J. G. A. Pocock, 'James Harrington and the Good Old Cause', *JBS*, 10 (1970), pp. 35–6; J. G. A. Pocock (ed.), *The Political Works of James Harrington* (Cambridge, 1977), p. 12. For the fifth monarchist see B. S. Capp, *The Fifth-Monarchy Men* (London, 1972), pp. 250, 288. A Rich. Goodgroom debated with the Quaker Edw. Burrough in West Drayton in 1658: Edward Burrough, *Something of Truth Made Manifest* (1658), pp. 1, 21; W. F., *The Quakers Rounds* (1658), *passim*. In 1659 a Rich. Goodgroome was appointed chaplain in Edm. Ludlow's foot regiment, and another nominated as cornet of a troop in Col. John Okey's regiment of horse: *CJ*, 7, pp. 668, 678, 697.

103 Pocock, *Harrington*, p. 12.

104 John Cloake, *Cottages and Common Fields of Richmond and Kew* (Chichester, 2001), pp. 56, 63, 138, 179, 184, 375.

105 TNA, LR2/297, fol. 190.

106 TNA, SC2/205/3; SHC, 2353/51/16/35, 37. A Rich. Pennard was buried in Richmond in August 1653: J. Challenor C. Smith (ed.), *The Parish Registers of Richmond, Surrey* (London, Surrey Parish Register Society, 1903), p. 209.

107 GL, 10,091/20, fol. 28.

108 TNA, SP28/179 (unfol.), Kingston assessment for 2nd moiety of the £400,000 tax, c. 1641; LMA, DW/PA/7/11, fol. 448; DW/PA/5/1664/92; KMHS, Kingston parish register transcripts; Daly, *Kingston Apprentices*, no. 571.

109 KMHS, KB12/1/1; KE1/1/14, p. 327. He was fined for absence from the meeting to elect officers in September 1650.

110 R. T. Vann, 'Diggers and quakers – a further note', *Journal of the Friends' Historical Society*, 50 (1962), p. 66.

111 LMA, DW/PA/7/9, fol. 265v; DW/PA/7/10, fol. 94.

112 Fielder, *Humble Petition and Appeal*, pp. 2–3.

113 SHC, 181/10/6; LMA, DW/PA/7/9, fol. 265v.

114 Powell and Jenkinson, *Surrey Quarter Sessions Records 1663–1666*, p. 176; Joseph Besse, *A Collection of the Sufferings of the People called Quakers* (London, 1753), vol. I, p. 699; Vann, 'Diggers and quakers', p. 66.

115 For problems with the surviving records, above, p. 10.

116 Cf. Vann, 'Diggers and quakers', p. 65.

117 TNA, ASSI35/91/4, 10; SP18/42/144; KMHS, KE1/1/14; Sabine, *Works*, pp. 17, 266, 277, 413–14, 440; Firth, *Clarke Papers*, 2, p. 217.

118 Sabine, *Works*, p. 434; Manning, *1649*, pp. 123–4.

119 Sabine, *Works*, p. 284.

120 SHC, 4398/1/11. The Coulton holding was estimated at 2 virgates in 1585, 25 acres in 1598, and *c.* 40 acres in 1694: K44/1/6; 181/17/5, pp. 102, 105; 2610/29/3, fols 19v–20.

121 TNA, SC12/22/34; SHC, 2610/29/3, fol. 20; 4398/1/11.

122 The entry fine for the Coultons' copyhold estate in 1695 was £45.

123 TNA, E41/117; Paget, *Whitgift Muniments*, pp. 127, 128–9; Paget, 'Manor of Croydon minute book', pp. 7, 12–13, 17–18, 20, 22, 24, 26–7, 29, 34, 38–9, 41, 45, 46–7.

124 Bannerman, *Visitations of Surrey 1530, 1572 and 1623*, p. 106.

125 Venn and Venn, *Alumni Cantabrigienses*, I, p. 148; G. F. Russell Barker and Alan H. Stenning (eds), *The Record of Old Westminsters* (London, 1928), p. 86; Walter Sterry (ed.), *The Eton College Register 1441–1698* (Eton, 1943), p. 34. His aunt was married to Michael Murgatroid, Archbishop Whitgift's secretary: F. A. Crisp, 'Surrey wills', *SAC*, 13 (1897), p. 178.

126 TNA, E317/Surrey/44, p. 9; GL, Skinners' Co. Register 1601–94, fols 48, 83; MF 317/11, p. 88; Ms 5255/1; Ms 5265/1, fol. 91; LMA, DW/PA/7/15 (Bickerstaffe, Wm); P. Hart (ed.), *Merchant Taylors' School Register*, I (London, 1936), *sub.* Edw., John and Rob. Bickerstaffe; T. C. Dale, *The Members of the City Companies in 1641*, (London, 1934), 1, fol. 87.

127 TNA, E317/Surrey/44, p. 9; LLRRO, DE728, 577, 579; G. E. Davis, *A History of Haslingfield* ([Haslingfield], 1968), p. 52. For Wendy, see also TNA, PROB11/346; PROB11/283, fols 74v–75; Somerset Archive and Record Service, DD/L 2/154/3; *VCH Cambridgeshire*, 5, p. 236; Henning, *House of Commons 1660–1690*, 3, pp. 603–4.

128 TNA, C2/CHASI/B170/46; C5/592/2; C6/164/16; C9/243/14; C10/468/162; C33/211, fols 40v, 128, 550, 563.

129 TNA, E179/251/22, fol. 222v; Dale, *Members of the City Companies in 1641* p. 18. (I am grateful to Robert Dalton for this reference.)

130 TNA, E317/Surrey/44, p. 9; PROB11/248, fols 393v–95; C9/243/14; C10/468/162. Anth. Bickerstaffe's son Jas stood to inherit these properties; Henry's male children were the next heirs.

131 GL, Ms 10,232, fols 10v, 11; SHC, COB/1/1. His wife's name is not known.

132 TNA, PROB11/248, fols 393v–95.

133 SHC, COB/1/1.

134 SHC, COB/1/1. Palmer had a daughter baptised in November 1641, and Webb, a son baptised in November 1642.

135 TNA, PROB11/269, fol. 219.

136 SHC, 2610/11/8/33, pp. 36–7.

137 See below, p. 193.

138 SHC, K145/19–20.

139 KMHS, KE1/1/14.

140 TNA, ASSI 35/94/8, 12.

141 SHC, 181/17/5, p. 72.

142 Wrightson and Levine, *Poverty and Piety*, pp. 134–9; Underdown, *Fire from Heaven*, pp. 72–5, 79–80.

143 Firth, *Clarke Papers*, 2, p. 217.

144 The general trend in early modern England was for the gradual withdrawal from involvement in popular protest of middling sorts and wealthier peasants, for which see Morrill and Walter, 'Order and disorder', pp. 151–4; Brian Manning, 'The peasantry and the English Revolution', *Journal of Peasant Studies*, 2 (1975), pp. 154–5.

145 Barry Reay, *The Quakers and the English Revolution* (London, 1985), pp. 9–11; Barry Reay, 'Quaker opposition to tithes 1652–1660', *P&P*, 86 (1980), pp. 99–107, 116; Barry Reay, 'The social origins of early Quakerism', *Journal of Interdisciplinary History*, 11 (1980), pp. 55–72.

146 Vann, 'Diggers and quakers', *passim*.

147 TNA, RG6/956, p. 7; RG6/1240, p. 3.

148 TNA, RG6/1240, p. 3; PROB11/505, fols 260–61v; LMA, DW/PA/5/1674/15.

149 Powell and Jenkinson, *Surrey Quarter Sessions Records 1663–66*, pp. 240–1. Among those arrested was Thos Barton of Cobham.

150 Vann, 'Diggers and quakers', pp. 50, 67.

151 William Urwick, *Nonconformity in Herts* (London, 1884), pp. 141, 832–33; *The Husbandmans Plea Against Tithes* (1647), p. 107; Besse, *Sufferings*, I, p. 77; Jonathan Scott, *Algernon Sidney and the Restoration Crisis, 1677–1683* (Cambridge, 1991), pp. 156, 175–8.

152 Sabine, *Works*, pp. 643–7. Thomason obtained a copy on 10 May; the pamphlet was also summarised in *The Kingdomes Faithfull Scout* of 4–11 May 1649.

153 Sabine, *Works*, pp. 646–47; Petegorsky, *Left-Wing Democracy*, p. 168; Lutaud, *Winstanley*, pp. 194–6.

154 Sabine, *Works*, p. 647.

155 Below, p. 142.

156 Above, pp. 109–10, 125.

157 Sabine, *Works*, pp. 627–39.

158 *Ibid.*, p. 607.

159 *The Kingdomes Faithfull and Impartiall Scout* (4–11 May 1649); Sabine, *Works*, p. 641.

160 Above, pp. 107–8, 123.

161 Hill, *World Turned Upside Down*, p. 95. Cf. Manning, *Far Left*, p. 52.

162 Hill, *World Turned Upside Down*, pp. 91–9; Manning, *Far Left*, pp. 1, 33, 36, 78. Cf. Aylmer, *Levellers*, pp. 48–9. For an important discussion of possible Leveller-Digger connections in Bucks, see Joan Thirsk, *The Rural Economy of England: Collected Essays* (London, 1984), vii–ix.

163 Sabine, *Works*, pp. 614, 616.

164 TNA, SP24/39, Chipping Wycombe v. Bradshaw; G. Eland (ed.), *Papers from an Iron Chest at Doddershall, Bucks* (Aylesbury, 1937), pp. 83–92.

165 *The Man in the Moon*, 21 (5–12 September), pp. 177–8; *Prince Charls Proclaimed King* ([September] 1649), p. 4.

166 Sabine, *Works*, pp. 619–20, 644–6.

167 *Ibid.*, p. 639. Cf. *ibid.*, pp. 637, 644–6; Manning, *1649*, pp. 198–9.

168 William Thompson, *Englands Standard Advanced* (1649).

169 Brailsford, *Levellers*, pp. 431–52; Manning, *English People*, pp. 393–9.

170 Brailsford, *Levellers*, p. 449.

171 Wood, *Politics of Social Conflict*, pp. 277–86; Lindley, *Fenland Riots*, pp. 188–222; Clive Holmes, 'Drainers and fenmen', in Anthony Fletcher and John Stevenson (eds), *Order and Disorder in Early Modern England, 1500–1750* (Cambridge, 1985), pp. 166–7.

172 Roger Howell, Jr and David E. Brewster, 'Reconsidering the Levellers: the evidence of *The Moderate*', *P&P*, 46 (1970), p. 86.

173 Hudson, 'Economic and social thought of Gerrard Winstanley', pp. 7, 9; Mulligan, Graham and Richards, 'Winstanley', pp. 57–75.

174 Above, p. 125 The hill was made up predominantly of Barton Beds, a mixture of sands, pebbles, ironstone and loams.

175 TNA, E317/40/6; LR2/226, fols 259–60.

176 Walter Blith, *The English Improver Improved* (1652), epistle to the reader; Hill, *World Turned Upside Down*, p. 89. Cf. Bodleian Library, MS Aubrey 4, fols 48, 53.

177 Mulligan, Graham and Richards, 'Winstanley', pp. 64–5, 68–9. Cf. Bradstock, *Faith in the Revolution*, pp. 102–3.

178 TNA, E134/29, 30 Eliz/M17; E317/Surrey/55, p. 10. For the bounds of Walton Heath, see LR2/197, fol. 192.

179 Firth, *Clarke Papers*, 2, p. 210.

180 TNA, E134/29, 30Eliz/M17; E134/32Eliz/E14.

181 TNA, E134/32Eliz/E14.

182 TNA, E317/Surrey/55; M. E. Blackman (ed.), *Customs of the manors of Walton Leigh and Walton Thames*, (Walton and Weybridge Local History, Monograph 12, 1971). For the general trend towards stinting in early 17th century England, see Manning, *Village Revolts*, pp. 20, 85–6, 311–12, 315.

183 TNA, E317/Surrey/55, p. 11.

184 Walton's population may have been only around 700 in 1649: Meekings, *Hearth Tax*.

185 TNA, E134/32/Eliz/E14; LR2/197, fol. 8v.

186 TNA, LR2/226, fols 259–60; E317/Surrey/55, pp. 10, 12.

187 For orders relating to the use of Walton's commons in the first half of the 17th century, SHC, 442, fols 42b-43, 50b, 53a.

188 *The Speeches of the Lord Generall Fairfax, and the Other Officers of the Armie, to the Diggers at St Georges Hill in Surrey* (1649).

189 Underdown, *Pride's Purge*, pp. 147, 168, 372; *The Names of the Justices of Peace in England and Wales* (1650), p. 54; TNA, SP28/214 (unfol.), county committee warrant to Henry Willcocks, 19 October 1648; C231/6; ASSI35/86–99.

190 TNA, SP28/291 (unfol.), papers regarding assessment dispute between Francis Drake and the parish of Walton.

191 TNA, SP28/335, fol. 473; SP28/244 (unfol.), answers of farmers, fee farmers and others, 21 November 1643; SP28/291 (unfol.), papers of Fras Lenthall.

192 BL, Harl. MS 164, fols 290–290v.

193 TNA, C3/441/5; C3/443/5; C6/147/9; LLRRO, 16 D 66/398–9; Norman E. Carlson, 'George Wither and the statute office', *N&Q*, (March 1969), p. 100. His partner in dealings with Jas Winstanley was Ralph Bovey, nephew of Gerrard Winstanley's business acquaintance Rich. Aldworth and beneficiary of the latter's will.

194 Sabine, *Works*, pp. 319–20.

195 TNA, ASSI35/89/5.

196 *Names of the Justices of Peace*, p. 54; Peter Le Fevre, 'Sir George Ayscue, commonwealth and restoration admiral', *Mariner's Mirror*, 68 (1982), pp. 191–2.

197 Gurney, 'Surrey and the English revolution', pp. 371–2; TNA, ASSI35/86–99.

198 Aubrey, *Surrey*, vol. I, 'Mr Evelyn's letter to Mr Aubrey'.

199 Brandon, *History of Surrey*, pp. 58–9, for Portnall Park; SHC, G70/38/4, for Witley manor.

200 TNA, REQ2/196/79. For similar provisions in a 1597 Abinger lease, see Brandon, 'Land, technology and water management', pp. 94–95.

201 TNA, E317/Surrey/44, pp. 2–6; E134/9JasI/H7; E134/19JasI/T2.

202 ESRO, GLY303.

203 Firth, *Clarke Papers*, 2, p. 210.

204 *Speeches of the Lord Generall*. Cf. Thirsk, *Rural Economy*, p. 189.

205 Thomas Fuller, *The Worthies of England* [1662], ed. John Freeman (London, 1952), p. 543.

206 Coulton, *Theoria Contigentium . . . 1653*; *Prognostes Astralis . . . 1654*; *Prognostae Astralis . . . 1655*, passim.

207 Brandon and Short, *South East*, p. 183; Thirsk, *Rural Economy*, p. 200.

208 TNA, E134/13 & 14Chas2/Hil7. I am indebted to Robert Dalton for this reference. For mid-17th century Surrey tithe customs, see SHC, 1304; 7000. Cf. Joan Thirsk, *Alternative Agriculture: a History* (Oxford, 1997), p. 36.

209 Malcolm Thick, 'Root crops and the feeding of London's poor in the late sixteenth and early seventeenth centuries', in John Chartres and David Hey (eds), *English Rural Society, 1500–1800: Essays in Honour of Joan Thirsk* (Cambridge, 1990), pp. 279–96; Thirsk, *Alternative Agriculture*, pp. 37–8, 41.

210 Fuller, *Worthies of England*, p. 543.

211 Thirsk, *Alternative Agriculture*, p. 41.

212 Thick, 'Root crops', pp. 291–3.

213 Thick, 'Root crops', p. 292; Thirsk, *Alternative Agriculture*, pp. 37–8. Gardiner's tract was reissued in 1603.

214 H[ugh] P[lat], *Sundrie New and Artificiall Remedies against Famine* (1596); Thick, 'Root crops', p. 291. For John Platt's lineage, see Armytage, *Visitation of Surrey 1662–68*; Manning and Bray, *Surrey*, I, p. 609; TNA, PROB11/175, fols 302ff; C5/588/62.

215 Above, pp. 112–13, 126–7; below, pp. 158, 170–1.

216 *Perfect Occurences*, 120 (13–20 April 1649), p. 452.

217 The interesting recent suggestion that a second Digger colony was actually established at Oatlands may reflect confusion in early press reports between St George's Hill and

the contiguous Oatlands Park: Ronald Hutton, *The British Republic 1649–1660* (2nd edn, London 2000), p. 31.

218 Sabine, *Works*, pp. 269–77.

219 *Ibid.*, pp. 272–4.

220 *Ibid.*, p. 272.

221 *Ibid.*, pp. 269–70, 272.

222 *Ibid.*, p. 274.

223 For the latter, see esp. Davis, *Utopia and the Ideal Society*, pp. 183–4; Hill, *Liberty against the Law*, pp. 285–6, 289, 295.

224 Sabine, *Works*, p. 272.

225 Ibid., p. 277; *Speeches of the Lord General; England's Moderate Messenger* (28 May-4 June 1649), p. 44.

Chapter 6

The Diggers and the local community

Assaults on the Diggers began almost immediately after they set to work on St George's Hill. In the first recorded attack, 'divers of the diggers' were, according to Winstanley, taken to the village of Walton and locked in the church, before being freed by a justice of the peace. On the second occasion, 'above a hundred rude people' forced the Diggers off the hill and took them first to Walton and then Kingston, where they were released again by a JP; in subsequent attacks Digger houses were pulled down, and their spades and hoes 'cut to pieces'.[1] During the first few days of the experiment, only a mistaken belief that the Diggers enjoyed the protection of the army saved them from further violence; but army officers soon 'endeavoured to undeceive the people of the bordering Towns'.[2] By 27 April, newsbooks were reporting confidently that the Diggers' 'new Plantation' was 'quite re-leveled, and their new Creation utterly destroyed, and by the Country people thereabouts, they are driven away'.[3]

The Diggers returned to the hill in greater numbers after the initial wave of attacks, and were subjected to further assaults in the succeeding weeks and months.[4] In the last week of May, a report in *Mercurius Republicus* described how 'those Levellers that be at Cobham, who dig upon St Georges Hill', were prevented by locals from fetching wood, being 'well beaten by an ambuscado of women and children, the horses hurt and killed that were to draw the same away'.[5] This was almost certainly the occasion when the Diggers attempted to take wood from Stoke Common, a cart being destroyed and a horse maimed in the attack.[6] Not long after, Winstanley accused soldiers quartered locally of assaulting a man and a boy on the hill, and of firing a Digger house.[7] On 11 June, local inhabitants joined together in a traditional, ritualised protest against the Diggers, with 'two free-holders, being on horseback' leading a group of men dressed in women's clothing and carrying staves and clubs; the four Diggers who were on the hill, 'fitting and preparing the ground for a winter season', were said by Winstanley to have been 'sore wounded' by the protestors.[8] Six weeks later, a Digger petition to parliament described how they had 'oftentimes bin molested', their crops being 'maliciously trodden down and trampled under foot' by their opponents.[9] It seems that disruption of the Diggers' activities continued until August when, under pressure from legal actions taken against them in Kingston's court of record, they abandoned St George's Hill and moved from there to Cobham's Little Heath.[10]

Much can be gleaned from Winstanley's writings about the opposition faced by the Diggers on St George's Hill. In a series of appeals to the authorities and to the nation, Winstanley protested forcefully and in great detail about the hostile treatment meted out to the Diggers while they remained on the hill.[11] In his *A New-Yeers Gift for the Parliament and Armie*, he also provided – in anticipation of Quaker practice – a 'bill of account' of the sufferings endured by the Diggers since 1 April.[12] The Diggers' opponents were presented in these writings as acting violently and irrationally, in contrast to the cheerful demeanour with which the Diggers, like the Quakers after them, faced their tormentors.[13] The two Diggers attacked by soldiers in June were described as 'naked men, peaceable men, Countrymen, that meddled not with the souldiers businesse'; the four men attacked by cross-dressing rioters were 'quiet and patient, willing and resolving to deliver up their lives unto their Creator', while their opponents 'would not speak like men',

> but like bruit beasts that have no understanding, they fell furiously upon them, beating and striking those foure naked men, beating them to the ground, breaking their heads, and sore bruising their bodies, whereof one is so sore bruised, that it is feared he will not escape with life.[14]

Winstanley's choice of imagery was clearly designed to elicit sympathy for the Diggers, and to present their opponents in the worst possible light; the language he used was both startling and heartfelt. What comes through strongly in Winstanley's account of the violence inflicted on the Diggers is that the opposition was made up not only of gentry and clergy – his targets in *The New Law of Righteousnes* and the first two Digger manifestos – but also of middling and poorer sorts. In the earliest attacks the chief perpetrators were described as 'rude people' or 'Countrey-people', while gentry involvement was not mentioned; 'bitter Professors' joined the 'rude multitude' in assaulting captive Diggers in Walton parish church, but when justices of the peace became involved it was in order to release the Diggers and quell the disorders.[15] Other terms used later by Winstanley to describe the Diggers' enemies – including 'sutlers', 'snapsack boyes, and ammunition drabs', and 'ignorant bawling women' – show his awareness of the widespread popular opposition generated by the occupation of St George's Hill.[16]

Local fears had been vividly expressed by Henry Sanders in April 1649, when he repeated claims that the Diggers had warned locals not to let their cattle near the plantation, for 'if they doe they will cutt their legges off'.[17] At the beginning of June, Winstanley felt compelled to assure Fairfax that rumours that 'we have intent to fortifie our selves, and afterwards to fight against others, and take away their goods from them', were wholly untrue.[18] The confrontational behaviour of some Diggers may also have caused alarm. In April a Digger was reported to have got together a 'great burden of thorns, and bryars' and 'thrust them into the pulpit at the Church at Walton, to stop out the Parson'.[19] This may have been William Everard, who had a reputation as an eccentric and conjuror, and who, as Ariel Hessayon has recently shown, had confronted the minister of Staines with a hedging bill in his church not long before the start of the digging.[20] The Diggers also had to contend with persistent rumours that they favoured sexual licentiousness and held partners as well as property in common, and accusations that they did 'not know God' and would not come to church.[21]

Even in the absence of such damaging rumours, the Diggers' presence on the commons was bound to provoke opposition. To Walton's inhabitants, the Diggers were outsiders, and although Walton's commons were extensive, and manorial control relatively lax, large-scale encroachments had been resisted before. Tenants of Walton manor had, for instance, taken legal action in 1587 and 1590 against the occupier of Apps Court, when he attempted to pasture his cattle on Walton heath.[22] In 1664, the astrologer William Lilly, as churchwarden of the 'distracted parish' of Walton, was to become involved in a legal dispute with the lord of the manor of Esher, after the latter put three hundred of his sheep on Walton's commons.[23] Digging and ploughing the commons, particularly on the scale envisaged by the Diggers at the start of their project, was also unprecedented. Piecemeal enclosure of the commons had taken place in Walton, but this had most often been enclosure by agreement. When Lakefield near Pains Hill was divided up and enclosed, it was done by 'mutuall consent', and was designed to reduce the number of 'quarrelles & bralles' among those who had interests in the field.[24] The Diggers' mass occupation of St George's Hill and their call for others to join them was quite unlike anything seen before in Walton. Despite obvious affinities between digging and older traditions of squatting on the commons, the new Digger settlement could not be confused with the kind of illegal encroachment by small cottagers that had for many years been tolerated by Walton's inhabitants.[25]

The most intense local opposition to the Diggers came from those Walton residents who lived near St George's Hill, and who had most to lose from incursions on that part of the heath. Winstanley identified two individuals, John Taylor and William Starr, as the leading participants in local campaigns against the Diggers. Taylor was, according to Winstanley, leader of the hundred or more 'rude people' who attacked the Diggers in the early days of the St George's Hill colony. In the ritualised protest of 11 June, Taylor was joined by Starr, the two of them riding on horseback at the head of the crowd of men dressed in women's clothing.[26] John Taylor was a prominent figure in the parish of Walton, and had been active during the Civil War in raising money for the parliamentary war effort; three of his brothers had fought for parliament.[27] Taylor belonged to a family of building workers and sheep farmers, and was, like his father and several others of his relatives, a carpenter.[28] The family may have had Cobham antecedents, but had settled in Walton by the mid-sixteenth century at the latest.[29] It is possible that some members of the family came to Walton as squatters, for John Taylor's grandfather was one of the cottage builders on Walton heath who had managed to acquire right of common without stint.[30] As small property holders and sheep farmers, the Taylors were heavily dependent on Walton's commons for their livelihood. They would understandably have been anxious to protect the commons from further incursions from outside the parish.[31]

William Starr was from a yeoman family that had long been settled near Pains Hill, on the Walton side of the boundary with the parish of Cobham.[32] The Starrs were neighbours of the Bickerstaffe family, and during the Civil War William Starr shared with the Digger Henry Bickerstaffe the costs of sending a soldier to the siege of Basing.[33] Starr was a member of the Surrey assize grand jury, and in September 1648 was high constable of Elmbridge hundred.[34] Like John Taylor, William Starr was a substantial sheep farmer, and seems to have shared Taylor's concerns about the threat posed by the Diggers to the commons around Pains Hill.[35] Starr was, according to Winstanley, one of those who claimed that the commons belonged to the poor, while being 'agrieved to see the poor make use of the Commons'.[36] What this suggests is that Starr feared that the rights of all Walton commoners – poor as well as rich – were endangered by the Diggers' claim to the common land of St George's Hill. If this was the case, he was drawing attention to one of the most intractable problems facing Winstanley and his companions, the difficulty of persuading poor commoners that it was in everyone's best interests to allow the Diggers to occupy their commons.[37] This was a problem highlighted in early newsbook reports of the digging, and Walter Blith would later return to it when he declared that 'though the poore are or ought to have advantage upon the Commons, yet I question whether they as a society gathered together from all parts of the Nation could claime a right to any particular Common'.[38]

Starr's hostility towards the Diggers may also have owed something to personal experience. His father, James Starr, had for many years been engaged in a bitter and sometimes violent dispute with the father of Henry Bickerstaffe. Robert Bickerstaffe had initiated several legal actions against James Starr in the Kingston court of record and the King's Bench in the years 1611–21, including six actions in the space of three years; and Starr was to claim that his wealthier neighbour's 'contynuall wronges, suits, and vexacons' had left him 'much decayed, and impoverished, in his poore estate'.[39] Bickerstaffe was also said to have blocked paths, forcibly encroached upon Starr's land, impounded cattle and ordered his servants to cut bushes on property belonging to Starr.[40] Matters had come to a head in November 1619, after Starr had tried to prevent Bickerstaffe carrying wood across his land. In exchequer depositions taken in Cobham in May 1621, witnesses described how Starr had been struck by Bickerstaffe before being beaten to the ground by the latter's servants. Winstanley's graphic account of the assault by William Starr, John Taylor and their companions upon the Diggers in June 1649 – 'beating with their long staves upon their bodies without mercie' – describes an incident not unlike the one that had taken place a short distance away thirty years before. On that occasion, according to Elizabeth Dalton of Weybridge, Bickerstaffe's servant John Otway knocked James Starr down 'that he colde not rise again till he was holpe upp'. Another witness to the incident was the ten-year-old William Starr, who two years later described on oath how he had seen one of Bickerstaffe's men, John Stephens alias Annis, beating his father 'with his fists lyenge upon the ground and Stephens uppermost and after that Stephens was upp this deponent sawe two stones in Stephens his hand'.[41] Violence of this sort was by no means uncommon in seventeenth-century land disputes, and we need not assume that there was a direct connection between the earlier incident and the attack on the St George's Hill Diggers in 1649. It is however possible that Starr's attitude towards the Diggers was coloured by memories of his family's dispute with the Bickerstaffes, and of his father's very public humiliation at the hands of the father of a leading Digger.[42]

In the face of local opposition, Winstanley attempted to defend the Diggers' actions in a series of pamphlets authored solely by him and addressed respectively to the Lord General and Council of War, the House of Commons and the City of London. By the time the first of these pamphlets appeared, William Everard had apparently left St George's Hill, and Winstanley was now the unchallenged leader and theoretician of the Diggers.[43] In the pamphlets addressed to the army and parliament, Winstanley emphasised the utility of the digging and to tried to play down the disruption that the Diggers' activities might cause to others. His purpose was, as he informed Fairfax in *A Letter to the Lord Fairfax and his Councell of War*, to 'lay open the bottome and intent of our businesse, as much as can be, that none may be troubled with doubtfull imaginations about us, but may be satisfied in the sincerity and universall righteousnesse of the work'.[44] *A Letter to the Lord Fairfax* also served to portray the Diggers as respectable members of society, whose views were listened to by the most powerful in the land. Winstanley made a point of reminding Fairfax – and by implication his readers – that the Diggers had received 'mildnesse and moderation' when they appeared before the Lord General and Council of War, and when Fairfax had visited St George's Hill in person; he also indicated that the pamphlet had been delivered before publication 'by the Authors own hand to the Generall, and the chief Officers', who 'very mildly promised they would read it, and consider of it'.[45] Winstanley clearly hoped to demonstrate that the Diggers' cause was of national importance – 'the talk of the whole Land' – and not an issue that was significant only to those immediately affected by the occupation of St George's Hill. Local opponents might think twice before launching their assaults if they thought that the Diggers had the ear of Fairfax and his senior officers.

In making the case to the army and parliament for official toleration of the Digger experiment, Winstanley insisted once more upon the Diggers' refusal to invade or expropriate private property, and he avoided any repetition of his earlier calls for a mass withdrawal of hired labour.[46] Although he still hoped that the spirit would work on the rich and induce them to surrender up their property to the community, he now placed greater emphasis on the Diggers' plans for the peaceful co-existence of two systems of land holding.[47] As he declared in *An Appeal to the House of Commons*:

> Let the Gentry have their inclosures free from all Norman enslaving intanglements whatsoever, and let the common people have their Commons and waste lands set free to them, from all Norman enslaving Lords of Mannors, that so both elder and younger brother, as we spring successively one from another, may live free and quiet one by, and with another, not burthening one another in this land of our Nativity.[48]

Similarly, Winstanley spelt out in *A Letter to the Lord Fairfax* the answer he had given to a question posed by Fairfax on St George's Hill:

> We told you (upon a question you put to us) that we were not against any that would have Magistrates and Laws to govern, as the Nations of the world are governed, but as for our parts we shall need neither the one nor the other in that nature of Government; for as our Land is common, so our Cattell is to be common, and our corn and fruits of the earth common, and are not to be bought and sold among us, but to remaine a standing portion of livelihood to us and our children, without that cheating intanglement of buying and selling, and we shall not arrest one another.[49]

The benefit to the nation of the digging was also stressed. The Diggers sought to 'sow corn for the succour of man', and to 'improve the Commons and waste Lands to our best advantage, for the relief of our selves and others'; the occupation of the commons would, among other things, encourage 'the quieting of the hearts of the poor oppressed that are groaning under burthens and straights'.[50]

Winstanley also used of these pamphlets to develop his own singular interpretation of Norman Yoke theory. Lords of manors were, for Winstanley, the successors of 'the Colonells and chief Officers' of William the Conqueror, and their powers derived from his conquest over the English; the execution of King Charles, the abolition of monarchy and creation of a free common-wealth should have invalidated the laws introduced since the conquest and have restored to the common people their legal right to the commons and wastes of England.[51] These arguments went hand in hand with arguments that emphasised the contractual obligations of the victorious parliament. Parliament's victory over the king could not have been achieved without the assistance of the common people: 'the Common People have joyned person and purse with you, to recover your selves from under the tyranny of Kings, and have prevailed'; they had been 'brought almost to a morsell of bread' and now demanded their 'bargain, which is 'freedom, with you in this Land of our Nativity'.[52] Those who dug on St George's Hill had, as Winstanley reminded Fairfax, 'ever been your friends in times of straits', and 'adventured estate and persons with you, to settle the Land in peace'; they had 'been ever friends to the Parliament'.[53] Parliament and people had subscribed to the Covenant to 'endeavour a Reformation according to the Word of God',

> which Reformation was to restore us to that Primitive freedom in the earth, in which the earth was first made and given to the sons of men, and that is to be a common treasury of livelihood to all, without working for hire, or paying rent to any, for this is the Reformation according to the Word of God before the fall of man, in which there is no respect of persons.[54]

Gentry and parliament would, he argued, be in breach of the Covenant if they kept to themselves the spoils of victory, shutting out the common people with whose support they had defeated the king:

> Let it not be said in the ears of posterity, That the Gentry of England assembled in Parliament, proved Covenant-breakers, Oaths, Protestations, and promise-breakers to God, and the Common people, after their own turn was served; and killed the King for his power and government, as a thief kils a true man for his money. I do not say you have done so, but for shame dally no longer, but cut off the bad laws, with the Kings head, and let the poor oppressed go free, as well as the Gentry and Clergy, and you will finde more peace.[55]

While it was relatively easy for Winstanley to advance the claims of the poor to common land, it was more difficult for him to account for the vehement popular opposition faced by the Diggers on St George's Hill. Winstanley's response to this problem was to direct his anger against those he termed 'ignorant, covetous, free-holders', to treat these 'violent bitter people' as separate from the bulk of the local population and to find a central place for them in his description of the social hierarchy that had emerged in the wake of the Norman Conquest.[56] When Fairfax visited St George's Hill, Winstanley told him that 'many of the Countrey-people that were offended at first, begin now to be moderate, and to see righteousnesse in our work, and to own it',

> excepting one or two covetous Free-holders, that would have all the Commons to themselves, and that would uphold the Norman Tyranny over us, which by that victorie that you have got over the Norman Successor, is plucked up by the roots, therefore ought to be cast away.[57]

In *A Declaration from the Poor Oppressed*, 'rich Free-holders' were accused with the gentry of making 'the most profit of the Commons, by your over-stocking of them with Sheep and Cattle; and the poor that have the name to own the Commons have the least share therein'; the poor 'are checked by you, if they cut Wood, Heath, Turf, or Furseys, in places about the Common, where you disallow'.[58] The selfishness and unreason of freeholders was, for Winstanley, embodied in the actions of those 'furious divells' William Starr and John Taylor, whose hostility towards the Diggers 'declares plainly, that they got their Lands, both they and their Fathers, by murder, violence, and theft, and they keep it by the same power'.[59] In Winstanley's social model, freeholders were portrayed as descendants of the Conqueror's inferior officers and soldiers, just as lords of manors were the successors to his colonels.[60] It was a simple but effective class analysis, and one that reflected the realities of a rural social structure in which the interests of the middling sorts were increasingly seen to be aligned with those of the gentry.[61] But it could do little to explain the manifest popular support for the local freeholders' campaigns against the Diggers.

Winstanley's antipathy towards his Walton yeoman opponents demonstrated the limits to the moderate approach he had sought to adopt in the St George's Hill pamphlets. His struggle to maintain a conciliatory tone in these writings could also be seen in the uncertain attitude he displayed towards the army and House of Commons. While he expressed confidence in Fairfax and the Council of War's 'moderation and friendship', he also felt constrained to warn them that if attacks by soldiers and freeholders continued, 'you and they shall be left without excuse in the day of Judgement, because you have been spoken to sufficiently'.[62] Parliament was expected to help advance the Digger cause, but MPs too would be 'left without excuse' if they allowed the poor to remain 'in the hands of oppression, and under the power of the old tyrannical laws'; already 'the hearts of people are much falling from you, for your breach of Promises when you have power to keep them, and for your neglect of giving them freedom, and removing burthens'.[63] Winstanley appears also to have become concerned about placing too great a reliance on Norman Yoke theory to argue the Diggers' case. The postscript to *A Letter to the Lord Fairfax*, which was presumably added after the letter had been delivered to Fairfax and his officers, attempted to clear up any misapprehension that the Diggers were now limiting their aims to the restoration of laws in force before the Conquest:

> The Reformation that England now is to endeavour, is not to remove the Norman Yoke only, and to bring us back to be governed by those Laws that were before William the Conqueror came in, as if that were the rule or mark we aime at: No, that is not it; but the Reformation is according to the Word of God, and that is the pure Law of righteousnesse before the fall, which made all things, unto which all things are to be restored: and he that endeavours not that, is a Covenant-breaker.[64]

It is clear that Winstanley remained committed to the radical programme of restoration he had expounded in *The New Law of Righteousnes* and *The True Levellers Standard Advanced*, and that he was anxious not to compromise this in his attempts to conciliate parliament, the army and the Diggers' local opponents.

The Diggers' attempts to overcome local hostility, and to extend their activities on St George's Hill, were dealt a further blow when their opponents adopted a new tactic in June 1649. On 23 June suits for trespass were filed against Winstanley, Henry Bickerstaffe, Thomas Starr, Henry Barton and five other Diggers in Kingston's court of record, the jurisdiction of which extended across Kingston and Elmbridge hundreds.[65] Although the plaintiffs' names were given as Thomas Lord Wenman, Sir Ralph Verney and Richard Winwood, the action was conducted on behalf of Francis Drake, the farmer of the manor of Walton.[66] It is not known whether Drake was acting to protect his own property rights, to protect the interests of those of his tenants who claimed right of common on St George's Hill, or to seek to limit the disorders that seemed bound to continue while the Diggers remained on the hill. Religion may also have played a part in his decision to rid his manor of the Diggers. Francis Drake was a man of strong religious views, as his later intervention in the case of the Quaker James Naylor testifies. In the debates in parliament in December 1656, Drake was one of the MPs who insisted that Naylor was guilty of horrid blasphemy and should be put to death, arguing that the obligation on MPs to vindicate the honour of God permitted nothing less than a death sentence.[67] The Drake family also had close connections with some of the leading godly ministers of early Stuart England. Drake was the son of the celebrated Joan Drake, who had become convinced that she was damned and 'by God's decree a reprobate'; and for many years the doors of the family homes at Esher, Walton and Blackfriars were opened to a succession of ministers who tried to convince her otherwise. These included John Dod, who visited many times, John Preston, James Ussher and Thomas Hooker; the 'thundering preacher' John Rogers of Dedham also became involved in her case.[68] Drake's father remembered Dod in his will, and named the renowned puritan ministers Richard Sibbes and William Gouge as overseers.[69] Drake also had close family connections with

John White, leader of the godly community of Dorchester, and with the puritan lawyer and MP John 'Century' White.[70]

Drake's action in the court of record was not concluded for several weeks, largely – it would seem – because the Diggers refused to fee an attorney.[71] Damages of £10 and costs were awarded on 28 July against Winstanley and Bickerstaffe, and damages of £3 or more against Starr; a writ of execution was issued on 11 August. [72] Bickerstaffe was imprisoned – though soon released by Drake – and orders were given for the distraint of Winstanley's goods. Starr, who Winstanley described as 'a poore man not worth ten pounds', appears to have evaded imprisonment, so a judgment was awarded against the mainpernor.[73] Four cows were distrained from Winstanley's home, but, as he later explained, 'strangers made rescue of those Cowes, and drove them astray out of the Bailiffes hands, so that the Bailiffes lost them'.[74] Winstanley claimed that the cows were not his, and nor were the seven cows and a bull taken from his home a fortnight later. Some apparently belonged to neighbours who had hired pasture, while the rest may have been the property of his parents-in-law.[75] He was presumably referring to this incident when he later described how goods that had been seized from the Diggers 'proved another mans, which one of the Diggers was Servant to'.[76] The owner of the distrained cattle was also 'the right owner' of the corn growing around Winstanley's home, which had been spoiled when the gates to the close were opened to allow in 'Hogs and common Cattell'.[77]

Much of what we know about the legal actions against the Diggers comes from Winstanley's *A Watch-Word to the City of London and the Armie*, which was dated 26 August 1649 and which had reached the London booksellers by 10 September.[78] In this, one of Winstanley's most powerful works from the Digger period, detailed accounts were provided of the proceedings in Kingston court under its 'covetous besotted, ignorant Atturney Mr Gilder', and of the several, unsuccessful attempts by bailiffs to execute the court's warrant against Winstanley.[79] Winstanley's vivid description of the seizure of his cows, and of the suffering inflicted upon them – the bailiffs 'beat them with their clubs, that the Cowes heads and sides did swell, which grieved tender hearts to see' – has often been remarked upon.[80] In previous pamphlets Winstanley had emphasised the irrationality of the Diggers' opponents by likening them to 'bruit beasts that have no understanding'; here he illustrated their inhumanity by reference to the ill-treatment of innocent cows that 'never were upon George Hill, nor never digged upon that ground', and that had suffered only 'because they give milk to feed me'.[81]

The court's attempt to prevent the Diggers pleading their own cause provided Winstanley with the opportunity to advance legal arguments of the sort he had first made use of when defending John Fielder at the assizes in February. Winstanley included in *A Watch-Word* a copy of a paper he had presented to the court of record to justify the digging and to condemn what he saw as the court's illegal proceedings, and which contained copious references to statute law, to Coke's *Institutes* and to *The Mirror of Justices*.[82] The covenant was invoked, as in the defence of Fielder, to support Winstanley's argument that 'old Norman tyrannicall and destructive Lawes' were now abrogated.[83] He repeated his argument that the activities of the Diggers were vindicated by the law of contract: 'all sorts, poor as well as rich, Tenant as well as Landlord, have paid Taxes, Free-quarter, Excise, or adventured their lives, to cast out that Kingly Office', and so it followed that 'all sorts of people ought to have freedom in the Land of this their nativity, without respecting persons, now the Kingly Office is cast out, by their joynt assistance'.[84]

Despite its confident tone, *A Watch-Word* displayed much of the same instability as Winstanley's two preceding pamphlets. Winstanley remained insistent that the Diggers were not about to take away the rights of others, and that freeholders need not fear the loss of their enclosures, but in his restatement of the aims of the Diggers he returned once again to the more militant language of the first Digger manifesto and his pre-Digger writings. The earth was 'a common treasury of livelihood for whole mankind in all his branches, without respect of persons', and no one 'ought to be Lord or landlord over another'.[85] While blame was placed on the Norman Conquest for the dispossession of the common people, elsewhere in the work Winstanley repeated his earlier, central claim that it was covetousness, following the fall of man, that had led to the rise of private property and the theft of land from the poor; in places he came close to conflating the two.[86]

A Watch-Word was in many ways more confrontational than *A Letter to the Lord Fairfax* and *An Appeal to the House of Commons*. In focusing upon the legal proceedings in Kingston's court of record, Winstanley was able to give expression to his growing frustration at the speed of change in the nation. Parliament's avowed determination to uphold existing laws had, he maintained, encouraged the plaintiffs in his case to embark upon their action, and the court to deny the Diggers their right to represent themselves without a lawyer. Some MPs had 'plaid fast and loose with this poor Nation', and while the office of king may have been abolished, kingly power remained.[87] In previous writings Winstanley had made little distinction between the kingly office and kingly power, and appeared at times to assume that both had been cast out with the abolition of monarchy.[88] Now he began to treat the concept of kingly power in the way the authors of *More Light Shining in Buckinghamshire* had done, as a force that existed independently of the king, and that had been allowed to survive the creation of the republic.[89] Kingly power, which was equated in *A Watch-Word* with covetousness, might be found 'in one or many mens hands'; its continuing strength served as a reminder of the fragility of England's new-found freedoms.[90]

In its emphasis on the continued strength of kingly power in the common-wealth – and in the legal system in particular – *A Watch-Word* showed some affinity with the concerns of other reformers. Moves in parliament for reform of the law had had only limited success in the spring and summer of 1649, and extra-parliamentary agitation for law reform continued at a heightened level.[91] On 24 August, two days before the completion of *A Watch-Word*, a Leveller-influenced petition from 'the oppressed of the County of Surrey, which have cast in their mite into the Treasury of this Commonwealth', was presented to the Commons. The petition expressed radicals' frustration at the pace of reform since the end of the wars, and called for, among other things, the abolition of tithes, the use of English in all legal proceedings, the speeding up of the court process, an end to MPs practising the law, and confirmation of the right of any individual to 'plead his own or Neighbors Cause before any Court of Justice, although no Lawyer'.[92] Only in its defence of juries did the petition differ significantly from the tenor of Winstanley's criticism of the legal system, Winstanley having become convinced that in Kingston at least juries were as corrupt as the court they served.[93]

The threat to freedom was a recurrent theme in *A Watch-Word*, and one that Winstanley hoped might encourage his readers to 'consider the case that England is in'.[94] No true freedom could be established in England 'but such a one as hath respect to the poor, as well as the rich', but 'the rich generally are enemies to true freedome'.[95] England's battles were now 'all spirituall. Dragon against the Lamb, and the power of love against the power of covetousnesse'; the Diggers' enemies sought to destroy their project so as to ensure that 'the name of community and freedome which is Christ, may not be known in earth.'[96] The importance of agency to advance freedom was again emphasised, as it had been in *The True Levellers Standard Advanced*, 'for action is the life of all, and if thou dost not act, thou dost nothing'.[97] 'Every one', Winstanley complained, 'talks of freedome, but there are but few that act for freedome, and the actors for freedome are oppressed by the talkers and verball professors of freedome.'[98] Freedoms that had been fought for were now in danger of being lost without a struggle, to those who 'lay close in action, waiting to trip up your heels by pollicy, when the sword could not do it'.[99] The problem lay partly in the unwillingness of many to recognise true freedom, for as Winstanley declared in his address to the City of London:

> all men have stood for freedom, thou hast kept fasting daies, and prayed in morning exercises for freedom; thou hast given thanks for victories, because hopes of freedome; plentie of Petitions and promises thereupon have been made for freedome, and now the common enemy is gone, you are all like men in a mist, seeking for freedom, and know not where, nor what it is: and those of the richer sort of you that see it, are ashamed and afraid to owne it, because it comes clothed in a clownish garment, and open to the best language that scoffing Ishmael can

afford, or that railing Rabsheka can speak, or furious Pharoah can act against him; for freedom is the man that will turn the world upside downe, therefore no wonder he hath enemies.[100]

Towards the end of *A Watch-Word*, Winstanley drew attention to the connections between this pamphlet and its two immediate predecessors. He had, he reminded his readers, 'dealt plainly with you all, and I have not flattered Parliament, Army, City, nor Countrey, but have declared in this and other writings the whole light of that truth revealed to me by the word of the Lord'.[101] The differences between the three works were, however, equally important – and in particular the contrast between the respectful, constructive tones of *A Letter to the Lord Fairfax* and the declamatory, combative style of *A Watch-Word* showed how quickly the Diggers had come to doubt their ability to persuade others to let them continue to work in peace on St George's Hill.

A Watch-Word contained much valuable, local detail, but there were also significant gaps in Winstanley's account of the persecution of the St George's Hill Diggers. There was nothing in the pamphlet, for example, to explain why Drake, the 'old Norman Prerogative Lord of the Mannour', should have released Henry Bickerstaffe after only three days in prison.[102] Nor was there anything to explain the precise nature of the incident in which 'Hogs and common Cattell' were allowed into Winstanley's grounds to feed on the corn growing there.[103] Was this – as Winstanley may have intended his readers to assume – another instance of mindless violence against the Diggers? Or was it something more troubling, a symbolic attempt perhaps to take Winstanley at his own word, to allow the local community free use of *his* land, and to commandeer his crops to feed the common cattle that would normally – in the absence of a Digger colony – have grazed on St George's Hill? If this were the case, and local Digger homes other than Winstanley's were also targeted in this way, it would have represented the most serious threat yet to the survival of the colony. It might help to explain why Henry Bickerstaffe, for instance, who had for the past eight years been responsible for the upkeep of his brother's estates in Walton and Cobham, soon gave up his active involvement in the digging and moved from Pains Hill to Kingston, where on 24 October he bought a house and settled with his family.[104] The incident may have been related to the other unexplained event to which Winstanley only briefly alluded in *A Watch-Word*, the abandonment by the Diggers of their colony on St George's Hill and their move to the parish of Cobham, where they set out to establish a new settlement on the Little Heath.

THE DIGGERS IN COBHAM

The work of digging still goes on, and stops not for a rest:
The Cowes were gone, but are return'd, and we are all at rest.
No money's paid, nor never shall, to a Lawyer or his man

> To plead our cause, for therein wee'll do the best we can.
> In Cobham on the little Heath our digging there goes on.
> And all our friends they live in love, as if they were but one.[105]

The exact date of the Diggers' move from St George's Hill to Cobham's Little Heath is not known, but the new plantation was almost certainly in existence by 24 August, when, according to Winstanley, a group of 'Knights, Gentlemen, and rich Freeholders' met at the White Lion in Cobham 'to advise together what course they should take to subdue the diggers'.[106] In spite of this meeting, and the setting up of a lecturer in Cobham to combat Digger propaganda, it seems that Winstanley and his companions were able to begin their work on the Little Heath without violent interruption.[107] Winstanley published nothing between August and late December, and he made no new complaints about popular opposition of the sort the Diggers had experienced on St George's Hill; there was no further mention of the Diggers or their opponents in London newsbooks before the autumn. The several acres worth of wheat and barley planted by the Diggers on the Little Heath apparently remained unmolested as late as December.[108] The Little Heath, which was situated in the east of the parish of Cobham close to the boundary with Stoke d'Abernon, was a relatively isolated spot and lay some distance from Cobham's chief settlements. If the Diggers hoped to avoid provoking the local community into action against them, the choice of the Little Heath as the site of their renewed activities was a sensible one.

In moving to Cobham, Winstanley and his companions were returning to the parish where the ideas behind the Digger movement had been developed, and where many of the Diggers originated. It is not surprising therefore that their reception in Cobham should have been very different from their reception on St George's Hill. The Diggers had been outsiders in Walton, and they had been subjected there to violent opposition from large sections of the local population. Popular hostility was much less evident in Cobham, and its force was blunted by the complex kinship and neighbourhood ties that linked Digger to non-Digger. Three-quarters of the Diggers who made the move from St George's Hill to the Little Heath were residents of Cobham or parishes in the immediate vicinity. These included Henry Barton, John Coulton, Thomas Edsaw, John Hayman, John Palmer, John South and Thomas Starr, as well as Winstanley himself.[109] Other local residents – including Daniel Freeland, Richard Maidley, John South junior, Thomas South and Anthony Wrenn – joined the Diggers in the succeeding months.[110] A majority of the Diggers associated with the St George's Hill colony had drifted away in the spring or early summer, but most of these had been only fleetingly involved with the movement and had no close connection with the locality. Three-quarters of those who left had put their names to just one manifesto, *A Declaration from the Poor Oppressed*, the work that contained by far the largest number of Digger names.[111] Henry Bickerstaffe was one of the few locals to leave around the time the Little Heath colony was established, and it seems likely that at least half of those who remained or who subsequently became active in the digging in Cobham were local inhabitants.[112]

Action against the Diggers did not begin again until the second week of October, when the Council of State was informed of 'a great number of persons gathered together about Cobham in a tumultuous and riotous manner'.[113] Surrey's JPs were instructed to investigate, and assistance was once again requested from Fairfax.[114] Newsbooks reported that around fifty rioters were ordered by justices to disperse, but the numbers of these 'planters of parsnips and carrats' may have been exaggerated.[115] Several Diggers were arrested, though on the return of a habeus corpus they were bailed by the court of King's Bench on a technicality, the sheriff not having been present at the finding of a riot.[116] It may have been on this or a later occasion that five Diggers were, according to Winstanley, imprisoned for over a month in the county gaol, the White Lion in Southwark.[117] Further proceedings were also begun against Winstanley and other Diggers in Kingston's court of record.[118]

Pressure on the Little Heath community increased in the last week of November, when soldiers and countrymen pulled down two Digger houses and carried away the building materials.[119] The incident sparked protests from Winstanley and other Diggers, who maintained that Fairfax had promised that his soldiers would not become involved in actions against the Diggers but would instead let the law take its course. The protests came in the form of two letters to Fairfax, one of them signed by Winstanley and the other bearing the names of seven other Diggers.[120] A slightly different version of the first letter, signed by Winstanley and John Palmer, was addressed to the Council of State.[121] What is clear from these letters, and from Winstanley's later, more detailed account of the November attacks in his *A New-Yeers Gift for the Parliament and Armie*, is the Diggers' impression that in Cobham they faced opposition of a markedly different character from what they had experienced in Walton. The local campaign in Cobham was tightly organised, led by local gentry and backed up by justices of the peace, the county's sheriff and detachments of soldiers; the autonomous popular opposition seen on St George's Hill was largely absent. Chief among the Diggers' new opponents was John Platt, rector of West Horsley and lord of the manor of Cobham by right of his wife, the former Margaret Gavell. In Platt, the Diggers now faced an articulate opponent who was apparently prepared to meet Winstanley's challenge to debate the issue of the digging with him, and who followed Winstanley's lead in appealing directly to the state authorities.[122] It was Platt, so Winstanley maintained, who was chiefly responsible for persuading Fairfax to send soldiers to assist the sheriff in removing the Diggers from the Little Heath. Winstanley now found himself having to defend the Diggers against accusations that they were 'a riotous people' and were holding 'a mans house by violence from him', that they were armed with guns and that they were 'drunkards, and Cavaleers waiteing an opportunity to helpe bring in the Prince, and such like'.[123]

While these allegations were largely baseless, there was, as has already been noted, a demonstrable connection between digging and drink.[124] Some Diggers also had royalist connections, which Platt and his allies may have been keen to exploit. Henry Bickerstaffe, for one, was related to several Surrey royalists, including members of the Hayward, Henn, Lambert and James families.[125] His uncle, Hayward Bickerstaffe, a page of the bedchamber to Charles I, had compounded on the Oxford articles and been fined £260 before mortgaging his estate and fleeing to Barbados.[126] Hayward Bickerstaffe's son, the future clerk of the privy seal Sir Charles Bickerstaffe, was to become an active royalist conspirator in Surrey during the 1650s, on one occasion marching with an armed band to a heath near Cobham before being driven away by the county forces.[127] Another royalist contact of Henry Bickerstaffe's may have been Thomas Ward, who acted as mainpernor for the Digger when he was prosecuted in the Kingston court of record.[128] In April 1650, the month the Digger colony was finally suppressed, a Thomas Ward of Cobham was accused of having been in arms against parliament during the Civil War.[129] Henry Bickerstaffe's elder brother, the London skinner and linen draper Anthony Bickerstaffe, was a well-known supporter of the high presbyterian cause in the City of London, and may also have been suspected of disaffection in 1649.[130] He had been a signatory to the City petition of 18 November 1645 in favour of increasing the powers of London's presbyterian elders, and in June 1647, when parliament was planning to disband the army, he was one of the treasurers appointed to help disburse £10,000 in payment to private soldiers.[131] He was to remain friends throughout the commonwealth period with the London minister William Jenkyn, who was implicated in the Christopher Love conspiracy in 1651.[132]

The Diggers reacted to the accusations made against them by branding their opponents as enemies of the commonwealth regime. Wood taken from the demolished Digger houses had, they claimed, been carried to 'a Gentleman's house who hath bin a Cavaleer all our tyme of wars'; among their opponents were some who 'were always Cavaleers, and had a hand in the Kentish riseing, and were cheife promoters of the offensive Surry petition'. Such people, they warned Fairfax, 'love you but from the teeth outwards, for their own ends'.[133] This was almost certainly a reference to Sir Anthony Vincent, whose wife was a prominent royalist and whose heir Sir Francis Vincent had been active the previous year in the Earl of Holland's rising.[134] John Platt, on the other hand, had demonstrated a strong commitment to the parliamentary cause in Surrey, and could not be so easily labelled a cavalier. As recently as August 1648 he had joined Surrey's leading parliamentarians in advancing money to raise a county troop in the aftermath of Holland's rising.[135] It was easier for the Diggers to attempt to exploit Platt's dual occupation of minister and manorial lord, and to portray him both as a hypocritical, uncharitable clergyman, and as an oppressive landlord who coerced his tenants and labourers into participating in the campaigns against the Diggers. Some of the most striking passages from Winstanley's Digger writings came in his account of Platt and Vincent's leadership of attacks on the Little Heath colony, the landlords' enthusiasm for the task being contrasted with the reluctance to act of those who carried out their orders. In *A New-Yeers Gift*, Winstanley described how 'the two Lords of Manor sat among the souldiers on horsback and coach, and commanded their fearfull tenants to pull down one of the Diggers houses before their faces, and rejoyced with shouting at the fall'; the 'poor tenants that pulled down the house, durst do no other, because their Land-lords and Lords looked on, for fear they should be turned out of service, or their livings':

> And when the poor enforced slaves had pulled down the house, then their Lords gave them ten shillings to drink, and there they smiled one upon another; being fearfull, like a dog that is kept in awe, when his Master gives him a bone, and stands over him with a whip; he will eat, and look up, and twinch his tail; for they durst not laugh out, lest their Lords should hear they jeer'd them openly; for in their hearts they are Diggers.[136]

Tenants and other local inhabitants were, Winstanley claimed, warned 'neither to give the Diggers lodging nor victuals', while those suspected of sympathising with the Diggers were threatened with eviction, as in the case of a 'poor honest man' given notice to quit 'because he looked with a cheerfull countenance upon the Diggers (though he was affraid to come neer, or affraid to speak openly . . .)'.[137]

Winstanley had good reason to emphasise the tensions between landlord and tenant in Cobham, and allowance must be made for exaggeration in his account of the uneasy relationship between gentry and non-gentry opponents of the Little Heath Digger colony. His depiction of a divided community is not, however, wholly unpersuasive. The Digger movement was rooted in local political culture, and the conflicts and discontents that helped generate support for Winstanley's programme had affected others besides those who became Diggers. Some of the Cobham Diggers were well established in the local community, and would have been linked by family and neighbourhood ties to those who were called upon to oppose them. A violent campaign against the Diggers in Cobham was always likely to be divisive, particularly if it were initiated and controlled by landowners rather than by the community as a whole. In Cobham, much more so than in Walton, the impetus for attacks on the Diggers seems to have come from landowners anxious to protect manorial resources to which they claimed title. Platt, for example, was even said to have considered leaving the Diggers alone if they stopped cutting wood upon the common.[138] Disputes over the respective rights of landowners and others to manorial resources were unlikely to unite the local community against the Diggers, and many inhabitants may have felt reluctant to engage in a campaign whose ultimate aim was to protect their landlords' property interests.

It is also possible that some Cobham inhabitants would have been prepared to tolerate the Digger experiment if it provided employment and food for local poor people who might otherwise turn to the parish for support.[139] In Wellingborough in Northamptonshire, where a Digger colony was established in 1650, some members of the middling sorts were said to have provided support for the venture.[140] In Cobham, local inhabitants may have felt unease at the prospect of demolishing the homes of poor local families, and depriving them of a livelihood, as winter approached in a year of scarcity. Winstanley made much of Platt's unchristian attitude in causing 'a poor old mans house that stood upon the Common, to be pulled down in the evening of a cold day', and in turning 'the old man, and his wife, and daughter to lie in the open field, because he was a Digger'; but it might also have made good economic sense for Platt to allow the house to stand.[141] When the Diggers were finally evicted from the Little Heath in April 1650, several apparently left their children on the parish before they set off to find work elsewhere.[142]

In their letters and pamphlets of November and December 1649, the Diggers played up once more those elements of their programme which drew on arguments from necessity, and which contained echoes of traditional languages of moral economy and reciprocity. It was these elements which might be expected to have most appeal in the local community. One of the justifications for digging provided by the Diggers in their letter to Fairfax was that 'wee digg upon the Common to make the earth a common treasury, because our necessity for food and rayment require it'.[143] Winstanley, in his letters to the Council of State and Fairfax, reminded them that 'we desire noe more of you then freedome to worke, and to enjoy the fruit of our labors, for here is wast land enough and to spare, to supplie all our wants'. Opening up the commons would help quieten the poor 'that ly under the great burden of poverty, and are alwayes complayning for want, and their miseries increased because they see noe meanes of releife found out'; if this freedom were denied them,

> then in rightesnes, you must rayse collections for the poore, out of your estates, and a masse of money will not supplie there wants; besides many are in want, that are ashamed to take collection money, and therefore they are desperate, and will rather rob and steale, and disturbe the land, and many are ashamed to beg, therefore would doe any worke for a livelihood, as it is the case of many of the diggers, who have bene good houskeepers.[144]

These arguments were repeated in *A New-Yeers Gift*, in which Winstanley emphasised that in digging the commons he hoped 'in time to obtain the

Freedom, to get Food and Raiment therefrom by righteous labour, which is all I desire'.[145] The Diggers were 'all poor People', who had 'suffered so much in one expence or other since they began'; poverty was 'their greatest burthen; and if any thing do break them from the Work, it will be that'.[146] Pleas of this sort might well have gained a sympathetic hearing from local inhabitants who were otherwise unpersuaded by Winstanley's teachings. Shorn of its more militant and mystical language, the Digger programme might appear scarcely more disruptive than the many other schemes for setting the local poor to work that were circulating in the late 1640s. By the time the Diggers moved to Cobham, they must also have appeared less threatening than they had in April, when fears were expressed that thousands would join them in bringing about a mass insurrection.[147] It would have been apparent to those who came into contact with the Little Heath Diggers that they were peaceful, few in number, and willing to restrict their activities to within the bounds of the commons they occupied.

What we know of those who joined Platt and Vincent in the campaigns of late 1649 and early 1650 provides support for the view that the local community was divided over the issue of the digging, and that several of those who joined in attacks on the Diggers were, as Winstanley claimed, local landowners, their dependents and hired men.[148] In *An Humble Request*, in which Winstanley described the final assault on the Little Heath colony in April 1650, he again named John Platt and Sir Anthony Vincent as the Diggers' chief antagonists, and also noted that the latter's 'Tenants and Servants, were most of them there'; others said to have been present were Thomas Sutton, the impropriator of the Cobham living, and William Starr of Walton.[149] From legal documents relating to the assault we can add other names. At the Croydon assizes in July 1650 a group of Diggers or local sympathisers attempted to prosecute twenty of the Diggers' assailants, but failed when the bills were thrown out by the grand jury. Those who launched the prosecution, and put their names to the bills as witnesses, were Matthew Mills, Elizabeth Barton, Jane Edsarr or Edsaw, John Palmer, one Lowry and Richard Maidley.[150] Palmer and Maidley were known Diggers; and if Elizabeth Barton and Jane Edsaw were also Diggers then these bills of indictment provide the sole surviving record of women Digger names.[151] Nothing is known of Lowry, but Mills came from a long-settled Cobham family and was well known to several of the Little Heath Diggers. He may himself have been a Digger, but since he signed no Digger manifestos we cannot be certain. If he was not part of the movement, his involvement in the attempted prosecution of the Diggers' opponents provides further evidence of local sympathy for their cause.[152]

What is immediately apparent about the names of accused listed in the bills of indictment is how few of the Diggers' assailants were from Cobham. Over a quarter of the accused were from Stoke d'Abernon, namely William Davey senior and junior, Henry Bird, Edward Bird, Thomas Shore, Thomas Lee and John Poore.[153] Davey was described in *An Humble Request* as 'Sir Anthony Vincents Servant', and Poore may be identified as the servant John Power to whom Vincent left £10 in his will.[154] Thomas Shore of Stoke d'Abernon was married to Mary, daughter of Nicholas Foster, a Cobham yeoman whose forebears had been servants of the Gavells.[155] Shore had been presented before the Cobham manorial court in April 1637 for carrying heath from the common, and during the Civil War he was active in raising money and men in his parish for parliament.[156] Thomas Lee was described in 1644 as a poor man after he failed to pay his two-month weekly assessment.[157] Henry Bird was to be exempted from the hearth tax in Stoke d'Abernon in 1670, as were widow Lee and widow Bird; William Davey was churchwarden that year.[158] Other opponents from outside Cobham were William Starr of Walton, Humphrey Stent or Stint and William Elliott. Elliott's place of residence has not been identified, but there was an Esher resident of that name in 1664.[159] Humphrey Stent was one of Platt's West Horsley parishioners. He was a yeoman farmer and customary tenant of the manor of West Horsley, and he died in April or May 1656.[160]

Most of the rest of the accused – possibly fewer than half the total – had Cobham connections.[161] At the head of the list was John Platt, and he was followed by Thomas Sutton and by the latter's kinsman Edward Sutton. Thomas Sutton had clashed with Winstanley before the digging, when in February he and John Downe of Cobham had acted as arbitrators for Kingston's bailiffs in their dispute with the separatist John Fielder.[162] Edward Sutton, who held the White Lion as a tenant of Ham Court manor, had been identified by Winstanley as an opponent of the Diggers in August.[163] John Greentree and Thomas Hill were living in Cobham in 1650, but little else is known about them except that a child of Greentree's was baptised in Cobham in May 1653.[164] Neither Greentree nor Hill seems to have been a manorial tenant or to have had strong roots in the parish. Robert Melsham, Thomas Parrish, William Honyard and John Goose are better documented.

Robert Melsham came from a family of tailors and yeomen that held property in the parishes of Cobham, Stoke d'Abernon and Esher. He was apparently originally from Esher, but was living in Cobham by 1650. He served as churchwarden in 1669–71 and died in 1674.[165] William Honyard or Whinyard was son of William Whinyard of Cobham, who died in 1627. He was a defaulter at the Cobham view of frankpledge in 1646 and 1648, and was elected tithingman for Cobham Downside in the latter year. In 1664 he was assessed at one hearth and was exempted from the hearth tax. He was in receipt of parochial relief in the years 1662–68 and died in 1668.[166] Thomas Parrish was a Cobham yeoman, who advanced £1 on the propositions in 1642 and was involved in raising weekly and monthly assessments in the parish during the

Civil War.[167] He was a juror at the Cobham court baron and view of frankpledge in 1647 and 1648 and was elected constable of Cobham Downside in 1648; he was high constable of Elmbridge hundred in 1651.[168] In September 1646 his son James was the first child to be baptised in the parish church according to the rules laid down in the Directory of Worship. Thomas Parrish was assessed at four hearths in 1664.[169]

John Goose came from a family of weavers and small copyholders that had settled in Cobham by the mid-sixteenth century at the latest.[170] It is possible that more than one person of this name was present in the parish in 1649, so there is some uncertainty as to which individual was accused of involvement in attacks on the Diggers. A John Goose of Cobham was pressed for a soldier in 1630, while in 1635 a John Goose, who was described as a poor child, was bound apprentice by the Cobham churchwardens John Coulton and Francis Stynt to a Kingston cordwainer.[171] John Goose was elected pinfold for Street Cobham in 1642 and 1646, and was – like Parrish – a juror at the manorial court in 1647 and 1648.[172] It is not certain whether this was the same John Goose of Cobham who fought for the king during the Civil War, and who was awarded a pension after the Restoration. He claimed in 1663 to have been wounded in the service of Charles I, and was 'att present very sicke and weake haveinge a wife and six Children and like to perish for want of reliefe'.[173] John Goose was assessed at one hearth in 1664 and was exempted from the hearth tax; he was in receipt of parish relief in the years 1662–64.[174]

Of the Cobham inhabitants accused of attacking the Digger colony, only four at most – Thomas Sutton, Edward Sutton, Thomas Pardar and John Goose – were manorial tenants at the time of the Digger incursion into their parish.[175] Thomas Sutton was a member of a leading local family, but he was originally from Byfleet and may only have settled in Cobham following his marriage in December 1631 to Katherine, widow of his kinsman James Sutton.[176] Thomas Sutton and Thomas Parrish both played a leading role in the parish during the Civil War, but Parrish did not begin serving on the homage at the manorial court until October 1642, and Sutton never attended on a regular basis; Edward Sutton's first appearance at the homage was not until 1658. John Goose was present at more meetings than any other of the Diggers' opponents, but he did not attend as regularly as did, for instance, Winstanley's friend John Coulton.[177] There was a noticeable absence from the draft bills of indictment, and also from Winstanley's accounts of the attacks on the Digger colony, of the names of those tenants whose attendance at the homage was most frequently recorded in manorial court rolls. It seems that while the Diggers' opponents in Cobham included some gentry, middling sorts and poorer tenants and inhabitants, a number of prominent figures in the local community steered clear of direct involvement in acts of violence against the colony. Several of those who did become involved were clearly quite marginal figures in the community, and some may have been there, as Winstanley suggested, as 'Tenants and Servants' of John Platt and other local gentlemen. The involvement of inhabitants of Stoke d'Abernon and West Horsley in the attacks suggests that the Diggers' Cobham opponents had need of outside help to carry through their campaign, and this may be a further indication of a lack of widespread support in the parish for the plans to destroy the Little Heath colony.

For further proof that the Diggers were not wholly isolated from the local community, we need only turn to an incident that occurred in Cobham's parish church in March 1650. It was probably around this time that Winstanley produced his *Englands Spirit Unfoulded*, a pamphlet that set out to encourage the taking of the Engagement in support of a constitution without king or House of Lords.[178] A version of this oath, which had originally been tendered to members of the council of state in February 1649, was from January 1650 to be taken by all males in England aged eighteen or over.[179] The decision to extend the oath to all adult males was taken partly in response to renewed fears of royalist risings; and in publicly offering his support for the Engagement Winstanley was again seeking to demonstrate the Diggers' commitment to the political changes that had taken place since December 1648. For Winstanley, the Engagement also served a similar purpose to the covenant in justifying the cause of national regeneration advanced by the Diggers, and in isolating those who continued to uphold kingly power by denying the poor their right to occupy the commons.[180] The Engagement encouraged internal regeneration, providing those who had hitherto resisted change – whether as royalists or lords of manors – with the incentive to cast out kingly power from within. In doing so they would liberate themselves as well as those they had oppressed – for 'these that would enslave others, are slaves themselves, to the Kingly Power within themselves' – and they would be protected from the popular anger that would follow any refusal to change their ways.[181] Running through the pamphlet was a belief that elections for a new representative were soon to take place, allowing the people – who 'now do generally understand their freedom' – to exert pressure on their representatives to ensure that true commonwealth's freedom triumphed over kingly power.[182]

Few lists of subscribers to the Engagement are known to have survived, but among the papers of the Hampshire MP Sir Thomas Jervoise of Herriard is a subscription book, endorsed by the commissioners Sir Thomas Evelyn of Long Ditton and Sackford Gunson of Kingston, which records the names of those who took the oath in the middle division of Surrey.[183] The Engagement was tendered to the adult male inhabitants of Kingston and Elmbridge hundreds in March 1650, with a subsequent attempt to collect subscriptions being made in November. Other names were added later, including those of Surrey inhabitants who had been reluctant to take the Engagement when it was first pressed on them. Sir Richard Onslow, for instance, who had dominated Surrey's parliamentarian administration before 1649, did not subscribe until January 1651.[184] Stoke d'Abernon's male parishioners took the Engagement on 9 March, and those of Walton-on-Thames and Cobham on Sunday 16 March. The Cobham list is one of the most comprehensive for Elmbridge Hundred, and includes the names of ninety-four men who subscribed on 16 March and of fifteen others who took the Engagement in November. What is striking about this list of names is not only who was included in it, but also the order in which the subscriptions were recorded. The list was headed by John Fuller, a yeoman and leading figure in the parish, and his name was immediately followed by those of John Coulton, Gerrard Winstanley and Thomas Starr. Other Diggers who took the Engagement that day were Anthony Wrenn, Thomas Barnett, John Hayman and William Taylor, their names interspered in the schedule with those of their kinsmen, neighbours and opponents. Thomas Parrish was the seventh parishioner to subscribe, following Hayman's father-in-law Laurence Johnson and John Downe, while other opponents who subscribed were Edward and Thomas Sutton, Thomas Hill, John Greentree, William Whinyard and Robert Melsham; John Goose did not subscribe until 23 November.[185] Thomas Shore, John Power, Thomas Lee and Edward Bird subscribed in Stoke d'Abernon, and William Starr and John Taylor in Walton.[186] John Platt's name was absent from the list, as was that of Sir Anthony Vincent from the Stoke list of subscribers. It is possible that Platt took the Engagement with his parishioners in West Horsley, but if he and Vincent were among those who had scruples about subscribing, this may provide a further explanation for Winstanley's very public endorsement of the Engagement.[187]

Englands Spirit Unfoulded was cast in what for Winstanley was the unusual form of a dramatic dialogue, the merits of the Engagement being discussed by two friends who had met by chance. This was one of several experimental forms adopted by the Diggers as they attempted to win support and spread their message in the winter of 1649–50. Also to appear in late 1649 and early 1650 were *The Diggers Mirth*, which included *The Diggers Christmass-Caroll*, and an unpublished Digger Song.[188] Whether Winstanley was responsible for all these works is uncertain, for other Diggers were now producing publications of their own. Both Lewis Berens and Olivier Lutaud have suggested that Robert Coster, a Digger who joined the colony after the move to Cobham, was involved with Winstanley in the composition of *The Diggers Mirth*.[189] Coster was certainly responsible for *A Mite Cast Into the Common Treasury*, a prose and verse pamphlet that appeared in December.[190] This work, which began by restating the Diggers' case in a style reminiscent of the *Light Shining* pamphlets, developed into a critique of the deferential behaviour spawned by inequalities of wealth and power. Digging would free the poor from having to 'go with Cap in hand, and bended knee, to Gentlemen and Farmers, begging and intreating to work with them for 8 d. or 10 d. a day, which doth give them an occasion to tyrannize over poor people'; if the poor refused to work for hire, landowners would no longer be able to let out parcels of land, and would be deprived of 'those great baggs of money'

> which are carried into them by their Tenants, who go in as slavish a posture as may be; namely, with Cap in hand, and bended knee, crouching and creeping from corner to corner, while his Lord (rather Tyrant) walkes up and down the Roome with his proud lookes, and with great swelling words questions him about his holding.

If 'Lords of Mannors, and other Gentlemen' were deprived of rental income, then 'down would fall the Lordliness of their spirits, and then poor men might speak to them; then there might be an acknowledging of one another to be fellow-Creatures'.[191]

In his concluding verses, Coster gave expression to the millenarian hopes that lay at the heart of the Digger programme and had helped sustain the Diggers in the months since April. 'Such community/As shall always indure' was shortly to appear, and 'The Rich and Poore/shall love each other/Respecting of Persons shall fall':

> The glorious State
> which I do relate
> Unspeakable comfort shall bring,
> The Corne will be greene
> And the Flowers seene
> Our store-houses they will be fill'd
> The Birds will rejoyce
> with a merry voice
> All things shall yield sweet increase
> Then let us sing
> And joy in our King,
> Which causeth all sorrowes to cease.[192]

With its combination of trenchant social criticism and expressions of confidence in the imminent regeneration of humanity, Coster's pamphlet contained echoes of *The New Law of Righteousnes* and of *The True Levellers Standard Advanced.* Winstanley also returned to some of the preoccupations of these and earlier works in his writings of the winter of 1649–50. Much of *A New-Yeers Gift* was taken up with a discourse on kingly power and with criticism of the clergy, lawyers and lords of manors, but this was expressed in an apocalyptic language reminiscent of Winstanley's pre-Digger works.[193] Christ was rising, and his 'power of Righteousness shall rise and spred from East to West, from North to South, and fill the Earth with himself' and cast out the 'Kingly power of darkness'; the conflicts troubling mankind, and afflicting each individual, were between love and covetousness, universal and particular love, and – in what was to become a persistent theme in the late Digger pamphlets – between light and darkness.[194] Imagination bred covetousness, which in turn bred fear; and from this came 'hypocrisie, subtlety, envie, and hardness of heart, which makes a man to break all promises and engagements, and to seek to save himself in others ruine, and to suppresse and oppresse every one that does not say as he sayes, and do as he does'.[195] Universal love was equated with community, and the power of self-love with covetousness and with inequality and oppression: 'And all this falling out or quarrelling among mankind, is about the earth who shall, and who shall not enjoy it, when indeed it is the portion of every one, and ought not to be striven for, nor bought, nor sold, whereby some are hedged in, and others hedged out.' The power of darkness was 'mans fall, or the night time of mankind':

> But Universall love hath declared that he will rise again, and he himself who is the Seed, will bruise that Serpents head, and reconcile mankind to himself again, and restore him to that Innocencie and Peace which he is fallen from. When this Son arises in more strength, and appears to be the Saviour indeed, he will then make mankind to be all of one heart and one mind, and make the Earth to be a common treasurie, though for the present in outward view there is nothing but darkness and confusion upon the face of the earth, mankind.[196]

Christ was the 'great Leveller' and the 'Spirit and power of universall love', and through his rising the prophecy that the poor shall inherit the earth was 'really and materially to be fullfilled'.[197] All would be saved, and the restoration of the creation would bring about community of mankind and community of the earth, 'that true Levelling which Christ will work at his most glorious appearance'; for 'Jesus Christ the Saviour of all men, is the greatest, first, and truest Leveller that ever was spoke of in the world'.[198]

It is possible that Winstanley's detailed exposition of his religious views in *A New-Yeers Gift* reflected in part a desire to engage in theological debate with John Platt and his fellow ministers, and to counter accusations that the Diggers' were unbelievers. The dispute with Platt may also explain, as Olivier Lutaud and David Boulton have suggested, the strong anticlerical focus of this work.[199] The religious turn was not however confined to *A New-Yeers Gift*, and it does seem that Winstanley was becoming concerned in late 1649 to reaffirm the religious underpinnings of the Digger programme, and perhaps also to re-assess his theological position in the light of the many setbacks experienced by the Diggers since April. On 20 December, only days before the appearance of *A New-Yeers Gift*, Winstanley had issued his *Several Pieces Gathered into one Volume*, a collection that brought together his first five publications and *The New Law of Righteousnes*, all of which dated from before the start of the digging. Winstanley's preface sought to emphasise the continuities between his pre-Digger and Digger writings, and to demonstrate that all he wrote arose from the spirit within, or from 'the light that is in me': those who disliked what he had published since *The Saints Paradise* 'know little of the Spirits inward workings; and truly what I have writ since or before that time, I was carried forth in the work by the same power, delivering it to others as I received it, and I received it not from books nor studie'.[200]

Winstanley's *Fire in the Bush*, which followed shortly after, was an avowedly apocalyptic work that has been described by Gerald Aylmer as 'perhaps the most obscure but possibly also the most important of his later writings'.[201] It was only in 1969 that its correct date of publication became known, when Sir Keith Thomas succeeded in establishing – from a recently rediscovered copy of George Thomason's – that the work had first appeared in March 1650. Many scholars had previously assumed that *Fire in the Bush* was written either before or after the Digger experiment, since it contained no certain references to the digging and bore many resemblances to Winstanley's early mystical writings.[202] Its closest resemblance was however to the religious passages of *A New-Yeers Gift*, many of the arguments of which were developed or reworked in the later publication. The internal conflicts between love and covetousness and between light and darkness were again outlined, and once more Winstanley asserted that 'all the strivings that is in Mankinde, is for the Earth, who shall have it; whether some particular persons shall have it, and the rest have none, or whether the Earth shall be a common treasury to all without respect of persons'.[203] Christ was again depicted as 'the true and faithfull Leveller', and imagination shown to be 'that God, which generally everyone worships and ownes', and which bred the fear that caused individuals to oppress others.[204]

Fire in the Bush was dedicated to the churches – 'in the Presbyterian, Independent, or any other forme of profession, in the service of God' – and predicted their destruction. Nothing should come between the individual and God, and all government 'set up by Imagination, shall be throwne downe'.[205] Most existing civil government belonged to the mystery of iniquity and was now as much in Winstanley's sights as the ministry, for 'the covetous, scoffing, covenant-breaking, thieves and murderers, that croud themselves under the name Magistracie, shall be sent empty away':

> You oppressing powers of the world, who think God hath blessed you, because you sit downe in that Chaire of Government, out of which the former Tyrants are gone: Doe you remember this? your overturning, overturning, overturning, is come on to you, as well as to your fellow break-promises, that are gone before; You that pretend to be saviours of the people, and to seeke the peace of the whole Nation; and yet serve your selves upon the peoples ruines, not regarding the crie of the poore, surely you must have your overturnings too.[206]

With its far-reaching scope *Fire in the Bush* recalled the millenialism of *The New Law of Righteousnes*, and it matched the earlier work in the strength of its denunciation of private property. The law of property was 'the shamefull nakednesse of Mankinde, and as farre from the Law of Christ, as light from darknesse'; and when Christ casts covetousness out of the heart 'so propriety is cast out from amongst men'.[207] The 'greatest sinnes in the world' were to lock up the treasuries of the earth, allowing it 'to rust or moulder, while others starve for want to whom it belongs, and it belongs to all'; and also to take and hold the earth by force, punishing by death 'any who takes the fruits of the Earth to supply his necessaries, from places or persons, where there is more then can be made use of by that particular family, where it is hoorded up'.[208] The present age was the last period of the Beast's reign, and England lay under the dividing of time; the struggle between Michael and the Dragon 'growes hotter and sharper then formerly', and 'the Lambe will cast the Dragon out, and bring all into Peace'.[209] Once more the emphasis was firmly on struggles taking place within each individual, rather than on any need to look to a 'Saviour that stands at a distance'; for 'that which hath by Imagination, or Judas Ministry, been held forth to us, to be without us' were 'within the heart of man clearly. And whether there was any such outward things or no, it matters not much, if thou seest all within, this will be thy life'.[210]

Winstanley's denunciation in *Fire in the Bush* of government founded upon the power of the sword, and his criticism of those who equated 'the state of nature' with the 'power in man, that causes divisions and war', has occasionally been seen as a possible allusion to Hobbes, whose *Leviathan* was to appear in print the following year.[211] It seems much more likely, however, that Winstanley was thinking of Anthony Ascham's *Of the Confusions and Revolutions of Government*, which had been published in November 1649 and which contained a detailed, though respectful rebuttal of Digger arguments.[212] Ascham expressed 'wonder not so much at this sort of arguing, as to find that they who would have such sort of Arguments in their mouths, should have spades in their hands'; for, as he pointed out, 'they conteine the most intricate points of the Constitution of societyes, of the Lawes of Nature and Nations'.[213] In seeking to defend the *de facto* powers of the republican regime, Ascham explored in detail the origins and ends of government and contrasted the virtues of civil government with a lawless state of nature.[214] For Ascham, the state of nature had been a state of community, with goods held in common, until in those anarchic conditions the weaker gave way to the stronger and 'inequality perfectly bred dominion, and that Property'; civil government had inevitably, and necessarily followed as fear bred 'generall compact or conditions for secure neighbour-hood, and for holding what was first laid hand on, though in unequall parts'.[215] Ascham appears to have assumed that the Diggers rejected all civil magistracy as well as private property, and that they wished for a return to a state of nature which they mistakenly believed to be characterised by 'simplicity and charity'.[216] In Ascham's view violence was the inevitable accompaniment to the state of nature, for without government there could be no peace:

> They who would live thus brutishly in meere Nature, have not yet considered that to avoyd Law, they must live in perpetuall war, (there is no such thing as *Salus populi*, or protection there) and that they can never find a way, how the fruits of the earth should be kept as a Common stock, and be equally distributed and spent according to the equality of worke done, whereby every one ought to have his Quantum.[217]

Although Winstanley could have replied to these arguments by insisting – as he had in other works – that the Diggers were not in principle against *all* civil government, he sought instead to deny the equation between the 'Law of darknesse' and the state of nature, and to emphasise humanity's natural goodness before it was corrupted by outward objects. This was the context for Winstanley's oft-quoted comment on the innocency of youth:

> Looke upon a childe that is new borne, or till he growes up to some few yeares, he is innocent, harmelesse, humble, patient, gentle, easie to be entreated, not envious; And this is Adam, or mankinde in his Innocency; and this continues till outward objects intice him to pleasure, or seeke content without him; And when he consents, or suffers the imaginary Covetousnesse within to close with the objects, Then he falls, and is taken captive, and falls lower and lower.[218]

Taken together, *A New-Yeers Gift, Several Pieces* and *Fire in the Bush* provided a comprehensive account of Winstanley's theology and political philosophy, on a scale that could not have been attempted in most of the Digger pamphlets. By publishing these works at this time, Winstanley was able to respond confidently to his critics among the clergy, to explain his views to readers who were unfamiliar with his pre-Digger writings, and also, it would seem, to address new challenges from fellow radicals seeking to compete with him for attention and support in the crowded world of post-civil war sectarian radicalism. Winstanley's claim in June 1649 that the digging 'is the talk of the whole Land' may not have been too much of an exaggeration, for it is evident that the Digger experiment did have an appreciable impact in radical circles.[219] The favourable response of some Buckinghamshire radicals to the digging upon St George's Hill has already been noted; and for a brief moment at least Winstanley's influence was to be felt among separatist groups over a wide area of southern and eastern England. Winstanley's writings were known in Warboys in Huntingdonshire, where Henry Denne had established his general baptist church in 1644, and members of the congregation there were said to have been led astray by the erroneous ideas of 'Diggers, Levellers and Ranters'.[220] The minister of Fenny Drayton in Leicestershire, Nathaniel Stephens, was another who became concerned about the local influence of

Winstanley's ideas. Stephens, who had laboured in vain to prevent the young George Fox from 'going after new lights', claimed to have seen Winstanley's *The New Law of Righteousnes* 'scattered abroad' by those he had once considered friends and 'of good hope', but who had since come to depart from the ministry, to slight the written word and to 'hang upon Revelations, and extraordinary Enthusiasms of the Spirit'.[221]

Several of the anti-formalist and spiritualist writers who flourished at the time of the Digger moment were clearly influenced by Winstanley or felt constrained to distance themselves from him. Abiezer Coppe, whose *A Fiery Flying Roll* had appeared before the end of December 1649, denied any connection with 'digging-levelling', while sharing with Winstanley a hatred of covetousness and a belief that 'the true communion amongst men, is to have all things common, and to call nothing one hath, ones own'.[222] George Foster's *The Sounding of the Last Trumpet* (1650) showed the unmistakeable influence of Winstanley in its vision of the restoration of the creation from bondage, the removal of the curse from the earth and 'the restitution of all things' – and in its prediction that the poor would become equal with the rich, 'all injoying the fruits of the earth and so no longer to worke for others, or others to have the benefit of their labours'.[223] Like Winstanley, Foster foresaw the destruction of existing, corrupt forms of civil as well as church government, and the coming of community and of 'universiall peace and freedome'.[224] Though published while the Diggers were active on Little Heath, Foster's pamphlet made no direct reference to Winstanley's writings, the views it contained being presented as the fruits of the author's own visions.[225] Later in the decade Fox and the early Quakers would fashion a movement which in its activism, spiritual millenarianism and striking language and imagery bore many resemblances to Winstanley's theology and writings, but which acknowledged no debt to the earlier thinker.[226]

The Surrey Digger commune no doubt received visits from sympathisers and the curious, some of whom may have spent time on St George's Hill or Little Heath. We should not assume that all who visited, or who were otherwise inspired by the Diggers' commitment to the advancement of community, were uncritical of every aspect of the Digger programme. Some may have applauded the Diggers' actions while resenting the intellectual control that Winstanley maintained over the movement, and resentment of this kind may even have been discernable within the colony itself. One person who may have come into contact with the Digger colony was the much-travelled seeker Laurence Clarkson, who was gaining a reputation as self-styled 'Captain of the Rant', and who was starting to espouse practical antinomian views far removed from Winstanley's understanding of the restoration from bondage.[227] Clarkson's views, as enunciated in his *A Single Eye* of 1650, offered a direct challenge to Winstanley's portrayal of the internal combat between love and covetousness and between light and darkness. While Winstanley hoped that light and love would triumph in individuals through their adoption of an activist religion of conduct, Clarkson insisted that as all powers derived from God, light and darkness were alike to God; darkness, and sinful acts, were such only in the imagination of fallen man, and to the pure all things were pure: 'there is no act whatsoever, that is impure in God, sinful with or before God'. For Clarkson:

> When as a man in purity in light, acts the same acts, in relation to the act, and not the title: this man (no this man) doth not swear, whore, nor steal: so that for want of this light, of this single pure eye, there appeareth Devil and God, Hell and Heaven, Sin and Holynesse, Damnation and Salvation; only, yea only from the esteemation and dark apprehension of the Creature.[228]

The concept of the single eye was a familiar one in radical mystical circles, but in Clarkson's formulation it became associated with an indifference to conduct which contrasted strongly with Winstanley's (and Coppe's) belief that an individual's behaviour towards others was all-important.

In asserting that 'for my part, till I acted that, so called sin, I could not predominate over sin', Clarkson came dangerously close, moreover, to endorsing the conventional, hostile equations of antinomianism with libertinism.[229] It was just this kind of extreme expression of practical antinomian doctrine, combined with reports of deliberately shocking and provocative behaviour, that encouraged the authorities later in 1650 to take action against what was seen as a growing 'Ranter' menace.[230] Clarkson's eagerness to put his doctrine into practice has been questioned by historians, but his own later testimony (in the admittedly untrustworthy form of a Muggletonian conversion narrative, published in 1660 as *The Lost Sheep Found*) suggests that he was not loth to act out this belief that 'none can be free from sin, till in purity it be acted as no sin'. Clarkson's choice of act, he later claimed, was adultery, since he apparently preferred this 'lustfull principle' to the 'ranting and swearing' practised by Coppe and his companions.[231]

It is not clear precisely what contacts there were between Clarkson and the Diggers, but it does seem that some sort of confrontation took place between him and Winstanley. As Clarkson remembered it in *A Lost Sheep Found*, he accused Winstanley of having 'a self-love and vain-glory nursed in his heart', and of seeking through the digging venture 'to have gained people to him, by which his name might become great among the poor Commonalty of the Nation'.[232] It is possible that this confrontation was connected with the unexpected appearance in Winstanley's writings in early 1650 of a series of condemnatory references to 'Ranters' and to 'the ranting power', which Winstanley clearly associated with the sort of excess and sexual licence then openly advocated, and possibly practised, by Clarkson. There is also evidence to suggest that Winstanley feared that this 'ranting power' had begun to cause dissention among his fellow Diggers, or at least among those he had had hopes of attracting to the Diggers' cause.

In *The New Law of Righteousnes* Winstanley had sought to respond to the age-old assertion that common ownership led inevitably to the holding of partners in common, and his sensitivity towards accusations of this sort continued to be seen throughout the Digger period.[233] Winstanley's defensive statements on this issue were, however, very different from his denunciations of a ranting power that he saw as threatening the spiritual wellbeing of actual or potential supporters of the digging venture. In *A Vindication of Those, Whose Endeavors is Only to Make the Earth a Common Treasury, Called Diggers*, a pamphlet devoted wholly to the 'ranting' threat, Winstanley sought not only to defend Diggers who had been 'slandered with the Ranting action', but also to warn of the consequences of following that path. Those most at risk were, he maintained:

> All you that are meerly civill, and that are of a loving and flexible disposition wanting the strength of reason: and the life of universall love, leading you forth to seeke the peace and preservation of every single body as of one's selfe; You are the People that are like to be tempted, and set upon and torne into peeces by this devouring Beast; the Ranting power.[234]

Tellingly, he insisted once more that 'these two men, one of Light, and the other of darknesse, now strives with great vehemencie'.[235]

Winstanley had attempted in *A New-Yeers Gift* to counter accusations that 'we Diggers hold women to be common, and live in that bestialnesse', while acknowledging that 'there have been some among the Diggers that have caused scandall, but we dis-own their wayes'.[236] *Englands Spirit Unfoulded* contained a 'watch-word' to women to beware 'the ranting crew', and a warning that 'if any of the Diggers fall into the practise of Ranting, they fall off from their principles, as some in all Churches does'.[237] In *Fire in the Bush*, Winstanley again condemned 'Lust of the flesh' as 'an excessive, or immoderate degree of covetousnesse'.[238] Whether these passages were written in response to the disruptive activities of Clarkson and his associates is not certain, and there were other acquaintances of Winstanley to whom the 'ranting' label was loosely applied in 1650. The former Digger William Everard, for instance, was described as 'Ranting Everard' when incarcerated in Bridewell in December of that year.[239] There were however passages in *Fire in the Bush* in which Winstanley appeared to engage directly with what seem very much like Clarksonian arguments. 'Some of you', Winstanley suggested, 'have got a speech':

> That those that see two powers within themselves, of darknesse and Light, Love and Envy, sorrow and comfort striving together, sees with two eyes: but you may say, you see every thing and power with a single eye, and nothing you see evill, but all things and actions are good, and as they must be.

Surely this is well, if you become all of you that speake these words, to eat of that Tree of Life; for my part Ile not condemne you. I can rejoyce to see the Resurrection of Christ in any, but I must watch some of you, to see if your conversations be so universally filled with Love, as shall make the darke world startle; and then I can say of a truth, Christ is risen indeed in you.

As usual, for Winstanley, it was by an individual's behaviour towards others that such claims to purity might be judged:

If your own eye be darke, that is, if darknesse rule your whole body; then all the actions of your body towards others are in darknesse, and builders up of selfishnesse, which is the one power you yet live in.

But if your eye be truly single, and full of Light, then the Light power wholly rules in you, and the actions of your outward man will be full of Light, and Life, and Love, towards every single branch of the whole Creation.[240]

THE END OF THE DIGGER COLONY

Winstanley's *A Vindication* contained further evidence of dissension in the Digger ranks, in an appendix which drew attention to attempts to raise money in the country from 'such as are friends to the Diggers'. Winstanley insisted that no such collections had been authorised, and he denied having signed the note carried by the collectors 'wherein my name and divers others are subscribed'.[241] It seems likely, given the context in which this was written, that the collections were being undertaken by former Diggers or Digger sympathisers who had fallen out with those who remained on the Little Heath. It was in response to these unauthorised activities that the Cobham Diggers sent out two emissaries, Thomas Heydon and Adam Knight, carrying a letter soliciting funds and asking sympathisers to send money directly to Cobham 'by some trusty friend of your owne'. The letter, which was published in *A Perfect Diurnal* after its bearers were arrested in the Northamptonshire town of Wellingborough on 4 April, provided a detailed picture of the state of the Diggers' cause at the end of the winter of 1649–50. The last summer's work had, the authors claimed, been lost as a result of their enemies' actions, but they had 'planted divers Acres of Corn and built 4. houses, and now this season time goes on digging , endeavouring to plant as much as they can; but in regard of poverty their work is like to flagge and droppe'. Money was needed to buy victuals and seed corn, and to 'keep alive the beginning of publique Freedom to the whole Land, which otherwise is ready to die again for want of help'. The letter was signed by Winstanley and twenty-one other male Diggers, 'Besides their Wives and Children, and many more if there were food for them'. Before they were arrested, Heydon and Knight had travelled through Buckinghamshire, Middlesex, Hertfordshire, Bedfordshire, Berkshire, Huntingdonshire and Northamptonshire, stopping at thirty-three towns and villages along the way.[242] Their route took them through, or close to, several places where support for the digging is known to have been forthcoming. These included Warboys, where members of Denne's church had expressed sympathy for the Digger project, and Colnbrook, Dunstable, Whetstone and Wellingborough, near to where Digger sympathisers were beginning to set up colonies of their own.[243] In Bedfordshire, they travelled through Caddington, a parish where prolonged conflicts over enclosure had taken place in the decades before the Civil War, as had mass trespasses involving digging and ploughing of the manorial waste.[244] In Cambridgeshire and Hertfordshire the Digger emissaries passed close to parishes where Quakerism was soon to make an appreciable impact.[245]

It may have been this evidence of growing support for the Digger programme that sealed the fate of the Cobham colony. By the time the Cobham Diggers issued *An Appeale to all Englishmen* on 26 March, digging was taking place in Wellingborough in Northamptonshire and was said to have started at 'Cox Hall in Kent'.[246] Another Digger community was soon established at Iver in Buckinghamshire, and by 1 May those involved in this new venture were claiming that digging activities had been extended to Barnet, Enfield and Dunstable, and to 'Bosworth old in Northamptonshire' and unspecified places in Buckinghamshire, Gloucestershire and Nottinghamshire.[247] With the exception of the Iver and Wellingborough communities (both of which issued manifestos) very little is known about digging activities outside Surrey. The site of the digging in Kent, for instance, cannot be identified with any certainty, since there appears to be no place named Cox Hall in that county.[248] The name given in *An Appeale to All Englishmen* may, as George H. Sabine believed, have been meant to refer to Cox Hill near Dover, or, as Christopher Hill suggested, to the unenclosed Cox Heath near Linton.[249] Peter Clark has plausibly suggested Cock Hill near Boxley, 'an old radical centre with Lollard and Brownist associations', and 'Cox Hall' may even be a reference to Coggeshall in Essex which – as Christopher Hill also pointed out – was often called Coxhall during the seventeenth century.[250] Similarly, the identity of 'Bosworth old in Northamptonshire' remains uncertain. Northamptonshire contains no Bosworth, and both Market Bosworth and Husbands Bosworth are in the neighbouring county of Leicestershire. Sir Keith Thomas was almost certainly correct in suggesting that the Iver Diggers were referring to Husbands Bosworth – which lies on the Northamptonshire border – rather than to Market Bosworth, but in the absence of further evidence it is impossible to be sure.[251] Nothing is known of the location of the Digger colonies in Gloucestershire and Nottinghamshire. Enclosure riots took place in the Gloucestershire parishes of Slimbridge and Frampton in June 1650, and the Forest of Dean was the site of agrarian conflict later in the decade, but again no evidence has been found to link the Diggers to these places.[252]

It seems clear from the Iver declaration that digging did get under way in Barnet and Enfield, and that the Iver Diggers managed to establish some sort of contact with the colonies there.[253] It is not known whether the Barnet Diggers were active in the Hertfordshire parish of High Barnet, or in the Middlesex parish of Friern Barnet, which included the hamlet of Whetstone through which Thomas Heydon and Adam Knight had passed. The manor of Whetstone or Friern Barnet was the scene of conflict over entry fines during the Interregnum, after the manorial rights, which had belonged to the Dean and Chapter of St Paul's, were sold in 1649 to the London draper Richard Utber.[254] Enfield, as David Pam has shown, also had experience of widespread agrarian conflicts during the 1640s and 1650s. Population pressures and the depletion of natural resources had led during the late sixteenth and early-seventeenth centuries to restrictions on commoners' rights on Enfield Chase, and sporadic outbreaks of fence breaking and wood stealing had taken place in the locality in the decades before the outbreak of war.[255] There were frequent reports during the war of deer killing and illegal tree felling on the chase and in Enfield Old Park, and armed gangs of deer stealers were still active on the chase and in Theobalds Park in 1649.[256] As in Cobham, manorial administration in Enfield continued to operate effectively in the mid- and late 1640s, and in 1644 and 1645 large numbers of inhabitants were apparently presented and fined at the Duchy manor court for wood stealing.[257] When the manor of Enfield was surveyed in 1650, inhabitants of the adjoining parishes and towns of Edmonton, Hadley and South Mimms petitioned for the protection of local rights of access to the commons, and warned that if existing customary rights were lost many hundreds of poor families would become an insupportable burden on their neighbours.[258] In 1659, after a large part of the chase had been divided up and sold, running battles took place between commoners and soldiers, some of whom had purchased land there.[259] The response by one Enfield resident, William Covell, to these 'tumults, madness, and confusions', was to propose settling commons and wastes on the poor, and establishing in Enfield a co-operative, moneyless community which would serve as a model for the rest of England and the World.[260] It seems that Enfield was very much the sort of place where Digger ideas might be expected to find a sympathetic audience.

Rather more is known about those involved in the Iver and Wellingborough Digger colonies. Iver, which was situated on the Buckinghamshire border with Middlesex, was a large parish of roughly seven miles in length and two miles in width, and with a population in the seventeenth century of between six and seven hundred.[261] Much of the northern half of the parish was taken up by Iver Heath, which was the most likely site of any Digger experiment in 1650. At the parish's southern end, and lying partly within its boundaries, was the town of Colnbrook, which has sometimes been described as a home of Winstanley. The suggestion that Winstanley settled in Colnbrook after his move from London was first made by L. H. Berens, who was apparently unaware of Winstanley's connection with Cobham.[262] No evidence of Winstanley's residence in the locality has ever come to light, and it is almost certainly a coincidence that Mansfield manor, a small estate in Iver, was owned in 1650 by Nicholas Grice, a kinsman of James Winstanley of Gray's Inn.[263] Links between mid-Surrey and this area were however quite strong. The sons of at least four Colnbrook inhabitants were apprenticed to Kingston tradespeople in the years 1630–45, and the estates of the Kingston Bridge endowment included lands in the parish of Iver.[264] Colnbrook was apparently the first town visited by Thomas Heydon and Adam Knight on their fund-raising tour of southern and Midland counties.[265]

The manor of Iver was part of a contiguous group of manors, which also included West Drayton and Harmondsworth, acquired by the Paget family in 1546 and 1547. The Pagets were for many years involved in disputes with their Middlesex and Buckinghamshire tenants over entry fines and other manorial customs, and they were apparently still in dispute with their West Drayton tenants at the end of the 1640s.[266] During the Civil War the manor of Iver had been subject to sequestration, along with other Paget properties, before William Lord Paget returned from the king's quarters late in 1644.[267] Iver was in an area that suffered the effects of the army's presence in 1647, and for a brief period in August 1647 Fairfax established his headquarters at Colnbrook.[268] Local tensions come through clearly in the 1650 Iver Digger declaration. The authors of the declaration emphasised their 'present necessity, and want of the comfort which belongs to our Creation', and pointed to the lack of adequate local support for the poor: 'we see no hope, comfort, or redresse to be had from any that are in Authority in our Parrish, who say they will do nothing but what they are forc'd to do'.[269] Like the Cobham Diggers, they argued that only by manuring the commons could the poor obtain a proper livelihood and not be confined to 'a distracted, languishing and miserable life'.[270]

The names of ten Iver Diggers are known, all of them signatories to the Iver Digger declaration. Sir Keith Thomas, who was responsible for bringing this work to light, demonstrated conclusively that the signatories all had connections with the parish in which they set to work.[271] A number of them were, like their Cobham counterparts, manorial tenants, and at least two had served as jurors at the manorial court in the 1640s.[272] Henry Slane or Slann was a regular member of the homage in 1644 and 1645, and had also served as churchwarden in 1643–44.[273] Several of the Iver Diggers had young families, as was the case in Cobham, and at least one may later have become a Quaker.[274] A similar pattern can be seen in Wellingborough, where nine individuals put their names to a Digger declaration published by Giles Calvert in March 1650.

The Wellingborough declaration conveyed the same sense of urgency as the Iver declaration had done, and again great emphasis was placed on the high incidence of poverty in the locality and on the absence of practical support for the poor:

> We are in Wellinborrow in one Parish 1169 persons that receive Alms, as the Officers have made it appear at the Quarter Sessions last: we have made our Case known to the Justices, the Justices have given Order that the Town should raise a Stock to set us on work, and that the Hundred should be enjoyned to assist them; but as yet we see nothing is done, nor any man that goeth about it; we have spent all we have, our trading is decayed, our wives and children cry for bread, our lives are a burden to us, divers of us having 5.6.7.8.9. in Family, and we cannot get bread for one of them by our labor; rich mens hearts are hardened, they will not give us if we beg at their doors; if we steal, the Law will end our lives, divers of the poor are starved to death already, and it were better for us that are living to dye by the Sword then by the Famine.[275]

The language of this passage was reminiscent of that used by the Midland 'Diggers' of 1607, who had declared that 'better it were in such case, wee manfully dye, then hereafter to be pined to death for want of yt wch these devouring Encroachers doe serve theyr fatt Hogges & Sheep withall'.[276]

Both the Wellingborough and Iver declarations echoed traditional concerns of rural rioters, and included specific demands that reflected local needs and preoccupations. The Iver Diggers, for instance, made demands relating to the regulation of fishing and the payment of soldiers' arrears, and they asked that mechanisms be established to control the activities of engrossers and to call churchwardens and overseers to account.[277] Both declarations, however, belonged unmistakably to the Digger canon, and contained the same potent combination of religious radicalism and arguments drawn from necessity that lay at the heart of Winstanley's message. The opening paragraphs of the Iver declaration were clearly modelled on those drawn up by their Wellingborough counterparts, and they in turn leant heavily on arguments advanced in the Surrey Digger manifestos. The earth had been made for the whole of mankind, but mankind had been deprived of its benefits; the scriptures however promised the end of oppression and the restoration of the creation. The Wellingborough Diggers made clear that restoration would take place 'in the last days', while the Iver Diggers defined the 'glorious liberty' to come as 'equality, community and fellowship with our own kind'.[278] Both groups followed Winstanley in emphasising the significance of the acts abolishing kingship and declaring England to be a commonwealth and free state; they were also careful to deny that they would invade their neighbours' property – at least, in the words of the Wellingborough Diggers, 'until they freely give us it'.[279] Like the St George's Hill Diggers before them, both groups invited others to join in the work or to provide assistance until their crops came up.[280] The Wellingborough Diggers echoed Winstanley in insisting that the commons and wastes belonged to the poor, and that 'we have a right to the common ground both from the Law of the Land, Reason and Scriptures', while the Iver Diggers invoked the Golden Rule and interpreted it as allowing all to have 'food and rayment, freely without being a slave to any of our fellow Creatures'.[281] They also adopted Winstanley's radical critique of custom, and, in describing how 'the great ones like Ratts and Mice drawe all the treasures and fruits of the earth into their nests and holes after them', borrowed a striking phrase used by Winstanley in the preface to *Fire in the Bush*.[282] Like the Surrey Diggers, the authors of the Wellingborough declaration sought to portray their most persistent opponents as 'such as have been constant enemies to the Parliaments Cause from first to last'.[283]

Eight of the nine signatories to the Wellingborough declaration can be traced in local records. There were possibly three individuals named Richard Smith living in Wellingborough in March 1650, one of them a glover and one (Richard Smith junior) a labourer. At least two of them had young families.[284] In 1655 a Quaker named Richard Smith went with the Wellingborough Quaker Francis Ellington to Findon, where both were assaulted by Bridget Makerines and others who threw water, stones and dirt at them and called them 'rogues, witches and Divels'. Ellington and Smith subsequently turned up unannounced at the home of Thomas Pentlow of Wilby, a JP whom the Northamptonshire Quakers identified as one of their chief persecutors and who was chiefly responsible for bringing the Wellingborough Digger venture to an end.[285]

Other Wellingborough Diggers with young children included John Avery, Joseph Hitchcock and Richard Pendred. Hitchcock and Pendred both had children of one-year-old or less at the time of the digging; Ann, a three-year-old daughter of John Avery, was buried in February 1650, only weeks before digging began. John Fartley alias Pie, Pye or Py married Elizabeth Fowler in 1644, and their children were baptised in 1645 and 1647. James Pittman, possibly a Wellingborough shepherd of that name, married Mary Bacon in 1635. They had four children, but the two youngest, born in 1642 and 1647 respectively, were both dead by March 1650; Mary Pittman died in 1654. Roger Tewes, a labourer, married Dorothy Skinner of Wellingborough in 1654, the ceremony taking place before the JP Thomas Pentlow.[286] 'Thomas Fardin' may have been Thomas Fardell or Fardill, a Wellingborough blacksmith who died, possibly unmarried, in 1659.[287] Only Edward Turner cannot be traced in the Wellingborough parish registers, but the surname was a common one in the town.

Also identifiable are three 'rich men' – John Freeman, Thomas Nottingham and John Clendon – who were praised by the Wellingborough Diggers for assisting their venture, having 'freely given us their share' in the common where the Diggers had begun planting corn.[288] Thomas Nottingham married Mary Hills in Wellingborough in 1624, and 'Mr John Freeman' married Margaret Mills in 1644; the will of a Wilby yeoman of this name was proved in 1657.[289] There were at least two John Clendons in Wellingborough in 1650, one of whom was buried in 1651 and the other in 1671. Both were bakers.[290] Thomas Nottingham was, as Richard Vann has shown, included in list drawn up by Northamptonshire Quakers in 1655 of men fit to be JPs, and he appears to have died a Quaker in 1670 or 1671.[291] All the evidence suggests that in character and social profile the Wellingborough Digger community bore marked similarities to those of Iver and Surrey, and that in each of these communities the same distinctive convergence of religious radicalism, egalitarianism and concern for the necessitous poor was to be found.

It seems that the Wellingborough Diggers were only able to occupy the commons for a brief period before their activities were curtailed by the JP Thomas Pentlow. In a letter of 15 April 1650, the Council of State assured Pentlow of its support in his 'proceedings with the Levellers in those parts', and instructed him to see that they were dealt with at the next sessions. The Council pointed out that laws existed to deal with 'those that intrude upon other men's properties' and to suppress 'all riotous assemblies and seditious and tumultuous meetings', and that if these laws were properly enforced the public peace would be preserved 'against the attempts of this sort of people'.[292] A reference to the Wellingborough Diggers in the Iver declaration suggests that nine of them were prosecuted at the Northampton quarter sessions on 16 and 17 April, and were kept in gaol despite being acquitted.[293] The Council of State's response to the digging in Wellingborough reflected the commonwealth government's preference for encouraging local elites to take the initiative in tackling individual outbreaks of disorder, while being willing to provide material assistance where necessary. A similar approach had been adopted in April and October 1649, when the Council responded to local appeals for help in dealing with the Surrey Diggers by asking Fairfax to assist Surrey's JPs and sheriff in dispersing them, but that strategy had failed as a result of the army's reluctance to use force against the Diggers. By 1650, however, it seems that the Council had become much more determined to ensure that effective measures were taken to suppress rural disorders, and the army had more reason to provide the necessary assistance. While Captain Gladman had been able to dismiss the St George's Hill Diggers as harmless eccentrics in April 1649, and Fairfax had been happy to visit St George's Hill and discuss with Winstanley the philosophy behind the digging, by the end of 1649 the Diggers' activities could be seen to represent a much greater challenge to the interests of the state and army. As new Digger communities began to appear in parishes across southern England and the Midlands, the government became increasingly willing to make connections between the Diggers' activities and the illegal activities of rural inhabitants quite unconnected with them. The Council of State and army also had a common interest in ensuring that the sale of crown land and decanal estates – the profits of which would help pay soldiers' arrears – might proceed as quickly and smoothly as possible. The presence of Diggers in areas with large quantities of such lands provided a further, compelling motive for action to be taken to bring their movement to an end.

Winstanley had challenged the right of the state to sell crown and church land in *A New-Yeers Gift*, when he argued that 'if there be a spoil to be gathered of crown Lands, Deans, Bishops, Forrests Lands and commons, that is to come to the poor commons freely':

> We that are the poor commons, that paid our Money, and gave you free Quarter, have as much Right in those crown Lands and Lands of the spoil as you; therefore we give no consent That you should buy and sell our crown Lands and waste Lands, for it is our purchased inheritance from under Oppression.[294]

These lands should, he suggested, be divided 'between them that stay'd at home, and them that went to Warr; for the Victory is for the whole Nation'.[295] By the time Winstanley wrote these words Ham Court manor (of which he was a tenant or sub-tenant), had been sold to its lessee Sir George Ayscue. Although Ayscue had been at sea when the lease came up for sale in August 1649, Cromwell had successfully intervened on his behalf in a letter to Speaker Lenthall, and the sale was delayed until his return to shore; Ayscue was able to secure the purchase on 13 November.[296] Parliamentary surveys of crown land in the vicinity of St George's Hill and Cobham began in February 1650, when the Bickerstaffe estate at Pains Hill was surveyed, and were to continue apace until November.[297] In Oatlands Park, which was surveyed in June 1650, the state suffered losses that it was apparently willing to associate – without proper evidence – with the activities of Winstanley and his companions. In December 1649 trees reserved for the use of the navy were felled by locals who then 'sold them away', and the accused, most of whom were from Walton or Weybridge, were sent for in safe custody.[298] Only one of the twelve or more accused – William Smith – bore a Digger name, and there is nothing to prove that he and the Digger were the same person. On 23 February, however, the Council of State wrote to Fairfax, informing him that 'great wasts and spoyles are made of the wood & timber belonging to the Comonwealth in the County of Surrey' and, in what may well have been a reference to the Diggers, reminding him that such actions encouraged 'the looser & disordered sort of people to the greater boldnesse in other designes against the Comonwealth by their impunitie in this'.[299] Surrey's JPs may also have had the Diggers in mind when in January 1650 they issued orders to suppress the illegal hunting of game in the county, which, they complained, was taking place 'to the great damage and preiudice of the Gent. of quality and Lords of Manors'.[300]

On 26 March, after it had become clear that Digger activities had spread beyond Surrey, the Little Heath Diggers produced their most confrontational work yet. *An Appeale to All Englishmen* was, like the Wellingborough and Iver declarations, published as a single broadsheet, and like the first of those it came from the press of Giles Calvert.[301] While Winstanley's involvement in writing the work is clearly evident, its style suggests that he may not have been the sole author. *An Appeale* repeated the familiar Digger claims that all 'Kingly and Lordly entanglements' had been declared against by army and parliament, and that the poor were now free to build upon and plant the commons.[302] The authors went further, however, in declaring explicitly that copyholders were now 'freed from obedience to their Lords of Mannors' and could no longer be compelled by manorial lords to 'come to their Court-Barons, nor to be of their Juries, nor take an Oath to be true to them, nor to pay fines, Heriots, quit-rent, nor any homage, as formerly, while the King and Lords were in their power'; and if tenants 'stand up to maintain their Freedom, against their Lords oppressing power, the Tenants forfeit nothing, but are protected by the Laws and Engagement of the Land'.[303]

The publication of this work may have been occasioned by the imminent sitting of manorial courts, which in many places, including Cobham, often took place in late March or April.[304] It was always possible that manorial court presentments against illegal encroachments might be used to drive the Diggers off the commons, and the authors of *An Appeale* were clearly anxious to dissuade tenants from attending court barons or finding themselves compelled by oath to carry out orders made there. Hence the Diggers' bold assertion that attendance at the manorial court was now illegal, and that

> if so be, that any fearfull or covetous Tenant, do obey their Court-Barons, and will be of their Jury, and will still pay Fines, Heriots, quit-Rents, or any homage as formerly, or take new Oaths, to be true to their Lords, or at the Command of their Lords, do beat the poor men off from planting the Commons; then they have broke the Engagement, and the Law of the Land, and both Lords and Tenants are conspiring to uphold or bring in the Kingly and Lordly Power again, and declare themselves enemies to the Army, and to the Parliament, and are traytors to the Commonwealth of England. And if so be they are to have no protection of the Lawes, that refused to tak the Engagement, surely they have lost their protection by breaking their Engagement, and stand lyable to answer for this their offence, to their great charge and trouble, if any will prosecute against them.[305]

The authors also drew once more on traditional discourses of popular protest, linking these – as Winstanley had done in his earlier pamphlets – with Norman Yoke theory and arguments from scripture. The iniquities of a legal system which filled prisons unnecessarily, and which brought about the 'hart breaking spectacle of seeing so many hanged every Sessions as there are', were again condemned; and the practical advantages of allowing the poor to share the spoils of military victory were stressed. Failure to reward the poor in victory – so that 'either they or their Children are like to be slaves still' – was 'the cause why many run away and faile our Armies in the time of need':

And so through the Gentries hardness of heart against the poor: The Land may be left to a forraigne enemy, for want of the poorers love sticking to them; for say they, we can as well live under a forraign enemy working for day wages, as under our own brethren, with whom we ought to have equal freedom by the Law of righteousness.[306]

Land held by 'the Norman Power' for the last six hundred years was now recovered by law, notwithstanding any arguments drawn from 'the old Lawes and Customes of the Land'; while in making their land a common treasury, the English had the example of the Israelites to follow, when 'the severall portions of the Land of Canaan, were the common Livelihood to such and such a Tribe; both the elder and younger Brother, without respect of persons'.[307]

It was shortly after the appearance of *An Appeale to All Englishmen* that the local campaign against the Surrey Diggers entered its final stages. Presentments were drawn up against four of the Diggers – John Hayman, Anthony Wrenn, Daniel Freeland and Henry Barton – for the illegal erection of cottages which lacked the requisite four acres of land and which were still standing on 1 March 1650.[308] At the Southwark assizes on 1 April fifteen Diggers were indicted for riot, illegal assembly and trespass and for digging up the commons to the detriment of the inhabitants of Walton and Weybridge.[309] This indictment related to the original occupation of St George's Hill the previous year, and those named in the bill included some – among them William Everard and Henry Bickerstaffe – who had abandoned the Digger colony long before.[310] The final assault on the Little Heath colony took place on Friday 19 April, in the week after Easter, and the timing of the action suggests that it may well have resulted from decisions made at Cobham's manorial court. We know the precise date of the attack from the assize indictment which some Diggers later tried to bring against their assailants.[311] The date also accords with Winstanley's suggestion that the events took place 'upon Fryday in Easter week'.[312] For the events themselves Winstanley provided most detail, though his account can be supplemented by information taken from the draft indictments.

In Winstanley's account John Platt and Thomas Sutton had first brought hired men to the Little Heath in the week before Easter, and had ordered them to 'pull down a poor mans house, that was built upon the Commons'. A woman occupant of the house was 'kikt and struck' and 'miscarried of her Child, and by the blowes and abuses they gave her, she kept her bed a week'.[313] There then followed discussions between Winstanley and Platt – the latter, according to Winstanley, using 'loving expressions, and words savouring of much moderation, tenderness and reason'.[314] Platt was said by Winstanley to have undertaken to leave the Diggers alone if they stopped cutting wood on the commons; he also agreed to read a newly-written tract of Winstanley's, which was subsequently printed as the first part of the final Digger pamphlet, *An*

Humble Request.[315] In this work Winstanley repeated the Diggers' case through arguments drawn from the scriptures and from recent history, and he insisted once more that scripture 'gives a full warrant to all poore men, to build them houses, and plant corne upon the Commons and unnurtured land'.[316] Any opponent of this work, so Winstanley maintained, 'doth deny God, Christ, and Scriptures, and overthrows true and pure undefiled religion'; it was 'not only the Gentry, but the Clergy generally are mad against this worke.[317] Platt, he said, 'promised me to read it over, and to give me an Answer'.[318]

The second part of *An Humble Request* was devoted to what Winstanley described as Platt's answer to his tract: the destruction by fire on 19 April of the Diggers' remaining six houses, and the putting in place of measures to prevent any attempt to rebuild the colony. Platt, Sutton and Sir Anthony Vincent were said by Winstanley to have been accompanied on 19 April by 'about 50 men', four or five of them having been hired specifically to burn down the Diggers' houses. The decision to fire the houses, rather than simply to pull them down, appears to have been made in order to prevent the Diggers using salvaged building materials to rebuild.[319] After the houses were destroyed, the 'hired men' were paid to remain on the heath 'to beat the Diggers, and to pull down their tents or houses, if they make any more'; the Diggers' eleven acres-worth of corn was abandoned and turned over to the commoners' cattle. Tenants and other local inhabitants were, according to Winstanley, forbidden from allowing any of the Diggers lodging in their houses, and from selling them victuals.[320] As in his previous accounts of attacks on the Diggers, Winstanley contrasted the passivity of the Diggers with the rage and fury of their assailants, who 'gnashed their tongues with vexation' while the Diggers remained 'patient, chearfull, quiet in spirit, loving to those that have burned their houses'.[321] Once more the Diggers' local origins were emphasised:

> Thereupon at the Command of this Parson Platt, they set fire to six houses, and burned them down, and burned likewise some of their housholdstuffe, and wearing Clothes, throwing their beds, stooles, and housholdstuffe, up and down the Common, not pittying the cries of many little Children, and their frighted Mothers, which are Parishioners borne in the Parish. And yet some of these hired men, lives not in the Parish, and some are strangers newly come into the Parish: and so were bewitched by the covetous make-bate Priests, to do this heathenish turkish act.[322]

We know from the draft assize indictments that among those whose houses were burnt were Henry Barton, Daniel Freeland, Thomas Adams and Robert Sawyer, at least two of whom were locals.[323] Barton and Freeland were also among those presented for illegally erecting cottages on the common.[324] As in December, Winstanley again argued that the local inhabitants who accompanied Platt and Vincent did so only under duress:

many of those that came were threatned by Vincent his chief men, to be turned out of their Livings, if they came not, so that this is not an act of the tenants by free consent, but the Gentlemen hired others to do it.[325]

Although it seems that Winstanley completed *An Humble Request* very soon after the 19 April attacks, it is evident from his narrative that he already recognised that the Little Heath experiment was at an end. With the destruction of the Digger houses and crops, and the measures taken to disperse the Diggers and to keep them off the commons, there can no longer have been any hope of a swift return to the heath. Winstanley was forced to acknowledge that the Diggers had been beaten, but he could at least claim a moral victory: 'And now they cry out the Diggers are routed, and they rang bells for joy; but stay Gentlemen, your selves are routed, and you have lost your Crown, and the poor Diggers have won the Crown of glory.'[326] The Diggers' enemies had gained their advantage only through a resort to violence and to 'the power of the Beast', but the Diggers still kept 'the field of patience, quietness, joy and sweet rest in their hearts'; the final choice between 'freedom and bondage' had yet to be made.[327]

It would be wrong to see the destruction of the Little Heath colony as the point at which the hopes sustaining the Digger experiment were extinguished. Although the Wellingborough colony had already been suppressed by 19 April, and its members brought before the sessions at Northampton, the Iver settlement remained in existence the following month. Other, smaller colonies about which little is known may also have continued their activities beyond April. Winstanley sought in *An Humble Request* to portray the destruction of the Cobham colony as a temporary defeat; it was 'for the present' that the Diggers' enemies had 'trod our weak flesh down'.[328] There was nothing in this pamphlet to suggest that the Diggers would not try to renew their work at a later date, in Cobham or elsewhere, and the arguments in the pamphlet's concluding paragraphs were no more pessimistic than those in *A New-Yeers Gift*, where Winstanley had hinted that some other means besides digging might have to be found to advance the cause of righteousness. In that work Winstanley offered what has since become the most widely-quoted epitaph of the Digger movement:

And here I end, having put my Arm as far as my strength will go to advance Righteousness: I have Writ, I have Acted, I have Peace: and now I must wait to see the Spirit do his own work in the hearts of others, and whether England shall be the first Land, or some other, wherein Truth shall sit down in triumph.[329]

A New-Yeers Gift was, however, published more than three-and-a-half months before the end of digging on the Little Heath, and it was written before *Fire in the Bush, Englands Spirit Unfoulded* and *An Appeale to All Englishmen*, in each of which Winstanley expressed the hope that the Digger venture would ultimately be successful. Winstanley's hopes of success were still evident in *An Humble Request*, and he reiterated there his confident belief that the destruction of the Beast was imminent:

> But though the Devill be let loose to swell against us, in these Gentry that rule over us, by Kingly Power, or Law of Norman Conquest, notwithstanding, they have taken the Engagement, to cast out Kingly Power: yet his time to be chained up drawes nigh: and then we are assured this righteous work of earthly community, shall have a most glorious resurrection out of his ashes.[330]

It is only with the benefit of hindsight that we date the end of the Digger movement to the spring of 1650; Winstanley and his fellow Diggers may not have felt so certain at the time. The Digger movement is often presented as part of a revolution that failed – an abortive, radical revolution that was quite distinct from the successful political revolution of 1648–49, and which inevitably fell victim to the more limited aims of the latter. In this view, the destruction of the Little Heath colony can be seen to have marked the moment when the Diggers' revolution ended, and the Diggers' subsequent careers and writings can conveniently be explained in terms of their reaction to defeat. If we adopt this approach, however, we risk detaching the Diggers from the experiences that moulded them and the events in which they played a part, and we risk losing sight of that sense of millenarian excitement, expectation and experiment which so characterised these years and had such a transformative effect.[331] Winstanley and the Diggers identified strongly with the profound and unexpected political changes that were taking place around them, and they were inspired by them to act; the Diggers were not mere bystanders to political developments with which they felt no affinity. To the Diggers, the Commonwealth government must in April 1650 have continued to represent the best hopes for future advance – despite their disappointment at finding soldiers participating in actions against them – and they would not have held the government to blame for the survival among their gentry opponents of the covetousness and kingly power that had brought them so many reverses. Kingly power had not triumphed; it had simply not yet been defeated. The hope of radical restoration remained in April 1650.

NOTES

1 Sabine, *Works*, p. 392.

2 *A Perfect Diurnall* (16–23 April 1649), p. 2450.

3 *A Perfect Summary of an Exact Dyarie* (23–30 April); *A Modest Narrative of Intelligence* (21–28 April 1649). Cf. BL, Add. MS 37,344, fol. 286.

4 *The Kingdomes Faithfull and Impartiall Scout* (20–27 April 1649).

5 *Mercurius Republicus* (22–29 May 1649), p. 5.

6 Sabine, *Works*, p. 392.

7 *Ibid.*, pp. 284–5, 392.

8 *Ibid.*, pp. 295–8; 393. For a discussion of this incident, see Christopher Kendrick, 'Preaching common grounds: Winstanley and the Diggers as concrete utopians', in William Zunder and Suzanne Trill (eds), *Writing and the English Renaissance* (London, 1996), pp. 217–21.

9 *The Moderate Messenger* (23–30 July); *The Kingdomes Faithfull and Impartial Scout* (20–27 July); *The Perfect Weekly Account* (18–25 July); *The Moderate Intelligencer*, 227 (19–26 July 1649).

10 Sabine, *Works*, pp. 150, 393.

11 *Ibid.*, pp. 284, 295–8, 302, 319–22, 327–35.

12 *Ibid.*, pp. 392–3.

13 Cf. John R. Knott, 'Joseph Besse and the Quaker culture of suffering', in Thomas N. Corns and David Loewenstein (eds), *The Emergence of Quaker Writing: Dissenting Literature in Seventeenth-Century England* (London, 1995), pp. 128, 130, 138–9.

14 Sabine, *Works*, pp. 285, 295.

15 *Ibid.*, pp. 282, 392.

16 *Ibid.*, pp. 330–1. Cf. Nigel Smith, 'Gerrard Winstanley and the literature of revolution', in Bradstock, *Winstanley and the Diggers*, pp. 50–1.

17 Firth, *Clarke Papers*, 2, p. 211.

18 Sabine, *Works*, p. 281.

19 *The Kingdomes Faithfull and Impartiall Scout* (20–27 April 1649); Petegorsky, *Left-Wing Democracy*, p. 164; Hill, *World Turned Upside Down*, p. 88.

20 Arial Hessayen, 'Everard, William', *ODNB* (2004).

21 Sabine, *Works*, pp. 366, 434; Manning, *1649*, pp. 130–1.

22 For resistance to encroachments, see TNA, E134/29, 30 Eliz/M17; E134/32 Eliz/E14.

23 William Lilly, *History of his Life and Times*, ed. E. Ashmole (London, 1715), p. 94.

24 TNA, E134/9JasI/H7.

25 Cf. Manning, *1649*, pp. 131–2.

26 Sabine, *Works*, pp. 295–8, 392–3.

27 TNA, SP28/35, fols 356, 359; SP28/291 (unfol.), certif. of Walton assessors, 11 March 1650; LMA, DW/PA/7/13, fol. 308.

28 TNA, PROB11/118, fol. 264; PROB11/272, fol. 346v; LR2/226, fol. 218; LMA, DW/PA/5/1575/42; DW/PA/7/11, fol. 442; DW/PA/7/12, fol. 100v; DW/PA/7/13, fol. 308; GL, 9051/6, fol. 143v; Ms 21742/1; SHC, 793/1; 3015 (unfol.), copy survey of Walton common fields, 25 February 1651; Blackman, *Ashley House Building Accounts*, xix, pp. 23, 54, 56–57, 68, 70; Cockburn, *Surrey Indictments: Eliz. I*, p. 510.

29 LMA, DW/PA/7/4, fol. 8v; DW/PA/7/5, fol. 15; HRO, 1587B/84/1.

30 TNA, E134/32 Eliz/E14.

31 Cf. John Gurney, '"Furious divells?" The Diggers and their opponents', in Bradstock, *Winstanley and the Diggers*, p. 76.

32 TNA, LR2/190, fol. 266; SC12/22/34; E317/Surrey/55; SHC, K44/1/6, 9; 4398/1/4, 11.

33 TNA, SP28/35, fol. 356. Starr witnessed Robt Bickerstaffe's will in 1640: LMA, DW/PA/7/13, fol. 95.

34 TNA, ASSI35/86/2; ASSI35/89/5.

35 SHC, 4398/1/11 for Starr's sheep farming activities.

36 Sabine, *Works*, p. 435.

37 Manning, *1649*, pp. 131–2; Joan Thirsk, 'Agrarian problems and the English revolution', in Richardson, *Town and Countryside*, pp. 183–4.

38 *A Perfect Summary of an Exact Diarie* (16–23 April 1649); Blith, *English Improver Improved*, epistle to the reader.

39 TNA, E134/9 JasI/H7; E134/19 JasI/Trin2, esp. depositions of Geo. Gyldon, Robt Best and Wm King.

40 TNA, E134/19 JasI/Trin2, esp. depositions of Nich. Lane, John Edsawe, Robt Best, Edw. Smith, Jas Sutton, John Hitches, Peter Barnard, Jas Arnold, Edw. Perryer and Abr. Terrill.

41 TNA, E134/19 JasI/T2, depositions of Eliz. Dalton and Wm Starr.

42 Cf. Gurney, 'Furious divells?', pp. 76–7.

43 Everard put his name only to the first Digger manifesto, in April 1649.

44 Sabine, *Works*, p. 281. Cf. *ibid.*, pp. 301, 317; Smith, 'Winstanley and the literature of revolution', p. 50.

45 Sabine, *Works*, pp. 281, 282, 285. Cf. *ibid.*, p. 326, for Winstanley's account of parliament's reception of *An Appeal to the House of Commons*: they 'have received our Appeal and promised an Answer'.

46 Cf. Kenyon, *Utopian Communism*, pp. 176, 178.

47 Sabine, *Works*, pp. 282, 283, 301, 305, 326.

48 *Ibid.*, p. 305.

49 *Ibid.*, pp. 282–3.

50 *Ibid.*, pp. 301, 303.

51 *Ibid.*, pp. 286–8, 305, 308, 311–12.

52 *Ibid.*, pp 286, 310. Cf. *ibid.*, pp. 276, 285, 296, 302, 304, 308, 325, 371; Hill, *Religion and Politics*, pp. 214–15; Bradstock, *Faith in the Revolution*, pp. 101–2.

53 Sabine, *Works*, pp. 285, 301.

54 *Ibid.*, p. 305.

55 *Ibid.*, p. 308.

56 *Ibid.*, pp. 259, 285. Cf. *ibid.*, pp. 282, 284, 288, 295, 296, 324, 326, 329–30, 385; Gurney, 'Digger movement', pp. 778–9.

57 Sabine, *Works*, p. 282.

58 *Ibid.*, p. 273. Cf. *ibid.*, p. 506.

59 *Ibid.*, p. 296.

60 *Ibid.*, pp. 56, 330. Cf. *ibid.*, p. 387.

61 Cf. Manning, *1649*, p. 124; Morrill, *Nature of the English Revolution*, pp. 375–8.

62 Sabine, *Works*, pp. 284, 285.

63 *Ibid.*, pp. 306–7, 310. Cf. *ibid.*, pp. 272, 317, 330.

64 *Ibid.*, p. 292. Cf. Aylmer, 'Religion of Gerrard Winstanley', p. 104; Bradstock, *Faith in the Revolution*, p. 129.

65 KMHS, KE1/1/14; Sabine, *Works*, p. 17. The others were John Barker, Edw. Longhurst, Sam. Webb, Abr. Pennard alias Goodgroome, and possibly Wm Hoggrill. All except Longhurst and Pennard were signatories to Digger manifestos. An Edw. Longhurst – not necessarily the Digger – was a tenant of West Horsley manor in 1649: JRULM, Nicholas MSS 5–6.

66 Sabine, *Works*, pp. 18, 302, 316, 319, 370.

67 Rutt, *Burton's Diary*, I, pp. 55–6, 107.

68 [John Hart], *Trodden Down Strength, By the God of Strength, or, Mrs Drake Revived* (1647), pp. 17–19, 21, 23, 26, 27–9, 36, 41–2, 44, 46, 67–8, 70, 72, 81, 83, 96–7, 108–9, 117–18, 128–9, 132, 135–46, 153–63.

69 TNA, PROB11/165, fols 340–1. He also remembered Hooker's daughter, then in New England.

70 Drake's elder brother William, who was bound with John White at the Middle Temple, does not appear to have shared his brother's puritan convictions: Kevin Sharpe, *Reading Revolutions: The Politics of Reading in Early Modern England* (New Haven, 2000), pp. 109, 231–4.

71 Sabine, *Works*, pp. 17, 319–27.

72 KMHS, KE1/1/14; Sabine, *Works*, pp. 327–8, 333. Winstanley's account of costs to the plaintiff of 'twenty nine shillings and a peny' is confirmed by the entry in the court of record book. Winstanley implied that the damages against Starr were also set at £10, though the court book suggests £3 plus costs; Sabine gives £4. Damages were apparently also awarded against the other Diggers, though possibly not followed up.

73 Sabine, *Works*, p. 328. Starr's mainpernor was John Allisome, Bickerstaffe stood surety for Winstanley and Thomas Ward for Bickerstaffe: KMHS, KE1/1/14.

74 Sabine, *Works*, p. 328.

75 *Ibid.*, pp. 328, 333.

76 *Ibid.*, p. 393.

77 *Ibid.*, p. 335.

78 *Ibid.*, p. 313.

79 *Ibid.*, pp. 316, 319–29, 331, 333–5. 'Mr Gilder' was George Gildon, who had been imprisoned in 1642 for his reluctance to assist in raising money for parliament.

80 *Ibid.*, p. 329. Cf. *ibid.*, pp. 331, 334, 336; Keith Thomas, *Man and the Natural World: Changing Attitudes in England 1500–1800* (Harmondsworth, 1983), p. 174; Lutaud, *Winstanley*, pp. 221–3; Hayes, *Winstanley*, pp. 158–9; Smith, 'Winstanley and the literature of revolution', p. 49.

81 Sabine, *Works*, pp. 295, 329. Cf. *ibid.*, pp. 282, 296, 338; Smith, 'Winstanley and the literature of revolution', p. 51.

82 Sabine, *Works*, pp. 321–7.

83 *Ibid.*, pp. 320–1, 325–6; above, p. 78.

84 Sabine, *Works*, p. 325.

85 *Ibid.*, p. 323. Cf. *ibid.*, pp. 316, 328–9.

86 *Ibid.*, pp. 323–4, 328, 330, 332, 335–6.

87 *Ibid.*, pp. 333, 335. Cf. *ibid.*, p. 302.

88 *Ibid.*, p. 287. Cf. *ibid.*, p. 322. For his earlier warnings that the Norman Yoke was still being upheld, see esp. *ibid.*, p. 259.

89 *Ibid.*, pp. 636–7.

90 *Ibid.*, p. 324. Cf. *ibid.*, pp. 332, 336.

91 Worden, *Rump Parliament*, pp. 198–206; Stuart E. Prall, *The Agitation for Law Reform During the Puritan Revolution 1640–1660* (The Hague, 1966), pp. 35, 52.

92 *The Perfect Weekly Account* (22–27 August), p. 280; *The Moderate*, 59 (21–28 August 1649) (the latter gives 23 August as the date the petition was presented).

93 Sabine, *Works*, pp. 327, 333, 360.

94 *Ibid.*, p. 316.

95 *Ibid.*, pp. 316, 337.

96 *Ibid.*, pp. 336, 337.

97 *Ibid.*, p. 315.

98 *Ibid.*, p. 317. Cf. *ibid.*, p. 365.

99 *Ibid.*, p. 336.

100 *Ibid.*, p. 316.

101 *Ibid.*, p. 337.

102 *Ibid.*, pp. 316, 327.

103 *Ibid.*, p. 335.

104 SHC, K145/19; Kingston parish registers (typed transcripts); above, p. 128.

105 Sabine, *Works*, p. 337.

106 *Ibid.*, pp. 331, 336.

107 *Ibid.*, p. 326; Gurney, 'Digger movement', p. 785.

108 Sabine, *Works*, pp. 369, 393.

109 12 Diggers are known to have been associated with both the St George's Hill and Little Heath colonies. (Figures in this and the following footnotes are based on the 70 Diggers who signed manifestos or were prosecuted for digging).

110 16 Diggers were associated only with the Little Heath settlement.

111 Sabine, *Works*, p. 277. 45 Diggers signed this work; 31 of these were no longer involved by the time of the move to Cobham. 32 of the 45 signatories put their names to this work only.

112 Possibly 14 of the 28 Diggers who were known to have been active on the Little Heath.

113 BL, Egerton MS 2618, fol. 38.

114 TNA, SP25/94, pp. 477–8.

115 *A Brief Relation*, 3 (16 October); *Mercurius Elenticus*, 25 (15–22 October 1649).

116 William Style, *Narrationes Modernae, Or Modern Reports* (1658), p.166; Hill, *World Turned Upside Down*, p. 91.

117 Sabine, *Works*, p. 393. This was possibly another occasion, since Winstanley implies the sheriff was present at the arrest.

118 KMHS, KE1/1/14, pp. 328, 336, 338; Sabine, *Works*, p. 360.

119 *Ibid.*, pp. 344, 367–8, 393.

120 Firth, *Clarke Papers*, 2, pp. 215–21; Sabine, *Works*, pp. 343–9. Signatories to the 2nd letter were John Hayman, Anth. Wrenn, Henry Barton, John Coulton, Robt Coster, John Palmer and Jacob Heard. The other letter was dated 8 December 1649.

121 TNA, SP18/42/144 (misfiled with state papers from 1653).

122 Sabine, *Works*, pp. 419, 433 for Platt's willingness to debate with Winstanley.

123 Firth, *Clarke Papers*, 2, p. 217. Cf. TNA, SP18/42/144; Sabine, *Works*, p. 366; Lutaud, *Winstanley*, pp. 227–8; Boulton, *Republic of Heaven*, p. 58.

124 Above. pp. 133–4.

125 Bannerman, *Visitations of Surrey 1530, 1572 and 1623*, pp. 149–50, 186; *CCC*, pp. 1238, 1973; *VCH Surrey*, 4, p. 257; *Family of Lambert*, pp. 5–6, 13–16; *LJ*, 5, p. 686; 6, p. 53.

126 TNA, SP23/186/890, 892,895–6, 898, 900; PROB11/207, fol. 101; *CCC*, p. 1468. It was through Hayward Bickerstaffe that the family had obtained the lease of the Pains Hill estate: TNA, E317/Surrey/44, pp. 7–8; NLW, Wynnstay 161, fol. 103v.

127 *Mercurius Politicus*, 583 (11–18 August 1659), p. 674; *Calendar of the Clarendon State Papers*, 4, pp. 328–55; David Underdown, *Royalist Conspiracy in England 1649–1660* (New Haven, 1960), pp. 280–1. For the later careers of Hayward Bickerstaffe's sons Sir Charles and Philip Bickerstaffe, see Henning, *House of Commons 1660–1690*, 1, pp. 648–9; J. C. Sainty and R. O. Bucholz, *Officials of the Royal Household 1660–1837*, Part 2 (London, 1998), p. 77.

128 KMHS, KE1/1/14.

129 TNA, SP19/22, p. 37. A Thos Ward of Kingston, possibly the same person, was awarded a pension in 1663 as a former royalist soldier: Powell and Jenkinson, *Surrey Quarter Sessions Records 1661–63*, p. 70.

130 Michael Mahony, 'Presbyterianism in the City of London, 1645–1647', *HJ*, 22 (1979), pp. 105, 111; Tai Liu, *Puritan London* (Newark, New Jersey, 1986), p. 95.

131 CLRO, Journal of the court of common council, 40, fol. 153v; *Five Orders and Ordinances of Parliament for Payment of Soldiers* (1647); *CJ*, 5, p. 216; *LJ*, 9, p. 279.

132 TNA, PROB11/248, fols 393v–95. Jenkin was one of the executors to his will.

133 Firth, *Clarke Papers*, 2, pp. 216–17, 218; TNA, SP18/42/144.

134 Above, pp. 33, 76. The suggestion sometimes made that Winstanley was wrong in identifying Sir Anthony (rather than Sir Francis) Vincent as an opponent is based on an error in Manning and Bray, *Surrey*, 2, pp. 724–5, repeated in *VCH Surrey*, 3, p. 286, where Sir Anthony's date of death is given as 1642. He did not in fact die until 1656: TNA, PROB11/260, fol. 379; Bannerman, *Stoke Parish Registers*, p. 34.

135 TNA, SP28/334 (unfol.), acct book of Rich. Wither, fol. 61.

136 Sabine, *Works*, pp. 365, 367–8. Cf. Manning, *1649*, pp. 126–7.

137 Sabine, *Works*, pp. 365, 367–8.

138 *Ibid.*, p. 433. Note also the carrying away of wood from demolished Digger homes to the homes of local gentlemen, above, p. 168.

139 Cf. Hindle, 'Persuasion and protest', pp. 71–3 for middling sorts opposition to enclosure in Caddington, Beds, generated partly by fears of an increase in poverty and consequent rise in poor rates.

140 Below, p. 189.

141 Sabine, *Works*, p. 365.

142 Thomas, 'Another Digger broadside', pp. 59, 65.

143 Firth, *Clarke Papers*, 2, p. 216.

144 TNA, SP18/42/144; Firth, *Clarke Papers*, 2, p. 220.

145 Sabine, *Works*, pp. 356–7, 359. Cf. *ibid.*, pp. 363, 364, 380, 388.

146 *Ibid.*, pp. 393–4.

147 *The Moderate Intelligencer*, 214 (19–26 April 1649). Cf. Gurney, 'Furious divells', pp. 78–9.

148 Sabine, *Works*, pp. 365, 368, 435.

149 *Ibid.*, p. 435.

150 TNA, ASSI35/91/10.

151 It is most likely that they were married to the Diggers Henry Barton of Cobham and Thos Edsaw of Stoke d'Abernon, but there is no independent evidence for this. If Eliz. Barton was the wife of Henry Barton, she may have been the widow Barton buried as a Quaker in 1672.

152 Above, pp. 5, 7, 50.

153 In the draft bills of indictment, all the accused were described as being from Cobham, the site of the alleged offence. All except Platt were described as labourers.

154 TNA, PROB 11/260, fol. 378v; Sabine, *Works*, p. 434. For Power see also SP16/501/37; SP28/244 (unfol.), warrant to high constables of Elmbridge hundred, 29 November 1643. John Power gent gave 10s and Wm Davye labourer 2s towards the free and voluntary present in 1661: E179/257/28.

155 SHC, COB/1/1; LMA, DW/PA/7/11, fol. 443; TNA, SP15/40/48.

156 SHC, 4398/1/6; TNA, SP28/35, fol. 359; SP28/159 , 177, 178 (unfol.), accts of Sackford Gunson; SP28/177 (unfol.), Stoke d'Abernon parish accts.

157 TNA, SP28/245 (unfol.), accts of Augustine Phillips.

158 TNA, E179/346 (unfol.), Stoke exemption certif., 11 November 1670. Davey was unable to sign his name on the certif.

159 Meekings, *Hearth Tax* (assessed at 3 hearths).

160 JRULM, Nicholas MS 6; TNA, PROB 11/255, fol. 213v.

161 One assailant, Leonard Collins, has escaped identification. If he was from Cobham, then precisely half of those accused were from that parish.

162 Above, p. 77.

163 Sabine, *Works*, p. 331; SHC, COB/1/1; St George's CAL, MS XI. M3, fols 110v, 117.

164 SHC, COB/1/1; HRO, 44M69/A6/3/1.

165 SHC, COB/1/1; COB/5/1; 1974/40; 4398/1/2; HRO, 44M69/A6/3/1; LMA, DW/PA/7/10, fol. 144.

166 SHC, COB/1/1; COB/5/1; 44/1/9; 4398/1/10; LMA, DW/PA/7/11, fol. 474; TNA, E179/188/481.

167 TNA, SP16/501/37; SP28/35, fol. 359; SP28/159 (unfol.), mid-Surrey assessments schedule, 1645/46; SP28/179 (unfol.), Cobham parish accts; accts of Henry Hastings and John Redfern.

168 SHC, K44/1/9; TNA, ASSI35/92/8.

169 SHC, COB/1/1; TNA, E179/188/481; E179/257/30.

170 TNA, SP12/50, fol. 44; SHC, K44/1/5; 2610/29/3; Cockburn, *Surrey Indictments: Eliz. I*, p. 50.

171 SHC, COB/1/1; COB/5/1; Daly, *Kingston Apprenticeship Registers*, 489.

172 SHC, K44/1/9; 4398/1/9.

173 Powell and Jenkinson, *Surrey Quarter Sessions Records 1661–63*, p. 19; 1663–66, p. 3.

174 TNA, E179/188/481; E179/258/4; E179/346 (unfol.), Cobham exemption certif. c. November 1670; SHC, COB/5/1. A John Goose was buried in Cobham in 1692: COB/1/1.

175 SHC, 4398/1/9, 11.

176 LMA, DW/PA/7/10, fols 20–21; TNA, PROB11/227, fols 134v–5; SHC, COB/1/1. It was through this marriage that Sutton became impropriator of the Cobham living.

177 SHC, K44/1/9; 2610/11/8/33; 4398/1/4–11.

178 For the date of this work see G. E. Aylmer, '*England's Spirit Unfoulded, Or an Incouragement to take* the Engagement: a newly discovered pamphlet by Gerrard Winstanley', *P&P*, 40 (1968), pp. 5–7.

179 Gardiner, *Constitutional Documents*, p. 391; Worden, *Rump Parliament*, pp. 222, 226–8.

180 Aylmer, '*England's Spirit Unfoulded*', pp. 9–14.

181 *Ibid.*, pp. 13–14.

182 *Ibid.*, pp. 9, 10, 12.

183 HRO, 44M69/A6/3/1. Although his political base was in Hampshire, Jervoise was active in Surrey as a JP and as a sequestration and militia commissioner in the years 1649–53.

184 HRO, 44M69/A6/3/1, p. 31.

185 HRO, 44M69/A6/3/1, p. 13. John Coulton junior, the almanac writer, also subscribed on 16 March.

186 HRO, 44M69/A6/3/1, pp. 14, 29–30.

187 Cf. Gardiner, *Commonwealth and Protectorate*, I, p. 246; Worden, *Rump Parliament*, pp. 231–2, for opposition among presbyterian clergymen to the Engagement.

188 Sabine, *Works*, pp. 663–75; Firth, *Clarke Papers*, 2, pp. 221–4.

189 Berens, *Digger Movement*, p. 129; Lutaud, *Winstanley*, p. 299. Cf. Hill, *Religion and Politics*, p. 209.

190 Sabine, *Works*, pp. 655–61.

191 *Ibid.*, pp. 656–7. Cf. Holstun, *Ehud's Dagger*, p. 392.

192 Sabine, *Works*, pp. 660–1.

193 *Ibid.*, pp. 353–62, 368–9.

194 *Ibid.*, pp. 355–6, 375, 377.

195 *Ibid.*, pp. 378–9.

196 *Ibid.*, pp. 380–1.

197 *Ibid.*, pp. 386, 389, 390–1.

198 *Ibid.*, pp. 381, 386.

199 Lutaud, *Winstanley*, p. 239; Boulton, *Republic of Heaven*, p. 60. The hostility to lawyers and denunciation of bad laws may, similarly, have reflected the Diggers' recent experiences before Kingston's court of record.

200 Winstanley, *Several Pieces*, sigs A2r–A4r.

201 Aylmer, 'Religion of Gerrard Winstanley', p. 105. *Fire in the Bush* was published by Calvert.

202 Keith Thomas, 'The date of Gerrard Winstanley's *Fire in the Bush*', *P&P*, 42 (1969), pp. 160–2.

203 Sabine, *Works*, pp. 452–4, 456–7, 458–9, 480, 482–3, 489–90, 493.

204 *Ibid.*, pp. 454, 456–61.

205 *Ibid.*, pp. 445, 463, 466–7, 470–1, 473–5. Cf. J. C. Davis, 'Religion and the struggle for freedom in the English Revolution', *HJ*, 35 (1992), pp. 507, 515–17, 519, 521, 523, 530.

206 Sabine, *Works*, pp. 472, 473–4. Cf. *ibid.*, p. 456.

207 *Ibid.*, pp. 492, 493.

208 *Ibid.*, pp. 496–7.

209 *Ibid.*, pp. 457, 485.

210 *Ibid.*, pp. 462, 496. Cf., *ibid.*, pp. 452, 454, 457, 470, 484, 495.

211 Hill, *World Turned Upside Down*, pp. 313, 315; Sabine, *Works*. pp. 492–3.

212 Anthony Ascham, *Of the Confusions and Revolutions of Governments* (1649), esp. pp. 18–26.

213 Ascham, *Confusions*, p. 19.

214 Cf. Zagorin, *Political Thought in the English Revolution*, pp. 64–7; Quentin Skinner, 'The ideological context of Hobbes's political thought', *HJ*, 9 (1966), pp. 308–11, 312; Quentin Skinner, 'Conquest and consent: Thomas Hobbes and the engagement controversy', in G. E. Aylmer, (ed.), *The Interregnum: The Quest for Settlement 1646–1660* (revised edn, London, 1974), pp. 87–95.

215 Ascham, *Confusions*, p. 21.

216 *Ibid.*, pp. 19, 21, 24.

217 *Ibid.*, p. 25.

218 Sabine, *Works*, pp. 493–4.

219 *Ibid.*, p. 281.

220 E. B. Underhill (ed.), *Records of the Churches of Christ, Fenstanton, Warboys and Hexham 1644–1720* (London, 1854), pp. 269–71. Winstanley was mentioned by name in the Warboys records, as was George Foster. Cf. Hill, *World Turned Upside Down*, p. 102.

221 Nathaniel Stephens, *A Plain and Easie Calculation of the Name, Mark and Number of the Name of the Beast* (1656), p. 267; George Fox, *The Journal*, ed. Nigel Smith (London, 1998), pp. 7–8, 11, 45–6. Alexander Gordon's suggestion in *DNB* that Winstanley visited Fenny Drayton and debated with Stephens appears to be based on a misreading of Stephens's account.

222 Smith, *Ranter Writings*, pp. 82, 114; Davis, *Fear, Myth and History*, p. 54.

223 Foster, *Sounding of the Last Trumpet*, pp. 42, 43. Cf. *ibid.*, pp. 14–15, 46–7; Gibbons, 'Fear, myth furore', p. 192; above, p. 109.

224 Foster, *Sounding of the Last Trumpet*, pp. 14, 17–19, 43, 49, 51, 52.

225 The preface was dated 14 January 1650, and Thomason had obtained a copy by 24 April. For the influence on Foster of other thinkers, notably Coppe and Clarkson, see Nigel Smith, 'Foster, George', *ODNB*.

226 Berens, *Digger Movement*, pp. 49–51, 67; W. S. Hudson, 'Gerrard Winstanley and the early Quakers', *Church History*, 12 (1943), pp. 191–4; Boulton, *Republic of Heaven*, pp. 114–15. Cf., for more sceptical views of the connections between Winstanley and early Quakerism, W. C. Braithwaite, *The Second Period of Quakerism* (2nd edn, ed. H. J. Cadbury, Cambridge, 1961), pp. 556–7, 709–10; Petegorsky, *Left-Wing Democracy*, p. 248; Hill, *Religion and Politics*, p. 229.

227 For Clarkson, see William Lamont, 'Clarkson, Laurence', *ODNB*; Barry Reay, 'Laurence Clarkson: an artisan and the English Revolution', in Christopher Hill, Barry Reay and William Lamont, *The World of the Muggletonians* (London, 1983), pp. 162–86.

228 Smith, *Ranter Writings*, pp. 165, 167, 169, 170, 173. Cf. Davis, *Fear, Myth and History*, pp. 61–4.

229 Smith, *Ranter Writings*, p. 173.

230 Lamont, 'Clarkson'; Davis, *Fear, Myth and History*, pp. 63, 77; McGregor, 'Fear, myth and furore', pp. 157–8, 160.

231 Smith, *Ranter Writings*, pp. 180–1. Cf. McGregor, 'Seekers and ranters', pp. 129–30. For doubts as to whether Clarkson went as far as he later claimed, see Davis, *Fear, Myth and History*, pp. 62, 71, 74, but see also Gibbons, 'Fear, myth and furore', p. 191.

232 Smith, *Ranter Writings*, p. 182.

233 Sabine, *Works*, pp. 185, 366–7. Cf. Davis, 'Fear, myth and furore', p. 196.

234 Sabine, *Works*, p. 403.

235 *Ibid.*, p. 402.

236 *Ibid.*, pp. 364, 366–7; Manning, *1649*, p. 131. (It is possible that Winstanley was not here referring to sexual licence.)

237 Aylmer, '*Englands Spirit Unfoulded*', pp. 14–15.

238 Sabine, *Works*, pp. 482–3.

239 Hessayon, 'Everard'.

240 Sabine, *Works*, pp. 477–8. Cf. Gibbons, 'Fear, myth and furore', p. 193. *A Single Eye* was in print by June 1650, but the views contained in it were apparently associated with Clarkson before then: Smith, *Ranter Writings*, p. 180–1.

241 Sabine, *Works*, p. 403. The main text of the pamphlet was dated 20 February, and the appendix 4 March 1650.

242 Sabine, *Works*, pp. 439–41, for the letter. Cf. Hill, *World Turned Upside Down*, pp. 101–3; Lutaud, *Winstanley*, pp. 296–8, 454. It is of course possible that other emissaries were sent out, travelling different routes. We only know of Heydon and Knight's journey because of their arrest in Wellingborough.

243 Below, pp. 186–190.

244 Hindle, 'Persuasion and protest', pp. 39, 52–3, 76–7. Hindle points out that the northern Chilterns were 'fertile territory for political radicalism': *ibid.*, p. 77.

245 For early Cambridgeshire Quakers see Margaret Spufford, *Contrasting Communities: English Villagers in the Sixteenth and Seventeenth Centuries* (Cambridge, 1974), pp. 281–4.

246 Sabine, *Works*, p. 411.

247 Thomas, 'Another Digger broadside', p. 65. I am inclined to believe that the statement that Diggers were 'at work at 'Dunstable, in Buckinghamshire also,' means that digging was taking place in both Dunstable *and* Buckinghamshire. It is usually taken to be a mistaken suggestion by the Iver Diggers that Dunstable was *in* Bucks rather than Beds.

248 Coxhall in Lamberhurst was a single property rather than a village or hamlet.

249 Sabine, *Works*, p. 411; Hill, *World Turned Upside Down*, p. 99. There are two Cox Hills in Kent, as well as a Cox Hill Mount and Cox Hill Wood. Sabine acknowledged that he knew of no evidence of digging in Cox Hill.

250 Peter Clark, *English Provincial Society* (Hassocks, 1977), p. 393; Hill, *World Turned Upside Down*, p. 99.

251 Thomas, 'Another Digger broadside', p. 65. For Husbands Bosworth see *VCH Leicestershire*, 5 (London, 1964), p. 28.

252 Petegorsky, *Left-Wing Democracy*, p. 174; *CSPD 1650*, p. 218; Thomas, 'Another Digger broadside', pp. 59, 65; Hill, *World Turned Upside Down*, pp. 100–1.

253 Thomas, 'Another Digger broadside', p. 65.

254 *VCH Middlesex*, 6 (London, 1980), p. 15.

255 D. O. Pam, *The Rude Multitude: Enfield and the Civil War* (Edmonton Hundred Historical Society, Occasional Paper (NS) 33, 1977), pp. 7, 10–11; Pam, *Parish Near London*, pp. 120–1; *VCH Middlesex*, 5 (London, 1976), pp. 233–6.

256 *CJ*, 2, p. 566; 3, p. 40; *LJ*, 5, p. 597; 6, pp. 235, 244, 254, 470; Pam, *Rude Multitude*, p. 10.

257 Pam, *Rude Multitude*, p. 11.

258 TNA, E317/Middx/17.

259 Pam, *Rude Multitude*, pp. 11–12; CJ, 7, p. 726; *A Relation of the Cruelties and Barbarous Murthers, and other Misdemeanours, Done and Committed by Some Foot-Souldiers, and Others* (1659); *A Relation of the Riotous Insurrection of Divers Inhabitants of Enfield, and Places Adjacent* (1659).

260 William Covell, *A Declaration unto the Parliament, Council of State and Army* (1659), pp. 9–12, 16, 20–1; J. M. Patrick, 'William Covell and the troubles at Enfield in 1659: a sequel to the Digger movement', *University of Toronto Quarterly*, 14 (1944–45), pp. 45–57; Pam, *Rude Multitude*, pp. 12–13.

261 W. H. Ward and K. S. Block, *A History of the Manor and Parish of Iver* (London, 1933), pp. 5, 193. I am indebted to Nicholas Cooper for drawing my attention to this work and for providing me with a copy.

262 Berens, *Digger Movement*, p. 79.

263 LLRRO, DE728/61–62, 615, 637; TNA, PROB11/276; Ward and Block, *History of Iver*, pp. 169–70; *VCH Bucks*, 3 (London, 1925), p. 291.

264 Daly, *Kingston Register of Apprentices*, pp. 43, 44, 50, 60; KMHS, KC2/4/5.

265 Sabine, *Works*, p. 441. Cf. Thomas, 'Another Digger broadside', p. 60.

266 LMA, ACC/0446/ED/101; EM/044; L/004; *VCH Bucks*, 3, p. 286; *VCH Middlesex*, (London, 1962), pp. 192, 197–99; Ward and Block, *History of Iver*, p. 104.

267 *LJ*, 7, pp. 42, 141.

268 *CJ*, 5, p. 263; *A Perfect Diurnall*, 210 (2–9 August 1647), p. 1685.

269 Thomas, 'Another Digger broadside', pp. 62, 63.

270 *Ibid.*, p. 62.

271 Thomas, 'Another Digger broadside', pp. 60, 67–8. The signatories were Henry Norman, Edw. Dun, Robt Dun, Benj. Dunt, Thos Taylor, Wm Saunders, Henry Slave, Thos Beedle younger, Rich. Moseley and John Currant.

272 *Ibid.*, pp. 60–1, 67–8.

273 LMA, ACC/0446/M/015; TNA, SP28/170 (unfol.), acct of money collected for the relief of Ireland, 1643–44. The other juror was Robt Dun, while Thos Beedle would serve as juror in 1665: Thomas, 'Another Digger broadside', pp. 67–8.

274 Thomas, 'Another Digger broadside', pp. 67–8. The Quaker was Edw. Dun. Biddle was also an Iver Quaker surname: Ward and Block, *History of Iver*, p. 181.

275 Sabine, *Works*, p. 650.

276 BL, Harl. MS 787, fol. 9v. Wellingborough was only a short distance from Pytchley, one of the centres of the Midland Rising.

277 Thomas, 'Another Digger broadside', pp. 64–5.

278 Sabine, *Works*, p. 649; Thomas, 'Another Digger broadside', pp. 61–2.

279 Sabine, *Works*, p. 650; Thomas, 'Another Digger broadside', pp. 63, 64.

280 Sabine, *Works*, p. 651; Thomas, 'Another Digger broadside', p. 64.

281 Sabine, *Works*, p. 650; Thomas, 'Another Digger broadside', pp. 63–4.

282 Thomas, 'Another Digger broadside', p. 62; Sabine, *Works*, p. 448.

283 *Ibid.*, p. 650. For a detailed discussion of the Wellingborough and Iver declarations, see also Wood, *Riot, Rebellion and Popular Politics*, pp. 157–63.

284 Northamptonshire Record Office (hereafter Northants RO), 350P/649. Rich. Smith sr died 1659 and Rich. Smith jr in 1660.

285 [Francis Ellington], *A True Discoverie of the Ground of the Imprisonment of Francis Ellington, Thomas Cocket, and Edward Ferman*, (1655), pp. 1–2. For Pentlow and the Quakers see also *A True Testimony of What Was Done Concerning the Servants of the Lord, at the Generall Assizes, Holden at Northampton* (1655), p. 10; William Dewsbury, *The Discovery of the Great Enmity of the Serpent Against the Seed of the Woman* (1655), p. 10.

286 Northants RO, 350P/649.

287 TNA, PROB11/301, fol. 270 (will signed as Fardill); Northants RO, 350P/649.

288 Sabine, *Works*, p. 650. The common was 'Bareshanke'. 'Bareshanke Leys' was mentioned in a 1612 libel from Wellingborough: Adam Fox, 'Ballads, libels and popular ridicule in Jacobean England', *P&P*, 145 (1994), pp. 67–8. A 'Bearshanks' was to be found in the neighbouring parish of Wilby.

289 TNA, PROB11/265, fols 327–7v; Northants RO, 350P/649.

290 Northants RO, 350P/649.

291 Vann, 'Diggers and quakers', p. 67.

292 *CSPD 1650*, p. 106; Petegorsky, *Left-Wing Democracy*, p. 174.

293 Thomas, 'Another Digger broadside', pp. 59, 67.

294 Sabine, *Works*, pp. 363–4.

295 *Ibid.*, p. 371.

296 *CJ*, 7, p. 236; Thomas Carlyle (ed.), *Oliver Cromwell's Letters and Speeches: with Elucidations* (copyright edn, London, nd), vol. 2, p. 138.

297 TNA, E317/Surrey/40–41; LR2/297, fols 129–40.

298 TNA, SP25/63, pp. 352, 414–15, 427, 429; LR2/297, fols 113–18.

299 TNA, SP25/95, p. 11; Petegorsky, *Left-Wing Democracy*, p. 175.

300 Cheshire and Chester Archives and Local Studies, CR63/2/702, p. 52.

301 Sabine, *Works*, pp. 407–15. It was dated 26 March, a fortnight after the Wellingborough declaration.

302 *Ibid.*, pp. 407, 412–13.

303 *Ibid.*, pp. 411–12. Cf. Hill, *Religion and Politics*, p. 218.

304 See above, p. 7.

305 Sabine, *Works*, p. 412.

306 *Ibid.*, pp. 414–15.

307 *Ibid.*, p. 413.

308 TNA, ASSI35/91/10. The presentments stated that the cottages remained occupied on 1 March 1650.

309 TNA, ASSI35/91/4.

310 The names were given as Gerrard Winstanley, Henry Barton, Thos Starr, John Cobham [i.e. Coulton?], Wm Everard, John Palmer, Jas Hall, Wm Comes, Adam Knight, Thos Edsaw, Rich. Goodgroome, Henry Bickerstaffe, Rich. Medley, Wm Boggerell and Edw. Longhurst.

311 TNA, ASSI35/91/10; above, p. 171.

312 Sabine, *Works*, p. 433. Easter Sunday was on 14 April.

313 *Ibid.*, p. 433.

314 *Ibid.*, p. 419.

315 *Ibid.*, p. 433. The opening address to the tract was dated 9 April.

316 *Ibid.*, p. 428.

317 *Ibid.*, pp. 428, 429.

318 *Ibid.*, p. 433.

319 *Ibid.*, pp. 433–4.

320 *Ibid.*, pp. 433, 435, 436–7.

321 *Ibid.*, p. 434. Cf. *ibid.*, pp. 436, 437.

322 *Ibid.*, p. 434.

323 TNA, ASSI35/91/10.

324 Above, p. 193.

325 Sabine, *Works*, pp. 435–6.

326 *Ibid.*, p. 436.

327 *Ibid.*, pp. 436, 437.

328 *Ibid.*, p. 437.
329 *Ibid.*, p. 395.
330 *Ibid.*, p. 435.
331 This point is made forcefully by William Lamont in 'The Left and its past: revisiting the 1650s', *History Workshop Journal*, 23 (1987), pp. 141–3, 150, 151.

Chapter 7

Aftermath

The story of the Digger movement did not end with the destruction of Digger colonies in April and May 1650. It seems that members of the different colonies had agreed beforehand on tactics to adopt in the event of their activities being curtailed. We know from the Iver Digger declaration at the end of April that some Surrey Diggers had left their children on the parish when their work was stopped, and that Diggers in Barnet and Enfield were threatening the same if their opponents prevented them planting and building on the commons.[1] The Iver Diggers also raised the question of whether it was a felony for 'any man to get some 30 or 40, or more together' and to go and set fire to '6 or 7 very poor men's houses that had set them up in some wast places' – as had recently happened in Cobham. The immediate context for raising this question was the campaign against the Diggers in Wellingborough, and the Iver Diggers appear to have been warning that action might be taken against perpetrators of such a crime if it were attempted in Wellingborough.[2] At the next Surrey Assizes, in July 1650, several Cobham Diggers and local sympathisers did make just such an attempt to prosecute their opponents for feloniously burning down Digger houses on the Little Heath on 19 April.[3]

It was at the time of the 1650 harvest that the Diggers renewed their activities in what seems to have been a co-ordinated, symbolic action. Their own crops having been destroyed, the Diggers sought out worthy individuals and offered them help in bringing in the year's crop. Winstanley and several of his companions made their way to Pirton in Hertfordshire, where the prophetess Lady Eleanor Davies or Douglas, who had declared 1650 to be a year of Jubilee and restitution, held the Rectory manor and impropriation.[4] Pirton was also the parish in which Henry Denne, founder of the Baptist churches at Fenstanton and Warboys, had until recently been curate.[5] The Diggers remained at Pirton from August until at least December, threshing wheat and assisting with general estate business; Winstanley also claimed to have helped to free the estate of a sequestration order.[6] Although Winstanley's role at Pirton is sometimes seen as that of estate steward, Winstanley later made it clear to Davies that 'I came not under your rooffe to earne money like a slave'; 'you know I asked you nothing'.[7] His aim, he told her, was 'the convertion of your spirit to true Nobilitie, which is falne in the earth'.[8]

While Winstanley and his companions set to work at Pirton, the former Digger William Everard appeared at the home of the Behmenists John and Mary Pordage at Bradfield Rectory in Berkshire. As John Pordage later explained, 'he came in Harvest-time with a new pair of Harvest-gloves on his hands, to shew his willingness and readiness to work; and asking to speak with me, told me, That if I pleased to employ him in Harvest-work, he came to offer his service: Hereupon I entertained him as a workman'.[9] Everard stayed for about three weeks, part of that time in the company of his fellow-prophet Thomas Tany.[10] Neither the Pirton nor the Bradfield venture was a success. Everard's presence at the Bradfield rectory was linked to 'very many and very strange apparitions' witnessed around the house, and to the sudden strange behaviour of its inhabitants, and rumours were spread locally that he was a conjuror, sorcerer or witch.[11] Pordage's entertainment of Everard was later used against him when in 1654 he was deprived of the Bradfield living.[12] At Pirton, Davies and Winstanley quarrelled over disputed threshing accounts, Davies confronting Winstanley on 3 December in the tithe barn in the guise of Melchizedek King of Salem.[13] Winstanley defended himself in two detailed, angry letters in which he accused Davies of having 'lost the Breeches, which is indeed true Reason, the strength of A man'; he promised nevertheless that 'tell your worke is done I will doe what I can for you in your proprietie bussines, and bring you up a clere accompt'.[14] If we must fix a date for the end of the Digger experiment, December 1650 may be as good a date as the preceding April.

It is not known how long Winstanley remained at Pirton after his dispute with Davies, but he and his companions may have had good reason to continue to stay away from Surrey for as long as possible. The Diggers had failed to appear at the Southwark Assizes in April 1650 to answer the charges made against them of riot and trespass, and orders to the sheriff to produce them before the assizes were issued regularly over the following two years.[15] Winstanley had returned to Cobham by 15 June 1652, when he witnessed the will of the elder John Coulton in the company of John Fuller and William Remnant of Cobham.[16] Coulton's son, the younger John Coulton, was also back in Cobham by 26 April 1652, on which date he put his name to the preface of his *Almanack and Prognostication* for the year 1653.[17] Other Diggers who returned to Cobham, and were admitted back into local society, included Henry Barton, Daniel Freeland, John Hayman, John Palmer and Thomas Starr.[18]

It was in 1651 that Winstanley completed his last, and most famous work, *The Law of Freedom in a Platform, or, True Magistracy Restored*. This was dedicated on 5 November to Oliver Cromwell, and it had appeared on booksellers' shelves by 20 February 1652.[19] Although published after the end of the digging venture, *The Law of Freedom* was, Winstanley suggested, at least partly written 'above two years' before the date of its dedication. He had, he claimed, then put it to one side until 1651, when he began 'to pick together as many of my scattered papers as I could finde'.[20] The work set out to advance the cause of 'Commonwealths Government' – Winstanley's new term for the alternative to kingly government and kingly power – and to suggest laws and constitutional arrangements by which it might be maintained. Cromwell was urged to do his utmost to support the implementation of commonwealth's government, for 'you are in place and power to see all Burthens taken off from your friends, the Commoners of England'.[21]

If Winstanley was correct in claiming that some of the contents of *The Law of Freedom* dated from 1649 or 1650, then the work can help us better understand the kinds of social arrangements, and means of production and distribution, that he may have envisaged for Digger communities had they spread as successfully as he had hoped. His proposals for family and household organisation, and for the operation of communal storehouses, are particularly important in this regard. While the earth would be worked in common, individual families would continue to live apart 'as they do; and every mans house, wife, children, and furniture for ornament of his house, or any thing which he hath fetched in from the Storehouses, or provided for the necessary use of his Family, is all a propriety to that Family, for the peace thereof'.[22] Fathers would be masters in their households, and would form one of the essential 'links of a Chain' of commonwealth's officers.[23] Each family might keep cows 'for their own use, about their own house', and have their own barns.[24] Most commodities – both agricultural produce and manufactured goods – would be held in storehouses, from where they would be 'delivered out again to particular Families, and to every one as they want for their own use', or be exported overseas in exchange for goods unavailable at home:

> And if any man or family want Corn, or other provision, they may go to the Store-houses, and fetch without money: If they want a Horse to ride, go into the fields in Summer, or to the Common Stables in Winter, and receive one from the Keepers, and when your Journey is performed, bring him where you had him, without money. If any want food or victuals, they may go to the Butchers shops, and receive what they want without money; or else go to the flocks of sheep, or herds of cattel, and take and kill what meat is needfull for their families, without buying and selling.[25]

The 'earth, and the labours thereupon', would be 'managed by common assistance of every family', and 'all the labours of Husbandmen and Trades-men, within the Land, or by Navigation to or from other Lands', would be 'all upon the common Stock'.[26] In each trade work would be guided by an overseer, while overseers in husbandry would ensure that every family participated in seasonal agricultural work.[27] Laws would be in place both to prevent idleness and to discourage excess and hording.[28]

What is most startling to modern readers of *The Law of Freedom* is the elaborate set of laws and the machinery of coercion described by Winstanley. Officers in his commonwealth included task-masters, peace makers, soldiers, judges and executioners; those who failed to play their part in the new society might lose their freedom and be forced to live – at least temporarily – in servitude; and the death penalty would apply to any who tried to buy or sell, who practised law for money, who made a trade of preaching or praying, or who were found guilty of rape.[29] In comparison with Winstanley's Digger writings, with their confident prediction of Christ's imminent rising in his sons and daughters, much greater emphasis was placed on institutionalised coercion and on the regulation of behaviour. Whether this should be seen as part of a pessimistic response to the failure of the Digger experiment, or fundamental shift in Winstanley's thought from millenarianism or anarchism to a belief that the state had the central role to play in effecting social change, is however less certain.[30] State action, as J.C. Davis has pointed out, always had a role to play in Winstanley's scheme, and he had often called on the army, parliament and Council of State to fulfil their obligations to cast out kingly power and keep their wartime promises to the common people.[31]

The sense of millenarian expectation at the heart of *The Law of Freedom* has also often been overlooked.[32] Winstanley continued to insist, as he had done in his Digger writings, that knowledge would 'spread to cover the Earth', and that kingly government – 'the great Man of Sin', the 'great Antichrist, and Mystery of Iniquity' – would fall.[33] The 'spirit of universal Righteousness dwelling in Mankind' was 'rising up to teach every one to do to another as he would have another do to him', though that spirit had been suppressed for many years by the spirit of self-love; the present times, Winstanley hoped, were to 'be the days of his resurrection to power . . . because the name of Commonwealth is risen and established in England by a Law'.[34] The choice for those in authority remained what it had been in 1649, between vainly holding on to kingly government and advancing the cause of commonwealth's government – or else between returning to Egypt and helping to 'bring in everlasting righteousness and peace into the earth'.[35] The crucial point was that kingly government was *bound* to fall, whether as a result of the righteous actions of those in authority or through divine intervention, for if the authorities failed to act their government too would perish, having gone 'no further but to the half day of the Beast, or to the dividing of Time, of which there must be an over-turn'.[36] The texts Winstanley chose to cite – Daniel 7.25 and Revelations 12.14 and 18.10 – ensured that his message could not be misunderstood by his readers.[37]

Clearly Winstanley now accepted that an effective implementation of good laws was necessary to bring about and sustain the new society; human fallibility might otherwise prove too strong a hindrance to progress.[38] Nevertheless, the focus in *The Law of Freedom* on law and government may have been less a reflection of Winstanley's preoccupations in the aftermath of the Digger venture – or of his pessimistic response to defeat – than of the very specific context in which the work saw the light of day. Whether the work was written afresh in 1651, or was drawn together from older notes, the occasion of its publication was, as Winstanley freely acknowledged, the debates over reform of the law, education and the ministry initiated by Hugh Peter in his 1651 treatise *Good Work for a Good Magistrate.*[39] Peter had sought, through reference to 'Scripture, Reason and Experience', to provide workable proposals for the settlement of the commonwealth in matters of religion, mercy and justice, and much of his treatise was taken up with proposals for the relief of the poor, the advancement of commerce and learning, the improvement of the ministry and reform of the law.[40] *Good Work* had first appeared in June 1651, but its reforming message had gained added significance following Cromwell's victory at Worcester and the growth in radical confidence in the likely implementation of major reforms.[41] In late 1651 and early 1652 the victorious Cromwell was also, as Blair Worden has shown, allowing himself to be portrayed as a 'champion of the radicals', and doing little to discourage the belief that he was not only sympathetic to reformist aims but keen to help carry them through.[42] Newsbooks confidently reported that there was soon to be a new representative and that the Lord General had 'declared for Liberty and Freedom', and radical pamphleteers praised Cromwell as a public figure whose 'heart was bent for the publique good'.[43] Parliament had also bowed to pressure to set up a commission to look into 'the inconveniences in the Law'; one of the commission's first nominees was Hugh Peter, whose proposals on law reform already included the advice to 'burn all the old Records yea, even those in the Tower, the Monuments of tyrannie'.[44] Thoroughgoing change in government and society seemed a realistic prospect for the first time since the spring of 1649. A number of writers, including Winstanley, took up the challenge laid down by Peter in his *Good Work* by offering their own contributions to the debate on what course reform should take, and Winstanley was not alone in optimistically dedicating his effort to Cromwell.[45]

The contents of Winstanley's *The Law of Freedom* appear to have been shaped – at least in part – by the debates to which the author was contributing. Scholars have often expressed surprise at Winstanley's claim in the preface that 'indeed the main Work of Reformation lies in this, to reform the Clergy, Lawyers, and Law; for all the Complaints of the Land are wrapped up within them three', but this comment makes perfect sense in the context of the debate initiated by Peter.[46] It is only when we insist on trying to understand the meaning of *The Law of Freedom* in relation to his earlier writings, rather than in the immediate context in which it was produced, that it looks at all remarkable. Winstanley's aim in *The Law of Freedom* was not to offer his mature reflections on the Digger venture or to record the shifts in his thought since 1649; rather, it seems that he was addressing a readership which may have had little familiarity with his Digger writings but which might – he hoped – now be receptive to suggestions for far-reaching reform. In his comments on law, education and government, Winstanley was picking up on themes already discussed by Peter and others, and offering his own singular suggestions for the reform of current abuses. In places he even borrowed directly from Peter, as in his advocacy of the use of peace-makers to settle disputes before the rigour of the law was applied.[47] Peter – perhaps drawing on his New England experience – had already called for the appointment of peace-makers to 'hear and determine all common-controversies between man and man'.[48] Peter had advocated the annual election of three peace-makers in every town or hundred, while Winstanley, who would have assigned to them a wider role, thought that three was the minimum number needed for a parish or town and that in some places more than six should be chosen.[49] Both Peter and Winstanley thought that the employment of peace-makers might be a means to avoid the unnecessary use of prisons, which both condemned for their cruelty.[50] Other writers involved in these debates also recognised the utility of Peter's peace-maker proposals, and saw in them a direct challenge to the power of lawyers. Samuel Duncon or Dunkon, for instance, whose *Severall Propositions of Publick Concernment* appeared a month after *The Law of Freedom*, advocated the annual election in every city, town and hundred of five, seven or eleven 'most understanding plain harted men' to be peace-makers, and, in an open letter to Peter, described his attempts at drafting an 'Act for Peace-making'.[51]

Much of *The Law of Freedom* reads like a commentary on Peter's proposals for reform, and on the literature inspired by them. Winstanley was aware that Peter 'and some others' had suggested that 'the Word of God might be consulted with to finde out a healing Government', and in publishing *The Law of Freedom* he was able to demonstrate from scripture, reason and experience the inadequacy of most of the reform proposals then circulating. For Winstanley, the essential point remained the utter incompatibility of kingly and commonwealth's government, and the futility of reforms that failed to remove all vestiges of kingly power. There was, Winstanley insisted, no 'middle path' between monarchy and commonwealth's government, 'for a man must either be a free and true Commonwealths man, or a Monarchial tyrannical Royalist'; 'you must either establish Commonwealths Freedom in Power, making provision for every ones Peace, which is Righteousness; or else you must set up Monarchy again'.[52] Those now in power had 'professed to the World a godly Righteousness, more purely then that of oppressing Kings', and 'without doubt their faithfulness and wisdom is required to be manifested in action, as well as in words'.[53] The reform debates of 1651–52 thus allowed Winstanley to publicly restate his case for the necessity of community, and for the establishment of a property-less, moneyless society from which clergymen and lawyers would be excluded. It was essentially the same case that he had made while pursuing his Digger experiment on St George's Hill and Cobham's Little Heath, and it can scarcely be seen as a retreat from the position he had adopted in 1649 and 1650.

For a short period Winstanley's became one of the most widely-heard voices in the reform debates, though not in the way he might have hoped. It is possible that he had difficulty in finding a publisher for *The Law of Freedom*, for he seems to have had to finance its publication himself.[54] Before the eventual appearance of the work, the manuscript (or part of it) fell into the hands of other publishers, and in the spring of 1652 large sections of it were issued anonymously by others, in a manner that can have borne little relation to Winstanley's original intentions.[55] The publisher George Horton issued lengthy unacknowledged extracts from *The Law of Freedom* in at least three reform pamphlets published in February and April 1652.[56] Daniel Border's *The Faithful Scout* also reprinted sections of the work in February 1652, as did the related newsbook *The French Intelligencer*.[57] While Winstanley's voice was being heard, his central argument was not. In each case the publishers ruthlessly edited out any mention of community, and left well-written, though largely unremarkable, passages on law reform, oppressive government and the role of a commonwealth's army in advancing the cause of freedom. On 21 April 1652 one of these pamphlets – apparently a mixture of extracts from *The Law of Freedom* and contributions from other radical authors – found its way into Cromwell's hands in the guise of 'Several Propositions' for 'the better regulating of the Law'. Cromwell was said to have 'seriously weighed and considered' these propositions and to have declared that it was 'his ardent affection and desire, that the Law might be so regulated, wherein true and impartial Justice may be freely administered, & that he was resolved to the utmost of his power to promote and propagate the same'.[58] Winstanley had finally received the approbation he had sought from Cromwell, but it was not for the cause he had set out to advance in *The Law of Freedom*.

It is in the months following the publication of *The Law of Freedom* that we see Winstanley attempting – like many of his fellow Diggers – to re-establish himself in the local community. In November 1652 he became involved in a case in the Mayor's Court relating to the estate of his brother-in-law Giles Hickes, who had died the previous August.[59] The case was ostensibly between William King and his daughter Mary Hickes, but it may have an attempt by the family to preserve the estate from creditors: Hickes had certainly been in debt to the governors of St Thomas's Hospital, who had distributed his last quarter's salary of £10 amongst themselves when he died.[60] Winstanley and William Forder, son-in-law of John Coulton of Cobham, were appointed to appraise Hickes's goods at his house in the parish of St Christopher le Stocks.[61] Given the paucity of information relating to this series of events, the significance of Winstanley's involvement in a court case of this kind cannot easily be assessed. What is evident, however, is that the years following the publication of *The Law of Freedom* were for Winstanley marked by what James Alsop has demonstrated to be a successful absorption back into local society.[62] It may have been this stage in Winstanley's life that Laurence Clarkson was referring to in 1660 when he accused him of 'a most shameful retreat from Georges-Hill with a spirit of pretended universality, to become a real Tithe-gatherer of propriety'.[63] The nature and extent of Winstanley's shift from radicalism to conformity should not however be exaggerated, for as late as the autumn of 1654 Winstanley was, as Barry Reay has shown, making contact with Quaker preachers at their first appearance in London, and apparently telling them that they were 'sent to perfect that worke which fell in their [the Diggers'] handes'.[64]

One reason why Winstanley should have needed to rebuild his livelihood so quickly was the sudden, and hitherto unnoticed, collapse in the mid-1650s of the King family's fortunes. It is usually thought that Winstanley owed the recovery of his own fortunes to his father-in-law William King, a well-established London surgeon and senior member of his City company. Yet by 1656 King had gone blind, retired from St Bartholomew's Hospital and become almost destitute of goods and land. In response to a suit brought against them by their daughter and son-in-law Christian and Robert Gill, William and Susan King had in 1655 and 1656 made over most their property in trust to their lodger, the musician John Stone, who subsequently became embroiled in a lengthy legal dispute with them.[65] In 1656 Stone surrendered to St Bartholomew's Hospital the leases of the Kings' house in St Bartholomew-the-Less, and obtained a new lease in his own name; he also later claimed that he had legitimately purchased from the Kings all their household goods.[66] When William King tried to return to his London house, he was 'arrested and carried away' by Stone's new lodger.[67] The Kings' Cobham property, on which Susan and Gerrard Winstanley were living, had been surrendered in April or May 1655 to the use of Stone and his heirs, and it was only in 1657 that they managed to recover it and surrender it into the hands of the manorial steward to their own use and after their deaths to the use of Gerrard and Susan.[68] With Susan King continuing to spend long periods away from home as a travelling midwife, William King became increasingly reliant on the hospitality of his daughter and son-in-law in Cobham, and he seems to have lived with them for stretches of a year or more at a time.[69] Although the Kings – with the help of the lawyer James Winstanley of Gray's Inn and Braunstone – won two court cases against Stone in 1658 and 1659, their dispute with him was still unresolved in 1663, and it may still have been continuing when William King drew up his will in 1664.[70] It seems likely that at the time of the Kings' deaths only their small copyhold estate in Cobham had been recovered from Stone.[71]

Evidence of Winstanley's reintegration into local society can be found in his willingness to hold parochial office in Cobham in the later 1650s and 60s.[72] He was elected surveyor or waywarden in 1659 and 1666 and overseer of the poor in 1660, and in 1667–68 and 1668–69 he served as churchwarden.[73] Although Winstanley must have been prepared to conform to the established church in order to serve as churchwarden, this need not be taken as proof of a complete abandonment of his earlier radicalism or social concern. Cobham's church-wardens played an active role in disbursing money from their many parochial charities, and the accounts surviving from Winstanley's time in office indicate that he took his responsibilities to the poor seriously. In both his years of office he appears to have disbursed more than he received, and entries in the accounts suggest a determination to ensure that receipts from charitable bequests were not diverted from their proper uses.[74] Among those who received money from Winstanley's hands while he was churchwarden were former Diggers and their opponents, and relatives of both these groups. Money was spent on John Palmer's youngest child and on Goodwife Goose and William Honyard in 1667–68, while 'Heman' received 17s 6d for 'making cloths'; 'Old South' and widow Coulton 'schooledame' were both in receipt of money from Winstanley in 1668–69.[75]

Winstanley was also prepared to engage in manorial land transactions in the 1650s. In October 1658, for instance, he was one of two tenants of Ham Court manor to whom Francis Sutton surrendered his customary holdings in the manor to the use of James Sutton. This surrender was however made out of court, and Winstanley was listed as a defaulter when the Dean and Canons of Windsor began holding manorial courts again in July 1662.[76] Like many members of Cobham's middling sorts before him, Winstanley also served as a juror at quarter sessions and as high constable of Elmbridge Hundred, to which post he was appointed in October 1671.[77] Other former Diggers also began holding local office again during the 1650s and 60s. Thomas Starr and John Hayman were, for instance, chosen tithingmen in Street Cobham and Church Cobham respectively in 1660; Hayman also served as parish waywarden in 1669–70 and Starr in 1672.[78] Henry Bickerstaffe, though remaining a resident of Kingston, collected rents in Walton and Cobham for his brother and nephew during the 1650s.[79] In September 1661 he became keeper of Kingston gaol.[80]

Local tensions, including tensions between landlord and tenant, were still in evidence in Cobham during the 1650s, despite the reabsorption into local society of many of the former Diggers. Large numbers of Cobham's manorial tenants were presented as defaulters at a court baron of 23 October 1657, at which only two tenants turned up to serve on the homage. At the view of frankpledge and court baron in April 1659 the defaulters were spared by the jury and homage, and the bailiff was amerced 10s for failing to give sufficient warning to the tenants to appear before the court baron. In April 1660 the Diggers' former antagonist William Starr was amerced 40s for putting five hundred sheep on Cobham's commons while holding no more than seven acres of land in the manor.[81] In 1655 a Chancery case was launched against John Platt and others by the former Cobham copyhold tenant William King, who claimed to have been defrauded following the sale of his estate to the Carleton family in 1631.[82] Platt was accused, among other things, of withholding relevant manorial documents from King, and of claiming that 'if any such things or writings were made they were lost in the late troubles among other things of the said Mannor'.[83] In 1661 Platt and his manorial steward were accused, with others, of fraudulently suggesting that certain of the Bickerstaffes' lands in Cobham were copyhold rather than freehold, thus enabling them to divert the profits away from trustees for Sarah Bickerstaffe.[84] The former Digger Henry Bickerstaffe was one of those who found himself embroiled in this complex series of actions.[85]

The growing influence of Quakerism also affected the local community. The connection between some Digger families and Quakers has already been noted, and other Cobham inhabitants also joined the Friends in the late 1650s and 1660s. Meetings were held at the house of Ephraim Carter, a butcher whose father had been a minor official of the Surrey county committee during the Civil War.[86] Like some of the former Diggers, Ephraim Carter was willing to hold manorial and parochial office, serving as constable of Street Cobham in 1658–9 and as parish overseer of the poor in 1664–5.[87] It was when a meeting at his house was broken up in 1665 that the former Digger Thomas Starr refused to assist the parish constable in making arrests.[88]

Another prominent Cobham figure who suffered the effects of the post-Restoration re-establishment of the church was John Platt, who was deprived of his West Horsley living in 1662.[89] He had however already bought the manor of Westbrook in Godalming, where he retired to after his ejection and where he died in November 1669.[90] While Platt was learning to embrace nonconformity, Gerrard Winstanley continued to conform to the established church. By 1664 Susan Winstanley was dead, and in July of that year, in the church of St Giles Cripplegate, Winstanley married Elizabeth Stanley or Standley, the daughter of Joan and Gabriel Stanley.[91] She was many years his junior, her parents having married only as recently as May 1642.[92] Three children – Jerrard, Elizabeth and Clement – were baptised in Cobham's parish church in 1665, 1668 and 1670.[93] It was through his marriage to Elizabeth Stanley that Winstanley became involved in a series of court cases that were to dog him until his death. Having in 1661 successfully fought off an attempt by the executors of the merchant taylor Richard Aldworth to prove in court that he still owed £114 from when he left off trading in 1643, Winstanley soon found himself legally responsible for the recovery of large sums of money to which his wife's uncle, Hugh Turner, had a claim when he died in 1665.[94] These sums related to the vast investments that Sampson Wise (to whose will Hugh Turner had acted as executor) had made in the estates of his royalist father-in-law Fitzwilliam Coningsby of Hampton Court, Herefordshire, in an attempt to save them from ruin in the aftermath of civil war.[95]

The Coningsbys had repaid only a negligible amount by the time Wise died in 1663, Wise having spent by some estimates as much as £30,000 in rebuilding the family's estates and paying off their debts. By 1665 the claim on the Coningsbys from Turner's estate stood, according to Winstanley, at £1,850.[96] Winstanley had been named an overseer of Turner's will, and since the executor Hugh Flood was still a minor in 1665 Winstanley effectively carried out the functions of executor and attempted to bring in the money owed to Turner's estate.[97] For a three-year period from 1666 Winstanley was said to have 'leavied and received many Rents and greate Sumes of money out of the issues and proffitts of the estate' of Fitzwilliam Coningsby, receiving by his own account £429 5s 8d from the tenants of the Hampton Court estates. By an agreement made between Winstanley and Coningsby, the former Digger was to allow the former monopolist, MP and leading civil war royalist one quarter of this income 'for and towards his maintenance'.[98]

It is usually thought that Winstanley first became involved in legal actions relating to this episode in 1675, the year before his death. It is evident however that he was a defendant in actions brought by another of Wise's executors and by members of the Coningsby family as early as 1668 and 1669, and it seems likely that the litigation continued for much of the remainder of his life.[99] His relative James Winstanley of Gray's Inn and Braunstone (who had successfully represented him in his court case against Richard Aldworth's executors, and the Kings in their actions against John Stone), had died in 1666, so Winstanley was forced to rely on others for legal advice and assistance.[100] In his last years, Winstanley was engaged in a series of court cases involving figures as diverse as members of the royalist Coningsby family, the London merchant and MP Sir Thomas Allen, Roger Boyle, Earl of Orrery, and the notorious Barbados merchant Ferdinando Gorges. It was Gorges, whose slave trading activities had earned him the nickname 'King of the Blacks', with whom Winstanley was in dispute in the months before his death, and it was Gorges who apparently emerged the main victor from the lengthy series of suits relating to the Coningsbys' estates.[101]

It is not certain how debilitating these actions were for Winstanley, or whether he had been able to benefit financially from having handled rental income from the Coningsby estates.[102] It has long been known that by 1675 he and Elizabeth had left Cobham for the Middlesex parish of St Giles-in-the-Fields, where he may have set up in business as a corn chandler.[103] What has escaped notice, however, is that that the Winstanleys lived there in a substantial house of ten hearths in the fashionable quarter of Bloomsbury. The size and situation of their house, which was located on the 'Street side' close to Bloomsbury Square, suggests that they had attained a considerable degree of prosperity by 1675.[104]

It was in this last phase of his life that Winstanley abandoned the established church and became involved with the Quakers. Winstanley died on 10 September 1676, the cause of death being recorded in the Westminster Monthly Meeting's burials register as 'gripes & vomiting', and he was buried in the Long Acre burial ground.[105] The significance of Winstanley's burial by the Quakers has often been questioned by scholars, since evidence of his active involvement in the Society of Friends was thought to be lacking.[106] There is, however, clear evidence that Winstanley attended the Savoy meeting in the months before his death. On 25 July 1676, for instance, his was the first name in a list of thirty friends present at the marriage of James Carter of St Andrew Holborn and Elizabeth Aplin of St Giles-in-the-Fields.[107] After his death his wife remained a Quaker. She married again in 1681, to Giles Stuchbury of Newington Butts, a cooper who was also active in the Society of Friends.[108] When Elizabeth and Gerrard Winstanley's sons Jerrard and Clement died in 1683 and 1684, they were given Quaker burials, as was Giles Stuchbury when he died in 1706.[109] Elizabeth Stuchbury lived until 1708, and in her will she left the residue of her estate, after several bequests to relatives had been made, for 'the putting out apprentice poore children of the people called Quakers in Southwarke' and 'toward the relief of the poor of the said People called Quakers in Southwark'. She too was given a Quaker burial.[110]

It seems fitting that some sixty years after Winstanley had first expressed his overriding concern for the poor, and his insistence on abiding by the Golden Rule, that his widow should seek to ensure that a substantial part of her estate went towards helping the poor. Outside the Winstanleys' immediate circles, however, memories of the Digger movement appear to have faded many years before. The evidence that survives of the reading or ownership of Digger tracts in late-seventeenth and early-eighteenth-century England is very scant, and would suggest that the ideas which inspired Winstanley and his companions were quickly forgotten. The Newcastle-upon-Tyne bookseller William London was still listing Winstanley's pre-Digger writings in his 1656 *Catalogue of the Most Vendible Books in England*, and copies of tracts from the Digger period were owned by the Quaker Benjamin Furly (1636–1714) and the radical merchant Samuel Jeake (1623–90) of Rye, both of whom had extensive libraries; Quakers in Kent were circulating Winstanley's *Several Pieces* in the 1720s.[111] But when, in the mid-eighteenth century, the Whig propagandist Thomas Hollis presented Sir John Fielding with a copy of *The Law of Freedom*, he probably saw it as something of a curiosity rather than as one of the works he wished to see stocked in his 'libraries of liberty'.[112] In 1673, when John Aubrey toured Surrey to gather information for his *Natural History and Antiquities* of that county, his journey took him past St George's Hill and he recalled that the hill had been the site of 'a great meeting of Levellers: which were like to have turned the world upside downe'.[113] Yet he made no mention of Winstanley's involvement in the episode, assuming instead that these 'Levellers' had been inspired by John Lilburne. Aubrey's editor, the Oxford antiquary Richard Rawlinson, later tidied up Aubrey's notes on the hill, omitting from the published version of the *Natural History* any reference to turning the world upside down, but he failed to spot or correct Aubrey's error in the identification of the Digger leader.[114] One local resident did however try to keep the memory of the Diggers alive for posterity. When the younger John Coulton published his series of almanacs in the 1650s, he followed the usual practice of including in them a list of the most significant events in world history since the Creation. Coulton's list contained many of the usual 'memorable accidents', such as the Norman Conquest, Luther's challenge to the Papacy, the Gunpowder Plot and the execution of Charles I. Among the most significant world events of recent times, however, was the one he included under the year 1649, the moment when 'the common people began to plant upon George Hill in Surrey, April I'.[115]

NOTES

1 Thomas, 'Another Digger broadside', pp. 59, 65. They threatened to leave seven children in Barnet and nine in Enfield.

2 *Ibid.*, pp. 66–7.

3 TNA, ASSI35/91/10. See above, p. 171.

4 Paul H. Hardacre, 'Gerrard Winstanley in 1650', *Huntington Library Quarterly*, 12 (1959). For Davies and the 1650 Jubilee, see Esther S. Cope (ed.), *Prophetic Writings of Lady Eleanor Davies* (Oxford, 1995), pp. 319, 329–31; Esther S. Cope, *Handmaid of the Holy Spirit: Dame Eleanor Davies, Never Soe Mad a Ladie* (Ann Arbor, 1992), p. 145.

5 Denne was still there in 1643: TNA, SP28/180 (unfol.), acct of money lent on ordinance of 30 January 1643 for relief of Ireland.

6 Esther Cope suggests that this sequestration was connected with a court order made in Michaelmas term 1650: Cope, *Handmaid*, p. 156.

7 Lutaud, *Winstanley*, p. 330. Cf. *ibid.*, pp. 329–31 for full transcripts of Winstanley's letters to Davies.

8 *Ibid.*, p. 330. Cf. Vann, 'Later life', p. 133. (In view of this combination of conversion of the spirit with actual harvest work, it is possible that the Diggers' actions were inspired by Matthew 9.37–8 or John 4.35–8.)

9 John Pordage, *Innocence Appearing Through the Dark Mists of Pretended Guilt* (1655), pp. 11–12; Howell, *State Trials*, 4, 552–3.

10 Pordage, *Innocence Appearing*, pp. 9, 11–12.

11 *Ibid.*, pp. 12, 68–9; *A Most Faithful Relation of Two Wonderful Passages* (1650), p. 4. Cf. Ariel Hessayon, 'Pordage, John', *ODNB*; Hessayon, 'Everard'.

12 Pordage, *Innocence Appearing*, p. 9; Howell, *State Trials*, 4, 549. Everard was not heard of again after March 1651: Hessayon, 'Everard'.

13 Cope, *Handmaid*, p. 155; Lutaud, *Winstanley*, pp. 329–31. Cf. Cope, *Prophetic Writings*, p. 311 for Davies's identification with Melchizadek. Melchizadeck was of course one of the first biblical figures to whom tithes were offered.

14 Lutaud, *Winstanley*, pp. 330–1.

15 TNA, ASSI35/91/4, 5; 92/7, 8; 93/5; 94/8.

16 TNA, PROB11/224, fol. 307v; Gurney, 'Digger movement', p. 794.

17 Coulton, *Theoria Contigentium . . . 1653* (preface written from Cobham).

18 Above, pp. 128, 129, 130.

19 Sabine, *Works*, p. 514 for the date of the dedication. The work went into two editions.

20 *Ibid.*, pp. 509–10. For scepticism about these claims, see Davis, *Utopia and the Ideal Society*, p. 171.

21 Sabine, *Works*, p. 503. Cf. Lamont, 'Left and its Past', p. 150; Richard Baxter, *A Holy Commonwealth*, ed. William Lamont (Cambridge, 1994), introduction, xi.

22 Sabine, *Works*, p. 512. Cf. *ibid.*, pp. 515, 526, 527, 546–7.

23 *Ibid.*, pp. 538–9, 544–5.

24 *Ibid.*, p. 549.

25 *Ibid.*, pp. 581, 582–3.

26 *Ibid.*, pp. 581, 582.

27 *Ibid.*, pp. 548–51.

28 *Ibid.*, 526–7, 583, 599.

29 *Ibid.*, pp. 591–9. For a detailed analysis of Winstanley's proposed legal system, see Michael Rogers, 'Gerrard Winstanley on crime and punishment', *Sixteenth Century Journal*, 27 (1996), pp. 735–47.

30 Cf., for debates about shifts in Winstanley's thought after the end of the Digger experiment, Zagorin, *Political Thought in the English Revolution*, pp. 52, 57; J. C. Davis, 'Gerrard Winstanley and the Restoration of True Magistracy', *P&P*, 70 (1976), pp. 78, 85, 90–3; Davis, *Utopia and the Ideal Society*, pp. 170, 180–1, 183, 189–203; Hill, *Religion and Politics*, pp. 207–8, 220–1, 223; Hill, 'Law of Freedom', pp. 41, 66; Christopher Hill, *The Experience of Defeat: Milton and Some Contemporaries* (London, 1984), p. 38; Aylmer, 'Religion of Gerrard Winstanley', pp. 108–14; Darren Webb, 'The Bitter Product of Defeat? Reflections on Winstanley's *Law of Freedom*', *Political Studies*, 52 (2004), pp. 199–215.

31 Davis, 'Restoration of True Magistracy', pp. 78–9.

32 An exception is Bradstock, *Faith in the Revolution*, pp. 90–2.

33 Sabine, *Works*, pp. 517, 530, 532, 565.

34 *Ibid.*, p. 534; Bradstock, *Faith in the Revolution*, p. 92.

35 Sabine, *Works*, pp. 534–5, 582.

36 *Ibid.*, pp. 535, 582.

37 *Ibid.*, pp. 535, 570; Bradstock, *Faith in the Revolution*, pp. 91–2.

38 Sabine, *Works*, pp. 515, 535–6. Cf. Davis, 'Restoration of True Magistracy', pp. 84–5, 87, 90–1.

39 Sabine, *Works*, p. 509.

40 Hugh Peter, *Good Work for a Good Magistrate* (1651). See also Raymond P. Stearns, *The Strenuous Puritan: Hugh Peter, 1598–1660* (Urbana, 1954), pp. 370–82.

41 The date of the work's dedication was 7 June 1651; Thomason had obtained a copy by 17 June.

42 Worden, *Rump Parliament*, pp. 274–5, 279. Cf. Austin Woolrych, *Commonwealth to Protectorate* (Oxford, 1982), pp. 28–9.

43 D. T., *Certain Queries, or Considerations Presented to the View of All that Desire Reformation of Grievances* (1651), dedication; *The French Intelligencer* (4–11 February 1652), p. 86; Worden, *Rump Parliament*, pp. 271–2, 275.

44 Worden, *Rump Parliament*, p. 272; Peter, *Good Work*, p. 33.

45 For instance Samuel Duncon, *Severall Propositions of Publick Concernment* (1652); S. D., *Certaine Assayes Propounded to the Consideration of the Honourable Committee for Regulating the Proceedings at Law* (1652); *Englands Doleful Complaint* (1651); D. T., *Certain Queries*; John Audley, *Englands Common-wealth* (1652). In October 1651 Lady Eleanor Davies dedicated her *The Benediction* to Cromwell, or 'Howl Rome': Cope, *Prophetic Writings*, pp. 341–2.

46 Sabine, *Works*, p. 505.

47 *Ibid.*, pp. 545–6, 547, 548.

48 Peter, *Good Work*, pp. 24, 29.

49 *Ibid.*, p. 29; Sabine, *Works*, pp. 545–6.

50 Peter, *Good Work*, p. 25; Sabine, *Works*, p. 553.

51 Duncan, *Severall Propositions*, pp. 4–6. Cf. Samuel Duncon, *Several Proposals* (1659), p. 2.

52 Sabine, *Works*, pp. 513, 527.

53 *Ibid.*, p. 528.

54 Though sold by Calvert, the work was 'printed for the Author'.

55 Cf. Berens, *Digger Movement*, p. 232; Petegorsky, *Left-Wing Democracy*, p. 232; Woolrych, *Commonwealth to Protectorate*, p. 39.

56 *A Declaration of the Commoners of England, to his Excellency The Lord General Cromwell* (1652); *Articles of High Treason* (1652); *A New Way to Pay Old Debts: Or, The Law and Freedom of the People Established* (1652).

57 *The Faithful Scout*, 56 (6–13 February), p. 439; 58 (20–27 February), pp. 454–5; *The French Intelligencer* (4–11 February), p. 87; (11–18 February 1652), p. 90.

58 *The Faithful Scout*, 66 (16–23 April 1652), pp. 518–19. See Sabine, *Works*, pp. 590–1 for those parts of *The Law of Freedom* borrowed for these 'Propositions'.

59 CLRO, MC1/83/232. The case is discussed in Dalton, 'Experience of fraud', pp. 979–80.

60 Parsons, *St Thomas's Hospital*, 2, p. 81. Wm King was plaintiff and Mary Hickes defendant in the case, and the dispute revolved around £200 which Giles Hickes owed his father-in-law at the time of his death.

61 CLRO, MC1/83/232. They also acted as pledges for restitution.

62 Alsop, 'Winstanley's later life', pp. 73–5; Alsop, 'Religion and respectability', pp. 705–9; Alsop, 'Winstanley: what do we know of his life?', pp. 30–3, where the need to exercise caution in explaining Winstanley's later life is emphasised.

63 Smith, *Ranter Writings*, p. 182. This may, on the other hand, have been a reference to Winstanley's time at Pirton: Aylmer, 'Religion of Gerrard Winstanley', p. 116; Vann, 'Later life', pp. 133–4.

64 Reay, *Quakers and the English Revolution*, p. 10; Alsop, 'Winstanley: what do we know of his life?', p. 32. It was the leading Quaker Edw. Burrough who reported Winstanley's words and who added 'hee hath bene with us'.

65 See also above, p. 69. At the time the property was made over to him it seemed likely that he would marry the Kings' sole remaining unmarried daughter, Sarah: TNA, C6/25/85. An unpaid marriage portion was also at issue in the dispute: C5/413/199.

66 TNA, C6/25/85; C6/26/73.

67 TNA, C6/25/85. The goods King left behind when arrested were carefully inventoried. They included 'one silver spoon with W:K:S: upon it', presumably representing Wm and Susan King.

68 TNA, C6/25/85; PROB11/320, fols 103–103v.

69 TNA, C6/25/85; C6/26/73. Stone claimed that King took most of his books with him to Cobham: C6/26/73.

70 TNA, C5/413/199. Stone was said in 1663 to have refused to hand over the St Bartholomew-the-Less lease, and to have threatened to take the lease overseas if put under pressure to surrender it or pay the sums determined by the court: C5/413/199, answer of Sarah King. King referred in his 1664 will to his real and personal estate 'which I have or can clayme any right or Tytle unto either in law or equity': PROB11/320, fol. 103v.

71 Susan King had died by October 1663; Wm King's will was proved in April 1666: TNA, C5/413/199; PROB11/320, fol. 104. Wm King died at Hornchurch, Essex, where Sarah King lived.

72 Alsop, 'Religion and respectability', p. 706.

73 SHC, COB/5/1.

74 SHC, COB/5/1, entries for 1657–58 and 1658–59. See the memoranda on the £1 due to the poor annually out of the Darnelly charity.

75 SHC, COB/5/1. The schoolteacher widow Coulton appears to have been widow of the younger John Coulton, the astrologer, who had died in 1659. His mother Jane, widow of John Coulton senior, had died in 1665: COB/1/1.

76 St George's CAL, MS XI.M3, fol. 116. Cf. Alsop, 'Religion and respectability', p. 707.

77 SHC, QS2/1/3, pp. 17, 121; QS2/5/X.

78 SHC, 4398/1/11; COB/5/1.

79 TNA, C9/243/14.

80 KMHS, KB13/3/4. Another keeper was appointed in 1662, which may mean that Bickerstaffe was a nonconformist: KB13/3/5.

81 SHC, 4398/1/11.

82 For this William King, who was not related to Winstanley's father-in-law, see above, pp. 19, 71, 73.

83 TNA, C10/22/86; above, p. 49. Some at least of these documents survive today in Surrey History Centre.

84 TNA, C10/468/162.

85 TNA, C9/243/14.

86 Powell and Jenkinson, *Surrey Quarter Sessions Records 1663–1666*, pp. 232, 240. Cf. KMHS, KE2/7/12. For Carter's father, see above, p. 39.

87 SHC, 4398/1/11; COB/5/1. For dissenters and office-holding, see esp. Bill Stevenson, 'The social integration of post-restoration dissenters, 1660–1725', in Margaret Spufford (ed.), *The World of the Rural Dissenters* (Cambridge, 1995), pp. 360–87; Marsh, *Family of Love*, pp. 188–96.

88 Powell and Jenkinson, *Surrey Quarter Sessions Records 1663–1666*, p. 241.

89 Matthews, *Calamy Revised*, p. 391.

90 TNA, PROB11/332, fols 200v–201; Manning and Bray, *Surrey*, I, p. 608; *VCH Surrey*, 3, p. 36.

91 GL, Ms 6419/7.

92 GL, Ms 4449/2, fol. 79. Gabriel Stanley and Joan Turner married on 3 May 1642 in St Stephen Coleman Street, London, on the same day as Edward Fflud and Joan's sister Elizabeth. Joan Stanley was a widow when she died in 1670 or 1671: LMA, DW/PC/5/1670/56.

93 SHC, COB/1/1. The untrustworthy 18th-cent parish register transcripts give the eldest child's name as Jeremiah.

94 For the Aldworth case, see above, pp. 65, 70, 86n. 99; Alsop, 'Ethics in the marketplace', pp. 100–12; Dalton, 'Experience of fraud', p. 975. The relevant case papers are TNA, C5/415/123; C6/44/101; C9/412/269; C24/867/102.

95 The case is discussed in Vann, 'Later life', p. 135; Alsop, 'Later life', pp. 77–9.

96 TNA, C6/188/19; C6/188/67; C6/217/31; PROB11/312; PROB11/316, fol. 398v. Cf. PROB11/322, fols 345–9v.

97 TNA, PROB11/316; C6/244/96; Alsop, 'Later life', p. 78. A £200 per annum rent charge on the Coningsby lands was also at issue.

98 TNA, C6/188/66; C6/192/31. Cf. C6/244/96. For Coningsby's career see Mary F. Keeler, *The Long Parliament, 1640–1641* (Philadelphia, 1954), pp. 139–40; Ian Atherton, *Ambition and Failure in Stuart England: the Career of John, First Viscount Scudamore* (Manchester, 1999), pp. 226–41.

99 TNA, C6/188/19, 66, 67; C6/192/31; C6/217/31.

100 TNA, C9/412/269; C24/867/102; Nichols, *History and Antiquities of the County of Leicester*, 4, p. 629.

101 TNA, C5/581/55; C6/188/67; C6/192/31; C6/244/96.

102 The evidence is assessed in Alsop, 'Later life', p. 79, where any suggestion that Winstanley profited from the episode is questioned.

103 Vann, 'Winstanley and friends', p. 42; Vann, 'Later life', p. 135. Legal constraints on the activities of corn chandlers had been lifted in 1673: Ray B. Westerfield, *Middlemen in English Business: particularly between 1660–1760* (New Haven, 1915), p. 167.

104 TNA, E179/143/370. James Winstanley's son-in-law Silius Titus was living around the corner in Bloomsbury Square at the time of this Middlesex hearth tax assessment.

105 TNA, RG6/827, p. 21.

106 See, for instance Hayes, *Winstanley*, p. 246.

107 TNA, RG6/825, p. 19.

108 Vann, 'Winstanley and friends', p. 42, where his name is given as Tuchbury. Cf. Powell and Jenkinson, *Surrey Quarter Sessions Records 1661–1663*, pp. 253, 259, 278 for Stuchbury's attendance at an unlawful meeting in Southwark in August 1662.

109 TNA, RG6/1100, pp. 88, 96, 251.

110 TNA, PROB11/505, fols 260–61v; RG6/1100. For Giles Stuchbury's will, see PROB11/491, fol. 315v.

111 William London, *Catalogue of the Most Vendible Books in England* (1658); W. P. D. Stebbing, 'Gerrard Winstanley's socialistic and religious discourses: a Kent Association volume', *Archaeologia Cantiana*, 66 (1944), pp. 70–1; Petegorsky, *Left-Wing Democracy*, p. 231; Hill, *Religion and Politics*, p. 186; Hill, *Experience of Defeat*, p. 42.

112 Barbara Taft (ed.), *Absolute Liberty: a Selection from the Articles and Papers of Caroline Robbins* (Hamden, Connecticut, 1982), p. 216. Cf. Hill, *Experience of Defeat*, p. 42, citing J. R. Jacob, *Henry Stubbe, Radicalism and Protestantism and the Early Enlightenment* (Cambridge, 1983), where Henry Fielding is named as the recipient.

113 Bodleian Library, MS Aubrey 4, fol. 60v.

114 Aubrey, *Surrey*, 3, p. 95.

115 Coulton, *Theoria Contigentium . . . 1653; Prognostes Astralis . . . 1654; Prognostae Astralis . . . 1655.*

Index

Index

Index